The Worldliness of a Co

MW00647826

Pinar positions himself against three pressing problems of the profession:

- the crime of collectivism that identity politics commits,
- the devaluation of academic knowledge by the programmatic preoccupations of teacher education, and
- the effacement of educational experience by standardized testing.

A cosmopolitan curriculum, Pinar argues, juxtaposes the abstract and the concrete, the collective and the individual, history and biography, politics and art, public service and private passion. Such a curriculum provides passages between the subjective and the social and, in so doing, engenders that worldliness a cosmopolitan education invites.

Such worldliness is vividly discernible in the lives of three heroic individuals: Jane Addams (1860–1935), Laura Bragg (1881–1978), and Pier Paolo Pasolini (1922–1975). What these disparate individuals demonstrate, Pinar argues, is the centrality of subjectivity in the cultivation of cosmopolitanism. Subjectivity takes form in the world, and the world is itself reconstructed by subjectivity's engagement with it.

The key curricular question—what knowledge is of most worth?—is posed by individuals existing at specific historical moments, in particular places, confronted by, infused with, reality that is itself ever shifting, in part as a consequence of one's engagement with it. Reality requires subjectivity: It is subjectivity that enables reality to speak.

In this intriguing, thought-provoking, nuanced volume, Pinar makes a crucial contribution to curriculum studies, providing compelling answers to key curricular questions concerning the inextricably interwoven relations among intellectual rigor, scholarly erudition, and intense but variegated engagement with the world.

William F. Pinar teaches curriculum theory at the University of British Columbia, where he holds a Canada Research Chair and directs the Centre for the Study of the Internationalization of Curriculum Studies.

Studies in Curriculum Theory
William F. Pinar, Series Editor

For additional information on titles in the Studies in Curriculum Theory series visit
www.routledge.com/education

The Worldliness of a Cosmopolitan Education
Passionate Lives in Public Service

William F. Pinar
University of British Columbia

 Routledge
Taylor & Francis Group

NEW YORK AND LONDON

First published 2009
by Routledge
270 Madison Ave, New York, NY 10016

Simultaneously published in the UK
by Routledge
2 Park Square, Milton Park, Abingdon, Oxon OX14 4RN

Routledge is an imprint of the Taylor & Francis Group, an informa business

© 2009 Taylor & Francis

Typeset in Sabon by
HWA Text and Data Management Ltd, London
Printed and bound in the United States of America on acid-free paper by
Walsworth Publishing Company, Marceline, MO

Library of Congress Cataloging in Publication Data
Pinar, William.
   The worldliness of a cosmopolitan education : passionate lives in public
   service / William F. Pinar.
       p. cm.
   1. Critical pedagogy. 2. Education–Curricula–Social aspects.
   3. Cosmopolitanism. 4. Addams, Jane, 1860–1935. 5. Bragg, Laura M.
   (Laura Mary), 1881–1978. 6. Pasolini, Pier Paolo, 1922–1975. I. Title.
   LC196.P56 2010
   370.11´5–dc22   2008046092

ISBN10: 0-415-99550-7 (hbk)
ISBN10: 0-415-99551-5 (pbk)
ISBN10: 0-203-87869-8 (ebk)

ISBN13: 978-0-415-99550-4 (hbk)
ISBN13: 978-0-415-99551-1 (pbk)
ISBN13: 978-0-203-87869-9 (ebk)

Contents

Definition of a Cosmopolitan Education

Preface

> A person who knows is a person who is engaged with the world.
> Madeleine R. Grumet (2006, 50)

Knowledge is about, presses us toward, into, the world (Young 2008, 95).[1]
Our private lives derive from our self-examined engagement with the world
(Nussbaum 1997, 9). Subjectivity takes form, achieves content and singularity,
in the world, itself reconstructed by subjectivity's engagement with it (Green
and Reid 2008, 20). Knowledge and engagement reconfigure subjectivity:
The persons we are and will become derive from our reconstructions of lived
experience in the world (Seigfried 1996, 57; Davies 2008, 173). Worldliness
summarizes the subjective consequences of such educational experience.
After the "linguistic turn" comes the "worldly turn" (Radhakrishnan 2008,
118). The key curricular question—what knowledge is of most worth?—is
a worldly question; it is posed by individuals existing at specific historical
moments, in particular places, confronted by, infused with, reality that is
itself ever shifting, in part according to our engagement with it. Reality
requires subjectivity: It is (not only) subjectivity that enables reality to speak
(Steimatsky 1998, 245).

   "What is the world and what is the human world," Radhakrishnan (2008,
24) asks, "and how does worldliness as a kind of becoming connect the
two?" A curriculum for cosmopolitanism juxtaposes the particular alongside
the abstract, creating collages of history and literature, politics and poetry,
science and art. Such a curriculum provides passages between the subjective
and the social, between "self-subjectivation" and "alterior interpellation"
(Radhakrishnan 2008, 8; see Muller 2000, 69). Focused less on institutional
allocations of coursework (Nussbaum 1997, 70, 77) than on its subjective
sources, a curriculum for cosmopolitanism cultivates comprehension of
alterity, including that self-knowledge that enables understanding of others
(Nussbaum 1997, 85). Such understanding can never be an "objective"
for which teachers can be held "accountable": It is always a retrospective
judgment rendered by those who been reconfigured by what they have studied
and how they have lived (Radhakrishnan 2008, 226; Seigfried 1996, 12).
Contrary to politicians' rhetoric, educational experience can be portrayed

but not mandated. Neither "models" nor "standards," these portraits of passionate lives in public service are testimonies to three cosmopolitan individuals: Jane Addams (1860–1935), Laura Bragg (1881–1978), and Pier Paolo Pasolini (1922–1975). These sketches (Chapters 5–7) refer us not only to further academic study—to the scholarly sources from which I have drawn them—but to ourselves, to the sometimes seemingly unsolvable puzzle of one's "life and flesh." Interesting and important in themselves, these three disparate individuals distance us from the reality of the present moment. "[T]he spell of the individual, meaningful image" (Schwenk 2005, 45) enables us to experience exile and estrangement (Nussbaum 1997, 57–58), thereby creating the existential conditions for "deeper knowledge through difference" (Gordon 1996, 79; Gilroy 2005, 24). Studying the alterity of actuality cultivates cosmopolitanism.

Not all need labor for distance from what is, of course: Diasporic peoples have been deported from it. Events expel even privileged subjects into strange spheres far from the familiar. For Pasolini, expulsion by the Communist Party in 1949 constituted such deportation; for Jane Addams, it was her father's death. The reconstruction of such traumatic lived experience for "the public work of subjectivity" (Gordon 1996, 80) takes variable forms, among them a civic commitment to difference. What Robert Gordon (1996, 81–82) says of Pasolini's tripartite self (poet, teacher, and outsider) might well extend to Addams and Bragg as well, as all three roles (and, I am suggesting, all three individuals) "share an origin in absolute 'love,' typically 'love for the world,' which sets them apart, gives them that privileged relationship with truth. All three attempt to shatter conventional modes of discourse *a priori*, through a form of scandalous difference." The public service of each can be understood as the project "to map the private work of subjectivity into history" (Gordon 1996, 82). A cosmopolitan curriculum relocates "the private work of subjectivity into history," as it underscores the "historicity of experience" (Cusset 2008, 156).

What does the concept of "subjectivity" suggest? Baudelaire associated subjectivity with "the invisible, the impalpable, the dream, the nerves, the *soul*" and, as such, in tension with facticity, with the objectivity of the present (quoted in Williams 2007, 34). Zola associated subjectivity with one's "heart" and "body," and, acknowledging its historical and social composition, with "civilization" and "locality" as well (quoted in Williams 2007, 34). What stands out here is the multiplicity of subjectivity, including "its internally heterogeneous interrelatedness" (Radhakrishnan 2008, 179). "Subjectivity is thus a *critical* resource," Robert Williams (2007, 35) points out, "and mobilizing it a strategy of opposition to the prevailing social and cultural order." Its cultivation constitutes a self-reflexive discipline of self-overcoming; it may even involve working against oneself (Williams 2007, 38; Garrison 1997, 38, 66). For those committed to this subjective discipline, self-reconstruction requires "cultivating solitude and independence of mind, distancing oneself from one's colleagues, or, if working in their company, doing so only in order to stimulate one's natural competitiveness and so spur oneself on to greater efforts" (Williams 2007, 37; Gallagher and Greenblatt 2000, 18). Collaboration means mediocrity if it compels conformity (Lepri 2005, 179; Seigfried 1996, 225; Popkewitz 2008, 125).

Cosmopolitanism confounds conformity, even contemporary and fashionable versions of it, such as identity politics (Chapter 2), with its commodification of subjectivity by culture (Foster 2005, 73). Cosmopolitanism, individuation, and self-knowledge are, I am suggesting, reciprocally related (Nussbaum 1997, 59). A cosmopolitan education invites an ongoing self-reflection associated with solitude while engaged with others in a world that is not only human and historical (Seigfried 1996, 195). For those mistaking the sign for the reality it signifies (Chapter 3), subjectivity is severed from the world, snared by slogans, substitutes for the knowledge to which they presumably refer. In our time, subjectivity is snared by the emergency of everyday life, wherein experience "[c]an neither be possessed nor internalized ... too 'large' to be contained within the boundaries of the individual self or ego" (Foster 2005, 176). Stripped of its sacred meaning, experience has been reduced to a means to an end.

Worldliness implies immanence rather than transcendence. Worldliness does not confine us to embodiment, however, trapped in "[p]articularity and thereby denied inclusion and participation in public life" (Foster 2005, 159). The magnetic medium of this immanence is subjectivity, as "the self becomes an emblem of the real" (Gordon 1996, 242). Passionate lives subjectively expressed through public service invite self-understanding through self-overcoming, as "it is only through history that man comes to know himself" (Jay 2005, 231). In our time, one also comes to know history through oneself, requiring declarations of independence from interpellation by powerful others, in U.S. schoolteachers' case, by politicians (Chapter 4).

Almost 50 years now into school deform—the conversion of academic institutions into businesses obsessed with "outputs," teachers downgraded to bureaucrats managing "learning," itself reduced to test taking—the sketch of Jane Addams' education (Chapter 5) reminds us that subjectivity structures social service. Addams built bridges between cultures through teaching the humanities and the arts while attending to the emergencies of everyday life in Chicago's Nineteenth Ward. In so doing, she made original contributions to American philosophy (Seigfried 1996, 44). Addams' passionate public service was sustained subjectively, a complex consequence of her relationship with her father and of her experience as mediator among family members, by her academic study at Rockford, by her experience of travel and disaffection, and by her intimate relationships with Ellen Gates Starr and, later, Mary Rozet Smith. A public intellectual whose classroom extended beyond Chicago to the nation and world, Addams personifies—in a singular, still echoing form—the worldliness a cosmopolitan education affords.

Here my representative for the anonymous teacher,[2] Laura Bragg, discovered that prosthetic extensions of her Yankee female body could teach lessons in local—early twentieth-century Southern—life her physical presence might have foreclosed. Like Addams, Bragg enacts subjectively her public service as reconstructions of the missionary legacy her father and the Progressive Era had imprinted. She found her "classroom"—the public—remarkably recalcitrant, whether in South Carolina or, later, in Massachusetts. Less a loud individual presence than Jane Addams or Pasolini, Bragg underscores the indirect expression of a "free" subjectivity through curricular materials—"transitional objects" (Pinar 2004, 248)—simultaneously self-expressive, communicative, testimonial. Through the complicated conversation that is the curriculum, subjectivity and that "instinctive, emotional cosmopolitanism" (Nava 2007, 69) it potentially expresses can be cultivated and come to form (Williams 2007, 39).

No one could know more keenly than Pasolini how contested subjectivity is, himself victim of vitriol from 1949 until his murder in 1975. Yet this post–World War II Renaissance man practiced a public pedagogy extolling subjectivity's capacity to reconstruct its interpellation through communicative media. First as a schoolteacher and as a Communist, a poet, playwright, and theoretician, always an outsider (Gordon 1996, 75), the legendary filmmaker understood his civic commitment as subjective expression of private passion. For Pasolini, political struggle was informed less by ideology (which always devolves into conformism) and more by passion expressed through reason to another individuals (Gordon 1996, 76). For him, "passion for the life of the body is also the passion for the absolute" (Viano 1993, 211). Indeed, for Pasolini, it is the body that enacts disruption of the abstract by the particular (Restivo 2002, 79). For him, "knowledge becomes possible only as experience and action" (Mariniello 1994, 121), including sexual experience and "action" undertaken esthetically. Informed by ongoing study, expressed critically and creatively through the arts, political action (like knowledge itself) was, for Pasolini, subjectively structured.

It is the primacy of subjectivity in education that is the through-line in my ongoing inquiry. With Madeleine Grumet, I devised an autobiographical method to study the subjectivity of educational experience. First drawing me to the study of literature and philosophy, then to history, politics, sexuality, gender, and race, last year my studies in subjectivity encountered cosmopolitanism. As rich and varied as the scholarly literature on cosmopolitanism is, I realized quickly that what it lacks is attention to subjectivity and its cultivation through education. I write this book to address that lack, invoking the lives of three passionate public intellectuals in service to us still. What they teach us is the centrality of subjectivity in the cultivation of cosmopolitanism.

esthetically

Organization of the Book

> Retrospection is now strategically deployed in an effort to grasp and transform the present.
>
> Robert S. C. Gordon (1996, 95)

> [P]rivate desires are fused with historical events.
>
> Charles Salas (2007, 27 n. 111)

In the first section of the book, I provide three problems of our not-exactly-cosmopolitan present, the first of which illustrates the wisdom of ideological mobility. When "identity" first dominated academic debates more than three decades ago, it was a welcome challenge to a patriarchal Eurocentrism, demanding and receiving recognition and inclusion of what had been before excluded knowledge: race-class-gender. The fact that these domains are now catechismal illustrates Pasolini's point about ideological devolution. Though the work of curriculum is never complete—the fundamental curriculum question[3] "what knowledge is of most worth?" is historically and subjectively stimulated—the labor of recognition and inclusion is elided by the indignation of contemporary identity politics (Nussbaum 1997, 109, 111). By substituting abstraction for particularity—ignoring the "reification of race" (Gilroy 2005, 151)—"the balkanized domain of identity politics" (Cusset 2008, 157) recapitulates the preference of prejudice for stereotypes (e.g., "whitestream thinkers" [Grande 2004, 33]). The reinscription of racism in identity politics and its catastrophic curricular cosmopolitics are the subject of Chapter 2.

It is abstraction that obliterates specificity in teacher education's emphasis upon signs stripped of scholarship. In this respect, teacher education—defiled by the Bush Administration's insistence on linking instruction to test scores—recapitulates the broader academic field of education's obsession with institutionalization. The school as an organization preoccupies many educational researchers, demonstrating an anti-intellectual, bureaucratic bias. The curriculum—after all, the point of the school—is systematically ignored, and the academic specialty devoted to it marginalized, as federal funding is targeted at the so-called "learning sciences" (Taubman 2009). In the obsession with outcomes, the intellectual quality of what we offer students is left to textbook writers and to teachers distracted by documenting "standards" and other bureaucratic markers of their "gracious submission." This mistaking of the institution for the process it houses is evident in one reviewer's criticism of my curriculum for reparation, as you will see in Chapter 3.

It is teachers' "gracious submission"—their interpellation by politicians and others determined to leave no child behind in their unregulated company (for a racial and gendered analysis see Pinar 2007d)—that I challenge in Chapter 4. This is a speech I gave two days after Independence Day 2006 to students in an arts-based masters program in educational administration. Having moved to Canada the year before had stimulated a patriotism I had

Each taking risks.

once forfeited to political conservatives, moving me to juxtapose Jefferson's formulation of the case for independence in 1776 and the teaching profession's need for it now.

In the second section, I present sketches of three passionate lives in public service. The three—Addams, Bragg, Pasolini—could not be more different from one another, but each was a most "excellent pedagogist" (Allen 1982, 35). Each sketch lays bare how academic study and lived experience subjectively reconstructed provide passages from private preoccupations to public service. Through academic engagement with the Western intellectual tradition, Addams, Bragg, and Pasolini found her or his way to those historically victimized by the racism, classicism, and misogyny that had accompanied that tradition's formation. Each took risks for the sake of "the Other," demonstrating moral[4] courage expressed pedagogically in the public interest. Despite sacrifice, each lived self-referentially, conscious that self-cultivation occurred through passionate engagement with the "world as history" (Radhakrishnan 2008, 212). That engagement transfigured these private individuals into public intellectuals, imprinting each with that worldliness a cosmopolitan education compels.

"The problem of my life and flesh" animates academic study and focuses ongoing reflection on lived experience. Structured subjectively and socially, educational experience enables engagement with the world always, as Jackson Pollock described his painting, "working from within" (Pinar 1994, 10). So understood, the private problem becomes worked out through public service conceived as forms of "intracultural education."[5] This phrase reminds us that the constitution of the subject occurs not through conformity to culture but through self-reflexive negotiations within and among alterities (Wang 2004, 92). Indeed: "[t]he only place in which the human subject dwells," Radhakrishnan (2008, 8) asserts, "is between." Summoned here to create "between" spaces within the surface of the present, the past is one such alterity. This is no poststructuralist performance of difference and undecidability. Though reality is composed like a text, the text of history functions here as a passage to the reality of the world. As Radhakrishnan (2008, 50) underscores, the "human subject can have no access to life except by way of history." Though "hidden in historical forms," life is not identical to it: the world—reality—exceeds our representations of it (Radhakrishnan 2008, 50, 130). I offer these biographical sketches of the past, then, to point us not only to history but as well to a "prediscursive, experiential, and phenomenological worldliness" (Radhakrishnan 2008, 130). Before reading Addams's, Bragg's, and Pasolini's personifications of such worldliness, let us survey three examples of the problem of the present to which these biographic sketches speak. "In the name of the political," Radhakrishnan (2008, 235) points out, "the lifeworld has been betrayed, even trashed." As identity is to interiority (Chapter 2), the "sign" is to academic knowledge (Chapter 3), and test-taking is to educational experience (Chapter 4). These substitutions of surface for substance is the problem of our not-exactly-cosmopolitan present.

Acknowledgments

[handwritten annotation: Influence of Father]

Earlier versions of Chapters 4 and 6 appeared elsewhere. I thank Alan Block, editor of the *Journal of the American Association for the Advancement of Curriculum Studies*, and Bill Clockel of Educator's International Press, for their permission to reprint these pieces. My debts are several: to Peter Taubman, for introducing me to Pasolini; to Petra Munro, whose devotion to Jane Addams' animated mine; to Madeleine Grumet (2006) for scolding schooling for being about itself and not the world; to Janet Miller (2005, 249, 114), whose conception of "worldliness" focused my initial inquiry, and for her conceptualization of "juxtaposition," which I hope I have put to good use, and not only in this book; to Mary Bryson, for bringing Rancière to campus and for recommending Kurasawa; and to Aditya Raj for the gift of Radhakrishnan. My thanks as well to the remarkable Naomi Silverman: How very much I appreciate our annual conversation.

In familial terms, my debt is to my parents. My professional life has been a consequence of my relationship with my father, to his repeated injunction during my childhood: "Whatever you seek in life, son, find understanding." For him—Frederick Eugene Pinar (1920–1988)—that quest was intellectual as well as lived, as he grappled with the trauma of having been orphaned at age 12. As a boy, I was entranced with his philosophizing; only later, after succeeding at school (as he relentlessly pressured me to do), did I imagine him naïve. Despite that rebellion, my intellectual life history testifies to the fact that I am my father's son. Those numerous and intense dispositions within me toward pleasure seeking derived from his considerable unconscious and from my mother, Malinda Brooke Pinar (1917–1982). A former nightclub singer, recording artist, and regional radio celebrity (with one appearance on national TV—"'The Kate Smith Variety Hour")—Malinda was a sometimes unenthusiastic but decidedly "good enough" mother (Zaretsky 2004, 272). Regularly she performed for us kids (my brother David and sister Mary), transfiguring our living room into a cabaret. Her sensual pleasure in singing, her raucous sense of humor, her profound emotion—in the last decade of her life, it was an inconsolable grief over her situation—left me with an internalized demand for pleasure that would drive me near death more than once. Sitting quietly in my sixties now, I am able to think about you calmly, Mom. It has been clear to me for some time that your victimization by a gender system that you – and, at the time, I—did not understand and personified in the one you (and I) loved, prepared me to become a feminist man, one working on your behalf, if belatedly and from a distance. Here I simply celebrate you, marvelous Malinda. This book is for you.

Introduction

To interpret the world is to change it

1 "The Problem of My Life and Flesh"

Subjectivity — inner life / sense of self

Individuality is not so much a state to be achieved as a mode of life to be pursued.

Kwame Anthony Appiah (2005, 5)

Consciousness also transforms.

Jane Mansbridge (2001, 5)

What is Subjectivity

Cosmopolitanism is often discussed in institutional and political terms, only relatively recently in gendered terms[1] or racial terms[2] and rarely in terms of subjectivity, as "a structure of feeling and aspiration" (Nava 2007, 98). By subjectivity, I mean the inner life, the lived sense of "self"—however non-unitary, dispersed, and fragmented—that is associated with what has been given and what one has chosen, those circumstances of everyday life, those residues of trauma and of fantasy, from which one reconstructs a life. Autobiography, biography, fiction, and poetry are all narrative modes of subjectivity, discursive means of self-disclosure and self-understanding (Garrison 1997, 191). However split off, interiority is always of and in the world. It is cosmopolitanism as subjectively being-in-the-the world that I sketch here, subjective engagement in and for the world that complicates the self and its narration as it challenges—even "changes"—the world (Jay 2005, 226, 231).

"You wouldn't be a cosmopolitan," Kwane Anthony Appiah (2005, 222) cautions, "if you were a humanitarian who (to invert Marx's slogan) sought to change the world but not to understand it." I suggest that to interpret the world *is* to change it. As the right-wing in America has long understood (Zimmerman 2002), the school curriculum is one crucial site of such interpretation. The school curriculum is where the world is explained to the young, where the very meaning of and impetus for "change" are elaborated. It is where, as Jane Addams appreciated, academic knowledge meets the neighborhood, where the abstraction of knowledge encounters the concrete specificity of students. The crucial character of the school curriculum is why even "democratic" governments have taken hold of the schools. Not explicitly, as that would disclose political agendas. Instead, "democratic" states take hold of schools indirectly, through standardized examinations whereby the curriculum becomes a means to an end. Rendered irrelevant in such "accountability" schemes is teachers' professional obligation to interpret their subjects—and through those subjects, the world—to their students. In Orwellian language, "Leave No Child Behind" is disguised as the political agenda to control what children know and can think: No child shall be left behind in the charge of intellectually independent teachers, now consigned to speak others' scripts (Taubman 2009).

Not only through the schools do governments attempt to control the "complicated conversation" that is the nation's private and public life. Through the media, citizens are conditioned to criticize, to assume, to trust. It is no accident that Pasolini conducted so much of his pedagogy through newspapers. Television, he felt certain, ensured somnolence; only through reading—and the subjectivity reading supports—was there a chance that truth might be discerned. Through his newspaper columns, through poetry, novels and, especially, through cinema, Pasolini taught the public. A man of, immersed in, the world, Pasolini is particularly appropriate to this textbook for teachers, as I emphasize the subjectivity of cosmopolitanism that is "worldliness." As a state of being between the local and the global, simultaneously self-engaged and worldly-wise, cause and consequence of a cosmopolitan education, worldliness is a subjective supplement to cosmopolitanism, more commonly discussed as a moral universalism or, more legally and diplomatically, as agreements among nation-states, expressed as concerns for human rights (Mayer, Luke and Luke 2008, 92).

One subtext of such conventions of cosmopolitanism is the primacy of "the individual" (it is the "individual" who is said to have human rights), a concept I recuperate from capitalism's capture as "possessive individualism" (the right to exploit in order to accumulate), from its disappearance in poststructuralism's emphasis upon discourse and textuality, and from its occlusion by identity politics' preference for collectivism, as I complain in Chapter 2. In his final years, even Foucault acknowledged the reality of the individual (Paras 2006, 123), as did Edward Said (Radhakrishnan 2008, 168-9), despite their disagreement over humanism (Radhakrishnan 2008, 147, 152). I work from the facticity of the concretely existing individual to sketch three personifications of cosmopolitanism: Jane Addams, Laura Bragg, Pier Paolo Pasolini. I intend these sketches as contributions to a "new" not necessarily Western (Radhakrishnan 2008, 178) indeed "planetary" humanism[3] that supports cosmopolitan ideals of justice expressed through culturally variable, individuated forms of subjectivity that education (especially in the humanities and the arts: Nussbaum 1997, 85, 97) invites, that the business model (in its misrepresentation of education as a measurable enterprise) obliterates.

Acknowledging that no predictable relationships exist between personality and politics (Young-Bruehl 1996, 57ff.), there *are* structures of subjectivity that can be socially significant. In particular, in the United States at the present time, the restructuring of subjectivity after conservative Christianity, with sexual abstinence linked with acceptance of biblical authority, reproduces persons inclined to do what they are told by their "born-again"—that often means uneducated—pastors. This predisposition to conformity cannot be captured by concepts such as the "authoritarian personality," but we can see the effects (or it is caused[4]): suspicion toward science, susceptibility to propaganda ("spin" as it is soft-pedaled today), and submission to authority. These predispositions are profoundly anti-democratic. Progressives have long appreciated that democratization depends upon reciprocal and responsive relations among individuals, ideals, and institutions. These reciprocal relations are reiterative, as individuals and institutions work their way through the past toward a future presumably more peaceful, more sustainable, more just than what that past and the present have produced.

Spirituality, sexuality, and sustainability are among those structures of subjectivity the present historical situation fractures. In contrast to (although intersecting with) religion ("institutional, creedal, orthodox"), spirituality ("individualistic, mystical, pluralist") I define simply as a subjective sense of the sacred (Robertson 2008, 4, 10; Lather 2007, 178 n. 4). This subjective sense of the sacred is not linked to a deity or to preachers posing as prophets (Jay 2005, 103ff.) but to life, and not only human life (Nussbaum 2006, 21). Such spirituality can inspire political action (Harris 2001, 57; Morris and Braine 2001, 37). But "pro-life" is a "decoy-concept" (Pasolini 2005 [1972], 125) for controlling women's bodies; many religious conservatives seem to be anything but religious or conservative, blocking, for instance, universal medical care as well as other forms of social and economic justice. It is a reverence for life that infuses the spiritual structure of subjectivity, including life that is past and life that is yet to come (Grande 2004, 57, 89 n. 8; Pitt 2008, 194). That respect for what is past and what is not yet requires "historical"—indeed "planetary"—"consciousness" (Seixas 2004; Gilroy 2005, 75; Morris 2001, 9; Kurasawa 2007, 17; Jay 2005, 257, 280, 282). For me, such a phrase includes specific (academic) knowledge of what has transpired but, as well, a temporal structure of subjectivity I have specified as regressive, progressive, analytic and synthetic.[5]

Such a temporally differentiated subjectivity supports remembrance and futuristic fantasy, grasped analytically as self-understanding, condensed as self-mobilization for engagement with the world. "If spirit is a name for the resistant and transcending faculties of the agent," Roberto Unger (2007, 38) suggests, "we can spiritualize society." Against the presentism compelled by consumer capitalism, such subjectivity means one always has one "foot" in the past, one in the future, while inhabiting the entire body, including mind and heart, in the present, ready to act in reverence for life (Robertson 2008, 12). Such an undertaking constitutes political action: Democratization of society toward economic justice and biospheric sustainability requires reconstruction of our racialized and gendered subjectivities. Such subjective democratization

Ecology ~ Sustainability / American Dream [handwritten annotation]

becomes evident in the lives of concretely existing individuals engaged with/in the world.

Sustainability does not mean the unregulated reproduction of the species. In fact, heterosexual copulation—with its potential for offspring—contributes to the crisis of sustainability, despite disbelief (Epstein 2008, 59). How can an ever-increasing human population mean anything but ever more deforestation, more carbon emissions, more destruction of habitats belonging to other species, more competition for scarce resources? "[T]he heterosexual couple is presented as an obsessively coercive model," Pasolini complained, "exactly along the lines, for example, of the pairing between consumer and motor car" (quoted in Caesar 1999, 372; Lawton 2005a, x). Separating heterosexuality from reproduction has not been accomplished by birth-control protocols; additional steps are required, including state regulation of reproduction and the promotion of homosexuality. Sexuality is, then, a second structure of cosmopolitan subjectivity for which the present historical situation calls. Especially those forms of sexual experimentation that enable self-restructuring can contribute to the democratization of subjectivity. If sexual experimentation is studied, that is. The structuring of academic study by lived experience—itself "interrogated as to its value for a richer, fuller, more expansive life" (Seigfried 1996, 57)—can dissolve the "snare of preparation" (Lasch 1965, 12), in our time mindless consumption and its compensatory concomitant, a narcissistic hedonism (Lepri 2005, 177). "Voluptuousness" is a state of mind, not a set of behaviors.

Split off from academic and self-knowledge, spirituality and sexuality—two sides of the same cultural coin—contribute little to sustainability. Indeed, by itself spirituality seems to turn in on itself, tending toward sectarianism. While providing comfort to desperate individuals, institutionalized religion has contributed considerably to the destruction of life on earth; it is to be engaged cautiously. By itself, sexuality becomes obsessive, its importance inflated as it is asked to carry more psychic freight than it can convey. It can even contribute to fascism through "repressive desublimation," where citizens trade civic sovereignty for sensual satiation (Savran 1998, 34-35; Caesar 1999, 369; Pedersen 1998). Presentistic sensualism cannot be understood apart from the capitalist commodification of everything. "Monstrously transformed by consumerism into a technique of domination," Walter Siti (1994, 67) laments, "eros leads people to the loss of self." What absorbs consumers are not matters of subjective meaning but opportunities for profit and acquisition. Lived experience is replaced by "lifestyle" (Restivo 2002, 149). The American Dream is no longer life, liberty, and the pursuit of happiness; it is owning a house whose market value constantly appreciates; it is winning a lottery. The American Nightmare is self-immolation through destruction of the biosphere for the sake of profit. "But few there are who have paused to question," Zitkala-Ša posed presciently, "whether real life or long-lasting death lies beneath this semblance of civilization" (quoted in Krupat 1994, 297). "Real life" is, I suggest, worldliness.

Worldliness is defined (the OED here) as "the condition of being worldly; devotion to worldly affairs to the neglect of religious duties or spiritual needs; love of the world and its pleasures." It is this binary worldliness[7] dissolves. It is love of this world—not only the human world—that enables experience of the spiritual, that faithful devotion to reality not split off in a separate sphere (an afterlife) but here and now (Jay 2005, 94; Robertson 2008, 19). Worldliness accepts death in life, accepts the reality of limits, respects necessity, stares evil in the eye without fear or faith. No religion, worldliness is a retrospective judgment, not an educational objective. "While [w]orldliness is no passive acceptance of the world as it is," Radhakrishnan 2008, 165) points out, neither does it imply faith in instrumentalism, or social engineering (Seigfried 1996, 193, 201). Rather, worldliness invites the "rigorous" enactment of "individual intentionality" and "critical consciousness" (Radhakrishnan 2008, 165). Because it follows from a subjectively structured creative engagement with the world eschewing "standards" or "models," worldliness is characterized by difference, diversity, diversion, and the personified and situated relations among these (Seigfried 1996, 145, 148). Historically, worldliness might represent a station on the historical path to a sacred humanism centered on the biosphere: "[H]istoricity is constitutive of our peculiarly human interactions with nature," Seigfried (1996, 151) notes. As for Walt Whitman, in worldliness the political and the spiritual are "completely intertwined" (Robertson 2008, 21; see Nussbaum 1995, 82, 119), in inextricable relation to both the "radical alterity" and "organic intimacy" of nature (Radhakrishnan 2008, 27).

With 1 billion human beings hungry, with the biosphere facing extinction, with the destruction of democracy the radical right has achieved in the United States, the pursuit of life and liberty becomes urgent. Personal happiness is precious in nightmare times. I do not share Marcuse's evocation of utopian ideals as creating the dissonance required for action; I focus on the actual, as "reality points to the absent ideal within it" (Rohdie 1995, 60). It is through the understanding of reality that we might find our way to the future (Seigfried 1996, 176). Because the educational potential of academic study "can be realized only in the service of a future implicated in the present but not yet apparent, imagination plays a central role in experimental understanding" (Seigfried 1996, 176; see Nussbaum 1997, 14). Central, yes, but even the "worldly imagination" (Radhakrishnan 2008, 13) is not necessarily benign (Pinar 2001, 1129 ff.). It is not to be encouraged uncritically, ungrounded by erudition (Greene 1995).

Fantasy structures sexuality. Despite repressive desublimation, evidently sex still portends a progressive politics: Witness the right's hysterical allegiance to abstinence. Sexuality must be studied (high-school courses on the history of sexuality are an obvious curricular offering now blocked by the right wing) and experienced (no curricular encouragement required). But experience without study can be stupid. Without study—knowledge, reason, self-reflexivity—one cannot experience subjective meaning or participate in one's self-formation, an idea centuries old (Jay 2005, 21–23, 89). Without academic study (in the public sphere justified by references to economics only), subjectivity can succumb to narcissism, presentism, and the commodification of experience consumer capitalism compels (Lasch 1978, 1984). Without a self-reflexive and temporally variegated subjectivity, the social collapses into conformity, individuals are rendered automata, and democracy becomes a cover for consumerism.

For those of us whose profession is academic study, maintaining a critical (if variable) distance[8] between our work and the society in which it occurs remains an obligation. Distance constitutes a prerequisite to the ongoing cultivation of disciplinary structures such as "verticality" (intellectual history) and "horizontality" (analysis of present circumstances). Disciplinarity enables fidelity to our collective intellectual advancement. While it is clear that the academic disciplines are also interdisciplinary, avowedly interdisciplinary movements—such as women's studies—have made possible not only new knowledge but revisions of existing disciplines (Nussbaum 1997, 186 ff.). The porousness of disciplinary boundaries—between disciplines, from social context—is variable according to academic field, historical moment, national culture, and even institutional setting (Anderson and Valente 2002). For me, this fact requires the cultivation of disciplinarity, even in interdisciplinary fields like curriculum studies (Pinar 2007a).

Academic labor can be subjectively animated and structured, a fact evident in the great humanistic tradition of study (Pinar 2006b, 109–120), now nearly extinguished by decades of school deform. "Standards" and "accountability" signify the rhetorical and material means by which study has come to connote only test preparation, not self-cultivation (Hlebowitsh 2005, 103). Replacing the professional prerogative—indeed, the obligation—to communicate a situated, singular understanding of one's discipline attuned to one's students, teachers are now scripted, delivering lessons not their own. Rather than students appreciating that academic study provides passages to understanding of the world in which their own subjectivities come to form, too many students (knowing only the business model of schooling) are now consumers of "educational services." This "anthropological" catastrophe, as Pasolini might say, means that humanity's historic vocation of humanization has been exchanged for unending ever-expanding exploitation.

A cosmopolitan curriculum enables students to grapple with (again borrowing Pasolini's language) the "problem of my life and flesh." That "problem" is autobiographical, historical, and biospheric. It is a problem to be studied as it is lived through and acted upon. The worldliness of a cosmopolitan curriculum implies that general education is more than an introduction to "great works," the memorization of "essential" knowledge, or a sampling of the primary disciplinary categories (three units in social science, three in natural science, etc.); it is subjectively structured academic study of this lived-historical problem of "my life and flesh," perhaps through great works, perhaps through sampling major intellectual traditions, no doubt involving memorization, organized around teachers' and students' questions expressed in creative curricular forms. Such a cosmopolitan curriculum may claim disciplinary and/or interdisciplinary identification (for one example, see Angier 2008); its educational significance is demonstrated by providing intellectual and lived bridges between self and society.

The possible consequences of study are best left unspecified, left to the retrospective judgment of those involved. In his rejection of claims made on behalf of the humanities, Stanley Fish (2008) makes the point that study has no predictable moral or economic effect. Rationalizing the humanities in terms apart from the humanities themselves (by references to career advancement, for instance) denigrates their educational significance, their intrinsic worth, the pleasure they give those who study them willingly. In my terms, such extra-educational rationales are indeed anti-intellectual, expressions of the social engineering pandemic accompanying the triumph of consumer capitalism. The humanities may have no "use," as Fish asserts, but I testify to their moral and ethical significance. The humanities express enduring human values to be reconstructed by each generation. Extracting those values for extra-educational remuneration, making them the tested outcomes of study, deforms academic knowledge as it reduces it to "information." Even when those value claims are entirely salutary—social and subjective reconstruction, for instance—we desecrate study by extracting use-values from the knowledge in which they are embedded.[9] This mistake is long-standing, and I discuss it in Chapter 3.

Some mistakes are not ours. The exploitation of public education as a political—indeed presidential campaign—issue after Sputnik's launching in 1957 is a calamity we can lay only at the feet of politicians, even the apparently well-meaning kind. Regardless of the Kennedy Administration's intentions, 1960s national curriculum reform achieved its negative apotheosis during the George W. Bush Administration when teachers were cast as accountable for students' scores on standardized examinations. As deferred and displaced racism and misogyny,[10] politicians' subjugation of America's schoolteachers also stripped the curriculum of its subjective animation and creative potential. As Madeleine R. Grumet (2007, x) observes: "The presence and individuality that are the markers of the inspired and inspiring teachers are expunged from the protocols that regulate teaching." Singled out as no profession has been, public school teaching is now so degraded that many teachers depart after only a few years of public service (Dillon 2007b). I express my outrage in Chapter 4.

Recasting Cosmopolitanism as Worldliness

What has happened to the fire inside?

Denise Taliaferro Baszile (2006, 8)

I am a correlate of this world.

Madeleine R. Grumet (2006, 50)

The crime of collectivism is the obliteration of the particular, the *individual*, that lived and legal basis of human rights (Jay 2005, 175). Erected on its grave are monuments to ethnic identity with concomitant claims to "martyrology" (Cusset 2008, 314; see Chapter 2), to signs stripped of academic knowledge (Chapter 3), and to politicians' Orwellian miseducation of the public, rendering teachers and students "non-persons" (i.e., test scores; Chapter 4). In this triumph of the abstract over the concrete (Stein 2001, 128), cosmopolitanism seems an elusive prospect, indeed. To depict the concept concretely, I provide portraits of three individuals whose passionate lives[11] were expressed in public service.[12] Each valued difference; each personified what Mica Nava (2007, 8) has characterized as an "intimate" and "visceral cosmopolitanism."

First and foremost, I remain a teacher, a secondary-school English teacher. Preparing for class, I look for material that speaks to and for me and might speak to my students, attending to my disciplinary preoccupations and obligations, animated, too, by my absorption in what we used to call "current events," a curiously detached phrase for "the pressing events of the day" (Seigfried 1996, 233). That adjective—"pressing"—more aptly conveys the phenomenological press of what happens even in Harare. (I have hated Mugabe since he likened gay people to "dogs" and "pigs" [Duke 1995, A19].) Here I mark "current events" by reference to newspaper articles. In 1930, Jane Addams remarked that "we gradually discovered that the use of the current event is valuable beyond all other methods of education" (quoted in Lasch 1965, 213). Like the reference to Mugabe, my teaching is subjectively animated *because* it is attuned to the historical moment.

My teaching was always structured by my academic training in literary criticism: by the close reading of texts, whether these were the various genres of literature or my students' writing, classroom statements and conduct or my own experience of all these. Owing to an undergraduate minor in psychology, I have rarely been impressed with social science; almost always it has seemed intellectually inferior to the humanities. Theory was the only subspecies of the social sciences that has held interest for me: In graduate school (two years of which coincided with my brief if imprinting high-school teaching experience) Alvin W. Gouldner's *The Coming Crisis of Western Sociology* seemed to provide a definitive epistemological critique of "social science" while encouraging my study of autobiography through his emphasis upon "domain assumptions" (1970, 31 ff.).

Complicated Conversation defines Curriculum

During the four decades since I taught high-school English, the academic subjects comprising the high-school curriculum threaten to become a casualty of politicians' obsession with what students "learn," that concept reduced to scores on standardized tests. During these decades I have studied (contrapuntally, as it were) the subjective experience of academic study, experience that is inevitably structured by life history, historical moment, and politics, including the politics of identity. From this focus upon self-formation through academic study and lived experience, I have come to a conception of curriculum development not as an institutional specification of "objectives" but as an intellectual-autobiographical matter of scholarship that engages teachers and students subjectively grappling with themselves in the world (Mayer, Luke and Luke 2008, 95). Curriculum design is not a matter of psychological manipulation but of the esthetic juxtaposition[13] of academic knowledge addressed to students who may already be worldly-wise.

"Complicated conversation" defines curriculum. By reintegrating "teaching" (or instruction or pedagogy) into the concept of curriculum, this phrase puts the teacher in his or her place: a participant in an ongoing multi-referenced conversation. Separating the teacher from curriculum reifies the role: Too easily teaching becomes inflated, one becomes a magician, mandated to a pull a rabbit out of a hat. Even conjoined conjunctively—as in curriculum *and* pedagogy—teaching becomes a topic in itself, thereby misconstrued as "technique," a bag of tricks to rescue a boring or irrelevant curriculum or a sales pitch student-consumers demand before they consider a "purchase." Given grade inflation, students' disinclination to study is likely reflected less in the grade received than in the score by which they evaluate the faculty (Lewis 1999). While always pedagogically appropriate to attend to the experience of the student, the ritualistic emphasis upon evaluation during the last 40 years has led to institutional neglect of the intellectual quality and character of the curriculum. The intellectual quality of the curriculum depends upon the erudition—only secondarily the savvy—of the teacher. Despite the profession's tragic assertion of the "priority of pedagogy over curriculum" (Green and Reid 2008, 23; see Pinar 2006b, 110), what matters is what teachers know.

The prominence of "teaching" in the concept and practice of education was turned against teachers by the Bush Administration, as it held them responsible for student learning.[14] Instead of educational opportunities offered, teaching became a contract promising to produce "results," that is, rising test scores. This catastrophe was made credible by those delusions of grandeur that an emphasis upon "teaching"—severed from the curriculum—supports. As one—albeit key—element in the complicated conversation that is the curriculum, teaching is not manipulation of "motivation" but a subjectively animated intellectual engagement with others over specific texts, a "characterological enactment" (Anderson 2006, 3) of passion in the public service.

Each individual I sketch here grappled ingenuously with the injustices of their time and place, enacting creatively their commitment to the education of the public. Each speaks to the problems of our not-exactly-cosmopolitan present. First and foremost, each was an individualist. Each took her or his individuality as a central medium of creative expression, whether in teaching (one form of Addams's public service) or curriculum development (Laura Bragg's boxes) or filmmaking (one form of Pasolini's public pedagogy). It is as if each appreciated that without the specificity of one's individuality, one has nothing original to say and, moreover, there is no one present to speak to anyway. None would have mistaken the sign for the signified (even if neither Addams nor Bragg would have used such terms), even if each appreciated the significance of "transitional objects"—Hull-House, Bragg's boxes, Pasolini's movies—as subjectively sculpted "curricular materials." As communicative media, these express the singularity of individuality as they address the alterity of the Other.

What is my relationship to the three and to the project itself? Obviously, it is not identificatory: I am not as compassionate as Addams, as clever as Bragg, as courageous as Pasolini. Studying these three figures inspires me to remain engaged with a world without hope. They refer me to the specificity of what I face, enabling me to thread the needle of intentionality that stitches me to the world. I chose Addams, Bragg, and Pasolini because they spoke to me and allowed me to speak through them. *Because* they were more compassionate, clever, and courageous than I, they stimulated my curiosity and, over time, commanded my attention. After Radhakrishnan (2008, 15), I also chose my subjects because each inhabited a "conjunctural space" in which the various constituent elements of each situation are reconstructed in specific, individuated ways that demonstrate the unrepeatable particularity of "worlding." In my terms, each enacts the worldliness of a cosmopolitan education.

Addams, Bragg, and Pasolini personify the three structures of subjectivity I have suggested as supplements to cosmopolitanism. While none faced the prospect of biospheric collapse, Pasolini exhibited an "ecological consciousness" following from his "enlarged notion of the sacred" (Viano 1993, 6). Addams invoked early Christianity as a courageous community of servants to humanity. Pasolini's sexuality was a public matter of intense controversy, while Bragg and Addams' sexual lives remained private (although not, I think, irrelevant). While private, none was content to stay at home; each understood that "home" was the world. In individuated ways, each expresses the worldliness of a cosmopolitan education.

Jane Addams' public service provides a compelling portrait of the "public intellectual" whose civic commitment meant not only meaningful and memorable participation in major public debates and events but "original" contributions to the "initial formulation" of American pragmatism (Seigfried 1996, 44). It is Addams's education that interests me especially, specifically her self-extrication from the "snare" her gender, class, and familial circumstances constructed for her. Addams herself blames academic preparation, but it is clear to me that study afforded her the concepts—and the experience—to name that (family) claim and to articulate another: the "social" (Brown 2004, 118). By displacing her submission to her stepmother onto the principal at Rockford Seminary, Addams was able to slowly sever the bonds that bind, reconstructing them into friendship with Ellen Gates Starr and, later, Mary Rozet Smith. As her biographers makes clear, Addams sought lived experience to supplement academic study, transposing her devotion to family into devotion to the world. From teaching her neighbors to teaching her fellow human beings, Addams's quietly passionate life was expressed in profound public service.

No larger-than-life figure, Laura Bragg suits my purpose in part because most public servants (including schoolteachers) will not be recognized with a Nobel Prize (as was Addams) or considered for one (as was, evidently, Pasolini: Schwartz 1992, 4). Most of us will not enjoy even the recognition a biography brings. Like Addams, Bragg was a daughter of progressivism; like Addams, she moved to a city estranged from the circumstances of her upbringing and education. Born in the South, Bragg was educated in Boston, then moved to Charleston, South Carolina, where she taught lessons in history, culture, and geography through prosthetic extensions of her female body. Bragg's displaced and restructured body becomes the site for historical action (Gordon 1996, 249). Her clever and committed interventions in the early twentieth-century segregated South not only testifies to the educational significance of "transitional objects" (Pinar 2004, 248), they illustrate the centrality of "free indirect subjectivity" (Rohdie 1995, 156) in public service. Through the public expression of private passion, teachers find their way through the labyrinth that is academic knowledge, historical moment, social structure, and professional obligation.

Few teachers have been as keenly conscious of this pedagogical puzzle as was Pasolini, a schoolteacher disbarred from his professional practice and excommunicated from his political party by sexual prejudice.[15] He would make Italy itself his classroom, as he translated his private passion into service to a public that often repudiated what he taught. First with translations of regional poetry, then with the composition of his own poems, novels, and films, Pasolini contested the anthropological catastrophe that was neocapitalistic consumerism as he feverishly fashioned lessons to lead us out of the ruins we have become (Jay 2005, 176). There are scholars (Barański 1999b, 22, 34) who complain about the "myth" of Pasolini. Like Addams, Pasolini *is* mythic: I found his accomplishment so astonishing it threatened to take over this book.

This autobiographical admission is not arbitrary or incidental. While "the personal"—sometimes felt to be located somewhere in the body (Salvio 2007, 4)—can be "relocated" where it is not immediately recognizable, it nonetheless structures one's engagement with the world, including through pedagogic participation in the curriculum. Such "relocation," Barbara Kamler (2001, 5) suggests, is "an embodied social and political act." The autobiographical can inform not only the teaching of writing—the subject of Kamler's intriguing text—but pedagogy, including the public kind (see Strong-Wilson 2007). In fact, subjectivity—not scripts written by others— must structure teaching if it is to acknowledge the centrality of erudition, intelligence, and professional judgment in education. Subjectivity must structure teaching if the curriculum is to convey the vitality of intellectual life. "[T]he intentionality that the teacher brings into the classroom must be directed toward the world, toward the phenomena that our knowledge points out," Grumet (2006, 51) points out, "if her interest in life is to be conveyed." To refocus these facts, I invoke Pasolini's conception of "free indirect subjectivity."

Free Indirect Subjectivity

> It is this primacy of style that, reanimating the speech of others, causes the material recovered in such a manner to assume an expressive function.
> Pier Paolo Pasolini (2005 [1972], 86)

Pasolini termed this reconfiguration of the author's subjectivity into his characters' speech "free indirect subjectivity," the communication of "expressive possibilities stifled by the convention of traditional narrative" (quoted in Greene 1990, 116).[16] Pasolini argued that at certain moments in cinema—brought to the viewer's attention by the "insistences" of the framings—we begin to sense the presence of a "second" film, expressed stylistically:

> Such an insistence on details, particularly on certain details in the digressions (excursus), represents a deviation from the system of the film: it is the temptation to make another film. In short, it is the presence of the author who, through an abnormal freedom, transcends his film and continually threatens to abandon it, detoured by a sudden inspiration - an inspiration of latent love for the poetic world of his own vital experiences (quoted in Greene 1990, 119).

Pasolini theorized a link between free indirect subjectivity—which implies a degree of mimesis between the author's vision and that of his protagonists (or, in our case, between the teacher's vision and her subjects, understood as both ideas and concrete individuals: her pupils, colleagues, parents)—and an "abnormal" stylistic freedom, in the teacher's case, academic or intellectual freedom (Ryan-Scheutz 2007, 143; Weis 2005, 61; Rohdie 1995, 136; Viano 1993, 93 ff.).

It is this stylistic freedom that is the core of Pasolini's "cinema of poetry" for, through it, the director creates the "second" film, an "authentic" and "irrational" film that springs from cinema's deepest, and perhaps most poetic, subtext. This "second" film—one that the "author would have wanted to make even without the visual mimesis of his protagonist"—is "totally and freely of an expressive-expressionist sort" (quoted in Greene 1990, 120). This "other" film is created through formal means. Its protagonist—and, by extension, the protagonist of the cinema of poetry—is style itself. And this style is understood, essentially, as a stylistic freedom that calls attention to itself by violating convention (Greene 1990).

While I assert no direct analogy between cinema and curriculum, Pasolini's conception helps us specify the educational potential of autobiographical labor.[17] While self-expressive, autobiography can create crevices in one's character to allow the "real" to surface and reconfigure the self being expressed. By focusing on the self-formation of Jane Addams, for instance, the reader's own self-formation becomes self-disclosing: the so-called dyadic effect. Indirect autobiography portrays certain "negatives" (in the photographic sense) of the autobiographer, and in so doing reincorporates the experience of "others," and, in the process, democratizing selfhood (Jay 2005, 162 ff.). Minority elements of the self return from the repressed and contribute to a reconstruction of a subjectivity more worldly than before.

Realizing the political potential of such reconstruction requires acts of creative representation in the public sphere (Mariniello 1994, 107). Through the juxtaposition of heteronymous elements, such representations translate the self-differentiating vitalism of subjective experience into reality itself. Translation names the relation between forms of representation - including montage - and the world to which it refers (Edgerton 1996, 54–55; Welle 1999, 93; Fabbri 1994, 80). Montage specifically holds out "the promise of creating new meaning" (Restivo 2002, 107). For Radhakrishnan (2008, 201), "all meaning makings are indeed acts of translation; ... the location at which translations lose and acquire their meanings is in the space of the between." This "between" is epistemological and historical: "[T]ranslation is primarily an act of historiography," Pasolini asserted (quoted in Welle 1999, 113). It is "the sacredness of the past" that must be salvaged from the wreckage of the present (quoted in Gordon 1996, 66). Without "translatability," there is "no meaning" (Radhakrishnan 2008, 200).

Language is key to this political-pedagogical project of translation, now that the expressive potential of language has been replaced by its technological function (Pasolini 2005 [1972], 19, 86, 95, 99). Belonging to another era yet audible still on the periphery (Pasolini believed), the political project becomes a linguistic-subjective one (Pasolini 2005 [1972], 59; Gordon 1996, 36), converging in indirect discourse (Rohdie 1995, 114). "[I]n indirect discourse," Fabbri (1994, 81) explains, "one is speaking unspeakable sentences. This kind of discourse does not take into account the objects or words or the images, but rather the relationship between images." There is in this relationship a form of "contamination," a key concept for Pasolini that specifies hybridity and transference (Stone 1994, 48). He writes: "On such material is enacted a violent and brutal laceration, a cut, from which erupts the *other* material which composes the objectivity, the real fabric of things which escaped the intellectual poet and also escaped, by and large, man" (quoted in Fabbri 1994, 83). Rather than simplistic schemes—historically (chronologically) or developmentally (from simple to complex)—Pasolini the filmmaker juxtaposes heteronymous elements in relations of "creative tensionality," rendering unstable self-same identity strung across discrete temporal conjunctures.[18]

By use of the concept "indirect," Pasolini emphasized that his films are no direct reflection (or representation) of something else, for instance in his 1964 *Comizi d'amore*, as if Italian faces were substitutes for "pure" sex. True, to Pasolini the face is sexual, as are speech and silence (Schwenk 2005, 47). But sex is not, as in the Christian dualism, "physical" while the soul resides elsewhere. At this stage in his thinking, sex was soulful; it was poetical. Pasolini's 1964 filmic inquiry is not only semiological, it is political and social. In this film, people are sometimes defensive and embarrassed about sex. In the face of their apparent (pretended?) indifference and complacency, even during eruptions of homophobia, Pasolini remains imperturbable, insistently encouraging, always the curious interviewer. Naomi Greene (1990, 69) characterizes the film as "a portrait of prejudice and conformism." Foucault suggested:

> What is running through the film (*Comizi d'amore*) is not, I think, an obsession with sex, but a kind of historical apprehension, a premonitory and confused hesitation in the face of a new regime that was taking place then in Italy, namely the regime of tolerance (quoted in Greene 1990, 73).

Pasolini felt only contempt for this regime of what he termed, ominously, "Power" (Ward 1999, 322; 1995, 25; Siti 1994, 57, 70). Power obliterates difference through a system of control so sophisticated that its effects go almost unnoticed (Ward 1999, 323; Lepri 2005, 179). Anticipating (informing?) the analysis of Foucault (Ward 1999, 325) and Baudrillard (Cusset 2008, 160), Pasolini appreciated how apparently oppositional practices are absorbed by "Power," reproducing the spectacle of the same (Ward 1999, 322, 326). Pasolini's response—*"Manifesto per un nuovo teatro"*—privileged "dialogue" focused on a text, cultivating "thoughtfulness" (Ward 1999, 327). In our time, the public sphere is so shredded that it sometimes seems to me that the only prospect for thoughtful "resistance" to a totalizing regime of commodification and exhibitionism is inner dialogue and study, academic versions of prayer.

Perhaps Pasolini would not completely disagree. After all, David Ward notes, it was the privileging of action over thought that Pasolini judged to be the fundamental mistake committed by protesting students in May 1968, thereby reproducing the obsessive emphasis upon "behavior" by which neo-capitalist Power eviscerates consciousness. "Action" becomes reactionary as it revalorizes practicality and utilitarianism, the means by which reality is reduced to means to other ends. What would be potentially revolutionary—Pasolini speculates—is to invert the hierarchy of action over thought and formulate new, as yet unidentified, ways of engendering post-bourgeois codes and practices (Ward 1999, 328). "Every Italian now comes out of the same mold," he decried (quoted in Caesar 1999, 364); what we suffer now is "a 'total' form of Fascism" (quoted in Caesar 1999, 367; Lepri 2005, 180). Because Pasolini knew first-hand that ideology devolves into orthodoxy (Ward 1999, 334), he searched for locations between intellectual traditions and practices from where subjectivity might be expressed indirectly. This is no naïve, unselfconscious subjectivity, unaware of its own inner otherness. "What he proposes," Ward (1999, 334) explains, "is a subject position which is aware of its status as an ideological construct, but whose constitutive element is an acute awareness of the danger of ideological sedimentations or perspectivism." This is, in a sense, a "negative freedom" that requires the unending embrace of exile and estrangement (Nussbaum 1997, 83), enabling subjective reconstruction and ideological mobility (Ward 1999, 337).

It is from such "negative freedom" I construct a montage confronting the fascism of the present. In the next three chapters, I decry the erasure of the individual by the collectivism of contemporary identity politics (in Chapter 2), the apparent incommensurability between academic knowledge and teacher education (in Chapter 3), and the effacement of educational experience by standardized testing regimes (in Chapter 4). While each ongoing calamity testifies to the total triumph of Power, there are locations between them Power has not yet incorporated. There the worldly stare steadily at the past whose sacred presence foreshadows a future in which subjectivity is freely, indirectly expressed in the curriculum we enact in schools. There we are not reduced to what others have made of us, as identity politics unwittingly espouses.

Part I

On Strategically Dysfunctional Essentialism, and Other Problems of the Not-Exactly-Cosmopolitan Present

2   On the Agony and Ecstasy of the Particular[1]

I Prologue: In Praise of Self-difference

"[I]dentity" has emerged as a pseudo-concept, which rephrases the questions we ask abut the world, and hence conditions the answers we produce.

Stefan Jonsson (2000, 15)

There is nothing inherently liberating about the recognition of difference. In fact, Orientalism feeds on it.

Mitsuhiro Yoshimoto (2002, 387)

I would supplement Yoshimoto's second sentence: It is also the misrecognition of difference that feeds fantasies such as Orientalism. And it is fantasy that feeds misrecognition. Not only the colonists and their descendants misapprehend the Other. The colonized and their descendents, Frantz Fanon predicted, would misapprehend themselves, and in so doing, usher in—Fanon was, of course, thinking of Africa, not Asia—a period of neocolonialism in which indigenous peoples would replay the genocidal roles assumed by European invaders. That prediction has been realized in post-colonial African genocides. In his study of Fanon, Ayo Sekyi-Otu (1996, 20) notes that in the "postcolonial world ... the agony and ecstasy of the particular—became the nightmare of absolutism." For Fanon, a "dying colonialism" foreshadowed black skin with white masks.

The binaries structuring colonialism's cultural cannibalism and genocide became reinscribed within postcolonial cultures. In the North American academy, such reinscription has been achieved through the establishment—and audible in the "rancor" (Grande 2004, 91) —of identity politics. "What ... are the political and ethical consequences of attributing centrality to race?" Sekyi-Otu (1996, 13-14) asks. He continues:

Does it result in an indiscriminate and genocidal antagonism toward the Other on the one hand, and, on the other, the tyrannizing protectionism of racial confraternity, a separatist chorus so mystified by its own chant of togetherness that it stifles the anguished cries of other languages of separation and subjugation, old and new—class, gender, ethnicity? (Otu 1996, 13–14)

The separatist chorus that is North American identity politics threatens to subsume the particular into "absolutes," including totalizing phrases such as "indigeneity." In such a phrase, where is acknowledgement of the diversity and hybridity of indigenous nations and cultures (Grande 2004, 3, 95; Ng-A-Fook 2007a)? Where is the recognition of internal differences? Do these not disappear into generalizing claims such as, for instance, indigenous cultures respect elders (Grant 1995, 212) or that African Americans (regardless of class or gender or region or historical moment) and "other ethnic groups of color" require for academic achievement so-called "culturally-responsive teaching" (Gay 2000, 13, 25), itself a totalizing instrumentalism (Gay 2000, 111).[2]

Through the self-righteous indignation of contemporary identity politics, the concrete "culture" one claims to represent disappears into abstractions, totalized into generalizations recapitulating, if through reversal, the stereotypes fabricated by the colonizers (Conn 2004, 196). Moreover, in the totalizing, nostalgic abstraction of "culture," the capacity for self-critique fades. "Sometimes," Harootunian (2002, 165) points out, "the mere enunciation of cultural difference and thus identity is made to appear as a political act of crowning importance when it usually means the disappearance of politics as such." In our time, "identity" (and not just the hybrid kind) has become a "closet idealism," as "cultural agency [becomes] unmoored from, or relatively independent of, the field of material forces that engender culture" (Cheah 2006, 94; Grande 2004, 92; Jay 2005, 60). The "psychic syntax" of identity politics is narcissistic exhibitionism.

Recall the 1930s *négritude* movement in France (Young-Bruehl 1996, 492; Kesteloot 1991) or more contemporary invocations of a pre-colonial African identity (Pinar 2001, 861 ff.), the former of which fantasized blackness as an unchanging cultural core of intuition, rhythm, sentiment, and creativity, the latter emphasizing manhood and morality. In both, blackness is always and everywhere beautifully and self-righteously non-European, non-technological, non-imperial. Having dismissed European cultures as monolithic and as only evil, there are descendents of the colonized—some of whom are our colleagues—who become trapped in a hall of mirrors, projecting onto the European-American Other the bifurcating elements they themselves have internalized through colonization. Speaking of this curse of colonialism, Masao Miyoshi (2002, 45) points out:

> Once survival and self-defense cease to be a desperate necessity, however, identity politics often turns into a policy of self-promotion, or, more exactly, a self-serving sales policy in which a history of victimization becomes a commodity that demands payment. It can pervert itself

Hatred resisted in inner thoughts.

into opportunism and cannibalism…. In the name of multiculturalism, one privileges one's own identity, while making merely a token acknowledgement of the other's whom one proceeds to disregard when an occasion for help arrives.

As a member of a victimized group claiming floor-space in the exhibition hall of multiculturalism, I know first-hand such temptations.

For many of us queers, it is the "straight world" that kills us or, at least, makes us over in its image. "Queer" and "straight" are abstractions and binaries queer theory itself claims to deconstruct. Never mind, "it is as if self-identity (quoting Miyoshi [2002, 45] again) were an article of private property, which the group—but more likely its elite leadership—claims to own and guard exclusively." Never able to shed the suspicion that my work has sometimes been dismissed due to homophobia and heterosexism, I have often felt, still feel, victimized, a strange self-pity, I remind myself, given Mathew Shepard and the daily assaults queers suffer worldwide (Barry 2008, for a recent instance). Almost any provocation scrapes off the scar of my social wound, and my vision is refracted through the pain of the old, ongoing injury. Identity politics is the privilege claimed by the academic elite to represent absent victimized others, justified in the name of suffering and social justice. As Jean Elshtain (2002, 201) points out (in a different but related context), "victimization does not confer moral rightness or political acuity." As it collectivizes identity, victimization immobilizes individuals.

"All told," Sandy Grande (2004, 104) admits, "essentialism fails the American Indian community. It fails to theorize the relational character of identity by denying the historicity and social comprehensiveness of American Indian subjectivity." The testimonial—indeed, political—labor of identity politics is more convincingly conducted by autobiography. After all, "the inner world of thought and speech is the place where, ultimately, hatred must be resisted" (Nussbaum 1997, 66). Rather than claiming for oneself a collective identity in which one presumes to be the representative absent Other, one might refocus one's moral obligation and pedagogical opportunity toward one's own individual decolonization, wherein those internalized binaries structured by colonialism might be reconstructed as multiple and linked identities, traversing the divides history and politics cut in our psychic terrain. These self-representations are singular—yes, even hybrid (the excess of this discourse, usually associated with the work of Homi Bhabha, was definitively critiqued a decade ago: Parry 2002)—and they testify to cultural as well as subjective survival and rejuvenation.

Consider the case of Zitkala-Ša (1876–1938). A Sioux educated in a boarding school, Zitkala-Ša taught briefly at the Carlisle Indian Industrial School, founded in Pennsylvania in 1879 by Richard Henry Pratt, an army officer. Carlisle became the model for federal Indian boarding schools designed to destroy tribal nations and strip Native children of their cultures, languages, and religions. A century ago, even those European-Americans who claimed to take a "pro-Indian" side in the national debate over how to solve "the Indian problem" assumed that the educational project was one of assimilation: the eventual elimination of tribal culture and identity. These white, usually Christian policy makers and philanthropists were convinced that Indians must finally disappear into the European-American population. They were considered "friends" because they opposed the complete physical extermination of native peoples, a position advocated by many (Katanski 2005, 3).

At Carlisle, Indian students were forbidden to speak native languages, wear traditional clothing, or practice ancestral religions. Because the student body was Pan-Indian, because the children had been taken away from their families when they were very young and kept away for years at a time, Indian students were, it was hoped by Pratt and others, severed from their tribal traditions (Katanski 2005, 4). The case of Zitkala-Ša demonstrates the disappointment of this hope. Her case speaks to the educational potential of autobiography, including its capacity to alert readers to and engage them in one's political cause. Because it portrays that cause not in abstract and totalizing terms but, rather, through vivid narratives of lived experience, potentially autobiography can traverse the divide between writer and reader.

After leaving her teaching position at Carlisle, Zitkala-Ša published three important autobiographical essays.[3] Appearing in *The Atlantic Monthly* in 1900, Zitkala-Ša recalled her early childhood on the reservation, followed by her experiences as a student at a Quaker off-reservation boarding school, then her brief stint as a teacher at Carlisle (Katanski 2005, 96). Zitkala-Ša's autobiographical narrative makes plain the genocidal character of the boarding schools, documenting specifically the tension between the representative Indian and the self-representing Indian. Exploiting the politics of self-representation by representing herself in different terms in different settings, Zitkala-Ša described herself as orator, musician, poet, storyteller, political activist, Dakota, half-blood, Indian, pagan, and Catholic (Katanski 2005, 113).

This variable and singular set of identities not only testified to her specific accomplishments (and accommodations), it advanced her political agenda of self-representation, contesting specifically the reductionism of the term *Indian*. Contrary to contemporary identity politics in which the individual disappears into the victimized category (now revalorized positively as "indigenous"), Zitkala-Ša emphasized her agency as an individual, reconstructing the self-annihilating process of assimilation as, in fact, self-enhancing. Unlike Paul Willis's "lads," this "victim" resisted "resistance" as well as assimilation. Contradicting Audre Lorde's warning (De Veaux 2004, 248), Zitkala-Ša employed the master's tools to dismantle the master's house.[4] As would both black revolutionaries and lesbian activists 60 years later, Zitkala-Ša rejected her given surname. In a simple but significant act of agency, Gertrude Simmons became Zitkala-Ša, a Lakota name that translates as Red Bird (Katanski 2005, 113, 114; Krupat 1994, 280).

This self-naming is significant in its testimony to and identification with her Indian ancestry, but Zitkala-Ša did not disappear into that collective identity. She continued to use her name Gertrude Simmons (later Gertrude Simmons Bonnin) in her private life. As a public intellectual and political activist, however, Simmons used her self-given Lakota name as a literary *nom de plume*, claiming in "School Days of an Indian Girl" that her muse, indeed her very voice, derived from her "Indian nature" (Katanski 2005, 114). Zitkala-Ša never mentions that her father was white, emphasizing in that essay her Dakota roots.[5] Through her choice of a Lakota name after years as a student and teacher in schools dedicated to the extinction of Indian cultures, and through her ascription of her authorial success to her Sioux heritage, Zitkala-Ša reverses the boarding-school teachers' practice of providing "savage" students with "civilized" English names, emphasizing that for her, education is no linear or bifurcated process of assimilation or resistance (Katanski 2005, 115) but a particular—in her case multicultural—reconstruction of who she was born to be and educated to become.

As her autobiographical essays make clear, Zitkala-Ša was hardly uneducated when she was taken to the boarding school. She was already a young woman in the process of being educated in the culture of her tribe. By testifying to her indigenous education, Zitkala-Ša negates Pratt's assertion that Indian students arrived at Carlisle like a blank slate, ready for imprinting with the text of civilization. Nor, however, does Zitkala-Ša represent her Dakota education as occurring in a pristine, precolonial past. She makes clear that her education—even at home with her mother—always occurred through accommodation to white encroachment (Katanski 2005, 116; Krupat 1994, 294). Although Dakota-identified during her childhood, Zitkala-Ša proclaims her multiplying adult identities: Indeed, she affirms self-difference (Katanski 2005, 118–119; Pitt 2003) through the articulation of her multiple and linked identities, listed earlier. These situated and singular identities constituting her multivariate individuality—" the problem of my inner self" (quoted in Krupat 1994, 297)—do not disappear into collective identifications such as "Indian" or "Indigenous." Nor does her criticism of whites become diffused by projection; she makes her criticism concrete and specific through autobiography, explaining in narrative detail, for instance, why she is a pagan.[6] Through her defiant and creative autobiographical reconstruction of the colonial culture she had internalized, Zitkala-Ša traversed, in Dwayne Donald's words, "the divides of the past and present" (2007, 6).

Juxtaposed with history, autobiography, not identity politics, testifies to injustice and injury, providing particular referents for totalizing abstractions that otherwise risk recapitulation of colonist binaries, if with reversed valences. Articulating subjective experience keeps a string on these conceptual kites that, in their distance from the everyday, enable more panoramic views of our location in the world. If unconnected to those to whom they bear witness, however, such totalizing phrases threaten to function as fatuous free-floating signifiers, scraping the scars off injuries ancient and ongoing, injuries at once individual and collective. That recognition of self-difference to which an autobiography of alterity testifies is prerequisite to the representation of the multivariate complexity of experience and identity. In so doing, autobiography makes plain that the Other is another person.[7]

II The Worldliness of Cosmopolitanism

> Inasmuch as understanding involves individualizing rather than normalizing, interpreting rather than objectifying, pluralizing rather than encompassing—in short, radically dialogic processes—we can free ourselves from our own potentially power-determined preunderstanding through an understanding of the other.
>
> Hans-Herbert Kögler (1999, 109)

> Genuine cosmopolitanism and individualistic particularism belong together.
>
> Karl Joachim Weintraub (1978, 339)

Another "person"? Does not such a word sound strangely "humanist" to postmodern ears wary of exhuming the "subject" in an era contemplating, after all, the "posthuman"? Is the cyborg what Fanon had in mind when he called for a "new man"? Acknowledging "the subjection of all individuals to preexisting systems of control and power" (Foster 2005, 77) and that the future—if there is a future, as the collapse of the biosphere is, apparently, well underway—looks grim, I employ this evidently old-fashioned concept ("person") to affirm not the abstraction of collective identity but the concrete variegated—even virtual (Foster 2005, 156)—character of embodied life. While out of fashion theoretically, the Law, at least, recognizes the individual. As Seyla Benhabib (2006, 16) points out, cosmopolitan norms of justice— even when articulated through treaty-like obligations among nations— "endow *individuals* rather than states and their agents with certain rights and claims." It is, she continues, "individuals as moral and legal persons" who comprise a "worldwide civil society" (Benhabib 2006, 16).

What structures of subjectivity might citizens of such a worldwide civil society cultivate and critique? Among these might be two interrelated structures many imagine as constructed (or at least made sophisticated) by formal education: the agency to remake ourselves and the world through rational activity and, more broadly, the transcendence of material limitations through the rational employment of our various resources, chief among them intelligence. "Transcend comes from the Latin," C. Fred Alford (2002, 82) reminds us, "meaning to climb over or go beyond the limits of something." Transcendence rationalizes—in the West, historically at least—the expectation that by moving beyond subjectivity one achieves objectivity, community, even universalism. This quasi-Christian conception of transcendence devalues individual lived experience—it is something to transcend—as it relocates ideality elsewhere, in an afterlife, for instance or, in its secular political form, after the revolution. I am suggesting that those ideals associated with "perpetual peace"—the title of Kant's canonical tract on cosmopolitanism—are subjectively served not by fantasies of transcendence[8] but by worldliness. The frank embrace of this world extends our conceptions of cosmopolitanism from the legal to include the lived. Through autobiographically focused educational experience of the material world might emerge the worldly-wise, a term whose cynical connotations I trade for the social ethics of, say, Jane Addams. In its preference for the abstract over the concrete, however, identity politics ensures that cosmopolitanism becomes a casualty of the curriculum, not its possible consequence.

Along with "empire" and "globalization," Benhabib (2006, 17) points out, "cosmopolitanism" has become one of the keywords of our times. Once associated with anti-Semitism (you recall that both Hitler and Stalin characterized Jews as "rootless cosmopolitans" [Appiah 2006, xvi; Gunew 2004, 8]), the term has, Jeremy Waldron (quoted in Benhabib 2006, 83) notes, "a number of meanings." Among these are the "love of mankind" and those "duties owed to every person in the world." Other meanings stress the "fluidity" and "evanescence" of culture, affirming the blurring of boundaries (between countries and cultures), welcoming one world of "fractured" and "mingled identities" (2006, 83).[9] Benhabib (2006, 175) summarizes:

> Whether cosmopolitanism is used to designate the hybridity, fluidity, intermingling, and interdependence of peoples, cultures, and practices, or a process of taming the nation-state such as to control the assertion of unbridled sovereignty, or even a politics of hospitality that challenges existing liberal democracies in order to examine their deepest self-understandings, this term and its derivates such as "cosmopolitics" grapple with the unique challenges of our times.

What is unique about "our times," Benhabib (2006, 175) offers, is the degree of "commercial, technological and functional interdependence" among sovereign states that still define the juridical status of the individual.

In his discussion of the concept, Appiah (2006, xv) acknowledges "obligations" owed to others while emphasizing the primacy of the particular. There will be times, he notes, when these two cosmopolitan ideals— "universal concern and respect for legitimate difference—clash" (2006, xv). Characterizing cosmopolitanism as the challenge, not the solution, Appiah (2006, xviii) posits conversation[10] as central to its cultivation. A shared vocabulary is no prerequisite for such conversation, he suggests, nor must such conversation be expected to lead to "consensus" about "anything, especially not values" (Appiah 2006, 85). What is the point, then? Appiah (2006, 78) explains:

I am urging that we should learn about people in other places, take an interest in their civilizations, their arguments, their errors, their achievements, not because that will bring us to agreement, but because it will help us get used to one another.

Given the horror of human history, getting used to one another is, I suppose, a lofty enough aspiration. As a teacher, however, one hopes for even more, namely the study of knowledge that transfigures the one and the other. Asserting that cosmopolitanism is a "philosophical project of mediations, not of reductions or of totalizations" (2006, 20), Benhabib (2006, 70) sketches what she terms "multiple processes of democratic iteration." A concept attributable to Derrida, "iteration" refers to the difference of repetition.[11] "In the process of repeating a term or a concept," Benhabib (2006, 47–48) explains,

> we never simply produce a replica of the original usage and its intended meaning: rather, every repetition is a form of variation. Every iteration transforms meaning, adds to it, enriches it in ever-so-subtle ways. In fact, there really is no "originary" source of meaning, or an "original" to which all subsequent forms must conform.

It is by means of "democratic iterations," then, that Benhabib postulates reconciliation between cosmopolitanism with the "unique legal, historical, and cultural traditions and memories of a people" (2006, 70).

Despite the considerable complication of "these unique traditions and memories of a people" by immigration and diasporas, despite the economic and political inequities of globalization that both undermine traditions and stimulate their reactionary reconstitution, it is the nation that remains the key context in which cosmopolitan norms are mediated. Despite the celebration and anxiety surrounding the supposed "retreat of the state" (Strange 1996), the contextual centrality of the nation-state—including its intervention in globalization (Mayer, Luke and Luke 2008, 90), including the forms of solidarity and self-protection it offers economically vulnerable countries (Cheah 2006, 46)—prompted me to organize the first international handbook of curriculum research around nation-states and to argue for the concept of "international" both in the establishment of the International Association for the Advancement of Curriculum Studies (modeled after the United Nations with a General Assembly populated by representatives of various nation-states) and in the concept of the Centre the University of British Columbia[12] established to institutionalize there the study of curriculum studies worldwide.[13] "Internationalization" captures the complexity of collective entities—nationally distinctive fields of curriculum studies—in disciplinary conversation with other collective entities through specific individuals.

Hannah Arendt promoted "worldliness" and, relatedly, "care for the world" (today understood as not only the human world) as "chief" among cosmopolitan virtues; these "trump her legalism," Bonnie Honig (in Benhabib 2006, 120) asserts. A cosmopolitanism contingent upon laws, states, and state-like and inter-state institutions marginalizes these virtues, Honig fears, effacing as it represents in collective terms "our voice, our desires, our aspirations, our solidarities." Benhabib wonders why these existential realities—what I would summarize as the sphere of the subjective—must replace rather than supplement the legal in the protection of human rights. I share this view (Kymlicka seems to agree as well: see Benhabib 2006, 169) that subjectivity supplements (not substitutes for) the social, that the cultivation of cosmopolitanism includes the establishment of what Benhabib terms "representative public institutions" (2006, 169). Such infrastructure can serve as "mechanisms of representation, accountability, participation, and deliberation" (2006, 169). Like professional societies (Pinar 2007a, xvi–xx), such organizations could also serve as "bearers of historical memory" (2006, 169).

In his critique of cosmopolitanism, Pheng Cheah (2006, 96) depicts Kant's conception of cosmopolitanism as predicated upon humanity's capacity "to free itself from the given," understood as those "passions and sensuous inclinations that subject human beings to nature," and, relatedly, as the "finitude" of human existence. Perhaps Kant's conception expresses a Christian bifurcation of the more ancient Greek—specifically Socratic—aspiration of living in harmony within nature, an archaic cosmopolitanism wherein "the rational cosmos had become one's true polis" (Weintraub 1978, 12).

Against Kant's universalism and moralism, queer theorists Guy Hocquenghem and René Schérer juxtaposed the early nineteenth-century utopian Charles Fourier's preference for perpetual peace predicated upon passion (Marshall 1997). "The passions," Fourier wrote, "believed to be the enemies of concord, in reality conduce to that unity from which we deem them so far removed."[14] For this utopian socialist, it was not the public sphere (wherein nation-states trade and negotiate agreements with each other) but the domestic sphere (for Fourier as it would be for Freud and Foucault a space of passion) that structures the political (Marshall 1997, 62; Elshtain 1993). Fourier's "subjects" of his utopia ("Harmony") need not emphasize the boundaries separating self and other, need not resist their own inclinations. For Fourier, Marshall explains, the "immorality" of the passions in "civilization" is due to their distortion, whereas in "Harmony" cosmopolitan citizens exercised a universal morality based not upon categorical imperatives, but upon sensation and pleasure.[15]

Sexual pleasure informs the Christian suspicion—indeed, warning—concerning worldliness.[16] We read in (I John 2:16–17 KJV): "For all that is in the world, the lust of the flesh, and the lust of the eyes, and the pride of life, is not of the Father, but is of the world. And the world passeth away, and the lust thereof, but he that doeth the will of God abideth forever." James is even blunter than John: "Know ye not that the friendship of the world is enmity with God? Whosoever therefore will be a friend of the world is an enemy of God" (James 4:4 KJV). Never mind that, according to Pastor Ray C. Stedman, "Christians isolate themselves from the world to avoid worldliness, and it inevitably results in more worldliness."[17] That self-deception—it always seems to accompany "commandments" and other prejudices masquerading as convictions—follows the false choice James commands us to make.

The ancient command to abandon desire—lust, as John would have it—for the sake of the Father precedes Christianity, of course; it structures, for example, Genesis 9:23, where, it is reported, that Noah rejected the son who visited him while he lay drunk and naked in his tent. In retaliation (for what is the resounding question; sexual assault is among the scholarly speculations), Noah condemns Ham's descendants to perpetual servitude. Recall that upon learning that their father was exposed, Noah's other sons (Shem and Japheth) took a garment, walked backward—in order to avoid seeing their father naked—into the tent and covered him. The narrator tells us: "Their faces were turned away, and they did not see their father's nakedness" (Gen. 9:23). Shem and Japheth—the sublimated sons—choose identification over desire, a choice that mutates into racism, that Curse of the Covenant (Pinar 2006a). It is the choice enabling what Kaja Silverman (1988, 215) terms a "secondary" identification, "leading to imaginary mastery and transcendence." In contrast to mastery and transcendence, I juxtapose worldliness.

The myth slaveholders and segregationists concocted was that Africans were the children of Ham, condemned by God Himself to perpetual servitude. Some number of descendents of these cursed children of Ham came to constitute the lumpenproletariat,[18] what Foucault (1995 [1979], 63) called, simply, "petty offenders—vagrants, false beggars, the indigent poor, pickpockets, receivers and dealers in stolen goods" against whom penal power was directed. The lumpenproletariat is also infamously associated with pimps and prostitutes (McCulloch 1983). The prominence of the sexual in this class is no accident; recall that in *Black Skin, White Masks* (1967a, 156), Fanon understands racism as the "product of a complex and diffuse historical process that is *initially motivated by sexual repression*" (McCulloch, 1983 141; emphasis added). During the 1960s, black radicals in the United States would fasten upon Fanon—and his faith in the lumpenproletariat—as inspiration for political activism. Black Panther Eldridge Cleaver, for instance, loudly limited his faith and trust to the black lumpenproletariat (Rout 1991, 136).[19] He and other black activists distrusted the white working class (Brown 1992, 399–400) long before many working-class whites—the so-called Reagan Democrats—began voting Republican in 1980.

Not only 1960s black radicals revalorized the mythic children of Ham. There has been—continues to be—a favorable fantasy of the black lumpenproletariat among titillated whites. In the 1950s, Norman Mailer imagined African Americans—specifically those "hipsters" associated with jazz culture—as not only cool but as capable of redeeming white culture. The

Beats—among them Kerouac, Ginsberg, and Burroughs—were "hip," dubbed by Mailer as examples of "the white negro" (Dearborn 1999, 132; Mailer 1957). Forty years later, Mailer's messianic jazz was replaced by gangsta rap, "a genre that relies on embellishing the menacing quality so often associated with the urban lumpenproletariat" (Boyd 1997, 62). Redeemers on the one hand and thugs on the other, African Americans remain ready to rough us up: Such (white) fantasies disclose the sexual politics of race.

Engels famously referred to the lumpenproletariat as "scum," as "depraved" (Hansen 1977, 158–159), judgments contemporary conservative Christians hurl at homosexuals. Evidently Marx regarded the lumpenproletariat as "thoroughly malleable, as capable of the most heroic deeds and the most exalted sacrifices as of the basest banditry and the foulest corruption" (Hansen 1977, 159), a view that anticipates the bifurcated fantasies of blacks many whites still fabricate. Focused on the former, Fanon discerned a revolutionary potential, describing the lumpenproletariat as "urged on from behind" (Hansen 1977, 163). Regardless of the location of the motivation, members of the lumpen class have sometimes realized their revolutionary potential, among them (in the United States—the list is Emmanuel Hansen's), Malcolm X, Eldridge Cleaver, and George Jackson. (Staying within the domain of late 1960s radical black politics, I would add to this list Elaine Brown.) Hansen acknowledges that these activists "did not acquire their revolutionary consciousness through armed conflict. They changed through intense mental contemplation made possible by long periods of confinement in prison" (Hansen 1977, 167). I add this acknowledgement not to remind us of Foucault's linking of the prison with the school but of his designation of writing—for me, study (Pinar 2006b, 109–120)—as the provocation of self-modification, the prerequisite for political action (Miller 1993, 33).

Fanon had more faith in the lumpenproletariat (due to the intensity of their cultural and economic crisis) and the African peasantry (because they felt a solidarity due their shared relationship to the means of production and because they harbored a nascent national culture) than in the urban masses to support indigenous political and cultural struggle (Zahar 1974). Both classes suffered owing to the atrophy of indigenous culture during colonialism (McCulloch 1983). For the Fanon of *The Wretched of the Earth*, the wounds of the lumpenproletariat are cultural as well as economic; the trauma they have undergone during colonialism is that of deculturation (McCulloch 1983).[20] Such an analysis recasts identity politics from self-righteous accusation to subjective decolonization. It is a point Fanon would, I think, have appreciated (Radhakrishnan 2008, 79; Pinar 2008b).

"What makes Fanon relevant today," Radhakrishnan (2008, 71) points out, "is the fact that he is interested both in the psychic and political dimensions of subject formation." Fanon (1967b, 103) declared, "An authentic national liberation exists only to the precise degree to which the individual has irreversibly begun his own liberation." National independence would only reinscribe colonial binaries, Fanon presciently predicted, if political action did not support the restructuring of the character of the individual.

Why would he emphasize the subjective in decolonization? Recall that Fanon[21] was trained as a psychiatrist under the direction of Professor François Tosquelles, a mentor who "had a great influence on Fanon's psychiatric work both in terms of method and in the nature of the problems on which Fanon chose to concentrate" (Gendzier 1973, 19). For two years, Fanon worked closely with Tosquelles, publishing three research papers with him directly and three with other students. From Tosquelles Fanon learned sociotherapy, a conception of psychiatry that emphasized the significance of the social context of individual pathology. When he moved to Blida-Joinville and later to Tunis to practice psychiatry, Fanon transposed the sociotherapeutic ideas of Tosquelles.[22] Central to his radicalization of Tosquelles was Fanon's conviction that seemingly private, individual pathology is often a socially induced and associated with political oppression (Bulhan 1985). In Radhakrishnan's (2008, 19) terms, Fanon "historicized the symptom as a specific pathology to be disalienated into legitimate belonging and representative sovereignty." Though the genesis of a particular pathology may have been systemic, its remedy was attempted on a smaller scale, addressed to the individual patient, both in solitude and as a member of the hospitalized community. Radhakrishnan (2008, 19) tells us that Fanon "allowed himself to dive into the immanent temporality of the symptom," enabling him to speak "within the phenomenology of the symptom, enjoying it as it were, even as he envisions the curing of the symptom by way of political interventions and revolutions." This juxtaposition of the political and the phenomenological is evident in Fanon's psychiatric protocol. In addition to the social and political activities Fanon planned—among them meetings, entertainment, a newspaper—for specific patients (especially for Algerian rebels exhausted by fighting the French) he prescribed sleep, sometimes a week of it (Geismar 1971).

Ah, the weariness of the flesh, the concreteness of community, of the inner life, of experience as lived: For the worldly, these are not avenues to somewhere else, another world wherein historical injury has been avenged, desire transcended. Sleep, self-expression, and conversation—Fanon's therapeutic protocol—constitute key modes of being in *this* world. As earthly creatures, it is the body wherein we live; the call for the posthuman seems to me curiously Christian. Moreover, to contradict the specularized and sexualized racism of whites, Fanon's (1968, 316) "new man" invokes for me a sensuous subjectivity in which voluptuousness democratizes desire.[23] Fanon's call invites a post-Christian, post-bourgeois sexualized subjectivity dedicated not to the renunciation of this world, but to its sensuous if creative and critical embrace.

Conclusion

> [R]acialization must be understood according to its historical locality and signification.
>
> Mica Nava (2007, 6)

> The term "conversation" comes from the Latin to convert, meaning to transform.
>
> C. Fred Alford (2002, 60)

What Robert Musil's *A Man Without Qualities* demonstrates, Stefan Jonsson suggests, is that "identity" is an effect, not a cause. As an effect of social and cultural history, identity has limited utility as a political or pedagogical device. Like other ideological phenomena, Jonsson (2000, 1617) explains, identities are constructed according to the psychic and material needs of "individuals" who use them "to recognize themselves and others as members of *their* group, nation, state, or culture." Constructed according to their function, then, collective identities have no ontological substance. In Marx's phrase, identity is "an ensemble of social relations" (quoted in Jonsson 2000, 17) and its function, Jonsson suggests, is to stabilize—I would add, mobilize—these relations. To be understood, collective identities cannot be detached from the communities that they bind together; it cannot, as even Judith Butler would acknowledge, be freely chosen or "performed" at will. To understand identity, Jonsson (2000, 17) concludes, we must focus upon its "historical origins" and "social functions," thereby studying how and why particular identities emerge in their current and specific forms. To do so, I would suggest (recalling Zitkala-Ša), we must singularize collective identity, thereby testifying to the individual subjectivities that give it substance and from which its forms can be reconstructed, as Zitkala-Ša demonstrates in her autobiographical essays.

For Jonsson (after Musil), "identity" refers to the intersection between the psychic and the social, a site of "negotiation" between subjectivity and society (2000, 17). For Jonsson (again, after Musil) "subjectivity" refers to that "ineffable agency that precedes [and, I would add, conveys as it constructs] language, culture, and ideology" (Jonsson 2000, 17). So sequenced, subjectivity surrounds and saturates identity. As ineffable, agency animates action but does not presume transcendence of the given, only the possibility of its reconstruction. Subjectivity enables engagement with the world, informed by study and experience. Such engagement means not only service to others but an othering of oneself as well. Such self-distanciation and complication invite "insight into usually hidden linkages between symbolic relations and social networks of power" (Kögler 1999, 252).

As epiphenomenal, identity both enables and constrains our capacity to articulate and thereby reconstruct our being-in-the-world. While something no one can do without, identity is no substitution for subjectivity. As the supplement to subjectivity, identity ought not be the foundational reality of our lives (Jonsson 2000, 17; Appiah 2005, 110). As a functional expression of lived experience, identity is a symbol, not a substitute, for the subjective complexity it summarizes. In this sense, identity politics risks recapitulating the error of idolatry. In subsuming oneself in a collective identity, one forfeits the agency subjectivity can create, thereby foreclosing a future not foretold by the hegemonic order (Jay 2005, 266).

By claiming to speak for the collective, scholars risk recapitulating that stereotypic Other racism creates. One becomes the contemporary version of the "race man" (Carby 1998) whites once demanded. Revalorized, the racial stereotype is unintentionally reinvigorated, now the occasion for self-righteous indignation and denigration of new "others": Now "white" becomes the stereotype, the reduction of European descent to a stigmatic badge of racialized inferiority. Recall that Zitkala-Ša rejected her interpellation as the "representative Indian" by claiming for herself the right to act as the self-representing Indian. By autobiographically asserting her individuality[24]—through acts of "passionate individualism" (Knight 2005, 13) we might say—she communicated the crime of collectivism while affirming the hybridity of even colonized individual experience.

The self-differentiating reflexivity of what William Earle termed "autobiographical consciousness" not only enables testimony to trauma and injustice but supports the social and subjective reconstruction that constitutes reparation. C. Fred Alford (2002, 144) points out that Levinas preserved individuality because "only the individual can see the other person's tears." It is for this reason that, the "individual is unique and valuable" (2006, 144). Because, for Levinas, otherness structures selfhood, it provides the subjective capacity for the acknowledgment of others' suffering and the invocation of one's own (Egéa-Kuehne 2008, 29). Neither empathy nor accusation supports the understanding of suffering or moves us to redress it; the interest in, the openness to, the other presumed by conversation can. The dialogic and solitary study of earlier epochs and cultures not one's own—such as the lumpenproletariat—acknowledges alterity as "an anchor and a point of departure for a new self-understanding within which we experience ourselves as other" (Kögler 1999, 174–175). Hongyu Wang (2004, 7) asks, "Isn't this relationship between the self and the stranger [including the stranger within: 2004, 8] one central theme of education?"

By reiterating the autobiographical, classifications, types, and stereotypes are forced out of the diffuse realm of the social (where they are too often taken for granted) and into the curriculum where they can be examined historically and analytically. In Kögler's (1999, 275) terms, the disclosure of abstract collective identity in the concreteness of individual lived experience (and vice versa) "constitutes the move away from the socially situated self toward the reflexively critical self." Because such intellectual movement renders "unrecognized distinctions" analytically available and thus capable of being "understood," Kögler (1999, 275) suggests, "it can be the starting point for directed and reflective social action." I don't know about that—I worry that such a tantalizing possibility is just another variation of the "outcome" obsession that denigrates intellectual activity as a means to an end—but such a subjectively focused conception of academic study (for Kögler dialogue is the more powerful concept; I would situate it within subjectivity) can reinstate the concrete in the abstract, thereby preserving the alterity of reality.

As educators, our calling is to participate in the complicated conversation that is the curriculum (Jay 2005, 189 ff.). Educational "content is otherness," Huebner (1999, 362) observed. "Through the symbolic discourse of other horizons of meaning," Kögler (1999, 91) suggests, "the phenomenon of worldhood becomes experienceable, and through the concrete experience of another worldhood, a reflective distance to one's own worldhood or horizon is effected." Studying the agony and ecstasy of the particular attunes us to the actuality of alterity. As study of the palimpsest that is the present, the curriculum can convey the immanence of everyday reality that transcendence splits off as futural or otherworldly. As the sentence opening this final section suggests, conversation carries the etymological suggestion that informed by the study and presence of the individuated Other educational experience can, if not convert us to cosmopolitanism, at least enable us to become more worldly (Appiah 2006, xviii). No ideal imposed from above, worldliness takes infinite earthy forms; it contradicts the universalism of Kant's cosmopolitanism by remaining a particularism, despite its ubiquity. Worldly-wise, sensuous, indeed, voluptuous, might we, as Appiah suggests, grow accustomed to one another?

3   Only the Sign is for Sale

How can one introduce unusual ideas that seem to go against consciousness without also calling forth the resistance?

Deborah P. Britzman (2006, 11)

In a recent review of my *Race, Religion and a Curriculum of Reparation*, Darren E. Lund[1] alleged that "a central shortcoming" of the book had to do with its failure to live up to its subtitle: *Teacher Education for a Multicultural Society*. Lund challenges readers to find "a single passage that suggests implications for teacher education, multiculturalism, or any direct attention whatsoever toward these pressing topics." He concludes that my "apparent avoidance of the lived world of teachers, and those who seek to educate them, constitutes a significant oversight considering the promise of the full title of the book."[2] What assumptions about "teacher education" and "multiculturalism" make such allegations possible?

Race, Religion and a Curriculum of Reparation provides teachers with a genealogy of whiteness in the West. I start with scholarship on the Curse of Ham, the founding and rationalizing moment in the mythology of race in the West. Curiously, Lund seems puzzled by my attention to Genesis 9:24; he admits that his memory of the Ark story is more vivid, an admission that questions his competence to review a book structured by a passage in which homosexual incest, not heterosexual reproduction, predominates. Actually, it is not clear what Ham did to his father—Noah—in order to provoke the curse. In Genesis 9:24, all we are told is: "And Noah awoke from his wine, and knew what his younger son had done unto him." Several scholars argue that the curse follows from the son viewing the naked body of the father; others allege that Ham raped or castrated his father. The severity of the latter transgression is obvious, but why would looking at the naked body of the father be so serious a violation that the son's progeny are condemned to perpetual servitude?

What is at stake in this encounter between father and son, I suggest, is patriarchy itself: that gendered system of power that projects sensuality and thereby vulnerability upon the body of Other, especially the bodies of women. Feminized as an embodied object by his son's gaze, the father responds defensively by repudiating that gendered, possibly sexualized, vulnerability by projecting that vulnerability onto the son's son, recasting the children's existence in terms of the embodied capacity to serve. Aside from the mistaken association of "Ham" with "dark" in ancient Hebrew, there is not the slightest textual reference to "race," after all a modern concept. Why would *that* passage be taken as biblical justification for slavery and, later, segregation?

Contemplating that question led me to sketch the genealogical structures of racism, gendered structures that originate, biblically at least, in the politics of patriarchy. Hegemonic white male masculinity, I argued, can be theorized as comprised of three interrelated elements: (1) the displacement of male self-same sexual difference onto a gendered Other (Genesis 2:21 and 2:22); (2) the social reorganization of dis-identification with the gendered Other as patriarchical reproduction (the Covenant: Genesis 17:10–13); and (3) and the externalization of alterity, later "verified" epistemologically and experienced as "race" via specularity, structured politically and economically as slavery and, later, as segregation. In summary, the repudiation of male self-same sexual difference (specifically father-son incest) became (retrospectively) a racialized alterity through specularity: The body of the father became the race of the son.

The color of sex, Mason Stokes (2001) asserts, is black. For many whites, the character of "black" is sexual. Though the phenomenology of "race" is hardly as simple as that sentence suggests, it cannot, I believe, be grasped or historically surpassed without understanding the relations among alterity, specularity, and sexuality, specifically the disavowal of patriarchal vulnerability (gendered as feminization). I am suggesting that the first two follow from the third and that they represent, in part, symbolic wounds of the father (once a son) as he (defensively) curses the son's son (one day a father perhaps, who then reproduces the curse). The Covenant, requiring filial obedience and heterosexual reproduction, institutionalized the repudiation of that homosexual incestuous desire visuality threatened to expose. The injuries this cover-up inflicts do not originate in a literal event but in a mythic one; nor are they contained there. They are restimulated and given aggressive, indeed, vicious social and political forms during specific moments in the history of the West, among them the hegemony of ocularcentrism in modernity—in particular its political expression as panopticism and surveillance (de Bolla 1996; Baker 2001; Hoffman 2008; Kovach 2008). These constitute the Curse, and not only that of Ham but of those sons (Shem and Japheth in Genesis) who sublimate (who do not look, who pretend Noah is not naked) and who are rewarded with the Kingdom of God, in secular terms that racialized patriarchal system wherein not only women constitute "units of currency" in "gracious submission" to men who imagine themselves white.

To Noah and his "stud" son Ham I juxtapose Daniel Paul Schreber and his (Godly) father, reporting scholarship not only concerning Schreber's infamous 1903 memoirs but also scholarship concerning Freud's theoretical appropriation of them during a historical period when European masculinity—not to mention the psychoanalytic movement Freud had fathered—was widely perceived to be in crisis. Schreber does not violate his father. Rather, Schreber is the son who succumbs sexually to him, becoming a "woman," and in the process experiencing what he describes as "soul voluptuousness." If, in the white male mind, "race" begins in father-son desire disavowed, can its cultural and, specifically, gendered reappropriation as "soul voluptuousness" inaugurate, in the white male mind, race's dissolution? Does the racialized and gendered self-shattering of white masculinity portend an era of racial democracy?

To these questions and the curriculum the book's structure outlines, Lund makes no reply, except that it leaves him feeling: "Well, I would not say I felt dirty after reading the book, but I did need to leave the tent for some fresh air a few times." He characterizes my analysis as a form of "hermeneutical self-pleasuring." Rather than masturbatory, reparation is "self-shattering" (2006a, 19, 47, 64, 74, 114, etc.), a "form of pedagogical consciousness" (Salvio 2007, 98). In disassembling the convoluted palimpsest that is "race," I am going beyond the tip of the rhetorical white hat—the ritualistic homage to race-class-gender—by disrobing race's sedimented genealogies in the Western (white) imagination, the canonical documentation of which is the Bible. My aspiration was to provide the knowledge that enables the interested student to "own" his or her "alienation" and "desire," by "confronting" him with "his own unconscious fantasy" (Newman 2004, 307). It is an incestuous fantasy recoded as racial.

Instead of composing a critique of this analysis, Lund focuses on (what he imagines is) a discrepancy between the advertising (specifically the subtitle) and the product sold. There is, he complains, no discussion of "teacher education" and "multiculturalism." Such a demand reminds me of Kierkegaard's complaint: What the philosophers say about Reality is often as disappointing as a sign one discovers in a shop window that reads: Pressing Done Here. If you brought your clothes to be pressed, you would be fooled; for only the sign is for sale.[3] Programmatic discussions of the topics "teacher education" and "multiculturalism" substitute for the subjects they signify.

Instead of self-righteously complaining about racism,[4] I prepared an inchoate curriculum (in Pasolini's terms, a screenplay) for teacher education emphasizing the genealogy of what today is institutionalized as "multiculturalism." As a curriculum developer, I provided a curriculum that provides knowledge of the subjects constitutive of "teacher education" and "multiculturalism", in particular, scholarship concerning the genesis of "race." *Race, Religion, and a Curriculum of Reparation* is not "about" teacher education as program: it *is* teacher education for a multicultural society.

Focusing on teacher education and multiculturalism as topics—rather than studying the subject matter summarized by these designations—substitutes institutional or programmatic preoccupations for academic knowledge. Is teacher education so organized around institutional "outcomes"—only the "best" teaching practices in adherence to "standards"—that academic knowledge and the subjective labor required to make that knowledge one's own have become subsidiary, in Lund's review unrecognizable, concerns? Has the curriculum question—what knowledge is of most worth?—been effaced by instruction organized around "topics" such as multiculturalism and commonsensical (if intellectually vacant) concepts such as "skills?"[5] Have decades of social engineering[6] emboldened us to imagine we can know teachers' "lived worlds" and those of our colleagues, as Lund implies? Are not those "lived worlds" also intellectual worlds composed of ideas? Is not teacher education finally an intellectual enterprise? Or it is now only a matter of the interpellation of teachers' identities through the inculcation of currently fashionable attitudes and practices?

Because racism is historically sedimented, subjectively structured, and culturally reproduced, I should have thought it obvious that anti-racist teacher education cannot be restricted to the confessions and (self-conferred) absolutions of racial guilt. To understand the Western phenomenon of racialization, one must theorize those racialized sediments—the fascination with the black body, for instance—visible today by devising new interpretations of ancient attitudes and practices. For those teachers who appreciate the centrality of academic knowledge in the cultivation of self-reflexive and ethical intelligence, in *Race, Religion, and a Curriculum of Reparation* I provided summaries of scholarship whose juxtaposition renders the genesis of those civilizational sediments discernible. In this revision of the synoptic text (Pinar 2006b), we gain what Lee Edelman (1994, 268) calls (not without a smile) "(be)hindsight." Such understanding dissolves that racism unconscious of itself.

Teaching for tolerance or encouraging activism is insufficient. We must work from within. As Françoise Verges (1999, 268) observes, "Reparation [is] about repairing oneself." Reparation is also about the acknowledgement of guilt, the asking for forgiveness, and the payment of compensation. (Periodically, my domestic partner quips: Where's my damned 40 acres and that mule?[7]) For those to occur, white subjectivity must be shattered so that "recognition" (Verges 1999, 268) is possible. Submerged in unresolved desire, desire becomes inverted as aggression and experienced as paranoia, as Bhabha (1996, 202) points out in his discussion of Fanon's *Black Skin, White Masks*:

> the paranoiac structure of "a man watching a man"… is his [Fanon's] surveillant model of racial colonial recognition…. In this relay of looks I read a process similar to Freud's transformative structure of paranoid projection, "I am a man who loves a man," that ends with "He hates me." [T]he differences of gender or sexuality—with their ambivalent and cross-dressed desires—are disavowed in a hymn to the originary Adamic male body, black or white.

As Freud suggested, "blacks" represent the white "unconscious." Racism becomes a "reaction-formation against one's own vices" (Zaretsky 2004, 89).

As self-knowledge and deferred collective action, reparation—in Britzman's formulation (2006, 100) "the urge to restore the goodness of the internal object and the self's relation to the external one"—can be taught only through a curriculum that engages intellectually the desire that animated the crime. Racism is the deferred and displaced consequence of homosexual incest punished by servitude, recast as filial obedience through the reproduction of patriarchy: that is the Covenant—marked by symbolic castration: circumcision—between Father and Son. Ned Lukacher (1986, 35) defines deferred action (*Nachtraglichkeit*) as "a mode of temporal spacing through which the randomness of a later event triggers the memory of an earlier event or image, which might never have come to consciousness had the later event never occurred." Too simply put: Only if we can remember the repudiated past can we will know how to repair the present.

Relegating Knowledge to Means to Extra-academic Ends

> Knowledge ... is not an epiphenomenon to the materiality of life but works in that materiality and is part of that phenomenon!
>
> Thomas S. Popkewitz (2008, 185)

> Teaching becomes a technique without object, rather than the mastery and transmission of content.
>
> François Cusset (2008, 46)

Teaching is participation in the complicated conversation that is curriculum. Split off as a "method"—even imagined as a "science"—teaching becomes technique. Isolated from the material to be studied and discussed, teaching devolves into manipulation, rationalized in bureaucratic terms as the "implementation" of "objectives." The segregation of teaching from curriculum devalues intellectual labor. For the teacher, this tragic emphasis upon teaching creates inflated expectations, including fantasies that no child will be left behind. Even parents cannot guarantee that their children will realize their potential, yet teachers are to be held "accountable" for doing so.

The quixotic quest created by an exaggerated emphasis on teaching is everywhere evident in teacher education. The academic disciplines are secondary, even slurred as teaching is tied to ideals even the Church (with God on its side) has failed to realize. Evidently a victim of these circumstances, Lund cannot discern the significance for teacher education of studying the cultural antecedents of present-day racism. He cannot appreciate that focusing on "signs" (e.g., topics, even those designed to encourage progressive beliefs and values) distracts prospective and practicing teachers from understanding the history of racialization in the West. Though academic knowledge is no guarantee of reparation, ignorance ensures the reproduction of the past prejudice. If racialization has its origins in gender and, specifically, in the son's desire for the father and the father's desire for the son, our resistance

Ignorance ensures the reproduction of the past prejudice

to the knowledge of reparation will be powerful indeed. One might flee from such obnoxious knowledge and fasten upon "action." Emphasizing activism over academic knowledge risks recapitulating the reckless righteousness of racists, if with a different set of values. Emphasizing topics over the academic scholarship they represent reduces the curriculum to rhetoric, politics not academics. Only the sign is for sale.

In Herbert Kliebard's critique of the infamous Tyler Rationale, there is another way to understand how Lund might have misunderstood *Race, Religion and a Curriculum of Reparation* as undeserving of its subtitle. Kliebard's critique—like the Tyler (1949) Rationale itself—is canonical (Pinar 2007a); here I will summarize the pertinent points. Kliebard suspects that the popularity of Tyler's rationale is due to its incorporation of several incompatible ideological perspectives—content-centeredness vs. child-centeredness, for instance—in the unfortunately unforgettable four questions: (1) what educational purposes should the school seek to attain? [objectives]; (2) what educational experiences can be provided that are likely to attain these purposes? [design]; (3) how can these educational experiences be effectively organized? [scope and sequence leading to instruction as implementation]; and (4) how can we determine whether these purposes are being attained? [evaluation]. "[S]imple eclecticism may not be the most efficacious way to proceed in theorizing," Kliebard (2000 [1970], 71) points out in understated terms, but there is no tolerance of eclecticism in Tyler's insistence upon objectives as the first and central step in curriculum development. Given the incommensurability of various educational viewpoints, Kliebard recalls, Dewey creatively reformulated them. No theorist (Tyler himself insists), indeed acting more like an accountant, Tyler lays them "all out side by side" (Kliebard 2000 [1970], 71).

Tyler misunderstands the Committee of Ten, Kliebard (2000 [1970], 72) continues, restating its emphasis upon "content" as "objectives." Kliebard (2000 [1970], 73–74) wonders about the wisdom of Tyler's definition of education as "changing behavior" and he characterizes this behaviorism as Pavlovian (2000 [1970], 78). However, Kliebard associates Tyler not with, for example, John B. Watson but with Franklin Bobbitt, his "spiritual ancestor" (2000 [1970], 76). Kliebard cites Bobbitt's resolution of the political problem of objectives—it was to seek "the common judgment of thoughtful men and women" (2000 [1970], 77)—as the conceptual antecedent to Tyler's suggestion that we strain objectives through a "philosophical screen," a concept Kliebard (2000 [1970], 77) judges as vacuous.

Perhaps Tyler's greatest mischief is his establishment of objectives as the first and most important step in curriculum and instruction (although tying these to evaluation is a very close second). Kliebard (2000 [1970], 80) "wonders" whether the idea has "any merit whatsoever." Kliebard is clear that the "simplistic" conception of evaluation as a matter of "matching objectives with outcomes leaves much to be desired," as it ignores "latent outcomes in favor of the manifest and anticipated ones, and it minimizes the vital relationship between ends and means." Objectives are devices disguising manipulation as professional practice, demoting curriculum and instruction to means to extra-educational ends. Matching outcomes to objectives ensures that educational experience is replaced with institutional control by measurement (Macedo 2007). The key curriculum question—what knowledge is of most worth?—becomes a calculation in social engineering's agenda to control the future. Determined to get from "here" to "there" (Lund 2007, 5), such instrumental rationality necessarily deforms the future into terms of the present (Seigfried 1996, 174). As anti-racist educators, a future forecast in terms of the present is exactly what we do not want.

Rather than forever playing the preacher pronouncing the values we wish the world held, rather than concocting activities we calculate will change students' hearts and minds, why not focus on the academic knowledge we deem important for students to study so that they can see for themselves the horrific legacies of our racist history? Why not spend our time studying scholarship in the humanities and social sciences as well as popular culture, summarizing and juxtaposing these in synopses prospective and practicing teachers might find informative? Let teachers decide to what extent they incorporate such material into the curriculum they devise. Should not teachers decide how they organize their classroom periods?

In assuming that our students (or teachers' in the public schools) are the ethical equivalent of "savages," are we not recapitulating the racist and xenophobic ideas associated with Herbert Spencer (Egan 2002, 28). While Spencer's ideas may be "outmoded, eccentric, and confused" (Egan 2002, 34), his question—what knowledge is of most worth?—remains the vibrant curriculum question. As an open and ongoing question, this question requires us to study academic knowledge to help us understand ourselves, our contemporaries, our historical-planetary situation (Jay 2005, 267 ff.). It is long past time we once again focus on "inputs" (in the ugly jargon of bureaucratism). Since Coleman's first report (Pinar 2006b, 124), the U.S. school curriculum has been eviscerated by politicians' obsession with "outputs," ugly jargon conflated with students' scores on standardized examinations. Not only a retrospective reductive judgment of educational achievement, such scores have, until recently (Lewin 2008), been used almost universally as a college entrance requirement, employed by conservatives as a weapon against other criteria of university admission, especially those associated with "affirmative action." By focusing on those analytic and mathematical "skills" measured (presumably) by such examinations, conservatives strip the curriculum of intellectual content, especially that knowledge they regard as unpatriotic (Zimmerman 2002; Revkin 2008). Theirs is no brief for impartiality, however: conservatives are hardly hesitant in adding material favorable to their cause (Banerjee 2008; Beil 2008), firing those who disagree (Blumenthal 2007). The quixotic search for "what works." in education is a secular version of salvation that, save the totalitarianism institutional religion invokes God's Law to rationalize, cannot succeed.[8]

Curriculum like Artwork

The Worldliness of Teacher Education

[T]he work of teacher education is not to resolve social problems, as if learning to teach can do that.

> Deborah P. Britzman and Jen Gilbert (2008, 212)

To rebuild teaching as a *cosmopolitan* form of work requires a major re-thinking of teacher education.

> Diane Mayer, Carmen Luke and Allan Luke (2008, 96)

To vitalize the curriculum is to emphasize its worldliness: how academic knowledge represents a symbolic and practical engagement with historical and planetary preoccupations (Hu 2008c). To emphasize worldliness is to encourage teachers to teach the curriculum animated by their subjective interests and those of their students, attentive to the communities (local and global[9]) in which they work and live (Garrison 1997, 98). "What knowledge is of most worth?" is an ongoing provocation to study according to subjective preoccupations, collective concerns, structured by academic knowledge discovered and created in universities and elsewhere.

Curriculum development is not, in this sense, programmatic, but intellectual, finally an individual affair, not a state (or province)-wide, not district-wide, not necessarily even a school-wide, bureaucratic undertaking. Like artwork, curriculum development is the teacher's opportunity to explore subjects informed by the academic knowledge and lived experience they and their students find compelling. Like artwork, then, curriculum is a form of self-expression that becomes, in its subjective meaning and social significance, "self-overcoming" in its "self-critical" (inter)disciplinarity (Williams 2007, 37).

With its echo of Nietzsche, "self-overcoming" bears emphasis, as teachers practice their profession by ongoing intellectual self-cultivation. Education is not a "service" rendered to consumers; it is an opportunity offered to students, the quality of which depends upon the intellectual sophistication of those who teach and the sincerity of those who study with them. Teachers' sophistication is, above all, intellectual, but it is also subjective, social, indeed, worldly. Teachers are not bureaucrats in gracious submission to the state; they are scholars-artists, private-and-public intellectuals willing to teach what they know, to acknowledge what they do not, and to encourage others to undertake what is, finally, a solitary journey in the company of others.

What Robert Williams describes as the Italian Renaissance painter's subjective discipline (he is writing about Leonardo da Vinci) communicates my sense of curriculum development as a public form of self-cultivation. "Schemes for the curriculum," Egan (2002, 123) reminds us, "are commonly a covert form of autobiographical writing." Like artwork, curriculum development aspires to the attainment of an objective truth but also to the fashioning of an ideal subjective disposition toward the world, an overall existential poise, and this disposition is fundamental *critical*. Art transforms subjectivity itself into a critical principle (Williams 2007, 38).

In pedagogical terms, such curriculum development can transform subjectivity into an ethical principle. As it was for late-nineteenth-century artists such as Zola and Baudelaire, the "native strength" and "abundance" of subjectivity can enable one "to cast off the fetters of convention, to create a new language, one that may be limited—in that it is his or her own—but one that is also capable of expressing the kind of truth we can all share" (Williams 2007, 35). Through the singularities of subjectivity the universal can be disclosed and created.

"What good is it for a man to gain the whole world, and yet lose or forfeit his very self?" (Luke 9:25). It is upon our (racialized) selves we might focus our anti-racist labor, and in so doing, provide opportunities for prospective and practicing teachers to study themselves through the academic disciplines that inform their profession. "You hypocrite, first take the log out of your own eye, and then you will clearly see to take the speck out of your brother's eye" (Matthew 7:5). Such self-scrutiny and ethical action requires autobiography, but for us educators life history is not separable from ongoing study of academic knowledge. Neither should topics or values—"signs"—be severed from the academic scholarship that inform them. No "empty promise" (Lund 2007, 6), such subjectively structured academic study *is* teacher education.

Structured
academic study
is teacher education

4   A Declaration of Independence[1]

The Declaration of Independence of the Thirteen Colonies

In CONGRESS, July 4, 1776

The unanimous Declaration of the thirteen united States of America,

When in the Course of human events, it becomes necessary for one people to dissolve the political bands which have connected them with another, and to assume among the powers of the earth, the separate and equal station to which the Laws of Nature and of Nature's God entitle them, a decent respect to the opinions of mankind requires that they should declare the causes which impel them to the separation.

We hold these truths to be self-evident, that all men are created equal, that they are endowed by their Creator with certain unalienable Rights, that among these are Life, Liberty and the pursuit of Happiness.

Maybe every generation wants to believe their time is the best time. It is, after all, one's time, the time of one's life. Life, or reality, is difficult all on its own: Discovering and deciding who one is, what one's to do, whom to love, the list is long in the West. And everything is made increasingly urgent with the coming of age. The meaning of our lives is, Martin Heidegger suggested, clarified as death approaches; we are, he reminded, being-toward-death. To lace this "original difficulty" of life (Pinar 2007a, 1) with political injustice aggravates the wound Heidegger believed animates our activity. The myth of progress—that especially technology can contradict, or at least compensate for, the original difficulty of life or reality—seems to many an inalienable right. Technology becomes the way of life (Mariniello 1994, 124).

With the legacy of what historians call American exceptionalism[2], many Americans believe their country is God's country. (Never mind British Columbia's assertion that *it* is the best place on earth.) Probably more than a few of us are prone to believe (certainly we are told) that progress is inevitable, that this moment is better than those preceding it, and that the best is yet to come. This optimism of our national character is a strength. As you know from your own experience, however, a strength can also be a fault. Optimism becomes a dysfunctional state when it obscures reality. Part of what I want to do today is to question the optimism I suspect many of us, and specifically as teachers, feel, or want to feel. Ours, after all, is a profession built on optimism, on the confidence that we can make a difference. Deriving from both our national character and from the confidence driving our profession, optimism is a strength that is now, at this present historical moment, a fault.

The opposite of optimism is, of course, pessimism, and I am not advocating that. Both states are dispositional responses (perhaps, in some individuals, genetically encoded) to the original complexity, uncertainty, difficulty of life. Being in reality, in life, as the founding fathers phrased it, is a prerequisite for the pursuit of happiness (Jay 2005, 171). That is obvious in our personal lives, is it not, as the countless romances that have gone wrong testify, at least for those of us who have loved individuals who didn't turn out to be the persons we thought them to be or the persons they pretended to be or because we weren't the persons we thought we were. Being in a state of denial, out of touch with reality, spells trouble. It invites unhappiness.

Commentators lament the high number of divorces, but for those of us who didn't get it right the first or second time, the statistic means, in addition to broken hearts and homes, an opportunity to try again, this time less "innocent," perhaps more savvy about ourselves, possibly more appreciative of the enigmatic and paradoxical reality of love. Through that declaration of independence that separation enacts, we exercise the liberty to pursue happiness alone and with another. Being in reality renders liberty concrete, not abstract, specific to our situation, not a general condition or a platitude. In the new realities declarations of independence establish, we undertake the pursuit of happiness. Free of unjust arrangements (like taxation without representation or, in personal terms, a relationship or marriage that no longer works) but still beset by the original difficulty of life, we summon our courage, we try again. We work to set our lives right.

It is—is it not?—long past time to set right our profession. To undertake that labor (simultaneously subjective and political, as I have argued: Pinar 2004), we must declare independence from those politicians and policymakers who betray us and the children we teach, who misrepresent us to the public and, in so doing, disable us from the practice of our profession, a profession of study (Pinar 2006b, 109–120) that requires liberty. Like our founding fathers, we are required to name the causes that compel us to declare independence. First among these is the misrepresentation of our profession by politicians who insist that education is a business, based on outcomes.

Like no other profession, we teachers have been singled out, made responsible (accountable in that ugly hypocritical word that seems to apply only to us) for social and economic realities for which we are not, as a profession, responsible. Those who scapegoat never acknowledge the nature of their game. Like lying, scapegoating doesn't work when you admit that is what you're doing. Instead, politicians insist they are concerned only for

Kennedy Caused the problem

America's children, that they are only representing the public, expressing the outrage of millions that we aren't doing our jobs: raising those test scores. (The political rhetoric is never over being educated any more; the last "outcome" politicians want is an educated public, capable of critical thinking, armed with facts, endowed with a memory. It is no surprise that politicians focus on standardized test scores, not educatedness.) Children must be tested, and teachers' conduct must be regulated if politicians are to protect a nation at risk, ensure that no child is left behind. In this Orwellian moment, politicians' words mean exactly the opposite.

The noose around teachers' and administrators' necks, around our necks as education professors, was placed there by the Democrats, more than 40 years ago during the Kennedy Administration. Exploiting Cold War tensions, relying on the first Coleman report (Sizer 2002, 10), liberal Democrats focused on outcomes in order to make the case for governmental intervention in the unequal social and economic circumstances in which America's children went to school. While Coleman's Equal Educational Opportunity Report emphasized outcomes, not inputs, the Kennedy Administration nonetheless initiated the first and thus far last national curriculum reform initiative, led by arts and science faculty, determined to bypass what politicians would later dismiss as the "education establishment." Even that liberal determination to create, through governmental programs, a "Great Society"—Kennedy's successor Lyndon B. Johnson's concept—was deemed insufficient by the late 1960s. Animated by the civil rights movement and anti-Vietnam War protests, by the late 1960s, the "output" many Americans were demanding was a socially just and subjectively meaningful society.

Expressive of that historical moment was the publication, in 1970, of *Crisis in the Classroom*. Written by Charles Silberman (a sociologist turned journalist who had served on the board of *Fortune* magazine), the book was produced for the Carnegie Corporation and had appeared in the *Atlantic Monthly* in a prepublication serial that included titles such as "Murder in the School Room" and "How the Public Schools Kill Dreams and Mutilate Minds." The accusatory, sensationalistic, character of Silberman's indignation foreshadowed those scapegoating strategies to be employed repeatedly in the decades that followed.

Silberman's indignation still seems strange to me. At the outset of the decade, he had been associated with the Kennedy Administration's effort to install teacher-proof curriculum designed to send presumably intellectually engaging curriculum straight to the students, bypassing their evidently incompetent teachers. By the time of *Crisis in the Classroom*, Silberman's views had, let us say, shifted. Children's spontaneity and the joy of learning preoccupied Silberman in 1970, not the structural verisimilitude of the school subjects and the university-based academic disciplines. A decade earlier, schools were failing because they weren't enough like the elite institutions JFK had attended (recall Kennedy first attended Princeton, then Harvard from which he graduated, and then, finally and briefly, Stanford's business school). By 1970, the public schools were awful not because they were insufficiently academic but because they weren't child-centered and spontaneous enough.

The school is a symbol for society. (Its status as an empty abstraction is indicated by the finding that the majority of Americans approve of their local schools and of their children's teachers [Medina 2008; Gootman 2007a]; it is only "schools" in general that distress and outrage Americans: Berliner and Biddle 1996.) Over the last 45 years, the school has become a projective screen for politicians' rhetoric, their empty canvas for conveying their ideological commitments and manipulating voters' emotions. For Kennedy Democrats, it was national curriculum reform for the sake of "getting the country moving again" (after the Sputnik humiliation)[3] as well as in the name of greater social and economic equality (Pinar 2006b, 122 ff). For the Republicans, since the election of Richard Nixon in 1968, it has been "back to the basics" in which the focus on outcomes is not employed to support government programs to equalize social and economic opportunity. The Republicans' focus on outcomes is a political tactic, displacing onto teachers responsibility for the increasing inequities their anti-welfare state policies have intensified (as the statistics showing increasing disparity between the rich and poor verify). Like the wives of abusive husbands, we teachers are to clean up the mess politicians make.

How? Through teaching to standards (presumably we didn't have them before), by operating schools like businesses, by being accountable. Are we to be accountable like those oil company executives who gauge the public with high gasoline prices while taking hundreds of millions of dollars in salary? Should we be accountable like the Bush Administration? Where is the accountability for miscalculating when the "mission" in Iraq would be "accomplished"? Where is the accountability for secret prisons, prisoner torture, for awarding exclusive government contracts to the company where the Vice President used to work? Where is the accountability for the Bush Administration's incompetent and racist response to Katrina? "With the dollar falling, the deficits rising," Madeleine Grumet (2006, 49) observes, "once again corporate America imposes an economy on the public schools that it cannot sustain in its own engorged and polluted balance books."

Not just we but the public has been gaslighted.[4] Nothing is what it appears. Conservatives meddle in the market they insist is "free." Take the ongoing crisis in health care. I am not thinking of the impending bankruptcy of Medicare but of the current crisis in hospital emergency rooms and the shortage of physicians, predicted to be 85,000 in another decade. Because "market-driven" conservatives believed managed (i.e., efficient, run-like-a-business) health care would reduce the demand for physicians, they reduced the funds available for students of medicine, specifically for residency programs. Medical schools reduced the number of applicants they accepted, and now injured and chronically ill patients are being turned away from emergency rooms in a number of large cities. In rural areas, physicians are not always available.

Never mind terrorism or a natural disaster or a pandemic: On a good day, thanks to accountability conservatives, people will die unnecessarily.

Speaking of medicine, where is the emphasis on "outcomes" in that profession? Despite pressure to make public statistics regarding the consequences of various treatment protocols, medical practice is not focused on outcomes. Medicine is predicated on those practices indicated by research, tempered by physicians' judgment. On more than one occasion (take Vioxx, for example), that research must be revised, owing to the cozy relationship between the Republican-dominated Food and Drug Administration and the pharmaceutical industry. The relationship between many doctors and the drug industry is not exactly distant either, is it?

Maybe if test preparation representatives took us golfing or to dinner or on holiday we might be more receptive to standardized exams. I hope not, as standardized tests measure mostly the ability of students to take tests, quantifying what psychologists call "skills," another empty abstraction, this one rationalizing a wide range of intellectually vacuous activities and the testing of them. Like the drug companies, the Educational Testing Service and other test manufacturers exploit the public for profit.

To return to medicine: I remember the first time I learned that approximately 80,000 patients die (and another 150,000 are injured) each year owing to medical errors (Berliner and Biddle 1996, 108). I was sure this was a misprint. (The number is, in fact, contested.) My effort at denial of this allegation was undermined when I heard the figure repeated, as fact, on the CBS Evening News in June (2006), and again on "Sixty Minutes (on March 16, 2008). Did you know that as many 80,000 Americans die owing to medical error each year? And politicians are on *our* case over a few points on standardized tests? Are these people completely crazy?

They're crazy like a fox. They play on parents' anxieties over their children's futures as they distract the public over the consequences of conservative social and fiscal policies, especially those targeting the working poor (McWilliam 2008, 35). Forty years of conservative policies have created conditions no teacher—even one with divine powers—can overcome. Speaking of the divine, where is the accountability for preachers, priests, and rabbis? Have they not been teaching pretty much the same lesson for thousands of years with, well, you have to admit, limited effectiveness. If politicians played the same scapegoating game with preachers, priests, and rabbis that they force on us, more than a few churches and synagogues would be closed for unacceptable outcomes. Where is the accountability for the religion business?

There is none. Instead, thousands of people in pulpits rave at millions of Americans each week. Many of these people—I am thinking of fundamentalist preachers for whom being "born again," not academic study, is the key qualification—are without college degrees, let alone advanced study of the Bible. Fuming and fussing over evolutionary theory, homosexuality, reproductive rights, these self-proclaimed representatives of God often take an obscure biblical passage to mean, well, just about anything they want it to mean. It *always* means sending more money to the ministry. For millions of Americans, the only "public intellectual" they hear is an uneducated, self-promoting and, I'd say, often delusional creature screaming at them to think as they command or risk eternal damnation. Nowhere does this happen more often than in the American South (although parts of the Midwest are not far behind).

I should say not the American South, which, for me, means Louisiana (where I lived for 20 years): beautiful landscapes, astonishing food, memorable music, and many remarkable individuals. So I should not say the South but, rather, the Confederacy, to specify that it is a political formation to which I refer, not a cultural one. (Admittedly, the boundaries between politics and culture blur.) It is clear to me that what we Americans suffer today is, in part, the triumph of the Confederacy (the South did rise again), laced as it is now (but was not 150 years ago) with religious fundamentalism and fascism, American style.[5] (The Bible Belt doesn't form until after the Civil War, as historian Joel Williamson makes clear.)

What elected George W. Bush were, do not forget, the Confederate states. These are the same 11 states that defeated the Equal Rights Amendment 25 years ago, and they are the same 11 states that would vote in favor of a Constitutional Amendment banning gay marriage. Eight of these 11 states voted against women's suffrage almost a century ago, once again claiming defense of the family, patriotism, and the inerrancy of the Bible. The failure of the U.S. government to stay the course in the post-bellum reconstruction of the South has proven to be a political disaster for American democracy, something that, despite the witch burning and capitalism, was more a Yankee than Confederate idea for the colonies.

It is, then, not only a culture war in which we are engaged. It is, alas, the Civil War. So-called conservative values are, in part, Confederate values. Just as conservatives lie about the founding fathers, converting them into Christians—they certainly were not: Jefferson was skeptical of Christ's divinity, Ben Franklin was largely indifferent, and Thomas Paine and Ethan Allen were evidently contemptuous of Christianity (Holmes 2006)—conservatives lie about what is at stake when their fellow citizens demand Constitutional protection of their civil rights. Last spring, for example, when legislation was proposed in California to require the teaching of gay and lesbian history in the public schools, a conservative spokesman complained *his* free speech was being violated.

Even if we could rid ourselves of the Republicans, we would still left with the Democrats. Many Democrats supported the passage of *No Child Left Behind*, now deserted by Democrats (Dillon 2007c, 2008c) and pronounced flawed even by the Bush Administration (Dillon 2008a). Unless we study the past, we cannot understand the present. It is a Confederate, not American, present, in which deferred and displaced gendered anxieties over Cold War confrontations and racist responses to Brown v. Board of Education and the civil rights movement have morphed into the nightmare that is the present: the evisceration of the curriculum through the political subjugation of teachers.[6] Not only have we lost control of the curriculum, we no longer devise the means by which we assess students' study of it: Without these, our profession is profoundly compromised.

The "regressive" moment of the method of *currere* is an ongoing act of remembrance and testimony, simultaneously a structure of subjectivity as well as the content of specific memories. Until we always keep, as it were, one foot in the past, we cannot, I believe, imagine the future or be in the present, in reality (Seigfried 1996, 198). Though in *What Is Curriculum Theory?* I remembered our collective history as a profession, the regressive moment is also individual, indeed, very personal. It is remembering who I am, may become, am now. For you, preparing to be a principal, I trust it means you will not forget you are a teacher, not a plant manager or CEO. Your obligation is not to the superintendent or to the school board—although you won't want to signal that to either body—but to the profession, to your colleagues and to the children they teach.

Without Liberty We Cannot Teach

> Art, like the curriculum, is the process of becoming and re-creating in each situation.
>
> Patrick Slattery (2006, 254)

> Translation (without a master) is a vital concept and capacity to the project of creating an anti-violent curriculum.
>
> Susan Edgerton (1996, 53)

Though we may be imprisoned in an abusive relationship, a bad marriage in which we have little power, we, and the academic knowledge we teach, can help our children, our students, find their way out. That is why we must teach individual courses of our own making rather than following others' directives in mass-produced textbooks linked to standardized exams. Our individual reconstructions of subject matter in conversation with our students constitute the prerequisite for teaching. Such curriculum is the expression of free indirect subjectivity. Unless we devise the curriculum we teach, we cannot demonstrate how academic knowledge enables understanding of the world. Academic knowledge can provide passages between the past and the future, between subjectivity and society, the local and the global. In knowledge, we can find freedom (Fabbri 1994, 82–83). Through the artistry of creative curriculum design, teachers can express their individuality and invite students to articulate theirs, through academic knowledge and inquiry (Williams 2007, 41; Seigfried 1996, 198).

What Is Curriculum Theory? is, in one sense, an elongated syllabus, summarizing scholarship salient to understanding the nightmare that is the present. It is a book composed as a course I teach. Not a book containing an airtight argument, it is a juxtaposition of readings, creating crevices wherein the reader can breathe. The emphasis upon autobiography provides a means by which you can reflect on yourself, including upon your gendered, racialized, and political positioning as a professional educator in society at this historical moment. As the individualized courses I am suggesting constitute the prerequisite for teaching, *What Is Curriculum Theory?* is a singular curriculum—standardization is the bane of education—which I would not necessarily expect another teacher to design.

It is our individuality, I have long argued (Pinar and Grumet 2006 [1976]), that configures educational experience. Intellectual work is psychological labor. Rather than being "noise" in the system, undermining its efficiency, what we feel, how we think, our relations to others configure our curiosity, animate our interests, drive our desire to explore and discover. What we offer our students when we engage them in conversation are, as Susan Edgerton has explained, translations, not copies of sacred, originary texts (the masters' words) but reconstructions of what others have studied in other times, in other places, for other purposes, for our time, this place, our purposes. Such translation constitutes the artistry of our profession, connecting subjectivity to society through academic knowledge, creating classrooms that are simultaneously civic squares and rooms of our own. In recreating each situation anew, as Patrick Slattery points out, we participate in a process of becoming, an educational process made immediate and vivid by our subjective presence in public.

It is precisely our singular subjective presence politicians have persistently muted. Since the heyday of educational radio in the late 1920s (Pinar et al. 1995, 707), politicians have worked to supplement (if not replace) flesh-and-blood teachers with equipment. Equipment costs less, or so the myth of mass production goes. But education, unlike manufacturing, is not a business. However much politicians would like us to turn out "products" to be sold in the global market-place, however much some parents would like their children to be clones, in conformity with their "values" (as they rename their preferences and prejudices), our students, as we know, are not products but singular subjectivities. Anyone paying attention knows a child's spirit—even when loved and nourished—is fragile and, finally, mysterious. The arrogance of trying to mold children after our ideas of what they should be fortunately fails, however often teachers are made to try. If parents—whose genetic and psychological material their children carry—can't get their kids to honor curfew, how do they expect us to make geniuses out of them? We offer educational opportunities; students (and their parents) are responsible for taking advantage of them. We cannot guarantee outcomes. Each generation must find its own way. We can help.

This is a conception of the teacher as a socially engaged artist-intellectual in complicated conversation not only with one's students but with oneself, one's subject, toward self-understanding and social reconstruction.[7] This is a conception in which the creativity and originality of the individual educator are key to the design of the curriculum. Maybe one doesn't know, in advance, what one aspires to accomplish or how one will assess students' study of what one teaches. Maybe one has only a hunch that juxtaposing the study of lynching to African American autobiographical practices to Cold War politics and school desegregation might enable students to understand the present political circumstances of their profession in ways they had not considered before, all the while introducing them to important bodies of scholarship, scholarship, one hopes, students will someday read in their original—not just summary—form. Such an apparent hodgepodge of topics may not a compelling argument make, but it becomes, one trusts, in the hands of a professional educator, a provocation to cultivate independence of mind (Nussbaum 1997, 19, 28).

Academic—that is, intellectual—freedom (to speak the truth as you understand it through the courses one is employed to teach, courses that reflect one's original and creative study of the subject as well as students' responses to it) is the prerequisite for teaching. It is, however, one of those necessary but insufficient conditions for the practice of our profession. The material conditions in which we teach must also change. Salaries and working conditions vary dramatically across the United States and across and even within districts but, in general, doubling teachers' salaries and cutting by half the number of classes and students they teach would improve working conditions considerably. Intellectual work can benefit from physical comfort and psychological stability (it should go without saying), neither of which is supported by the ongoing obsession with "what works."[8]

I suppose I am slipping into the progressive moment of the method of *currere* (otherwise known as fantasy of the future), where I will also imagine paid—at full salary, thank you—sabbaticals every five to seven years. Nor will I forget to provide each school with a teachers' reading room, comfortably furnished with overstuffed chairs, good reading lamps, a library really, where teachers can read and think and nap, where they can be served coffee and snacks by a well-paid and respectful staff. Do you still want to be principals?

That job would change, too. As Ted Aoki (Pinar and Irwin 2005) pointed out, the concept of principal used to mean the principal teacher. It was an honorary and, still in a few countries today, an elected position, reserved for the most respected members of the faculty who accept the burden of serving the faculty as its academic secretary and for a limited period of time, after which they return to the faculty. It is a position not modeled after businessmen but after teachers, themselves modeled after artists, scholars, and intellectuals, emphasizing creativity, originality, and individuality expressed through service to others. Dwayne Huebner (1999, 385) reminds us that "to administer is to minister to, to serve." Working from a Christian tradition (after leaving Teachers College, Columbia University, he taught at Yale Divinity School), Huebner asks principals to think not in terms of organizations but of communities in open and candid conversation with themselves and their constituencies.

The Pursuit of Happiness

> [P]olitics can be a projective area for feelings and impulses that are only marginally related to the manifest issues.
>
> Richard Hofstadter (1996 [1965], ix)

> What operates at the level of cultural fantasy is not finally dissociable from the ways in which material life is organized.
>
> Judith Butler (2004, 214)

In the nightmare that is the present, such a community of colleagues is precisely what is not likely. As you may have done as a teacher, as a future principal you might "close the door" and proceed on your own, paying lip service to the ridiculous demands made by others far removed from and, it is clear, not really interested in education. I am suggesting that you say what you must to your supervisors but that you remain private in your professional convictions, acting on them as circumstances allow. You cannot be candid; you are behind enemy lines.

Contrary to military events 140 ago, the Civil War was lost. Confederates—today known as conservatives—have triumphed. They salute the flag, but it is the stars and bars, not the stars and stripes, they see. The idea of democracy—in part, private sacrifice for the common good—has been replaced by the Confederate compulsion for privilege and possession, in which the "American dream" is wealth, not equality of opportunity. It is not the country my ancestors fought to hold together. It carries the name, but not the reality. The reality—Gauntanamo, Abu Ghraib, Enron, *No Child Left Behind*—might seem distant to you this July morning in this beautiful place, engaged in a remarkable academic program with remarkable teachers. This intensely artful place, removed from your home classroom and your future principal's office, can become the reality you affirm, however, can become the reality you remember when you return home. Form friendships here, create Massachusetts College of Liberal Arts alumni networks, meet again and regularly back home: Remember and affirm this reality.

In affirming the reality of your experience here, I am hardly asking you to retreat from the public sphere that is the school in which you work. As the brilliant Christopher Lasch (1978, 1984) famously argued, such retreat, a maneuver made out of alienation in the name of self-protection, creates the political and psychic conditions in which the "outcome" one wanted to avoid—unhappiness—necessarily occurs. In concentrating on one's private pleasures, in retreat from the unpleasantness of the public sphere, one loses, Lasch argues, the possibility of that one pleasure that can persist, namely satisfaction. Narcissism is the concept Lasch invokes to depict the condition of the socially withdrawn, politically passive individual in pursuit of private pleasures only. As a consequence, the narcissist devolves into an atrophied or minimal self, a fragile self, vulnerable to the original difficulties of life, not to mention to the pain of oppressive political realities. As Franz Kafka put it, in trying to avoid pain one incurs the only suffering one might have avoided.

This realization—that the pursuit of happiness must be conducted in public, as well as private, life, and that it incurs political risks a well as private pleasures—links the three inalienable rights our founding fathers proclaimed as a curricular sequence, in which the achievement of one becomes the prerequisite to the experience and attainment of the one that follows. What the founding fathers called life is reality, that in-your-face, behind-your-back, everywhere and nowhere truth of our ever-mutating lived experience. Our lived experience is structured inequitably by the legacies of our ancestors' greed and idiocy. Life—reality—teaches us the necessity of liberty in human affairs. Unless we are free to correct the injustices into which we are born and the mistakes we ourselves make, unless we are free to think creatively, originally, passionately and to teach what we know and explore what we do not know with our students, without the inalienable right of liberty, we cannot pursue happiness. Experiencing life, that is, being in reality, we exercise liberty in the pursuit of happiness, a public, not only private, state of satisfaction. Happiness cannot be achieved without liberty and justice for all. This July, in historic Massachusetts, in this remarkable academic program, I ask you to declare your independence from politicians, affirm your inalienable right to practice your profession, creatively, as an artist, teaching and ministering in the public good, in the pursuit of happiness, for the sake of the nation.

Part II

Passionate Lives in Public Service

5 Jane Addams

A "Person of Marked Individuality"[1]

[T]he processes of life are as important as its aims.

Jane Addams (2002 [1902], 48)

In her brief for Jane Addams as canonical in curriculum history,[2] Petra Munro (1999) emphasized Addams' courage in defending immigrants, vilified especially during World War I (as was she, for her pacifism). Though immigrants—her neighbors in Chicago's Nineteenth Ward—remained her lifelong concern, African Americans also engaged her ethical commitment to democracy in America (Munro 1999, 42–43). Influenced by her father, by her study at Rockford (Seminary, then College), by her tours abroad (including her momentous visit to Toynbee Hall), Addams arrived at this commitment to democracy quite on her own. Louise Knight (2005, 296–297) underscores Addams's intellectual independence:

> [Addams] was ferociously determined to think through matters on her own. There was intellectual hubris in this position—she was clearly confident of her ability to reason things out for herself and reluctant to consider that her class origins blinded her in any way—but there was moral courage in it, too. Many of the most difficult and defining moments in Jane Addams' life would rise because she insisted on speaking the truth as she saw it. This was one tenet of individualism that she would never abandon.[3]

It is a tenet central to the academic enterprise, one threatened by right-wing—and specifically the Bush Administration's—assaults on schools and universities (Chapter 4) and undermined from within the profession by what sometimes seems an intensifying bureaucratism (Chapter 3).

In this chapter, I recount Jane Addams's experience of academic study as a "snare of preparation."[4] Missing, she felt, was experience in the world, experience outside the claims of the family and the confines of institutions. It was, I suggest, the worldliness that accrued from her two tours of Europe[5] (like academic study, opportunities for acquiring culture: Knight 2005, 127) as well as her emotional (and possibly sexual) engagement with Ellen Gates Starr (Brown 2004, 194; Knight 2005, 218) and Mary Rozet Smith (Brown 2005, 255–259) that enabled her to honor the "social claim." Her acceptance of that claim resulted in a courageous career of social work and intellectual accomplishment, a passionate[6] life devoted to public service. It is evident in her relationship with John Dewey, her support of W. E. B. Du Bois, and long-term colleagueship with Ida B. Wells.

A Cosmopolitan Education

> To create a life ... is to interpret the materials that history has given you.
> Kwane Anthony Appiah (2005, 163)

Addams was always attentive to the "evolutionary process by which an individual or a social condition came to be," one of her most perceptive biographers—Victoria Bissell Brown (2004, 8)—points out. If Addams could know the genesis of a situation, she thought, more likely it was that she could devise interventions precisely appropriate to its resolution. "By tracing the evolution of Addams' own approach from arrogant heroics to democratic process," Brown (2004, 8) writes, "we can appreciate why her lived experience convinced her that we learn best about life from life itself." While I think Brown draws too sharp a line between Addams's early embrace of a heroic individualism and her later apparently selfless service, her point about learning from life itself specifies the source of Jane Addams's worldliness.[7]

When the self-centered ego—what Addams called "the great I"—shatters, the specific subjectivity that is oneself hardly disappears. That subjectivity structures as it animates one's engagement with the world, as it is stimulated and reconstructed by that engagement. When, in Christopher Lasch's (1984) terms, the "minimal self" (contracted, he argues, by self-protective, survivalist retreat from the world) "expands" into one's lived—and civic—space, it risks dissolution by engaging with the world. Such experience—lived experience, informed by academic study, self-reflectively reconstructed—is primary in the production of worldliness.[8]

The two tours of Europe gave Addams a taste for what experience could yield, but her postgraduation period of fidelity to the "family claim" upon her she would later depict as "the nadir of my nervous depression and sense of maladjustment" (quoted in Brown 2004, 148) seemed to her a suspension of educational experience. Brown, however, emphasizes this period as also one of education. It was during this period, for instance, that Addams began reading Leo Tolstoy's religious and social criticism, affirming her focus on the historical Jesus. Reading Tolstoy confirmed Addams's sense that true Christianity demanded faith in Jesus' message about human salvation on earth, not faith in a supernatural Jesus or promises of life after death (Brown 2004, 164). It was Christianity's meaning for *this* world that preoccupied Jane Addams.[9]

Possibly even more crucial in her self-formation was Addams' supplementation of her Rockford persona as student leader and intellectual with sustained attention to "women's personal style" and "emotional authenticity" (Brown 2004, 176). Addams was critical of what she worried was higher education's tendency to engender women's detachment from the world. Education, she felt sure, ought not undermine women's ability to notice people's faces, to be "bread givers," to preserve "the softer graces" (2004, 176). This was a period, Brown (2004, 177) suggests, of Addams' affirmation of women's culture. Her attachment to her sisters and to other women, among them her teachers Sarah Blaisdell and Sarah Anderson, and fellow alumnae, prominently among them Ellen Gates Starr, signified an "embrace of female culture" (Brown 2004, 183). It was during this time that Addams realized that, as Brown (2004, 177) notes, "any heroism she aspired to would draw upon the connections that women fostered in their relationships." This was no incipient separatism; in fact, during her second tour of Europe, it was the study of Auguste Comte—specifically "his belief in a supreme 'fellowship' of all humanity based on lived experience rather than metaphysics" (Brown 2004, 195)—that provided Addams a rationale for extending her embrace of "female culture" to humanity itself.

It was the juxtaposition of study and experience that enabled Addams to imagine opening—with Ellen Gates Starr—a settlement house. Brown (2004, 203–204) tells us that Addams was reading Walter Besant's popular 1882 novel, *All Sorts and Conditions of Men*, the same week (in June 1888) she visited Toynbee Hall. The novel's plot seemed to reproduce the main points of Addams' life: The heroine, Angela Messenger, a wealthy heiress who felt lost after graduation from Newnham College, moves to East London to live and learn (and fall in love) among the working classes. There she builds there a People's Palace as a center for culture. After reading *All Sorts and Conditions of Men*, Brown continues, Addams visited the actual "People's Palace," a new East London youth center built with private and public funds. The Palace's classrooms, meeting rooms, billiard rooms, music and dance rooms, and library were, Brown (2004, 203–204) suggests, "an important model" for Hull-House, a settlement house that would be much more "alive with the sounds of youth than Toynbee Hall."[10] There was to be no simple mimicry: Moved by her experience in London, informed by her ongoing academic study, she was able to imagine her future course of action. However shared that course would be, it would be distinctively hers; Hull-House[11] would bear the subjective stamp[12] of the young woman from Cedarville, Illinois.

In her eulogy delivered at the memorial service for Anna Peck Sill[13] (the founder and headmistress of Rockford Female Seminary) a year after her return from Europe, Jane Addams asserted that a college education was nothing more than a "mountain of mere straw and stubble" if it did not give graduates "a moral purpose" (quoted in Brown 2004, 206). From Brown's depiction of Addams' post-Rockford period—she describes it as a "postgraduate education in humanity and humility" (2004, 206)—we are reminded it was Addams who restructured the subjectivity her upbringing and education had formed. That subjectivity proved to the sustaining source for her commitment to learn from experience. In one of many beautifully crafted passages, Brown (2004, 205) summarizes the shifts Addams underwent during the period after her undergraduate education and before the founding of Hull-House:

> Those years of "ever-lasting preparation" taught her to value the caring and intimacy fostered by female culture, directed her eye away from the hero on stage and toward the individual on the street, and forced her to realize that in a world of bent backs, dying children, filthy factories, and selfish power, heroism was not a romantic flight of the disembodied but a daily decision to show up and hold on. She knew none of this when she left Rockford, and without the intervening years she could not have grasped, replicated, or—most important—improved upon what she saw at Toynbee Hall.

As this passage (and Brown's biography) makes clear, becoming worldly-wise is part accident of circumstances and part subjective capacity made conscious and articulate through academic and self-study.[14] From experience and self-reflective academic study, Addams synthesized a coherent self capable of sustained, critical, and creative engagement with the world.

By 1912—when she becomes the first women to second a presidential nomination (at the Progressive Party Convention)—Addams's reputation had grown far beyond Hull-House; she was widely acknowledged as "one[15] of the most articulate voices for progressive reform on the American scene," appreciated for her "prodemocratic" and "promediation" commitments for which she was, by then, "well known" and "widely respected" (Brown 2004, 293). When Addams confessed, in her 1910 autobiography, that she longed for "a definite social creed," Brown (2004, 293) believes that

> she seriously underestimated her own achievement in fashioning—out of the bits and pieces of a scattered, self-directed education—a coherent, consistent social philosophy of democratic mediation that suited her temperament, caught the spirit of her time, and gave her the authenticity for which she had longed.

In this sentence is conveyed the confluence of lived experience,[16] autobiographical consciousness (Earle 1972), and academic study attuned to the historical moment and grounded in "place" (Pinar 1991) that the concept of "study" communicates.

Worldliness is no educational "objective" for which teachers can be held "accountable." Juxtaposing autobiographical and academic study, situated socially and attuned historically, is no formula for student success or teaching effectiveness. As Brown's perceptive observation makes explicit, worldliness is a retrospective judgment on a life already lived, one that Addams felt was, for a time, lost. That she fashioned a progressive selfhood out of what she felt was the provincialism of her late nineteenth-century academic and family experience is a testimony to her genius but also to that experience and those who figured so prominently in it: her father; Ellen Gates Starr; her teachers (discussed momentarily); and, later, to fortuitous events (the infamous bullfight, for instance: Lasch 1965, 8; Brown 2004, 7, 198–199; Knight 2005, 163–164). Her genius drew upon her fidelity—her intellectual and emotional honesty—to her lived experience, self-reflectively reconstructed through study and attuned to the historical moment in which and the place where she lived.

Worldliness is not only a function of openness to the world but, as well, openness to the world of one's interiority. The distinctiveness of one's genetic legacy, individual life history, and present experience is not only one's curse to bear but one's ongoing opportunity to act. It is the gift of life from one's parents and those who cared for and taught one. That distinctiveness—an individuated sense of dependence on and independence from others, on the biosphere, enmeshed in history, facing one's fate—is one's obligation to cultivate. It is also one's ongoing knot to unravel—as Pasolini put it, "the problem of my flesh and life" (quoted in Greene 1990, 14)—tying us to those preceding us, those around us now, finally, if indirectly, to everyone on the planet. That Addams appreciated the inextricable relation between subjectivity and sociality is evident in her acknowledgement that "a righteous life cannot be lived in a society that is not righteous" (quoted in Brown 2004, 243). Addams's life contradicted this assertion.

A passionate life in public service among Chicago's working-class poor represented no sacrifice of Addams's life to "the other" nor, Brown suggests, was it any simple expression of duty in expectation of gratitude. Addams's life at Hull-House was "freely chosen and exuberantly embraced" (Brown 2004, 297). That choice was not immediately obvious; years of study at school and experience at home and abroad provided the knowledge she needed to solve her puzzle. What she discovered was that the knot to be unraveled was simultaneously social and subjective. What "Jane Addams carried out of her education and into her career," Brown (2004, 297) tells us, was "the certain knowledge that democracy—as daily practice—was the path to joy, and it was the experience of joy that guided the next forty years of her democratic endeavor." It was a life of passionate public service that won her the Nobel Peace Prize in 1931 and the accusation, by the paranoid right-wing (Hofstadter 1996 [1965]), that she was the most "dangerous woman in America" (Munro 1999, 40).

As Munro (1999, 39) points out, Addams's life among Chicago's immigrants forced upon her a keen sense of the limitations of American democracy. While contradicted by political facts, Addams's faith in humanity was, Brown (2004, 297) argues, finally spiritual: "[I]t was a hard-won and deeply felt spiritual conviction from which arose all her other convictions." That conviction did not follow from "gracious submission" to others, but from an insistence on thinking things through for herself. "It was," Knight (2005, 404, emphasis added) concludes,

> this persistent *rethinking*, and not only the experiences, that produced her profoundest insights and taught her the most about her class, her gender, and herself. Addams' love of abstract theory, of sweeping generality, of uplifting philosophy had almost trapped her in her given life of reading, but it was the same passion for larger meaning that drove her to break free of that life, to struggle to integrate her experiences with her thought, and to change her mind.

Through this independence of mind, Addams became engaged with the world, threaded through her own distinctive life history and individual character, placed in the Nineteenth Ward of Chicago. Note that "rethinking" is no technical cognitive process educational researchers are forever attempting to specify; self-reflexively such rumination integrates lived experience with one's points of view and thereby reconstructs subjectivity. In so doing, Addams reconstructed the world.

Early in the research for her biography, Knight found a passage in Addams' writings that remained one of her favorites: "[W]e are under a moral obligation in choosing our experiences," she wrote, " since the result of those experiences must ultimately determine our understanding of life" (quoted in 2005, 1). "Her experiences"—most of which were not chosen—"along with key books she read" provided the passage from the "individualistic, absolutist, benevolent ethics of her father and her own class in favor of what she perceived to be the working-class ethic of cooperative justice, which she found less selfish and self-righteous" (Knight 2005, 4; Lasch 1965, xxi). Though no doubt idealized, such an ethic enabled Addams to distance herself from the self her upbringing had formed, thereby providing the self-reflective opportunity to restructure her subjectivity according to the commitments she had acquired and cultivated through study and experience. As Knight (2004, 4) points out, Addams came to believe that a nation's (and a person's) ethics ought to be revised in light of new experience and insight.[17]

Addams' courage to relinquish the past and embrace the future in the present was exceptional. The order of moral and intellectual courage worldliness requires was an order of courage Addams mustered over and over again. "Addams earns our greatest respect as a profound student of life and as a moral and political philosopher[18] of what it means to be fully human," Knight (2005, 4) asserts. As her nephew, Weber Linn, recalled, her "real eagerness" was for understanding. Addams used the word "interpretation" to describe her soul-searching analysis of experience. "Many experiences in those early years," she later wrote, "although vivid, seemed to contain no illumination" (quoted in Knight 2005, 4). It is self-reflection—including social and self-criticism—that enables experience to be illuminated. It was illuminated not according to one light—an absolutist ethics, for instance, or, thinking of U.S. teachers' dilemma, by adherence to "standards" or "best practices"—but according to the distinctive kaleidoscopic prism her individual insight permitted. She was committed, Knight (2004, 13) notes, to a "passionate individualism."

For Knight (2005, 50), that "passionate individualism" contained two sides: a "solemn moral earnestness" and a "fascination with the imaginary and mystical." Perhaps the former disposition provided a mooring for the latter. Academic study provided opportunities for the ongoing articulation of these dispositions; without such study they might well have remained silent, inactive, self-enclosed. In addition to her formal study at Rockford, the books the young Jane Addams read in the family library "taught … that private passions, nurtured by the flights of one's imagination, brought one closest to spiritual understanding and to happiness" (Knight 2005, 50). Later, Addams would express those passions through service to others. Through that public service, she experienced spiritual understanding and happiness. How? In a vividly imagistic passage, Knight (2005, 70) explains:

> Entirely private, it [reading] linked her through her imagination to the world. Its effects, as future developments will show, were various. Sometimes reading flooded her mind like a tide that swept into a shallow inlet and set swirling eddies of confusion in motion; sometimes reading exploded in her mind like a bomb, perhaps when an idea was first met, perhaps later, when it collided with another idea and there was a double explosion; sometimes reading corroded her mind with a steady drip of acidic doubts, tiny "what ifs" that, over the years, would eat away the iron framework of surely built by her parents, church, and school; eventually, reading would transform her mind from a sponge that absorbed to an engine of initiating, discriminating energy, from a receiver to a transmitter, from an organ of her body to an instrument of her soul. In the 1870s, reading was changing Jane Addams. From then on, because she wished it to, but even when she did not, it would never stop changing her.

I would be hard pressed to produce a more succinct statement of the phenomenology of study. Study does not just yield new "information," it restructures one's subjectivity, animating and focusing one's engagement with the world. That potential acknowledged, how study in fact functions cannot be predicted in advance or generalized across individuals. Had she been forced to funnel her attention according to "objectives" and the attainment of "skills," Addams's genius might well have not achieved articulation.

Among the teachers Addams found inspiring was Caroline Potter, who taught rhetoric and history. Potter became her favorite teacher. In her second year at Rockford, Addams took Potter's required ancient history and modern

What it means to have character

history courses. Potter met with each student individually to discuss her essays. Fifty years later, Addams recalled that "[t]he hours spent with her ... are still surrounded with a sort of enchantment" (quoted in Knight 2005, 85). In addition to history and rhetoric, Potter also taught literature and composition, but her "real responsibility," Knight (2005, 86) reports,

> was to teach character, the force that, to her mind, shaped history and supplied the central theme in the study of Western civilization. Character was an expansive concept. A man of character was decisive, bold, creative, original, engaged with this times, able to withstand pressures to compromise his integrity, responsible, courageous, and determined. Potter's entire curriculum was an intense and lengthy seminar on the heroic.

What was Addams response? She was "entranced" (2005, 86).

Though Knight employs the generic "man" in the foregoing passage, she emphasizes that Potter taught the heroic as a virtue for women. She was always looking for students who showed promise of fulfilling women's "grand potential." Those were students capable of "discipline" and who were willing, "if she found the right course of study for them" (Knight 2005 86), could (in Potter's own words) "exhaust [their] strength in [study's] pursuit." She also looked for originality and for the willingness to act "upon the demand of the occasion" (quoted in Knight 2006, 83). Knight tells us that Potter was quite conscious that those students, particularly women who fell in love with learning, might fail to take the ideas "back into the world." For Potter, "learning was not for its own sake" (2005, 86). Given the enforced domesticity the separate-spheres ideology rationalized, one appreciates Potter's call for worldly engagement as "progressive." In our time of vulgar vocationalism, however, learning for its own sake seems a progressive idea.

"Encouraged by Potter's woman-affirming curriculum," Knight (2005, 99) tells us, Addams explored the potential of female power and began to appreciate "women's feelings as useful in the world of public action." Potter's influence is discernible in an essay Addams wrote in her sophomore year in which she employed George Sand in an argument for women's rights. "This splendid ... woman," Addams wrote, "declares the social independence and equality of woman [in] her relations to man, society and destiny." Like Sand, she continued, today's woman "wishes not to be a man or like a man but she claims the same right to independent thought and action" (quoted passages in Knight 2005, 87). Though she comes to the suffrage campaign late, these lines leave no doubt that Jane Addams appreciated at age 18 the injustice of the separate-spheres arrangement. As Knight (2005, 87) notes, these lines also convey as well "her confidence in the power of ideas to change the world." Addams' linking of social and intellectual independence with equality is also significant; it presages the gendered character of U.S. teachers' "gracious submission" to scripted curricula, standardized examinations, and to "best practices" they themselves have not devised. To this situation of political and intellectual subjugation, a declaration of independence is required.

"No list survives of all the books that Jane Addams read at Rockford Seminary," Knight (2005, 88) reports, "but she undoubtedly read a great many." Knight suggests Addams had come to Rockford in order to read as "widely and as fruitfully as possible, ... to pursue culture" (2005, 88–89). The moral significance of such a pursuit was articulated by, among others, Matthew Arnold[20] in his 1869 essay, *Culture and Anarchy*, which Addams read at Rockford. By studying "the best which has been thought and said in the world," one strengthened one's commitment to improving society: a "moral and social passion for doing good" (quoted in Knight 2005, 89). In effect, Knight notes, culture was Christianity's replacement, the means by which one redeemed oneself and others. This promise of secular salvation Addams would articulate in two early essays: "The Subjective Necessity for Social Settlements" and "The Objective Value of a Social Settlement" (both dated 1892). For Addams, Knight (2005, 90), explains this conception of culture "both challenged her to escape her class and racial biases and reinforced their claim on her." Significantly, these essays link self-reconstruction to the reconstruction of society. In so doing, it demonstrated culture's—indeed, education's—"deepest appeal: its ability to awaken her profoundest longings and desires" (Knight 2005, 137).

In addition to Arnold, several other texts were influential in Addams's intellectual formation. The first she read in Baltimore after returning in 1885 from her first trip to Europe; it was Giuseppe Mazzini's *Duties of Man*. Mazzini (1805–1872) was critical of the family's demands on one's loyalty and interests, insisting that "your first duties ... are ... towards Humanity" (quoted in Appiah 2005, 240). Mazzini reverses the order Addams had learned; for him it was selfish to serve the family and in doing so fail to serve strangers. Reading Mazzini, Knight (2005, 142) reports, was for Addams an "unsettling, even shocking, experience." Serving others, Mazzini argued, was a Christian duty because Christ's love was directed toward humanity. It was also a democratic duty because through democracy each person can become "better than he is" (quoted in Knight 2005, 142–143). (This idea—that self-realization depends upon social justice and vice versa—would later become a keystone of U.S. curriculum theory: Pinar 2004, 247). For Mazzini, education was also central, but so was the opportunity for people from social classes to come to know each other. Addams would combine those two ideas.

The Christian element in Mazzini's tract would become amplified for Addams when she read Leo Tolstoy's *My Religion*, which was published in the United Sates in 1885. Knight (2005, 142) tells us that "it touched her as no other book had." Decades later (1927), Addams would identify *My Religion* as "the book that changed my life" (quoted in Knight 2005, 142). What Addams remembered those many years later, Knight suggests, was that at age 50 Tolstoy felt himself a failure; after converting to Christianity, he was able to transform his life rather than sink into an immobilizing despair. That

Christ's love toward All humanity

Addams was reading Tolstoy during the depth of her own despair[21] illustrates the "biographic function" (Pinar 1994, 46–57) of study, the confluence of life history and intellectual interest in provoking movement in one's life.

Though Tolstoy's book was pivotal, others influenced Addams's formation as social theorist-activist as well, among them W. H. Fremantle's *The World as the Subject of Redemption* (1885) and Brooke Foss Westcott's *The Social Aspects of Christianity* (1883). Fremantle wrote that "the main object of effort is not … either … the saving of individual souls out of a ruined world, or … the organization of a separate society destined always to be held aloof from the world, but … the saving of the world itself." This would be accomplished by abandoning selfishness and "imbu[ing] all human relations with the spirit of Christ's self-renouncing love" (quoted in Knight 2005, 173). Westcott called upon his readers to find fellowship with the poor and thereby learn the significance of duty: "The end of labor is not material well-being but that larger, deeper, more abiding delight which comes from successfully administering to the good of others" (quoted in Knight 2005, 173). Knight (2005, 174) observes that Addams found these ideas "consistent" with her own desire to transform the world.[22]

Not only did Tolstoy inspire a discouraged Jane Addams, he introduced her to the concept of nonviolence, or "non-resistance." Addams would make this idea her own. (In the introduction to her 1907 *Newer Ideals of Peace*, she declares "non-resistance" to be "too feeble." She prefers a more "aggressive ideal of peace" [quoted in Lasch 1965, 221, 219].) Tolstoy had written that anger "is an abnormal, pernicious, and morbid state" (quoted in Knight 2005, 145). Knight (2005, 145) reminds us that anger was a familiar experience for Jane Addams, as living with her "willful" and "relentless" stepmother meant living with "Anna's anger and her own." Her practice of non-resistance[23] required, Knight notes, a willingness to undergo suffering. By the time she arrived at Hull-House in 1889, but possibly as early as 1886, Knight tells us (2005, 145) that the concept of nonviolence had become central to her theory and practice.

Nonviolence was a feminist issue. Knight (2005, 148) reports that during this period, two books challenged her thinking about women: John Stuart Mill's *The Subjection of Women* and Leo Tolstoy's *What Shall We Do?* Each undercut those beliefs about gender she had acquired during childhood. Each asked her to question the assumptions she held about gender, including the primacy of the family's claim upon a daughter's life.[24] It was Tolstoy's book that enabled Addams to affirm that an upper-middle-class, educated young woman could not ignore the social problem of poverty (Knight 2004, 149). As she read, Knight (2005, 148) writes (again providing a phenomenology of study), "her mind, which had earlier been sabotaging her with self-criticism, became her ally."

Almost 20 years later, when members of women's organizations gathered in Washington, D.C. in 1915 to create the Women's Peace Party, they asked Jane Addams to give the keynote address. Then they elected her chair. Not

Tolstoy
Tolstoy Homeward

Reconstruct Subjectivity

limited to war, the party's platform proclaimed a feminist agenda. When World War I ended in 1918, the Party was absorbed into a new organization, the Women's International League for Peace and Freedom (Brown 2004, 5). Jane Addams was elected president. In recognition of her efforts, Jane Addams would be awarded the Nobel Peace Prize in 1931 (Knight 2005, 395; Elshtain 2002, 224). For Christopher Lasch (1965, 218), "Jane Addams made her greatest contribution to the cause of peace."[25]

Perhaps Addams was overstating her dilemma when she declared herself to be snared by preparation. Despite her confinement in a Rockford Female Seminary and in a family who asserted that her significance was limited to the family, Addams reconstructed her subjectivity through reading. Perhaps reading alone would have been insufficient: Without the experience of the "bullfight" and of Toynbee Hall—without her teachers at Rockford (emphasizing, for instance, the feminine heroic)—Addams would have been unable to mobilize herself and find her way out. Without reading, without study—that intersection of subjective longing with scholarship and theory ("culture")—it is difficult to imagine the bullfight incident provoking the moral crisis to which Toynbee Hall provided a solution. Once again, Louise Knight (2005, 156) provides us with an insightful and detailed depiction of Addams's subjective and intellectual passage out of the family into society:

> During the seven years since she had graduated from seminary, culture in the form of books—that is, the humanities—had continued to change her. Books had freed her from a too narrowly defined duty to family, shown her that society's restrictions on women's responsibilities were artificial and cruel, allowed her to examine the responsibilities that accompanied her inherited wealth, deepened her ideas about class, capitalism, and poverty, revised her understanding of Christianity, and helped her reinterpret the meaning of her interest in the poor. These were large gifts. In her childhood, culture—in the broader sense of society's teachings—had placed her in a necessary prison of unexamined assumptions. But as she grew older, culture—in the sense of "higher" learning—also gave her the key to unlock the door. From culture she received the ability to stand back and examine those assumptions and consciously and selectively reject them.

This subjective undergoing of estrangement and exile (Wang 2004) that study affords enables self-reconstruction (Nussbaum 1997, 29), one perquisite to political activism and cultural politics dedicated to social reconstruction (Mansbridge and Morris 2001; Goodwin, Jasper and Polletta 2001).

For Addams, education provided the passage between subjectivity and society. At Hull-House, the first subjects offered—all "academically substantive" (Knight 2005, 205)—were in the humanities. The students who took them were factory workers, teachers, bank tellers, clerks, and others who, Addams thought, had "some education" and had "kept up an intellectual life and are keen for books" in spite of "adverse circumstances" (quoted in Knight 2005, 2005). "Defiant of cultural barriers," Knight (2005, 206) suggests, the curriculum was composed of—after Arnold—the "best" of European civilization. Ellen Gates Starr taught George Eliot's novel *Romola* (and the history of art, in which she specialized) while Addams (who remained the generalist: Knight 2005, 224) taught Mazzini's *Duties of Man* in English translation to a group of Italian men, several of whom had fought in Italy's struggle for nationhood. Later these men presented Hull House with a bust of Mazzini, causing Addams (in Lasch 1965, 214) to quip: "perhaps in gratitude that the course was over!" By teaching art, literature, and music, Brown (2004, 237) suggests,

> Jane and Ellen accidentally tapped into a feature of immigrant life which too often went unrecognized: that immigrants had not only ambition for their future lives but deep connections to their past lives which were often culturally, if not materially, rich.

Rather than reducing the gap[26] between immigrants' culture and life in Chicago, Addams and Starr provided passages between the two.

As more volunteer teachers joined Addams and Starr, additional offerings— in French, Latin, German, Greek, painting, music, mathematics, rhetoric and Roman history—were formalized as "College Extension Classes," the first adult college extension courses in Chicago (Knight 2005, 206, 223; Brown 2004, 233). Indeed, during the early years of Hull-House there developed, Addams (in Lasch 1965, 212) suggested, "a cordial cooperation" between settlements and universities, one that Charles Beard described as "as exerting beyond all question a direct and immediate influence on American thinking about industrial questions, and on the course of social practice" (quoted in Lasch 1965, 212). Settlement houses were, Munro (1999, 19) suggests, "curricular experiments that contested dominant notions of education." In 1891, Addams launched a working people's summer school, held for four weeks in July on the campus of her alma mater. A liberal arts curriculum was taught to the same working-class women who took college extension classes at Hull-House: factory workers, public school teachers, seamstresses, and others. About 90 women, most of them first- or second-generation Chicagoans of Irish, German, Jewish, or English descent, attended the summer school that first year, staying for two weeks or a month; they paid $2 a week. Taught by Starr, Addams, and several volunteers, the curriculum included Browning, Emerson, Victor Hugo, Ruskin, as well as botany, gymnastics, tennis, singing, and German conversation. Addams and Starr were offering workingwomen intellectual opportunities they themselves had been offered and at the same place. It was possibly the first time a residential liberal arts college experience had been offered to workingwomen; the school would continue for 10 years (Knight 2005, 225–226). As Adams (in Lasch 1965, 201) knew, cultural reconstruction "depend[s] upon fresh knowledge and must further be equipped with a wide and familiar acquaintance with the human spirit and its productions." Throughout her life Addams continued to learn; she regarded herself, Brown (2004, 6) suggests, as a "reformer ever in need of reform."

The concept of education had a broad meaning for Jane Addams, Lasch (1965, 175) points out. Though education may have been institutionalized in the form of classroom instruction, it was hardly contained there, for it was Addams's contention (shared by other progressive educators), that education was ongoing and inhered in any situation that brought one into contact with "the unexpected and the unfamiliar." For Addams, education was as broad as experience itself, Lasch notes. Education *was* experience. It was the failure of professional educators to come to grips with this fact, in Addams's view, that accounted for the sterility of what progressives would pillory as *traditional* education. Such education had divorced itself from "life," and the task of educators was to reestablish the connection (Lasch 1965, 175).

Traditional Education

These ideas derived from Addams's judgment that her own college training left her within "the snare of preparation," a self-contained cognitive affair that had kept her from engagement with the world. During her long years of waiting for such engagement—they start during her time at Rockford (Knight 2005, 91)—Addams reflected on the consequences of acquiring culture without having experience. "I gradually reached a conviction," Addams (in Lasch 1965, 16-17) concluded,

> that the first generation of college women had taken their learning too quickly, had departed too suddenly from the active, emotional life led by their grandmothers and great-grandmothers; that the contemporary education of young women had developed too exclusively the power of acquiring knowledge and of merely receiving impressions; that somewhere in the process of "being educated" they had lost that simple and almost automatic response to the human appeal, that old healthful reaction resulting in activity from the mere presence of suffering or of helplessness; that they are so sheltered and pampered they have no chance even to make "the great refusal."

Such shelter created—in dialectical fashion—the "subjective necessity of settlements," Addams would later assert (Lasch 1965, 29). That subjective necessity required acknowledgement that "the dependence of classes on each other is reciprocal" (quoted in Lasch 1965, 29; Seigfried 1996, 225).

Addams did not think of Hull-House as a charity but as educational institution, Lasch (1965, 175) points out, one in which she and the other residents were pupils; her immigrant neighbors were teachers. From this experience, she theorized that education must be conceived as a mutual relation. No one-way transmission of knowledge insulated from lived experience, education occurred for Addams during ongoing conversation between teacher and student; it was embedded in the conditions of life itself.

Such a conception, Lasch (1965, 175) notes, "paralleled" and "supported" the educational theories of John Dewey.

It is clear that Jane Addams influenced Dewey and that Dewey influenced Addams (Knight 2005, 258; Lasch 1965, 175; Seigfried 1996, 47, 58). Each acknowledged intellectual debts to the other.[27] Hull-House and Dewey's experimental school at the University of Chicago "constantly exchanged ideas and personnel" (Lasch 1965, 175). One of the teachers in Dewey's school was a resident at Hull-House, and Dewey himself delivered a series of lectures at Hull-House, even before moving to Chicago in 1894. "But Hull House was not so much an example of Dewey's theory of education," Charlene Haddock Seigfried (1996, 74) suggests, "as it was already exemplary of what Dewey sought to theorize." Pragmatism itself may have developed directly from these intellectual exchanges and interpersonal collaborations (Seigfried 1996, 44, 47–48).

While still teaching at the University of Michigan, Dewey spent a week at Hull-House in January 1892; he and Addams talked for hours. Knight (2005, 238) tells us "they connected immediately." Like Addams and others of their generation, Dewey, while estranged from the Church,[28] was nonetheless inspired by Jesus' teachings and thought they could transform the world, not via psychological experiences associated with personal salvation but through cooperative action. When Addams explained to him that the point of Hull-House was the "bridging of class cultures" (Westbrook 1991, 85) by embodying the Christian spirit through cooperation, Dewey was appreciative, even enthusiastic. "I am confident that twenty-five years from now," he wrote her after his visit, "the forces now turned in upon themselves in various church[es] or agencies will be finding [an] outlet very largely through such channels as you have opened" (quoted in Knight 2005, 238–239).

"Fascinated" with Hull-House and Addams's ideas, Dewey expressed his gratitude for the visit. "I cannot tell you," he wrote afterward, "how much good I got from my stay at Hull House. My indebtedness to you for giving me an insight into matters there is great. I think I got a pretty good idea of the general spirit and methods. Every day I stayed there only added to my conviction that you [have] taken the right way" (quoted in Knight 2005, 240). In March 1892, Dewey would delivered a paper entitled "Christianity and Democracy" to the Christian Student Association at the University of Michigan. Evidently he sent Addams a copy, as she used several of his phrases in "The Subjective Necessity of Settlements" (1892). Given that the two had discussed the relations between Christianity and democracy during their January meeting, Knight (2005, 254) concludes that Dewey's paper may been "partly inspired by their conversations."

After the visit to Hull-House, Dewey came to appreciate the social settlement as an educational institution. After moving to Chicago in 1894, Dewey found Hull-House to be "one of the more lively intellectual centers" in Chicago (Brown 2004, 292). In "The School as Social Centre," Dewey

Culture taken away from children *(handwritten annotation)*

focused on those psychic strains immigration created: "[W]ise observers in New York and Chicago have recently sounded a note of alarm. They call attention to the fact that in some respect the children are too rapidly, I will not say Americanized, but too rapidly de-nationalized" (quoted in Ryan 1995, 152). As Dewey indirectly acknowledges, Addams had "already embraced" this concern; Ryan (1995, 152) reports she was "very depressed" by the facts of deculturation.

After 1894, John Dewey and Jane Addams saw each other "often," engaging in, Knight (2005, 240) suggests, "some of the most fascinating conversations ever conducted in the history of American social ethics." Though these conversations went unrecorded, a thematic trace is evident in the exchange between the two over the role of conflict, a conversation they held following the violence of the Pullman strike.[29] Was class antagonism inevitable? Committed to Tolstoyan and Christian nonviolence, social Christian cooperation, and Comtean societal unity, Addams could only answer in the negative (Knight 2005, 322–323). Opposites, Addams insisted, were never really opposites; they were elements of "unity in its growth" (quoted in Brown 2004, 293).

Addams's conviction—that antagonism functioned to block movement toward unity, conferring personal belligerence with a philosophical legitimacy that served no common end (Brown 2004, 292)—challenged the views of her new friend. In a letter to his wife, Alice, John Dewey reported replying to Addams that conflict was not only inevitable but possibly beneficial: "[A]ntagonism," he told Addams, "was necessary to an appreciation of the truth and to a consciousness of growth"; it was a requisite step toward "the reconciliation of opposites," expressing the Hegelianism of his graduate training.[30] A persuasive presence, Addams persuaded him that he had "the dialectic wrong end up" (quoted passages in Brown 2004, 292).

Addams "had always believed and still believed," he reported, that "antagonism was not only useless and harmful, but entirely unnecessary." Antagonisms were caused (in Dewey's words) not by "objective differences" but by "a person's mixing in his own personal reactions." One became antagonistic either because he took pleasure in opposing others, because he desired not to be a "moral coward," or because he felt hurt or insulted (quoted passages in Knight 2005, 322). These were emotional reactions in which one could intervene. Only evil, Addams declared, followed from antagonism (Knight 2005, 322). Dewey confessed that Addams had "converted me internally, but not really, I fear." In the aftermath of the Pullman strike, Dewey simply could not believe that "all this conflict ... had no functional value." Two years later, however, when Jane was circulating among her friends a revised version of her meditation on the Pullman strike—what would become "A Modern Lear"—Dewey declared it "one of the greatest things I have read both as to its form and ethical philosophy" (quoted passages in Brown 2004, 293; Lasch 1965, 175). "I never had anything take hold of me so," Dewey acknowledged; Addams's convictions amounted to "the most magnificent exhibition of intellectual & moral faith" that he had ever encountered (quoted passages in Knight 2005, 323).

Despite his admiration for Addams' reasoning, Dewey did not abandon his conviction that "antagonism" had functional value: It helped one to discover the truth (Knight 2005, 324). Despite her disagreement with him, in time Addams herself may have been persuaded, as she argued later, that strikes can be useful and necessary. Strikes are often "the only method of arresting attention to [the workers'] demands"; they offered the permanent benefits of solidifying the ties of "brotherhood" among the strikers and enabling (at least when successful) a more "democratic" relation between workers and their employer (quoted in Knight 2005, 327). (Addams would insist that a "democratic" relation should also obtain in "race relations," as we will see.) From a definition of democracy that had stressed the educational potential of citizens encountering each other socially, by the aftermath of the Pullman strike, it was clear to her that democracy also required citizens working together to correct unjust conditions (Knight 2005, 399). The practice of democracy depended upon cooperation with and learning from those who were different from oneself (Knight 2005, 401). The cosmopolitan person is "a citizen of the world because of his growing understanding of all kinds of people and their varying experiences" (quoted in Knight 2005, 402).

The beneficiary of a cosmopolitan education—including the one she afforded herself—Jane Addams sought to "understand humanity as presented in the flesh in the way she had once sought to understand it as presented in literature and the arts" (Knight 2005, 402). In addition to reading, now Addams relied on listening. Those who met her were struck by her "questioning eyes" and "gentle inquisitiveness." A new young resident was moved by her commitment "to understand and interpret [everyone] correctly and generously" (quoted in Knight 2005, 368). Informing her "striking personal manner," Knight (2005, 368, emphasis added) tells us, was the knowledge that "democracy was as much an *inward* process as an outer one," and that if one was to "learn from others, to reap the benefits of free speech, as it were, mind would need to be open to being changed." Service to others depended upon "self-improvement" (Knight 2005, 377).

Now an old-fashioned, even discredited, concept, self-improvement was then associated with public service conducted as a "subjective necessity" (Jay 2005, 174). The contrary of the defensive and compensatory preoccupation with psychological survival that Lasch (1978) depicts as the culture of narcissism, Addams's worldliness stretched her subjective boundaries by attaching them to her neighbors and fellow citizens. Addams's cosmopolitan citizenship was an "achievement that she and the world accomplished together, and she would not have had it otherwise" (Knight 2005, 404). Her worldliness was evident in her experience of immigrants as neighbors whose distinctiveness she acknowledged, even celebrated, never collapsed into her own distinctiveness as an individual.

Derrida quote must be strong!!

For Addams, Munro (1999, 41) underscores, social democracy meant that immigrants brought their values into the community; it did not demand conformity, the erasure of their native cultures. Thus, "the identification with the common lot, which is the essential idea of democracy, becomes the source and expression of social ethics" (Addams 1902, 11; quoted in Munro 1999, 41). The "recognition" phase of late twentieth-century identity politics performed precisely that inclusion; the separatist self-righteousness of later (contemporary) phases of identity politics is anti-democratic as it automatically elevates victims (rather, their self-appointed representatives) into morally superior denizens demonizing everyone else. In *Democracy and Social Ethics*, Addams wrote, "We know instinctively that if we grow contemptuous of our fellows, and consciously limit our intercourse to certain kinds of people whom we previously decided to respect, we not only tremendously circumscribe our range of life, but limit the scope of our ethics" (1902, 10; quoted in Munro 1999, 41). Addams's observation remains salient today, not only for racists but for self-appointed representatives of their victims as well.

Sure she meant interaction not sex

Addressing Race in Science

The Anti-racist Activism of Jane Addams

In fact, it has already been discovered at The Hague that many difficulties formerly called international were in reality interracial.

Jane Addams, "The Progressive Party and the Negro"
(1912; quoted in Lasch 1965, 173)

"There is no question," Petra Munro (1999, 42) points out, "that Addams addressed the issue of race relations." When Jane Addams and Ellen Gates Starr opened Hull-House in 1889, there were few African Americans living in the "congested" and cosmopolitan Nineteenth Ward (Elshtain 2002, 202). Of its 44,380 residents, only 120 were designated "colored," the umbrella term the U.S. Bureau of the Census used for "Negroes, Chinese, Japanese, and civilized Indians." The remaining inhabitants were nearly all European immigrants: southern Italians and Germans but also Irish, Polish and Russian Jews, Bohemians, French Canadians, English, and others; 18 nationalities altogether were represented (Knight 2005, 179, 194; Brown 2004, 212, 217). Decades later the second largest black neighborhood in Chicago developed around Hull-House (Munro 1999, 43).

Despite the absence of African American neighbors, Addams found opportunities to work for racial equality. Between 1895 and 1902, she supported the nomination of the first African American woman, Fannie Barrier Williams, to the Chicago Woman's Club; she hosted, with Ida B. Wells's help, the officers of the National Council of Colored Women at a luncheon at Hull-House when it held its biennial meeting in Chicago (this was how Wells met Addams—Addams contacted Wells for assistance); and she advocated, unsuccessfully, for the National Convention of Women's Club to admit African American clubs to their meetings (Knight 2005, 389; Seigfried 1996, 235; Munro 1999, 42).

Among the cooperative projects that Hull-House undertook was a free health clinic. Three women—a physician with a general practice in the neighborhood, a nurse from the Visiting Nurses Association, and a newly arrived Hull-House resident with a medical degree, Harriet Rice—staffed it. An African American, Rice was, in 1893, the settlement's first black resident (Knight 2005, 289). Rice's resistance to serving the poor first became apparent in 1893 when she was staffing the settlement's public dispensary and caring for its mostly immigrant clients. Also evident was Rice resistance to practicing medicine among poor black people living elsewhere in the city. In 1895, Addams and Julia Lathrop suggested that Rice work at the new Provident Hospital, founded to provide medical care to African Americans, including those who were impoverished. Rice declined (Knight 2005, 387–388).

Knight (2005, 388) suggests that Rice's reasons for not wanting to practice charity medicine followed from her ambition. The 1890s represented a new low in post-bellum race relations in the United States: Black disenfranchisement and lynching were at their most intense. Indeed, 1892 saw more black victims of white mobs than any other year. Rice must have been eager to show what her race could do, Knight speculates, both as a confirmation of her self-respect and as a way to dispel prejudice. Proud of her accomplishments, Knight continues, Rice may have felt discomfort when asked to associate with poor people. To Rice, working among the poor meant returning to that class from which her family had only recently escaped. Economically, in fact, she had not moved up. Knight tells us that she lived at Hull-House, which was, recall, in a poor neighborhood, because she could not afford to live elsewhere. With these motives, I wonder why Addams accepted her. Were there other residents who did not share the settlement-house cause?

As for Addams's reasons for failing to understand how Rice felt, Knight (2005, 388) speculates that Addams could not see that an ambitious young person from a working-class background might seek escape from lower-class associations. In addition, Addams could not appreciate that when that person was African American, the stakes were even higher. To my mind, Knight—whose biography of Addams seems superb in almost every respect—has climbed out on a limb with these efforts to reconstruct Rice's and Addams's reasoning. The only fact of which I am confident is that Addams accepted a black resident at Hull-House in 1893, a resident who did not share her values. That fact testifies to her commitment to cooperation and inclusiveness.

"This same class blindness"—the phrase is Knight's (2005, 388)—also informed Addams' initial response to lynching. By the time Addams gave her first speech about it in 1899, lynching had become a national scandal. Addams expanded her remarks in an article for the *Independent* published two years later, in which she erroneously assumed that the white men's charges—that lynched black men had raped white women—were accurate. Her mistake was hardly hers alone; many white middle-class Northerners assumed the men were guilty, that the outrage was, rather, lawlessness on the part of whites. In fact, as her "friend" (Knight 2005, 389)—I am not confident they were *friends*; colleagues may have been a more circumspect choice of words; certainly they enjoyed an "ongoing relationship" lasting 35 years (Munro 1999, 21; 23)—Ida B. Wells carefully documented (in 1892 and again in the 1901 article she published in the *Independent* in reply to Addams's essay on the subject) that those southern white women whose cases led to lynching had sometimes willingly entered into interracial liaisons. Addams had failed to do her homework, Knight (2005, 388; Pinar 2001, 532–542) observes.

Although Addams did not, during the 1890s, know the facts of lynching—and the complexities of racism more generally, Knight adds—she had long appreciated that racial prejudice was a crucial social issue. In 1892, at the Plymouth Conference (sponsored by the Ethical Culture Society: Robertson 2008, 239), Addams reminded her white audience that "we are quite unmoved by the fact that [the Negro] lives among us in a practical social ostracism" (quoted in Knight 2005, 389). Her interest in the issue may have originated, Knight points out, in her father's opposition to slavery and, in particular, in her brief encounter (in her father's house when she was not yet four years old) with an escaped slave. The intellectual foundation of her concern, Knight tells us, was her "moral universalism" (Knight 2005, 389). That moral universalism led her to join with Ida B. Wells in fighting the segregation of Chicago's public schools.

In 1900 a series of articles appeared in the *Chicago Tribune* advocating a segregated public school system in the city. In her autobiography, Ida B. Wells (1970, 274) remembers:

> For a period extending over two weeks interviews were printed, first with parents of children who had struck in one of the schools of Chicago against having a colored teacher. Second, articles were written containing interviews from superintendents of separate school systems in Saint Louis, Baltimore, Washington, D.C., and other places of smaller note. The only places from which there were not interviews on the subject were those in which the mixed school system prevailed. And not a single colored person was quoted on the subject.

Outraged, Wells wrote to the *Tribune* editor, but he ignored her. Not to be silenced, Wells went to his office. She recalls that

> When Mr. Robert W. Patterson came in I walked up to him and stood waiting for him to finish reading a letter before he entered his private office. He glanced up and said, "I have nothing for you today." I replied that I did not understand what he meant and told him who I was and

why I was there. He said, "Oh, I thought you were one of the women from one of the colored churches coming to solicit a contribution, as they very frequently do."

I laughed and said, "It therefore seems natural that whenever you see a colored woman she is begging for her church. I happen to be begging, Mr. Patterson, but not for money." I then said that, not hearing from my letter, I had come down to have a talk with him about the matter. (Wells 1970, 275).

Wells discovers that his views on "race" had been influenced by southern whites who had gained his ear during times of relaxation. (Patterson wintered in Thomasville, Georgia: Wells 1970, 275). While her tone is calm, Wells is outraged:

> He said he did not believe that it was right that ignorant Negroes should have the right to vote and to rule white people because they were in the majority. My reply to him was that I did not think it was any more fair for that type of Negro to rule than it was for that same class of white men in the First Ward flophouses who cast a ruling vote for the Great First Ward of Chicago. Even so, I was not disposed to condemn all white people because of that situation nor deprive the better class of them of their rights in the premises.

Mr. Patterson further informed me that he did not have time to listen to a lot of colored people on the subject but that he would publish as much of my letter as he could find space for, when he got around to it (Wells 1970, 275–276).

"That was as much as I could get out of him," Wells concludes in her matter-of-fact fashion. Her thoughts turned to economic boycott but she realizes the impact of a black boycott on the *Tribune* would be "so small" as to have no effect. Quickly she resolved to seek the assistance of those whose opinion and influence the *Tribune* would notice. Wells reports:

> I went to the phone and called up Miss Jane Addams of Hull House and asked if she would see me. When I called upon her and explained the situation I said, "Miss Addams, there are plenty of people in Chicago who would not sanction such a move if they knew about it. Will you undertake to reach those of influence who would be willing to do for us what we cannot do for ourselves"? (all passages from Wells 1970, 276).

Addams "very readily agreed" to help, and on "the following Sunday evening there were gathered at Hull House representative men and women of the white race, who listened to my story. There were editors of other daily papers in the city, ministers of the gospel, and social service workers" (Wells 1970, 276). Among those present was a progressive member of the Board of Education. Wells made her case plainly, persuasively.

After the Hull House meeting, Jane Addams headed a delegation of white citizens who met with the editors of the *Tribune*. Wells (1970, 278) writes, "I do not know what they did or what argument was brought to bear, but I do know that the series of articles ceased and from that day until this there has been no further effort made by the Chicago *Tribune* to separate the schoolchildren on the basis of race." Wells's political acumen coupled with Addams's willingness to help spelled a successful struggle against segregation in Chicago, a relatively rare victory during those decades of radical racism (Williamson 1984).

In addition to supporting Ida B. Wells' efforts to stop segregation in Chicago's public schools, Addams was an early supporter of W. E. B. Du Bois. Probably Addams attended the Atlanta University Conference on the Negro Church in May 1903 that Du Bois had organized (Aptheker 1977). It is likely that the publication of Addams' *Hull House Papers and Maps* in 1895 influenced Du Bois as he wrote his study of *The Philadelphia Negro* the following year. Addams asked Du Bois to speak at Hull-House in February 1907 on the occasion of Abraham Lincoln's birthday, a president who had referred to lynching as the "mobocratic spirit" and the "ill-omen amongst us" (quoted in Brundage 1997, 2; Elshtain 2002, 21).

In February 1908, on the centennial of Lincoln's birth, Jane Addams and Ida B. Wells organized a mass meeting to be held at Orchestra Hall in Chicago. Du Bois was the featured speaker. The celebration served as a call to action against lynching and the convict-lease system, disfranchisement and segregation (Pinar 2007b). A year later, Wells and Addams were among the 40 signers of the call to found what would become the N.A.A.C.P. In 1911, Addams was among the American representatives who signed the call for the First Universal Races Congress held in London. Her civil-rights activism earned her the appreciative recognition of N.A.A.C.P. leaders, who appointed her to the executive committee. In 1913, acting on behalf of the National Board of the N.A.A.C.P., Oswald Garrison Villard recommended that Jane Addams be one of 15 people selected to serve on a National Race Commission to be appointed by President Woodrow Wilson. No friend of African Americans, Wilson refused to appoint such a commission. Instead, he (with the support of his mostly southern cabinet, prominently among them William G. McAdoo) introduced the segregation of federal employees in government offices for the first time in U.S. history (Kellogg 1967; Friedman 1970). "[I]n the context of American politics at the turn of the century and after," Bettina Aptheker (1977, 8) points out, "Addams' affirmative actions on civil rights were courageous, even radical."

Addams joined the campaign of the Illinois branch of the Niagara Movement (Pinar 2001, 626). In addition to the N.A.A.C.P., Addams was also a member of the Chicago Urban League. In 1912, as a member of the platform committee for the Progressive Party, she protested Theodore Roosevelt's decision not to seat the African American delegates from several southern states (an incident to which I return in the next paragraph). When the Marines occupied Haiti in 1916, she joined others in supporting self-government there. Despite her misunderstanding of lynching, Addams was, Louise Knight (2006, 389) concludes, committed to racial equality. Addams was also clear about the necessity of compromise.[31] Jean Elshtain (2002, 186) points out that "Addams was no abstract dreamer or revolutionary filled with wroth; for her, politics was the realm of the best possible, not the perfect." Elshtain's observation is evident in Addams's efforts to seat a "colored delegation" from Mississippi to the 1912 Progressive Party national convention.

African Americans were present at that convention as members of integrated delegations from Rhode Island, West Virginia, Maryland, Tennessee, and Kentucky. Two delegations—one black, one white—vied for accreditation from Mississippi. (Fifty-two years later at the 1964 Democratic Party Convention, an integrated Mississippi Freedom Democratic Party challenged an all-white delegation sent by the regular Mississippi Democratic Party.[32]) Demanding that the Black Mississippians be seated, Addams participated in an all-night debate among members of the Convention's resolutions committee. She lost that battle; the white delegation was seated. Addams acquiesced in the removal of the black delegates (Aptheker 1977). Upon learning of her compromise, several of her friends "stood outside the door at the Congress Hotel and wept in the night hours." It seemed as though she could not do anything," said a former Hull-House resident, "that was in the nature of an exercise of compulsion or control" (quoted in Lasch 1965, 162).

Addams rationalized the Convention's action a few months later in an article in the *Crisis* (the official publication of the N.A.A.C.P.).[33] Seating the black delegation was, Addams argued, a necessary action in order to bring the Progressive Party into the South as the opposition party to the Democrats who controlled the region, "without the bitterness and old hatred evoked by the Republicans" (quoted in Aptheker 1977, 5). The Republicans, she contended, paid lip service to equality; the silence of the Progressives seemed to her preferable. By avoiding a direct challenge to white supremacy in the South, she reasoned, the Progressives might eventually establish themselves in that region, thereby challenging the hegemony of the Democrats. Only then, she reasoned, would it be possible to overthrow white supremacy. As Lasch (1965, 169–170) points out, her arguments assumed that the Progressive Party would remain a viable force in U.S. politics. In fact, the Party turned out to be overly identified with Theodore Roosevelt; when Roosevelt led his followers back to the Republicans in 1916, the Progressive Party collapsed, and with it, Addams' dream of a two-party South.

Conclusion

In the 2008 presidential candidacy of Barack Obama, Jane Addams may have taken consolation not only for the symbolic statement that a black candidate makes but as well in Obama's rhetoric of inclusion. Addams was, in general, unwilling to leave anyone out; only in "A Modern Lear" does she take another to task and then by today's standards somewhat indirectly. (Her campaign against Nineteenth Ward boss Johnny Powers *is* an example of Addams's capacity for criticism.) In that commitment to inclusion and mediation Addams communicated her cosmopolitanism.

The period in which Jane Addams lived Lasch (1965, xxvi) characterizes as an era of "social exploration," during which the "submerged tenth" of society was "discovered" by the middle and upper classes. Because this discovery involved the "shock" and the "reversal" of common assumptions about immigrants, African Americans, women and men, Lasch (1965, xxvi) suggests that "autobiography was on the whole well-suited to such a time." This charting of "discovery"—what I am characterizing as a cosmopolitan education—was best documented by autobiography and biography.

What has intrigued me is the movement of Jane Addams from Cedarville to Chicago, from the provincial to the cosmopolitan. There is no simple adoption of "sophisticated" attitudes, no knee-jerk rejection of her past, no fantasies of "us" versus "them," no disappearance into a collective identity. The cosmopolitan education of Jane Addams resulted from her study at home, at Rockford, abroad, and with friends. Addams incorporated as she reconstructed her lived experience. There was not always a direct open path ahead: Given the constraints upon young women of her class at that time, that path led to an apparent cul-de-sac. The struggle against her confinement within the family was feminist in both intention and result: The affirmation of women's culture, as Brown points out, was an essential consequence of this period of her life. It was a feminism appreciative of men's thought and activism, as her reading and visits to Russia and England confirm. Identity politics would have struck Addams as a phase—as Sartre saw *négritude*—to be moved through swiftly, in part because it sacrifices the individual to the collective, the concrete to the abstract. For Lasch, it is the unique interplay between the two that implies

> the distinctive quality of Jane Addams' intelligence. She loved the concrete, but she was always earnestly seeking the general. She theorized about every subject she ever touched, but without arriving at a general theory of modern society—doubtless because she distrusted the dogmatism with which such theories are often association (Lasch 1965, xxv–xxvi).

Doubtless she distrusted dogmatism of any kind. Addams's method was, Lasch (1965, xxvi) asserts, "essentially autobiographical," and the "virtues" and "defects" of her work were those associated with writing from one's experience. He acknowledges that she wrote "superbly" about the revolt of youth, the plight of women, the estrangement immigrants suffered, and the disintegration of family life under the assaults of industrialism. On subjects such as prostitution, he continues, Addams's writing was less effective, perhaps because there was no parallel in her experience. Whether writing from experience directly or imaginatively, Addams's writing is often compelling, in part owing to the heartfelt—passionate—commitment she obviously felt. The illustrations are vivid; they lend the writing an immediacy that other forms of prose lack. It is her subjective presence—in her writing, in her public service—that sculpts its distinctiveness.

The social theories of the progressive period have not held up very well over the years, Lasch (1965, xxvi) concludes. If he meant that they have not met a favorable fate, he might well amend that sentence today, in even stronger terms. In autumn 1995, over lunch at "The Virginian" across from the University of Virginia campus, Richard Rorty expressed to me his hope that the conservative restoration was at its end, that a resurrection of liberalism was at hand. Rorty has not lived to see that happy day. Nor, I suspect, will I, despite the candidacy of Barack Obama. Whatever the final fate of progressivism and the liberal democratic policies it supported, Rorty will not soon be forgotten and nor will Jane Addams. No sophisticated academic philosopher like Rorty, Addams however lived "philosophically," theorizing her way out of confinement and into service to others. That ongoing cosmopolitan education is recorded in Addams's various statements, including her autobiographies. "Where the discovery of the poor was bound up with the discovery of the self," Lasch (1965, xxvi) concludes, "the result was a literature notable for its clarity, its immediacy, and its power to evoke in the reader sympathies whose existence he scarcely suspected." That is teaching worthy of the name.

6   Religion, Love, and Democracy
in Laura Bragg's Boxes

Ida B. Wells

> What does it mean to do curriculum history at this particular juncture?
>
> Petra Munro (1998, 263)

Born in Massachusetts on October 9, 1881, the eldest daughter of a Protestant minister, Laura Bragg spent a year of her childhood in Holly Springs, Mississippi, the birthplace of Ida B. Wells, elementary-school teacher, journalist and, most famously, anti-lynching activist. When Bragg lived in Holly Springs (1890), Wells had already moved to Memphis and was no longer a teacher but a journalist, soon to be mobilized into activism by the lynching of one of her friends (Pinar 2001, 464). After briefly (the Bragg family remained in Mississippi for two years: Allen 2002, 180) teaching mathematics at Rust University (where Ida B. Wells had studied), a black school in Holly Springs founded in 1866 by the Freedman's Aid Society of the Methodist Episcopal Church (still in session today), the Reverend Lyman Bragg returned to New England, where Laura Bragg would study first in her father's library[1]—as did Jane Addams (Knight 2005, 50)—and then at Simmons College, where she studied the liberal arts and became a librarian.

Bragg worked as librarian after her graduation in 1906, first on Orr's Island off the coast of Maine, then in Charleston, South Carolina, where she also taught science, both at the Museum and at a local private girls' school.[2] At the Museum, she created traveling school exhibits—later known as Bragg's Boxes—that became the major focus of the Museum's educational program. They were a key element of her responsibilities[3] (Allen 2001, 36).

In 1920, Laura Bragg was appointed director of the Charleston Museum, the first woman so appointed. After serving 11 years, Bragg took up the directorship of the Pittsfield, Massachusetts Museum, where she introduced to the often artistically conservative local patrons not only the avant-garde—among them the sculptor Alexander Calder (1898–1976)—but socially progressive exhibits focused on contemporary social problems. Bragg retired after one such exhibit—the "World of Today," staged in 1939 (see note 15)—and returned to Charleston, where she lived a long life, still teaching not only classes but informally at her evening salons, held nearly every night before her illness and death (Allen 2001, 201). Outliving all of her immediate family

too radical

and her closest friends, Bragg was almost 97 when she died on May 16, 1978 (Allen 2001, 212; 199).

These are only the main points in the life of Laura Bragg, points discussed in detail in Louise Anderson Allen's (2001) fine biography. Here I focus on what I take to be the educational expression of Bragg's homoeroticism through her progressive pedagogical politics, specifically materialized in the traveling school exhibits. Informing my sense of the interrelatedness of her private desire and public pedagogy is the poetic political sense of American democracy expressed by Walt Whitman, whose work Harold Bloom (1994; Tröhler 2006, 94) declared as central to the American canon of literature and poetry. In one of his later dedicatory poems, "Staring From Paumanok," Whitman wrote:

> My comrade! For you to share with me two greatnesses, and a third one rising inclusive and more resplendent, The greatnesses of Love and Democracy, and the greatness of Religion (1881, 23; quoted in Tröhler 2006, 95).

Like other progressives (Tröhler 2006) but no disciple (Anderson 2008), John Dewey was taken with Whitman's democratic vision.[4] These three interconnected "greatnesses"—love, democracy, and religion—are materialized, I suggest, in Laura Bragg's Boxes.

Protestantism and Progressivism

> Bragg was always the teacher.
>
> Louise A. Allen (2001, 202)

Toward the end of the nineteenth century, Daniel Tröhler (2006, 92) explains, liberal movements in U.S. theology encouraged "worldly redemption," translating Christianity[5] into a "secular religion." Protestantism, Tröhler (2006, 99) argues, comprised "a fundamental part of the American mentality" during the Progressive Era (1890–1920). Tröhler stresses the non-dogmatic character of this religious understanding, not specific to any denomination or church; it is best understood, he suggests, as an "all-encompassing certainty rather than as a sect" (2006, 99).

Reacting to modernization (especially industrialization) and inspired by Protestantism, early progressives committed themselves to building—through education—the kingdom of God on earth. To personify the point, Tröhler (2006, 105) quotes Dewey: "I believe that in this way the teacher is always the prophet of the true God and the usherer in of the true kingdom of God." For progressives, then, democracy *was* social redemption (Tröhler 2006, 102), an idea not entirely unique to the nineteenth century, as McKnight (2003) makes clear.

As Freud appreciated, the distinction between earthly and heavenly fathers often blurs in the psychic lives of children. Laura Bragg was never especially devoted to her heavenly father (Allen 2001, 48). Like Jane Addams, it was her earthly father who was the primary male figure in her life, Bragg's confidant until his death in April 1927. Allen (2001, 12) points out that Bragg's intimacy with her father mirrors other early twentieth-century progressive women's relationships with their fathers, recalling Grumet's (1988) argument that late nineteenth-century women teachers were rejecting enforced domesticity when they embraced the independence and worldliness associated with public school teaching. While hardly a prerequisite for public service, did the rejection of women's (and some men's, as Kevin Murphy points out, as we see later) traditional gender and sex roles prove helpful to these fin de siècle activists in appreciating the plight of "others"?

Like her minister father, Laura Bragg moved to the American South "to do missionary work" (Allen 2001, 26). Allen (2001, 35) characterizes Bragg as "a self-proclaimed social missionary and reformer" who saw in museums institutional opportunities for self-improvement and social reconstruction. Though Allen says "self" and not "social," the two were interrelated, if not conflated. If wealth was the sign of salvation in certain strands of Protestantism, a life of public service was the secular sign of self-improvement. Like a supplicant, Bragg was, Allen (2001, 205) tells us, "always learning, studying intensely." For Bragg, learning was a "continuous process" (Allen 2001, 205). For Bragg, "life was always under construction," Allen (2001, 205) continues, "and so was understanding." This constructed character of Bragg's understanding was materialized in her traveling school exhibits.

Bragg's Boxes

Bragg boxes were unique.

Louise A. Allen (2001, 171)

Upon Bragg's arrival in Charleston, the Museum's educational program included one traveling school exhibit. It was, Allen (2001, 41) tells us, an "unimaginative exhibit of loose items." In addition to increasing the number of exhibits—by the close of 1914, under Bragg's leadership, the Museum's Department of Public Instruction had constructed 63 traveling school exhibits—Bragg added stories for teachers to read to students. Housed in green wooden boxes with handles and hinged doors, when opened the exhibits displayed staged scenes affording children glimpses, for example, of the wildlife within their region or of the people and their customs in other countries.

Rather than waiting for requests, Bragg shipped the exhibits automatically, enabling more of the exhibits to be in circulation. Beginning in 1913, Bragg sent the exhibits to both white and black schools (Allen 2002, 185). Providing the same educational services to both black and white children during the second decade of the twentieth century in Charleston, South Carolina was "both fearless and brazen" (Allen 2001, 42). Allen (2001, 50)

suggests that Bragg recognized that the ignorance and apathy of Charleston's population followed from the political and social stranglehold conservatives who controlled the city and state maintained. Rather than confront this state apparatus directly, Bragg focused on teaching, realizing, as many social progressives did, that "it is absurd to expect the public ... to rise above the intellectual level of its average constituents" (Dewey 1991 [1927], 60).

Tireless (she fell ill regularly, evidently owing to overwork), Bragg taught nature study courses for first-, second-, and third-grade public school teachers. Later (Allen 2001, 56), Bragg taught summer school for teachers at the Museum, offering courses on geography, nature study, and local history. Bragg's classroom teaching was extended through the traveling school exhibits. The natural history exhibits were regularly used in the elementary grades while the industrial exhibits were typically used in the sixth and seventh grades. There were several public schools, however, wherein the principals directed that the exhibits be used in all the grades. Fourteen private schools in Charleston borrowed them (Allen 2001, 50).

Not only Bragg appreciated the exhibits' "drawing power" (Allen 2001, 50). The Museum's work with the public schools so impressed the Board of Public School Commissioners, Allen (2001, 50) reports, that they passed a special resolution on January 26, 1914 requesting extension of the Museum's work with the city schools and seeking formal affiliation with the Museum. By 1916, every primary teacher was directed to use Bragg's nature study curriculum. The traveling school exhibits were aligned with Bragg's curriculum; teachers also brought their students to the Museum for classes. At the Museum, Bragg taught summer school for teachers on subjects, with credit given as if the course had been provided by a normal school or a university summer school (Allen 2002, 184).

By the fall of 1919 (Allen 2001, 57), Bragg had increased the circulation of the traveling school exhibits to all the white schools in the county, with the parcel post costs assumed by the county school commissioners. Seven of the city's public schools (both black and white) received the exhibits, as did 10 of the private schools. Additionally, the Museum was shipping the exhibits to more distant places across the state, among them the Greenville Woman's College, where they were employed as a demonstration of grammar-school teaching methods.

During the period 1925–1930, every school in the city was involved in the educational program at the Museum to some degree (Allen 2001, 118). In 1926, for instance (Allen 2001, 120), Bragg was shipping 147 exhibits to 30 city and county public schools and nine private schools. Accompanying the exhibits were 100 traveling school libraries. By 1927, Bragg's traveling school exhibits were being shipped to all the schools in the city and the county and, for the first time, they were systematically circulated to the county's black schools as well. In 1928, Bragg worked to become directly involved with the black community by securing books for use in black schools (Allen 2001, 122). By 1928 (Allen 2001, 123), there were 160 traveling exhibits

No Blacks allowed in museum

circulating regularly in the city schools (white, black, and private) and in the country schools.

Despite white resistance, Bragg continued to press against the color line: In 1917, the Museum's trustees agreed to allow classes of black students to visit the Museum when accompanied by a teacher. (They disallowed admission to black adults, however, even to black maids accompanying white children under the age of five [Allen 2001, 63]). During her first year as director, however, with the mayor's support, Bragg succeeded in opening the Museum to black patrons, if only on Saturday afternoons.[6] "Crossing the color line was beyond the pale," Allen (2001, 80) comments, "and her conduct provoked many Charlestonians."

African Americans were not the only minority in whom Bragg took an interest.[7] For a time, Bragg became interested in Indians native to South Carolina and, specifically, to the "low country." She participated in excavating various Indian mounds around the area and planned to publish a survey of them (Allen 2001, 99). American archeology is sometimes credited as starting with Thomas Jefferson's sponsorship of excavations of Indian mounds (Conn 2004, 9); through much of the nineteenth century, American archaeology and mounds were "virtually cotermininous" (Conn 2004, 120).

Gullah

As noted, Bragg also took an interest in Chinese culture and religion through her "China Boy" (quoted Allen 2001, 111). Despite the patronizing phrase, Chia Mei became important to Bragg.[8] In the fall of 1927, just after the arrival of the other five Chinese students, it was rumored that Bragg had applied for Poetry Society membership for all her "babies" (Allen 2001, 113). Unsurprisingly, there was resistance among whites. In response, Bragg formed the Ta T'ung Club. When Bragg invited "respectable young ladies" to meet the Chinese cadets at her home or at picnics, she "set many tongues wagging." Whites in Charleston considering the Chinese "colored" (Allen 2001, 114).

The traveling school exhibits did not rely on visuality alone. Perhaps sensitized by her own deafness (Allen 2001, 123), Bragg appreciated the significance of touch as "a real asset in teaching." In an interview conducted many years later, Bragg spoke of the importance of children touching, even handling, the items in the exhibits. Birds and other animals had to be replaced regularly in the exhibits as they were "petted to death" (Allen 2001, 123). Her work was recognized by the Rosenwald Fund,[10] which granted Bragg $5,000 for the traveling school exhibits (Allen 2001, 126).

Bragg also focused on exhibits at the Museum. During 1915, Bragg planned for a history of man exhibit, illustrating the "development of civilization from the most primitive peoples through the Egyptians and Assyrians to modern times" (quoted in Allen 2001, 59), including large casts of Egyptian and Assyrian sculpture. Though the scheme seemed to echo the 1893 Chicago World's Fair—in which the summit of civilization (The White City) was located at the opposite end of the fairway from those exhibitions of presumably primitive societies (Pinar 2001, 487 ff.)—Bragg, as Allen (2001,

94) points out, held "no brief for the Nordic race theory." Indeed, Bragg felt that culture museums can "change our supercilious attitude toward the rest of the world" (quoted in Allen, 2001, 95).

After moving to Pittsfield in 1931, Bragg continued this educational work. Though Bragg's educational labor did not prove controversial in Pittsfield, her art exhibitions did. Despite favorable publicity in *The New Yorker* and *Art News*, many local patrons found the modern art Bragg exhibited distasteful, even objectionable (Allen 2001, 167). In 1933 (Allen 2001, 177), Bragg exhibited the work of Alexander Calder, his first exhibit in the United States. The first American museum director to recognize Calder's genius, Bragg purchased for the Museum two motorized sculptures, *The Arc and the Quadrant* and *Dancing Torpedo Shape*. In 1934, Gertrude Stein lectured at the Museum during her two-and-a-half-month tour of the United States. Stein praised Picasso and dismissed Thomas Hart, Diego Rivera, and James Whistler. Local patrons admired Hart and Whistler, and Stein's dismissal of them was not well received (Allen 2001, 184).

Demonstrating that her progressive vision for the Berkshire Museum extended beyond challenging exhibits, Bragg invited Richard Lull, professor of paleontology at Yale, to lecture on evolution (Allen 2001, 182). The lectures and the exhibits would lead to intensifying controversy over Bragg and her leadership (Allen 2001, 184).

It was in Pittsfield, Allen (2001, 171) reports, that the traveling school exhibits became known as Bragg's Boxes. Built in boxes, the exhibits opened "like stage sets" (Allen 2001, 171). Now on display were objects and scenes representing various subjects in the curriculum, among them cultural history, geography, and natural history as well as industrial subjects and topics specific to Berkshire County. Exhibits included pictures (often from a government bulletin or an issue of *National Geographic*) as well as other items related to the topic of the exhibit (such as stamps or post cards: Allen 2002, 185). As in Charleston, each exhibit included a teacher's story and items for students to touch.

For children who rarely came to the Museum, Bragg's Boxes represented "windows on the world" (Allen's phrase: 2001, 171). They functioned as well to socialize rural and immigrant families to the "prevailing American values," Allen (2001, 171) suggests. Given that Bragg was invited to speak to the national Progressive Education Association meeting in Baltimore in February 1932, it seems the American values to which Bragg's Boxes socialized students were values associated with social reconstruction rather than those associated with social efficiency.[11] Traveling school exhibits were the major focus of the Museum's educational activities during this period, as indicated in Bragg's 1934 report (Allen 2001, 173). In 1936, *The New York Times* reported on the boxes, citing Bragg's conviction that if the people cannot come to the museum, the museum must go to the people. Adopted by museums in several sections of the country, Bragg boxes were now nationally known.

The success of the traveling school exhibits and the Berkshire Museum's other educational opportunities affirmed Bragg's conviction that museums could contribute to social change. Indeed, Bragg called museum work "the work of the people" (quoted in Allen 2002, 188), asserting that "Museum exhibits are for the purpose of creating understanding, not teaching facts" (quoted in Allen 2001, 104).[12] Bragg believed education to be the primary point of the museum, functioning to equalize "opportunities between the rich and poor" (quoted in Allen 2001, 74). That fantasy persists, now among conservatives.[13]

Romantic Mentorship

> Romantic friendships offered women an alternative to be married without replicating their mothers' domestic roles.
>
> Louise Allen (2001, 47)

Bragg believed that one should "be an opener of doors for those who come after you" (quoted in Allen 2001, 205). Though the emphasis in that sentence is on the agency of the actor, there is acknowledgement that the agency of the actor is expressed in service to those just now appearing: the young. This generational sense is evident in Bragg's pedagogical and affectional relationships with younger women whom she mentored.

Soon after arriving in Charleston, Bragg befriended two young women: Anita Pollitzer (who later became a leader of the National Woman's Party: Allen 2001, 54) and Josephine Pinckney. Anita Pollitzer attended the first Natural History Society meeting in October 1909, forming a friendship with Bragg that lasted until Pollitzer's death in 1975. Josephine Pinckney's father was president of the trustees. Josephine Pinckney and Bragg became lifelong friends as well as next-door neighbors on Chalmers Street in Charleston, where Bragg bought a house in 1927 (Allen 2001, 37).

Allen (2001, 47) describes Bragg's relationship with Hester Gaillard and her subsequent relationship with Belle Heyward as romantic friendships (Pinar 2001, 332 ff.), also known as "Boston marriages." In an interview many years later, Bragg identified Belle as a lesbian and recalled that lots of

> women were lesbians when I came to Charleston. It was all very innocent. I had at least five friends who were... There was just a shortage of men and it was though the women were married (quoted in Allen 2001, 57).

One suspects "shortage of men" had little to do with it. Even in prisons, "situational homosexuality" has proven to be an insubstantial concept (Pinar 2001, 1049).

In February 1915, Bragg moved into Belle Heyward's home. Among the reasons Bragg chose to leave Hester Gaillard for Heyward were financial and psychological ones: The Gaillard family dairy had gone into bankruptcy. This financial disaster, Allen (2001, 55) tells us, meant that the "atmosphere" was more pleasant in the Heyward house. Belle Heyward became, Allen continues (2001, 55), "Bragg's supporter, protector, and partner who provided Bragg with a warm, loving, and emotionally supportive home."

While still involved with Heyward, Bragg met Helen McCormick, a woman even younger than the other "bright young things" (quoted in Allen 2001, 102) Bragg befriended. McCormick first worked at the Museum as a volunteer in 1923 while still a student at the College of Charleston, from which she graduated with a degree in English. By August 1925, McCormick was working at the Museum, the replacement for the curator of children's work, Anne Porcher, who had become ill. Helen McCormick and Bragg became increasingly close while Belle Heyward was in Europe. By the time Heyward returned from a six-month trip to Europe (in January 1926), McCormick was on staff at the Museum and very much a part of Bragg's world (Allen 2001, 102). In response, Heyward appears to have committed suicide (Allen 2001, 106).

Helen McCormick fell in love with her mentor (Allen 2001, 112). After leaving Charleston for Pittsfield, she wrote to Bragg:

> Though I haven't my arms about you as I have so often in reality—my love is there like a warm mantle around you. Can't you feel it dear? I have loved you, dear, as I have loved no one else.... Remember that I love you always and always—your Helen (quoted in Allen 2001, 162).

Allen (2001, 211) describes McCormick as Bragg's "most successful student." She was also Bragg's confidant and nurturer. "In times of sorrow," Allen (2001, 187) tells us, "Bragg sought solace from Helen, who was always there, waiting to fill the role of Bragg's admirer and supporter." In retirement, living alone in Charleston, McCormick's photograph was the only one on Bragg's desk, "placed where she could see it from her bed" (Allen 2001, 202).

To what extent can we accept Bragg's assertion that "I am deeply tender, but I have never been much interested in sex" (quoted Allen 2001, 57)? Allen (2001, 57) characterizes Bragg's statement as "paradoxical," perhaps an "unconscious denial of her own sexuality." Despite Bragg's self-description as a person, not a woman, the truth is, in Allen's (2001, 57) words, that Bragg chose to be "supported by and nurtured [by], and loved and [was] loved [by] women exclusively."

There were other young women—and young men—Bragg mentored. Prominent among "Bragg's boys," as Allen (2001, 112) terms them, was Ned Jennings, who had appeared at the Museum in 1911. Jennings shared Bragg's passions for culture and same-sex affection (Allen 2001, 112). After becoming the curator of art, Jennings conducted handwork classes and assisted students in the illustration of geography projects. Years later, Jennings was found dead from a gunshot wound to the head. The official ruling was death by suicide, but Bragg recalled in 1976 that a "detective had told her that Ned's body had been moved, and so he could not have shot himself," and she was "completely convinced that Ned's male lover had murdered him" (quoted in Allen 2001, 154). Bragg honored her protégé in Pittsfield, mounting a memorial exhibit of Ned Jennings' paintings and masks (Allen 2001, 168).

The Homoerotics of Progressivism

> In the long view, she [Bragg] could be viewed ... as attempting an intellectual revolution through the traveling school exhibits, libraries, art classes, lectures, films, music, and other aspects of the educational programs she instituted.
>
> Louise Anderson Allen (2001, 216)

> [D]esire is itself a mode of entry into history.
>
> Angelo Restivo (2002, 3)

Laura Bragg was one among many progressive women working to reform U.S. institutions during the first decades of the twentieth century. Like other progressive women who were feminists, Allen (2001, 214) suggests, Bragg chose to act as an individual rather than through collective organizations. In this regard, she would seem to anticipate the later twentieth-century feminist assertion that the personal is political (Allen 2001, 217). Bragg also worked through institutions—the museum, the school—to educate a citizenry suspicious of experimentation.

Progressives were convinced that the very character and function of museums must change. Museums ought not to be, as Allen (2001, 214) nicely phrases it, "mausoleums of preserved relics," reserved for the elite. Allen attributes the progressive reconceptualization of the museum from mausoleums to educational institutions to the arrival of immigrants, requiring them to join the public school in Americanizing the new citizens.[14]

Bragg first came to appreciate relation between immigration and the reconstruction of the museum as educational institution when she visited Boston-area museums during her time at Simmons. Allen (2001, 215) reports that at that time, Bragg saw firsthand how museum personnel responded to immigrants by writing new exhibition labels in everyday English, "words that would both illuminate and instruct." It was this pedagogical challenge, Allen continues, that provoked the professionalism of museum work.

Such professionalism was not only instructional but curricular, and it required courage. As Allen suggests, Bragg's risk taking in making the Boxes available to black students recalls her father's post-bellum educational work in Mississippi at Rust. This same legacy of social reconstruction (a term recalling the post-bellum Reconstruction) must have been in play in exhibits such as the 1939 "World of Today" exhibit.[15] Might we understand Bragg's interest in avant-garde art as not only an expression of her artistic sophistication, but also as a symbolic activism on behalf of marginalized groups, including sexual minorities, of which, as Allen points out at several points in the book, the public was becoming increasingly conscious?

Bragg's educational programs were designed, Allen (2001, 215) emphasizes, for "ordinary citizens," animated by progressives' devotion to "uplift and progress." Committed to the museum as an "engine for social change," Allen (2001, 215) continues, "Bragg turned both museums into social settlement houses by offering plays, lectures, art classes, and educational programs." The settlement house claim may not be entirely mistaken, but it does seem exaggerated. Certainly Bragg did not live with the underclass, as did Jane Addams, and her penchant for the privileged classes seems more than a shrewd choice of affiliation for fundraising purposes.[16] The choice of "bluestocking" in the book's title recalls ladies of leisure, not street activists, as Addams sometimes was (Elshtain 2002, 173).

Describing her as a missionary and social worker, Allen (2001, 215) argues that Bragg was committed to "social change, even though she had come to the city intending to be a librarian and botanist." The traveling school exhibits were, Allen (2001, 216) concludes, "among her greatest accomplishments." Bragg's Boxes represented "an attempt to end the apathy and ignorance of schoolchildren" (2001, 216). An educated citizenry, she hoped, would bring their children to the museum.

In addition to the pragmatism-as-Protestantism thesis advanced so persuasively by Daniel Tröhler and others, I want to suggest that for some progressives such as Bragg, gendered, and specifically homoerotic, elements were also in play in their social humanitarianism and activism (Pinar 2001, 348 ff.). Louise Allen accords gender almost definitive status in her concluding remarks:

> Bragg's story is about gender, as all stories about women are; it is about race, racism, and class and how this early feminist confronted those issues; and it is about Bragg's sexuality and her ambivalence about it (2001, 214).

My question is: Were these elements interrelated, and how did Bragg's boxes enable her to confront, express, and disguise these elements?

I will suggest a general answer to that specific question first. I will point to two scholarly narratives that suggest, if not an interrelation among sexuality, social activism, and religion, at least that sexuality was also an element in the "mentality" that bound many progressives in the common cause of social redemption through democracy.

The first narrative—that of historian Kevin P. Murphy—concerns the settlement house movement. Though women—Jane Addams most conspicuously—were the leaders in that movement, many men also lived and worked in urban settlement houses. Murphy (1998) focuses on two: Charles B. Stover, head of the University Settlement on New York's Lower East Side (where Eleanor Roosevelt worked when she was 17), and John Lovejoy Elliott of the Hudson Guild, located on Manhattan's West Side. Stover and Elliott drew on the same intellectual traditions Addams did, embracing social democratic ideas of cross-class "human brotherhood" grounded in humanist ethical theory. Also like Addams, Stover and Elliott became involved in national politics (Murphy 1998).

Like Addams, Lillian Wald, and other settlement women, Elliott and Stover included a critique of middle-class gender roles within their ideal of human brotherhood. Like many settlement women, these men created their primary emotional and erotic relationships with members of the same gender. Stover and Elliott regarded settlement houses as experiments in alternative families wherein sexuality was not necessarily linked to reproduction. In so doing, Murphy (1998) points out, the two men performed a cultural and pedagogical politics of same-sex eroticism very different from emerging medical models of homosexual pathology and heterosexual normativity.

Though the historical moment (the 1960s) and geographical place (Mississippi) are quite different in the second narrative, the interrelation of social activism and same-sex desire remains the same. Mississippi's best-known black leader, Aaron Henry, and liberal white attorney Bill Higgs were often present in gay settings, and this fact was seized upon by white supremacists committed to discrediting the civil rights movement. "By 1965," historian John Howard (1999, xvii) concludes, "homosexuality was linked to the specter of racial justice." This is a negative formulation of the interrelated elements of love and democracy—in Howard's account, we are minus the third element: religion—evident in Bragg's life and work.

As civil rights activists questioned white racist assumptions about justice and equality, Howard (1999, 118) argues, an "atmosphere"—Tröhler (2006, 99) would term it a "mentality"—was created that was "conducive to queer thought and, sometimes, queer desire." More than a few of those activists who fought for racial justice—most visibly Aaron Henry and Bill Higgs—expressed "queer thought" and "queer desire," reports Howard (1999, 118).

Among those white volunteers who came to Mississippi for 1964's "freedom summer" was Amber Hollibaugh. A lesbian, Hollibaugh later realized that she and her college student friends "put the Black community in even more danger because of that heterosexual racism" (Howard 1999, 119). During "freedom summer," straight white college men were among those who experimented while sharing beds with young black men (Howard 1999, 119).

The white supremacist conflation of racial justice with sexual deviance was most dramatically expressed by the White Knights of the Ku Klux Klan of Mississippi, who added communism to the mix. In a public letter to President Lyndon Johnson, the Klan described his "Great Society" programs as "full of

* Daddy said Pappy kept KKK from going down street + through his property

treason, blood, and perversion." They attacked his "homosexual associates," the "sex perverts and atheistic murderers ... engaged in the deliberate, criminal destruction of this Nation under color of unConstitutional, unLawful statutes and decrees." Johnson's proxies—those northern college student volunteers pouring into the state in 1964—were dismissed as "commies" and queers. As Imperial Wizard Sam Bowers put it:

> The heretics, the enemies of Christ in the early spring of 1964 [were the] false prophets ... from the pagan academies, with "the whores of the media" in tow. Communists, homosexuals, and Jews, fornicators and liberals and angry blacks—infidels all (quoted passages in Howard 1999, 149).

Though overstating the presence of Communists in the civil rights movement, Bowers understood precisely, if negatively, the interrelatedness of love, democracy, and religion in progressive racial politics.

Though communism and a Jewish conspiracy (themselves conflated by many, especially during the decades following 1917: for an autobiographical account see Mosse 2000) were fantasies of the paranoid right wing (Hofstadter 1996 [1965]), Howard (1999, 150) points out that homosexual civil rights activists were "not simply figments of a paranoid white Mississippi imagination." He reports that:

> Queer sexuality was not an import, brought into the region by an invading army of misfits. Support for sexual difference existed alongside varied reformist tendencies within the movement. And in the heart of the lynching and Bible Belt, queer Mississippians were at the forefront of the civil rights struggle (Howard 1999, 150).

Racism is now taboo as a public political discourse even in the South; it is now expressed indirectly as anti-gay hysteria. That is not all the contemporary anti-gay movement is—there are other ingredients such as a contemporary crisis of masculinity (Pinar 2001, 1139 ff.), including homophobia—but it cannot be understood apart from the convoluted conflation of racialized and sexualized hatreds Sam Bowers expressed 40 years ago.

The Bragg Box as Fetish

> The fetish is compensation for this lost female body,
>   making sexual access to (other) women's bodies possible.
>   Elizabeth Grosz (1994, 291)

In his 1927 essay "Fetishism," Freud theorized that men, traumatized by the sight of female anatomical difference (by what they perceive as castration), devise a fetish (a surrogate penis) and project it onto women's bodies as a substitute object (Eng 2001, 2). Freud limits his best-known discussion of fetishism to its role in sustaining a "disavowal" of castration (Laplanche and Pontalis 1973, 118–119). The fetish (usually an unremarkable quotidian object invested, by the fetishist, with an extraordinary quotient of libidinal cathexis) is defined as a substitute for the missing maternal phallus (Johnston 2004, 265). Without this prosthetic defense, Johnston (2004, 265) suggests, the fetishist's very sense of reality itself collapses.

Though Freud limited fetishism to masculine development (Grosz 1995, 147), given Laura Bragg's identification with her own father, we cannot judge her ineligible to participate in this general psychic formation. Certainly the concept has been used widely and not necessarily in gender-specific ways,[17] most famously in the Marxian concept of "commodity fetishism" and, more recently, as racial fetishism (Eng 2001, 32; Stoler 1995, 124).

The "essence" of commodity fetishism, Jonathan Flatley (1996, 117) explains (in his discussion of Andy Warhol, an artist Bragg might have exhibited if their generations had more closely coincided), is the "ascription to objects of the characteristics of persons," a "transformation of human social relations into an abstract thing." Commodity fetishism endows specific objects—money, works of art, traveling school exhibits— with sometimes considerable significance, and it does so by disguising the social nexus in which the object comes to form. For Flatley (1996, 117), "the personification of exchange value is literalized most clearly perhaps in the portraits that adorn our money, one of the many forms of everyday portraiture that made its way into Warhol's art." The everyday forms of natural history and other subjects found their way to—were exhibited in— Bragg's Boxes.

Commodity fetishism not only disguises the social nexus in which the objects come to form; it also disguises the psychic processes that structure its specific materialization. This function of the fetish recalls what D. W. Winnicott calls a "transitional object," which, he suggests, may in later life become a fetish object. Winnicott (1990, 9; Derrick 1997, 229 n. 20) suggested that "the transitional object stands for the breast, or the object of the first relationship." In this view, the fetish thus is constructed from the maternal body against loss, rather than given to the mother to defend against the spectacle of "lack."[18]

Fetishism, as Kobena Mercer (1994, 190) observes in a different context, is not necessarily "a bad thing." No simple reproduction of the maternal breast (or paternal phallus), fetishism invites, Mercer (1994, 190) imagines, "a deconstructive strategy which begins to lay bare the psychic and social relations of ambivalence at play in cultural representations." Not having viewed the Boxes that remain, I am unable to specify how Bragg's choice of objects for display inside them may have expressed those "psychic and social relations of ambivalence" that were "at play" in the "cultural representations" school children viewed when the boxes were opened. What I can suggest— contrary to Freud's initial formulation[19]—is that the boxes represented two organs of gendered significance: the breast and the penis, themselves conflated at various historical moments (Pinar 2006b, 34 ff.).

In this fetishistic sense, Bragg's Boxes were symbolic expressions of maternal care *and* patriarchal power, the former disguising Bragg's non-reproductive sexuality and career-focused, paternally identified life, the latter contradicting her "castration" (or lack or vulnerability) as a progressive—lesbian?—woman from the North in the Deep South. By extending the "maternal museum"— in which objects are, in a sense, nurtured as they are archived, shown to the world as they are shielded from it—to children trapped in public places away from their mothers, did Bragg promote not only the museum and the education of children but, at the same time, represent herself as mythically maternal (and hence heteronormative) and with a "phallus" (with patriarchal power)? Revising David Eng's (2001, 157) question (itself revising Freud), I ask: "Can the fetish serve to deny [while it affirms] [fe-]male homosexuality rather than female castration?"

The boxes—substituting for pieces of Bragg's psychic (if not anatomical) terrain—not only afforded school children a visual experience of the displaced and disguised maternal object. Recall that Bragg wanted children to touch "parts" of the exhibit. Not only compensations for lost objects— the breast symbolizing maternal love, the phallus symbolizing patriarchal power—Laura Bragg's Boxes functioned as material contradictions of her own vulnerability and lack as a woman working in a gendered and racialized society inhospitable to progressive women. Bragg's Boxes afforded, as Kaja Silverman (1988, 5) suggests in a different context, a "simulated real" of the "absent real." Silverman (1988, 20) reminds us that "the fetish classically functions not so much to conceal woman's castration as to deny man's," making historical as well as gendered sense given the simultaneity of a late nineteenth-century Western "crisis of masculinity" (Pinar 2001, 321 ff.) with the primacy (since the 1870s) of fetishism as the "preeminent example of all the perversions" (Crary 1999, 12), a decade, incidentally, associated with the birth of progressivism (Pinar et al. 1995, 103 ff).

Like the appearance of the figure of the "homosexual" in late nineteenth-century Europe (sensationalized in the person of Oscar Wilde), the appearance of the fetish functioned to "release *sexuality from its embeddedness in reproduction,* and thus demonstrates that reproduction is not a feature of sexuality as such, but rather an effect of the construction of sexuality in modern Western cultures" (de Lauretis 1994, 309). As I suggest in the first chapter, it is also a structure of subjectivity associated with the cultivation of cosmopolitanism. Not only in Western cultures (Gilmore 2001), but sexuality became politicized in the West with the emergence of sexualized identity politics just over a century ago.

My point is not historical but educational and, specifically, curricular. I am not reducing Bragg's Boxes to their fetishistic functions. So conceived, however, they shed their quaint and antiquated status—indeed, as items to be stored in a museum—and display another and still relevant view of enduring and vital educational questions, among them: What is the curricular significance of curiosity? What are the relations among attention, arousal, and study? What is the relation between academic study and subjective formation? What are the relations between intellectual understanding and the intersubjective bonds (the transference and counter-transference relationships) between teacher and student, between students and those absent ones whose objects (books or boxes) students touch and visually examine as they study?

Though failing to provide specific answers to these questions, the concept of the fetish (and of the fetishist) enables us to discern the displaced and deferred status of curricular artifacts and the libidinal status of our attention to them. Structured around interest, arousal, and shared passions, academic knowledge can enchant as it complicates and thereby can contribute to changing the world. Substitute "student" or "teacher" for "fetishist" in the following quoted passage, and what is at stake in expressing one's subjectivity through the school curriculum becomes obvious:

> [T]he fetishist enters a universe of the animated, intensified object as rich and complex as any sexual relation (perhaps more so than). The point is that both a world and a body are opened up for redistribution, disorganization, transformation; each is metamorphosed in the encounter, both become something other, something incapable of being determined in advance, and perhaps even in retrospect, but which nonetheless have perceptibly shifted and realigned. The sexual encounter cannot be regarded as an expedition, an adventure, a goal, or an investment, for it is a directionless mobilization of excitations with no guaranteed outcomes or "results" (not even orgasm) (Grosz 1995, 200).

Certainly study's "outcome" cannot be expressed in standardized test scores, a fetish of another, political kind.

To suggest, then, that Laura Bragg's Boxes were fetishized objects is to invoke an image of education as erotic,[20] as excitation, without direction (at least at the outset), as stimulating metamorphosis. Using language evocative of complexity theory (Doll et al. 2005)—specifically, the terms *disorganization* and *transformation*—Grosz's depiction of the fetishist reminds us not only of students set free to study where desire takes them (guided by teachers), it reminds us of Laura Bragg and her remarkable Boxes.

Conclusion

> I do not trust thought that liberates itself from sex.
>
> Witold Gombrowicz (1989, 201)

> I never see what I want or exhibit what is desired in the fetishistic masquerade, whose effects are ambiguous.
>
> Carole-Anne Tyler (1994, 226)

Laura Bragg was a courageous and committed progressive woman driven by personal ambition, same-sex desire, and a secular faith in social redemption. In her life and accomplishment, we see Whitman's triumvirate—love, democracy, and religion—intertwined and materialized in those traveling school exhibits. Combining sight and touch—two modes of fetishistic satisfaction—the exhibitionism of the boxes enabled Bragg to penetrate the public through maternal nurturance of their children. There is the additional kinky element of offering teachers something to say, a fetishistic fantasy of substitution (of self) through ventriloquism, staff development through lesbian love.

Published in 1855, *Leaves of Grass* suggested a utopia of masculine comradeship that would bind American men together in a democratic society (Robertson 2008, 195–196, 251). (Whitman lost his job at the U.S. Interior Department when *Leaves of Grass* was published [Greenberg 1988].) In the "Calamus" poems, Whitman sexualized those bonds, making himself, Murphy (1998, 279) suggests, both "the poet of homosexual love and the bard of democracy." Whitman himself appreciated the political significance of his "Calamus" poems:

> Important as they are in my purpose as emotional expression for humanity, the special meaning of Calamus cluster of *Leaves of Grass* ... mainly resides in its Political significance. In my opinion it is by a fervent, accepted development of Comradeship, the beautiful and sane affection of man for man, latent in all the young fellows, North and South, East and West—it is by this, I say ... that the United States of the future (I cannot too often repeat), are to be most effectually welded together, intercalated, anneal'd into a Living Union (quoted in Murphy 1998, 279–280).

For Bragg, it was the love of women for women and the secularization of religion in social redemption that animated her political activism, materialized in those Boxes. For Bragg, as for Whitman, private desire and public pedagogy were "welded together ... into a Living Union." Are we speaking here of a homosexual union? Are prosthetic extensions of the public pedagogue sex toys to stimulate the (intellectual) senses, shattering the somnolence of even (or is it especially) democratic society? Such shattering may be what Pier Paolo Pasolini had in mind when he devised prosthetic extensions of his body.

7 Pier Paolo Pasolini

A Most "Excellent Pedagogist" *Polemical?*

[P]asolini continues to be a "living" and authoritative force in Italy.
Zygmunt G. Barański (1999b, 14)

The Western heritage is nowhere thicker on the ground than in Italy.
Elizabeth Boa (1996, 236)

Known primarily as a filmmaker in the United States, Pier Paolo Pasolini was regarded by Italians as an equally important poet, "first and foremost a poet" (Ryan-Scheutz 2007, 4), "a great civic poet" (Volponi 2007 [1976], 124), "our greatest poet of the postwar period" (Moravia 2007 [1978], 109). He was also a novelist, theoretician, journalist, translator, playwright, actor, painter, songwriter, and illustrator (Schwenk and Semff 2005, 19; Gordon 1996, 21; Welle 1999, 93; Borgna 2007, 140). Pasolini was probably "the most polemical figure in Italian cultural and political life" (Greene 1990, 3). As Italy's "major post-war intellectual" (Barański 1999a, 7), "probably Italy's major intellectual of the twentieth century" (Duncan 2006, 83), Pasolini was "relentlessly introspective and restlessly experimental" (Gordon 1996, 1). One of the founders of the review *Officina*,[1] he engaged the Italian public through regular columns in a wide range of newspapers (Barański 1999c, 255). More than thirty years after his death, Pasolini "continues to exert [influence] over the cultural and emotional sensibilities of his compatriots" (Barański 1999b, 14). His *oeuvre* continues to generate a "rich and steady" stream of scholarship worldwide; the field of Pasolini studies is "vast" (Ryan-Scheutz 2007, 9). In the field of Italian Studies, Pasolini's literary and cinematic oeuvre is "quietly becoming canonical" (Viano 1993, vii). "Pasolini is dead," Ben Lawton (2005a, x) points out, "but he has not been silenced."

Pasolini was born on March 5 or 6, 1922 in Bologna. A native of Ravenna, his father was a career officer in the Italian military; his mother, of peasant origins, was an elementary schoolteacher from Friuli. During his early years, the family lived in various northern Italian cities where his father was stationed (Snyder 1980). Pasolini completed high school in Bologna. There he read Rimbaud, the French symbolists, and Gungaretti's *Sentimento del tempo* (Chiesi and Mancini 2007, 83); he developed friendships with other young intellectuals, friendships that would last for decades. "And there," Pasolini recalled, "is where my Marxism began, materially, poetically, and physically" (quoted in Chiesi and Mancini 2007, 84).

Each summer the family returned to Pasolini's mother's home in Casarsa della Delizia in the province of Udine. In Casarsa—along with his mother and older brother Guido—he spent most of the years of the war. In 1942, Pasolini registered in the Faculty of Letters of the University of Bologna, where he discovered psychoanalysis, poetry, painting, and soccer (Schwartz, 1992, 41). Also in 1942, he published his first book of poems, *Poesie di Casarsa*, composed in the Friulian dialect, praised by renowned philologist Gianfranco Contini (Ryan-Scheutz 2007, 233 n. 16) whose influence on Pasolini was "singular" (Welle 1999, 98; De Mauro 1999, 89 n. 17). His "mother's tongue," Friulian was an acquired language for Pasolini (Rohdie 1995, 28).

In 1943, Pasolini was inducted into the army. Like Sartre and Althusser, Pasolini was captured by the Germans but, in contrast to those famous French prisoners of war, Pasolini managed to escape. The war was a catastrophe for his family. During resistance fighting, the elder son Guido was "traitorously murdered by rival communist partisans" (Ahern 1983/1984, 104). His father was also a prisoner of war, from which he never recovered psychologically; he drank himself to death during the postwar years. One consequence of the war experience—coupled with his reading as a high-school student (noted earlier: see Chiesi and Mancini 2007, 83–84; Ryan-Scheutz 2007, 233 n. 24)—was Pasolini's lifelong and passionate opposition to fascism. Indeed, Pasolini's anti-fascism was a major motive in all that he did (Greene 1990).

Pasolini received his Laurea in 1945 with a thesis on Pascoli.[2] He had written part of an earlier thesis on twentieth-century Italian painting, directed by art historian Roberto Longhi[3] (Schwartz 1992, 120), but it was lost during the war. Turning 24 in March 1946, Pasolini looked forward to a respectable and secure career as a local schoolteacher. He held an excellent degree, something rare enough for schoolteachers in Friuli, and even had classroom experience to his credit, having taught peasant children in 1945 (Viano 1993, xvi; Schwartz 1992, 165). During this period—May 1946 to August 8, 1947—Pasolini kept a diary "against my will (maybe this, and nothing else, is divine punishment)"; he had decided, however, that he must write about himself as part of a project of self-study (Schwartz 1992, 166).[4]

Pasolini became a member of the Italian Communist Party (*Partito Communista Italiana: PCI*) in 1947; soon after he was appointed secretary of the local section of the Party. At this time, he taught in the middle school at Valvasone. He made the daily commute of six kilometers roundtrip by bicycle in the company of a fellow teacher, Sergio Vacher. Years later, Vacher recalled spending long hours with him every day, utterly unaware of his "tendencies" (Schwartz 1992, 191). It was years later, too, that Pasolini's two short novels—composed during this period—were published: They constitute "confessions of his own homosexuality" (Ward 1995, 28).

Pasolini was, evidently, a "natural teacher," envisaging "teaching as an act of love for the child and for the world" (Gordon 1996, 77). His principal called him a *maestro mirabile*, "one ready and able to manage a classroom with unheard-of student participation, open experimentalism, along the lines of the newly influential Carleton Washburne and John Dewey" (Schwartz 1992, 191). Before the "genial analytic mind" became a concept in his film theory, it was, it seems, Pasolini's pedagogical persona (Ward 1994, 134). His was "a poetics of pedagogy" (Stone 1994, 41).

Pasolini taught Italian literature and grammar: "[T]he question of pedagogy in Italian culture is inseparable from the question of language" (Stone 1994, 40). His students wrote poems in *Friulano*, John Ahern (1983/1984, 104) tells us, memorized the "witty didactic verses" he had composed for them, and "listened to him read Verga, Chekhov, Black Spirituals, and *The Spoon River Anthology*." He coached soccer, "made a small garden in the courtyard of the school and taught the Latin names of the plants; he drew posters with colored figures and invented fables like that of the monster *Userum*, so that the children would have a good time learning the endings of the substantives of the second declension, -us, -er, -um" (Zanzotto, quoted in Schwartz 1992, 191). His inventiveness in the classroom disclosed a devotion to his students[5] that many of his students felt for him. Decades later, two of his students published a "Souvenir of Pasolini" that details their fascination with a teacher who was, by one account, "serious to the point of fierceness" (Schwartz 1992, 192).

In 1949, after allegations of sexual misconduct with local boys (aged 14–16), Pasolini was expelled from the Communist Party, a scandal he had "predicted" in an early, unfinished novel (Duncan 2006, 89). Guilt and innocence were irrelevant; charges and bad publicity for the Party[6] were enough to justify expelling him on grounds of "moral unfitness" (Schwartz 1992, 223). A priest had blackmailed him: Either resign from the Communist Party or his affairs with boys would be made public (Ahern 1983/1984, 104). Within 48 hours, he was stripped of his teaching post (Schwartz 1992, 224). With his mother, and joined later by his father, he fled to Rome, where they moved into the city's historic if impoverished center (Rhodes 2007, 21). There, after struggling to find a job, he taught in a private school in Ciampino (Volponi 2007 [1976], 124; Rumble and Testa 1994a), where he taught "tough city types" Dante as well as songs, rhymes, sayings, and proverbs that Pasolini asked them to bring to class from home (Schwartz 1992, 249; Ahern 1983/1984, 108). In effect, he was transposing "his" Friuli to Rome (Barański 1999c, 264; Rhodes 2007, 164 n. 6).

In Rome, Pasolini met Attilio Bertolucci[7], Alberto Moravia[8], Elsa Morante[9], Paolo Volponi[10], and other important writers, artists, and intellectuals. In 1952, he published an anthology of dialect poetry entitled *Poesia dialettale del Novecento* and began to work as a screenwriter, collaborating on screenplays for directors such as Frederico Fellini,[11] Mauro Bolognini,[12] Franco Rossi,[13] Florestano Vancini,[14] and Bernardo Bertolucci[15] (whom he had known since Bertolucci's childhood). In 1955, he published his first novel, *Ragazzi di vita*,[16] for which he was brought to trial. Along with Roberto Roversi,[17] Francesco Leonetti,[18] and Franco Fortini,[19] he founded the journal *Officina*. In 1957, he won the Premio Viareggio for a collection of poems entitled *The Ashes of Gramsci*. In 1959, he won the *Premio Crotone* for his second novel, *Una vita violenta* (Rumble and Testa 1994a).

In 1961, Pasolini focused his "urban pedagogy" (Gordon 1996, 100) on cinema, directing his first film, *Accattone*, employing boys he had met (often sexually) in the *borgate* or slums of Rome, "the heart of Pasolini's cinema" (Rhodes 2007, ix). For the next decade, he averaged almost one feature-length film per year. During this period, Pasolini was repeatedly brought to trial for his films. He continued to write poetry and criticism, and a collection of theoretical essays, *Heretical Empiricism*,[20] was released in 1972. From the late 1960s, he worked on the journal *Nuovi argomenti*. In the early seventies, his journalistic activities intensified (Gordon 1996).[21] Most notable was his weekly column for the newspaper *Il Corriere della Sera*. These essays were collected and published later under the titles *Scritti corsari* and *Lettere luterane*. Pasolini was violently murdered on November 2, 1975 at Ostia, near Rome, by a young male prostitute named Giuseppe Pelosi, although the circumstances of his death remain mysterious.[22] After a massive public display of grief in Rome by thousands of mourners, he was buried in Casarsa. Pasolini's last film, *Salò o le 120 giornate di Sodoma*, was released posthumously in 1975. "[A]rguably the darkest and most disturbing film ever made" (Rich 2007, 80), *Salò* was greeted with a series of court injunctions that effectively removed the film from circulation for years. In 1992, his last, unfinished novel, *Petrolio*,[23] was published in Italy, again resulting in controversy and scandal in the Italian press.

Pasolini expressed his political commitments early on. In 1947, he sided with peasants in their struggle with landowners: "As for me," he asserted simply, "I am on the side of victims" (quoted in Greene 1990, 138). Inspired by Antonio Gramsci ("my teacher" [quoted in De Mauro 1999, 81]), Pasolini joined the Communist Party. He wrote a poem addressed to the deceased Gramsci, whose theories of organic intellectuality—with its dynamic links to the life to the masses—influenced Pasolini's perceptions of himself, his work, and the world: "The resonances of Gramsci's work within me were decisive" (quoted in Greene 1990, 54). Like Fanon, Gramsci underscored the importance of the peasantry, but he also ascribed a revolutionary role to culture and intellectuals. Moreover, he did so without de-emphasizing the value of art (Greene 1990).

Pasolini was a writer before he was a film director; his writing continued throughout his remarkable career. For example, his film *Teorema* appeared also as a book. Alberto Moravia compared Pasolini to the legendary French playwright Jean Genet; others judged him to be more important than Genet. Sartre, De Lauretis, Calvino, Barthes, Deleuze, Guattari, and Foucault, among others, wrote appreciatively about Pasolini. Pasolini, Naomi Greene

(1990, 223) suggests, is "one of the most radical and prophetic voices of our century." In this chapter, I focus upon his early life and his theory of free indirect subjectivity. A theory of artistic production as well as (I will suggest) curriculum development, a subjectivity that is "free" and "indirect" welcomes the worldliness of a cosmopolitan education.

Early Life

> [T]here are things—even the most abstract or spiritual—that are lived *only through the body.*
>
> Pier Paolo Pasolini (1997, 224)

> Ah, may life
> Always be a girl....
>
> Pier Paolo Pasolini (quoted in Ryan-Scheutz 2007, 27)

His parents' differing social origins and outlooks would be reflected in Pasolini's persistently binary view of the world. His parents' arguments echoed in him, psychologically and politically. Pasolini remembered: "He [father] reproached her with having her head in the clouds. The simple truth is that he was a Fascist; she was not. Being in the clouds meant, for him, being anti-conformist, in disagreement with the laws of the State, with the ideas of those in power" (quoted in Greene 1990, 4). This anti-conformism, this oedipal battle with his father, with fascism, on behalf of his mother, would characterize his life's work.[24] He always found it easier to express his love for his mother (with whom he lived all his life) than his feelings for his father (Ryan-Scheutz 2007, 14 ff.). An avid reader of Freud (and later of Jung: Viano 1993, 12, 239–240), Pasolini spoke with self-irony: "As you know, the last person to know oneself is oneself. What I can say is that I had a great love for my mother" (quoted in Stack 1969, 11). Pasolini admitted he was influenced by his mother's respect for "authority"—a respect he would internalize and which would complicate his commitment to rebellion (Greene 1990; Snyder 1980). A former elementary schoolteacher (Ryan-Scheutz 2007, 16; Zigaina 2005, 33), Susanna played an important role—the Old Virgin—his *Il Vangelo secondo Matteo*[25]; she "stands out for her silent communication and compelling facial expressions" (Ryan-Scheutz 2007, 147).

About his father, Carlo Alberto, Pasolini confessed that the relationship was "only a question of rivalry and hatred" (quoted in Greene 1990, 5). Probably Pasolini's father detested his son's homosexuality. Not only did it express a rejection of himself (and his fascist values) but, in his eyes, it converted the ritualized relationship between mother and son into a more "mysterious, possibly erotic, symbiosis. Through this homosexuality Pasolini threatened his father's virility and his sense of being-in-the-world" (Siciliano 1982, 37). Pasolini's childhood, then, both within the family and the Italian state, was torn between fascism and democracy. And in the middle between these opposing ways of life was his sexuality. As Greene (1990, 5) writes: "At the heart of his deeply ambivalent nexus of conformism and rebellion lay his homosexuality." Pasolini's perception of the disjuncture between reality and representation—history and culture—is also traceable to his homosexuality (Viano 1993, 15; Lawton 1980–81, 170–171), which he regarded as "an *alterity*, not an identity" (Restivo 2002, 90).

Pasolini understood his eroticization of otherness early on. Later, Pasolini would recall when, at the age of three, he was excited sexually by the knees of young boys at play nearby. He wrote:

> Now I know that it was an intensely sensual feeling. If I re-experience it I feel it precisely in my insides the melting, sadness, and a violence of desire. It was the sense of the unobtainable, of the carnal—a sense for which no name had yet been invented. I invented it then and it was "teta veleta." Just seeing the legs bent in the throes of the game I said to myself that I felt "teta veleta," something which was like a tickling, a seduction, a humiliation (quoted in Greene 1990, 5).

Fetishism, violence, and sadness would surface in many of his films, in his poetry, in his novels, and in his theory (Viano 1993, 16).

In addition to Gramsci, there were other influences. Pasolini was also drawn to Rimbaud, especially to his "passion and rebellion," his "scandalous and doomed" love affair with the married poet Paul Verlaine and, finally, his "romantic flight from Europe into the dark heart of Africa" (Greene 1990, 6). What Greene (1990, 7) terms "the fierceness of his desire" is evident in his struggle for self-expression, a struggle intensified and complicated owing to the pervasiveness of Catholicism in Italy. Pasolini confessed:

> In a mystical nakedness, the terror-creating nakedness of the soul, perhaps I can find some way of justifying myself: if I *had to* sin, that is to follow the road of the Christian in reverse. It is known that a convert normally has one obstacle to overcome: the state of sin. I had to go from an innocence that was imposed to one that was willed (quoted in Greene 1990, 7).

These themes of transfiguration and self-purification, of the sin of innocence and the moral superiority of decadence, would characterize the cosmopolitan curriculum Pasolini taught.

The Teacher

> [T]he intellectual's role is not to have any role—to be the living contradiction to every role.
>
> Pier Paolo Pasolini (quoted in Schwartz 1992, 10)

> A life of Socrates would be ideally my ultimate film—I would like it to be the culmination of my cinema experience.
>
> Pier Paolo Pasolini (quoted in Schwartz 1992, 610)

Immediately after the fall of the Mussolini government, Pasolini wrote of the "pedagogical duty" (quoted in Francese 1994, 31) that called intellectuals of his generation. In 1944, Pasolini established a small school for those children who could no longer travel in safety to their usual schools. With friends and help from his mother (Ryan-Scheutz 2007, 19), he had launched the year before a similar school in Casarsa. Pasolini loved teaching these children. "I believe," he remarked in his diary, "that I never gave of myself with such dedication as I did to these students during the lessons of Italian and history" (quoted in Greene 1990, 7).

Despite the pleasure he took in teaching, education was hardly self-enclosed. Pasolini was quite clear about the political nature of schooling. In an interview conducted 30 years later, Pasolini observed,

> Power is a system of education that divides us into the subjugated and the subjugators. A single educational system that forms us all, from the so-called ruling classes to the poor. In a certain sense, all are weak because all are victims. And all are guilty because all are ready for the massacre game (quoted in Allen 1982, 30).

Pasolini rarely understated the reality he discerned about him. It was a world to be signified, designated by his neologism *Significando*, a term that renders reality simultaneously subjective and objective (Viano 1993, 33).

The language of reality is ideological, characterized, as Viano (1993, 34) nicely puts it, "by the social intonations through which it gains historical specificity." Consequently, Pasolini called compulsory or "common education, obligatory and mistaken," during "late-capitalist cannibalism … pushes us all into the arena." The apparent innocence of the classroom and the apparent good will of the teacher's role disguise the pivotal role of the school in the formation of desire and dependence. Pasolini believed that the school infiltrated, in vampirical fashion, the inner world of the child by its "caricatural doubles of some primary authenticities" (quoted passages in Allen 1982, 31), dramatic language reminding me of the violence of the school (Block 1997; Pinar et al. 1995, 518), now not only psychological but physical (Webber 2003; AP 2008). For Pasolini, corporeality constitutes the initial and imprinting instance of subjectivity; "branded" by a "sedimented pile" of "marks" and "traces" that comprise the subject's semiotic history, the body constitutes an "archive" that informs—indeed, overdetermines— human action (Viano 1993, 38; Bruno 1994, 99).

Despite the social role performed by the school, the idealistic aspiration of the teacher was very strong in Pasolini; it was, perhaps, "the sublimated form of a homoerotic drive" (Sicioliano 1982, 74–75). By all reports, he was a most "excellent pedagogist" (Allen 1982, 35). The erotic animated the curriculum: "Pasolini, being an excellent teacher, knew all the same that he had to change the cultural and social canons in order to be at (relative) peace with himself, and to be able to forgive himself his pedagogic love-violence," Zanzotto comments (quoted in Sicioliano 1982, 104). Self-shattering accompanied public pedagogy. In post–World War II Italy (as in the early twenty-first century United States), a commitment to the truth required an inconsumable curriculum (Rohdie 1995, 197; Pinar 2001, 24).

As the War ended, Pasolini began to read political theory: Marx and Engels and, crucially, Gramsci. Noting that he found Marx "distant," Pasolini remarked that "Gramsci's ideas coincided with mine; they won me over immediately, and he had a fundamental role in my formation" (quoted in Greene 1990, 12; Mariniello 1994, 107). Viano (1993, 14) suggests it was Marx's inability to understand sexuality that led Pasolini to emphasize subjectivity as a primary terrain of political struggle. Despite this reservation about Marx, Pasolini joined the Communist Party in a region so conservative and Catholic that, it was said, "only the radishes were red" (quoted in Greene 1990, 221). For Pasolini, a key aspect of Gramsci's political theory was its central concern for the subaltern classes, whose cultural identity was being effaced by post–World War II bourgeoisification (Ryan-Scheutz 2007, 4). Pasolini's first films—his "national-popular Gramscian" phase (Rohdie 1995, 121—were made in the slums of Rome, the place structuring his cinematic vision (Rhodes 2007).[26]

Pasolini's activism was the target of the first and, possibly, the most traumatic of the many "scandals" he was fated to suffer, his expulsion from the Communist Party and dismissal as a teacher in 1949 (noted earlier). We have some sense of the situation when we read a March 1949 letter Pasolini wrote to a close friend, Silvana Mauri.[27] In this letter, Pasolini reports that the "priests of the area slander me from the altars." Despite this threat, he continued his political work, "for me believing in Communism is a great thing." At one point, an important prelate warned had him that he would be ruined if he did not stop his political activities. This warning came true in the fall of 1949. During a local festival in the countryside on September 30, Pasolini disappeared into the bushes with several young men. On October 22, he was publicly accused of "corrupting minors and obscene acts in public" (quoted passages in Greene 1990, 13).

In recounting the incident, his cousin Nico Naldini insists that only "a masturbation" took place. This not-exactly-uncommon act led first to an anonymous letter and then to a police report that Pasolini's political enemies were quick to inflate into legal charges. Although acquitted of the corruption charge, Pasolini was convicted of "obscene acts." Two years later, the appeals court reversed the conviction for insufficient evidence, but by then the damage had been done. The Communist paper *l'Unità* stated,

> The facts which have provoked a serious disciplinary measure against the poet Pasolini give us the opportunity to once again denounce the deleterious influence of certain ideological and philosophical currents [represented] by Gide, Sartre, and other decadent poets and men of letters who try to seem progressive but who, in reality, take on the most harmful aspects of bourgeois degeneration (quoted by Greene 1990, 13).

Incidentally, Sartre had been branded "a typing hyena" by Stalin's Soviet Union (quoted in Schwartz 1992, 223), a catty comment echoed (strangely enough) by the distinguished U.S. political theorist Jean Elshtain (2002, 281, n. 9).

Devastated by this political excommunication, Pasolini responded with a moving letter to Ferdinando Mautino, author of the expulsion decree. After reminding Mautino that the scandal had been provoked by the right-wing, Pasolini wrote of his suffering and his continuing political faith:

> Yesterday morning my mother almost went crazy, my father is in an indescribable state—I heard them crying and moaning all night long. I'm without work, that is, reduced to begging. Simply because *I am a Communist*. I am astonished by your inhumanity. You must understand that any talk of ideological deviation is idiotic. In spite of you, I remain and shall remain a Communist, in the most authentic meaning of word. For this I have betrayed my class and what you people call my bourgeois education; now those betrayed have revenged themselves in the most ruthless and frightful way. And I remain alone with the mortal grief of my father and mother (quoted in Greene 1990, 14).

There was no sympathy from the self-righteous homophobic Communists.[28] In fact, Mautino did not bother to even reply to the letter. However, he did keep it in his possession for 28 years, releasing the letter to the press after Pasolini death (Schwartz 1992).

The cruelty of the Communists made him despair; he wrote to a friend, "My future is not even black; it does not exist" (quoted in Greene 1990, 14). He continued to write but without any means of support. Unwilling to be supported by his alcoholic father, Pasolini made what would prove to be a momentous decision: He would move to Rome. Abandoning the father, he and his mother left Casarsa for the home of one of his uncles in Rome. Some 20 years later he would remember:

> With the end of the war began the most tragic period of my life ... my brother's death and my mother's superhuman grief; my father's

return from prison—an ill veteran, poisoned by the defeat of Fascism ...
destroyed, ferocious, a powerless tyrant, crazed by bad wine, more and
more in love with my mother who had never loved him very much and
who was now wrapped up in her own grief. And to all this was added the
problem of my life and flesh. As in a novel, in the winter of '49, I fled
with my mother to Rome (quoted in Greene 1990, 14).

Nico Naldini (1994, 21) remembers another reason for the move to Rome:
"More than once I saw Pier Paolo risk lynching, and indeed it was this risk
that precipitated his move to Rome." Though I would reserve the use of
that term to events in the United States (Pinar 2001), evidently the threat to
Pasolini's life was real.

Rome

The ravishment of Rome in early summer!

James Merrill (1993, 9)

The Rome Pasolini encountered was a city recovering from war: poor and
hungry. Life did not become easier, not right away, anyway. Pasolini recalled:
"For two years I was a desperate person out of work, like those who wind up
killing themselves" (quoted in Greene 1990, 15). He did some proofreading,
listed himself as an "extra" at local film studios, sold books from his library.
His father's arrival intensified the difficulty: "My father is always there, alone
in the poor little kitchen, elbows on the table, face in his hands, immobile,
mean, grieving; he fills up the space of the tiny room with the huge size
of dead bodies" (quoted in Greene 1990, 15). Despite this physical and
psychological stress, he continued to write: journalism, poetry, and fiction.
In 1953, Pasolini enjoyed a definite change of fortunes: His *Poesia dialettale
del Novecento* was well received, and a second anthology appeared two years
later. In 1953, he published a volume of verse in Friulian and a short story—
"Ragazzi di vita"—that would become a chapter in his first novel.

   He became close to established writers, including Alberto Moravia and
Attilio Bertolucci. For a time, the Bertolucci and the Pasolini families lived in
the same apartment building. Bernardo Bertolucci remembered his friendship
with Pasolini:

   I wrote poems and I was used to a kind of ritual: as soon as I finished
   writing them, I ran from the fifth floor where we lived to the second
   floor where Pier Paolo lived. I rang his door and if Pier Paolo was home,
   I immediately had him read them. In a certain way I even saw Pier Paolo
   as a paternal figure. I tended to absorb his way of seeing reality and even
   a little of his style. There are certain poems of mine that I believe I never
   published because they were very Pasolinian, really written in Pasolini's
   manner (quoted in Greene 1990, 16).

What was the Pasolinian manner? Pasolini was drawn to the world of "the other," first Friulian peasants and, once in Rome, to the inhabitants of the slums. "The direct experience of the problems of others," he would write later, "radically transformed my own problems: for this reason I feel that at the root of the communism of a bourgeois there is always an ethical, in some sense, an evangelical, impulse" (quoted in Greene 1990, 12). Like Jane Addams and Laura Bragg, Pasolini secularized his spirituality through political commitment and public service. Others have observed that Pasolini's poetry and politics were rooted in spiritual passion: "Critics have been obsessed with his Marxism or presumed Freudianism, ignoring his criticism of both, and forgetting that his deepest passions were spiritual" (Snyder 1980, 10). As Pasolini himself observed: "I followed the only two paths that could take me to anti-Fascism: that of hermeticism and decadentism, that is, essentially [the path] of good taste and, secondly, the path which led me into contact with the humble and Christian way of life of the peasants in my mother's region, a way of life expressing a mentality totally different from the style of Fascism" (quoted in Greene 1990, 10). Recall that it had been the humility of the early Christians that enabled Jane Addams to express her spirituality socially.

Pasolini's poetic style and images from this early period are expressed in a poem he wrote much later, entitled "But It Was A Naked And Swarming Italy." In that poem, he tells us about teaching in a private school for $27 a month, suffering and working "voraciously," living with his parents in a house without a roof, next to a jail, "But it was Italy, naked and swarming Italy,/with its boys, its women,/…—and as for me, my poetry-dreams intact" (Pasolini 1986, 111). Expressed sexually and politically and focused on the earth and its landscapes, spirituality testifies to Pasolini's worldliness. Living among the ruins of Rome, his sense of historicity was acute; everyday reality was a palimpsest. Pasolini would later analyze his attraction to the world of the Friulian peasants, and especially to their dialect; he insisted that the nature of his attraction was that to past civilizations. This attraction– it was political, sexual, familial, spiritual—would become, in later years, an intense longing, the other psychic side of the pain he experienced living through the crisis of his own civilization (Greene 1990, 9; Duncan 2006, 92-94, 98).

True, the sheer "otherness" of the Friulians drew him—"their psychology, their education, their mentality, their soul, their sexuality were all different" (quoted in Greene 1990, 11)—and this otherness, as Greene (1990, 11) notes, "heightened his class consciousness, his acute awareness of his own bourgeois core. Gradually the use of dialect became less an aesthetic device and more a political and social one." Nathaniel Rich (2007, 78) notes that "Pasolini's Friulian is purposefully blunt, truncated, and cacophonous." Why? "In his expression of sacred and romantic themes through a crude vernacular," (Rich 2007, 78) concludes, "Pasolini had discovered a successful formula for provocation." It was the sacred and sexual "otherness" of the "ragazzi," those who lived in the *borgate* or "desolate wastelands" (Greene

1990, 17), that drew him to those who would provide him with a "crude vernacular" for "sacred" and "romantic" themes.

The slums were populated by the poorer-than-poor, by the sub-proletariat, mostly southerners who had migrated north to Rome in search of work. Pasolini had lived in these areas. It was there he encountered the boys to whom he was sexually, politically, and aesthetically drawn. Though he would be criticized in later years for sexually soliciting young men of this underclass, it is clear to me his relation to them was not, at least not simply or solely, exploitative. Pasolini would become friends with more than a few of the young men he met there; two in particular became closely associated with his cinema. Sergio Citti (who later became a director in his own right) often collaborated with him behind the camera. A 15-year-old Calabrian from a Roman slum and "love of his life" (Ahern 1983/1984, 117), Ninetto Davoli acted in many of Pasolini's films. Sergio's brother Franco Citti also became one of Pasolini's favorite actors (Greene 1990).

Pasolini's first novels (*Ragazzi di vita*, 1955) and (*Una vita violenta*, 1959), were set in the *borgate*—a world that, before then, had remained invisible to most Romans. These novels and a major collection of poetry (*Le Ceneri di Gramsci*, 1957) made Pasolini famous. Just as in Casarsa years earlier, with visibility came scandal. The appearance of *Ragazzi di vita* brought legal charges; the novel was alleged to be an "obscene publication." Later, the charges were dropped, but this event foreshadowed the intense controversy and legal challenges Pasolini's work would encounter over the coming years. Pasolini would be the object of constant attacks in the right-wing press. Nine of his films were censored. Pasolini himself was hauled into court 33 times to face lurid charges, among them public brawling, corrupting minors, armed robbery, and contempt for the state religion (by virtue of making of *La ricotta*). Found guilty of this last charge, he was sentenced to four months in jail, but the conviction was later overturned (Lawton 2005a, ix; Greene 1990).

At the core of this persecution was hatred of his homosexuality. "With *very* few exceptions," Maurizio Viano (1993, xiii) asserts, even critics (except gay critics: Viano 1993, 14) have been "reticent" about Pasolini's homosexuality. As early as 1950 (in a letter to Silvana Mauri), Pasolini discerned the struggle (internally and in public) homosexuality would entail:

> My future life will certainly not be that of a university professor: by now I have the mark of Rimbaud on me, or Campana,[29] or even a Wilde, whether I like it or not, whether others accept it or not. It is something uncomfortable, irritating, and inadmissible, but that's how it is, and I, like you, do not give up (quoted in Sicioliano 1982, 159).

In this statement, Sicioliano (1982, 159) suggests, we do not read a "Catholic resignation" but, instead, a "Pauline fury," a rage in the tradition of "decadent revolt." Viano (1993, 2) discerns a more complex "authorial intertext," informed primarily (but not only: Viano 1993, 178) by homosexuality, humanism, Catholicism, Marxism, and psychoanalysis.

Pasolini foresees his destiny clearly, Greene believes, a destiny of provocation and tragedy. In oedipal terms, she speculates, the son has assumed responsibility for his transgressions, and in accepting his guilt, he accepts the moral responsibility of a person in the world. Consequently, Sicioliano (1982, 159) suggests, Pasolini can "permit himself everything, from the urinal along the Tiber to the film extra's union card." In accepting one's guilt, in pledging allegiance to the mutilated "other," one is granted the license for pleasure. These are among the psychodynamics of worldliness.

Why is Pasolini's lifelong provocation, to use Scioliano's phrase, a "decadent revolt"? Decadence communicates rejection of the bourgeois life of respectability, life characterized by the mistaking of fastidiousness and self-righteousness for morality. In living decadently and in a public way, Pasolini could render "performative" not only this rejection but his revolutionary search for new life, new patterns of living, patterns woven by desire and courage. Pasolini's worldliness was profoundly political as well as esthetic and sexual.

Though accurate, such a formula is not sufficiently nuanced to capture Pasolini's complicated, ambivalent, engaged struggle with himself and the world. We see something of this complexity in his thoughts on his homosexuality, which he also expressed in a 1950 letter to Silvana Mauri:

> I have never accepted my sin, I have never made a truce with my nature and I am not even used to it. I was born to be calm, balanced, and natural: my homosexuality was something extra, it was outside, it had nothing to do with me. I always saw it beside me like an enemy; I never felt it within me (quoted in Greene 1990, 16).

This frank acknowledgement would bring criticism from gay liberationists years later, but I admire his candor, his commitment to truth. It acknowledges that one's most intimate and life-structuring desire is also a form of Otherness (Alford 2002, 68).

This letter did not express his final or only view of the matter. Pasolini's feelings changed, Greene (1990) tells us, sometimes it would seem from day to day, from letter to letter. As the hardships and deprivations of those first years in Rome came to a close, Pasolini wrote Mauri in 1952 of his gratitude to "stupendous, miserable" (Jewell 1992, 97) Rome and to the almost Nietzschean life it made possible: "Here [in Rome] I am living a life that is all muscles ... here none of the Christian attitudes—forgiveness, humility, etc.—are known, and egotism takes legitimate, virile forms" (quoted in Greene 1990, 17). Though now free to follow his desire, this was no life of ease: "But in me, the difficulty of loving has made the need for loving an obsession" (quoted in Greene 1990, 16).

Early Films

> Still surviving, in a long extension
> of unexhausted, inexhaustible passion
> that almost has its roots in another time.
>
> Pier Paolo Pasolini (quoted in Ryan-Scheutz 2007, 29)

Pasolini's success as a novelist and poet brought him invitations to collaborate on films, the making of which he regarded as a poetical labor.[30] He worked first as a screenwriter with a number of respected directors. The best-known film on which he worked as a screenwriter was Frederico Fellini's *The Nights of Cabria* (1956). With a young man he met in the *borgate*—Sergio Citti (who served as his "linguistic consultant")—Pasolini had responsibility for writing "low life" parts of the film (Greene 1990, 18). Pasolini became known as an authority on prostitutes and pimps, above all as a student of their language. It was Fellini who would offer to produce Pasolini's first directed film, *Accattone*, but he backed out on the deal when he saw test footage (Sitney 1994).

Filmmaking was a medium enabling him to work with those young men of the lumpenproletariat to whom he was sexually attracted and about whom he had written in his novels (Schwartz 1992, 334). It was an erotic and, apparently, inebriating, act: "Shooting films is a little bit like a drug for me. It's like being drunk on reality. I like it so much in an erotic, panicked, or ... religious way. When I make a film I am in reality and I make reality" (quoted in Snyder 1980, 29). Confronting reality became carnal: "Cinema permits me to maintain contact with reality—a physical, carnal contact, and even one, I'd say, of a sensual kind" (quoted in Greene 1990, 19). Heat, light, carnality, religiosity: These were among the modalities of reality for Pasolini (Rohdie 1999, 177). "In essence," he remarked in 1962, "cinema is a question of the sun" (quoted in Greene 1990, 21). Filmmaking was a solar event making visible the world others could—would—not see. "So in practice the cinema was an explosion of my love for reality" (quoted in Stack, 1969, p. 29). In his first film, reality was the *borgate*.

Despite his expulsion from the Communist Party, like Sartre Pasolini felt keenly the claim Marxism made upon intellectuals in the postwar period. In an essay written in 1954, he wrote,

> Whether we cannot be, or do not want to be, Communists ... the very fact of having to face this new, implicit, social and moral measure, this new configuration of the past and this new perspective of the future ... works within us. That is, it works within those of us who have remained bourgeois with the violence and the inertia of a psychology which has been historically determined. But, in our view, the situation which confronts us daily seems sufficiently dramatic to produce a new poetry (quoted in Greene 1990, 38).

A "new poetry" is precisely what Pasolini would compose. Recall that Pasolini's Marxism was influenced by Gramsci's concern with the *language* of literary works (Welle 1999, 111; Mariniello 1994, 107, 113). Partly from this concern, Pasolini would construct what Greene (1990) terms a sociolinguistic approach. Anticipating the fascination with cultural politics in North America some 40 years later, Pasolini asserted that political practice in a bourgeois democracy is a broadly cultural, not a narrowly political, task: "The only hope is a cultural one, to be an intellectual" (quoted in Stack 1969, 124).

For Pasolini, then, politics was no insulated domain; its boundaries were porous. Because political, and specifically Marxian, aspiration arises in dissatisfaction with this world and yearning for another, it is not unlike religion (Yack 1986). In a profoundly Catholic nation such as Italy, the impulses of the two were bound to intermingle: "The adoption of Marxist philosophy originally comes from a sentimental and moralistic impetus and is therefore continually permeable to the rising of the religious, and naturally of the catholic, spirit" (Pasolini, quoted in Greene 1990, 36).

Pasolini believed that Catholicism differed from Protestantism in part in its punitiveness. This difference is reflected in the hardness of the Reichian "armor" of the bourgeoisie:

> The petit bourgeoisie, on the other hand, is naturally repressed, like everywhere, but it is basically not a very sincere repression, it isn't very much felt; it's rather superficial. Repression is not so pathological as it is in other bourgeois societies which don't have Catholicism, which is basically not a rigid religion. There hasn't been a Protestant revolution in Italy, in fact in a sense there hasn't been a religious revolution at all: Catholicism has superimposed itself on paganism, particularly among the ordinary people, without changing them in the slightest (quoted in Stack 1969, 67).

This theme of civilizations layered upon each other is repeated in Pasolini's work; he will take as his task the unearthing of those buried and ancient civilizations that the present obliterates, a breaking through the outer shells of culture's repressive armor. Cultural archeology and political activism intertwine in his esthetic and pedagogical project.

In the postwar period of consumer capitalism,[31] the Italian past was being obliterated, Pasolini pointed out. Political and spiritual aspiration was displaced by greed, civilization by barbarism (Rohdie 1995, 89). The authority of the Church was replaced by a reactionary state apparatus. Nowhere was this development more evident to Pasolini than in language, that "skin" of culture where private and public spheres are separated, and culture reconstructed.[32] Pasolini lamented: "In a period of reactionary, centralist State politics, language achieved a maximum of 'fixation' perhaps never before in Italy" (quoted in Greene 1990, 36). In such a situation, innovative forms of political and pedagogical practice are required, ones that stimulate the skin of culture and stimulate new expressions: "The world which was, at first, a pure source of sensations expressed by means of a ratiocinative and precious irrationalism, has now become an object of ideological, if not philosophical, awareness, and, as such, demands stylistic experiments of a radically new type" (quoted in Greene 1990, 37).

Postwar cinematic neorealists had waited patiently for reality to unveil itself, a narrative with its own internal logic.[33] Pasolini insisted on meeting "reality" head-on. He remarked, "I hate naturalness. I reconstruct everything" (quoted in Greene, 1990, p. 41). In Pasolini's world, the banal and the trivial—the raw material of neorealism—are banished. Characters are not gradually established but, instead, captured at moments of crisis when their lives are at stake. In his rejection of neorealism, in his jarring shots as well as in mythic narrative moments, Pasolini shatters the somnolence of daily life in bureaucratic capitalism, where television,[34] movies, and advertising images create the illusion of repetition, security, even while their presence position us as provisional, tentative, minimal (Lasch 1984).

Pasolini's cinematic technique represents not only a political practice; it is also a subjective expression of his worldliness. "[I]t is through technique that Pasolini inserts the subjective voice," Gordon (1996, 206) suggests. "My fetishistic love for the 'things' of the world," Pasolini once explained, "prevents me from considering them natural. It consecrates them or desecrates them, violently, one by one: it does not link them in a correct flow, it does not accept this flow. Rather, it isolates them and idolizes them one by one, more or less intensely" (quoted in Greene 1990, 40). Regarding this tension between passion and rationalism (expressed as political commitment), Greene (1990, 39) comments, "Although I think that the balance between passion and ideology was, indeed, precarious—and the scales were always tipped toward passion—I also believe that much of the special tone of Pasolini's work comes, precisely, from this tension." It derived, one might say, from a state of "creative tensionality," recalling a key curriculum concept devised by Aoki (Pinar 2007a, 18) and practiced to perfection by Hongyu Wang (2004).

Subjective expressions of passion were simultaneously political, autobiographical, and esthetic: Each time Pasolini included Ninetto Davoli in one of his films, the audience knew exactly who this young man was and what he represented. In one film (*The Gospel According to St. Matthew*), Pasolini employed his mother, Susanna, as Mary the mother of God, an immodest move one might observe but one that signed his film autobiographically. These "mascot-faces," to borrow a term proposed by Jean Sémoulé (quoted in Greene 1990, 42), functioned as an artistic signature, registering the autobiographical presence of the author within the film. Pasolini's populist politics were unacceptable to conservative critics; they were regarded as horrifying confessions of sexual compulsion rather than as heroic gestures of political commitment (Greene 1990).

Esthetic Technique

Pasolini employed a number of stylistic innovations in the service of both esthetic and political aspirations. He rejected the neorealist preference for the linear unfolding of narrative. He had little patience for the artistic autonomy of the actor, but given his insistence on extensive editing, patience would not have mattered much. As he himself observed, "Besides, I attach such importance to editing that nothing much remains of a 'personal acting style'" (quoted in Greene 1990, 42). Pasolini viewed cinematic reality *as* reality, so the use of professional actors was in fact unnecessary. Boys from the *borgate* were just right.[35]

Pasolini employed music deliberately and effectively (Borgna 2007, 140 ff.). As Greene (1990) explains, Pasolini applied music contrapuntally or, to use his adverb, "vertically" to transform the images on the screen. This technique Pasolini termed "contamination" (see note 32), and its point was to create contrast. For example, in *Accattone*, Pasolini used the music of Bach contrapuntally; it functions to mythologize the meaningless brutality of the *borgate* (Rohdie 1995, 31; Ryan-Scheutz 2007, 79; Viano 1993, 197). Prehistoric in the Marxian sense, subproletarian culture could thus achieve the status of myth or epic: "The sub-proletariat is only apparently contemporary with our history; the characteristics of the sub-proletariat are prehistoric, directly pre-Christian; the moral world of a sub-proletarian has no awareness of Christianity" (Pasolini, quoted in Rohdie 1995, 49). A Marxist and a Communist, Pasolini was also a mythologist: "My vision of the world is essentially an epic-religious sort. Misery is always—because of its deepest nature—epic" (quoted in Greene 1990, 43). It was for political, indeed, Marxian reasons that Pasolini would place, as one interviewer explained, "increasing stress on the need to restore an epic and mythological dimension to life, a sense of awe and reverence to the world: a sense which, he believes, the peasantry still sustain, though the bourgeoisie has done all in its power to destroy it" (Stack 1969, 9). This may be what Deleuze means when he says that the most difficult thing to do is to believe in the world. Worldliness signifies its accomplishment.

Though Pasolini's films conveyed thematic material sometimes quite didactically (Viano 1993, 100), these works of arts functioned more indirectly, more stylistically one might say. McLuhan's notion of the "medium is the message" (an idea to be devised later in the decade, across the Atlantic in Toronto) and John Ciardi's elaboration of "how a poem means" are evident in Pasolini's conviction that style teaches. The real "message" of *Accattone*, he insisted, lay in its style, specifically in the sacred quality of this film that conveys life in the *borgate*. The narrative line does not convey this spiritual quality, which rests

> less in the character's overwhelming need for personal salvation (from pimp to thief!), or in the external fatality that determines and concludes

everything … than in the way of "seeing the world": in the technical sacredness of seeing it. Nothing is more sacred, technically, than a slow panorama. Sacredness, front view (*frontalita*). And thus religion (quoted in Greene 1990, 44).

Greene (1990, 44) notes: "If the film's 'technical sacredness' is created by prolonged frontal shots and slow panorama, it is further underscored by a deliberate avoidance of motion. A pervasive sense of immobility gives a hieratic and ritualistic cast to Pasolini's films even as it, too, works against the illusion of naturalism." Like Bach's *St. Matthew's Passion*, it is the contrapuntal juxtaposition of immobility and action that consecrates the mundane.

Pasolini drew upon his extensive knowledge of European and, especially, Italian painting. Allusions to specific works as well as plays on whole schools of painting operate throughout his films. Pasolini commented, "At least for an Italian like me painting has had an enormous importance in these two thousand years, indeed it is the major element in the Christological tradition" (quoted in Stack 1969, 91). Certainly through layering works of art upon each other, so that when (especially an Italian) viewer saw a specific shot, centuries of Italian painting reverberated in that moment. Through this means, Pasolini reminded his modern audience of the ancient civilizations underneath their feet, disguised by their commodification as tourist sites.[36]

Pasolini performed this thematic preoccupation stylistically. "By fixing and isolating segments of what is visible," Greene (1990, 45) notes, "Pasolini creates the sense that what we see is merely one part of reality, and that the truly essential—and sacred—remains unseen." The emphasis here is less on reminders that consumer capitalism erases the localisms of earlier social formations. Instead, Pasolini teaches his audience that the appearance of a smooth social surface is just that, an appearance. What we see in everyday life occludes a vast universe operating just underneath what we know as everyday reality. How does Pasolini achieve this insight stylistically? Greene (1990, 47) explains: "Through frontal shots and obsessive close-ups Pasolini separates his characters from the known world even as he suggests the (invisible) presence of spiritual realities, of what Deleuze calls a 'radical Elsewhere.'" This idea is not unlike Musil's notion of "truth" residing outside the everyday, in *Young Torless* (Musil 1955 [1905]; Pinar 2006c) in an attic room.

How does Pasolini work to break our identification with the everyday? *Accattone* begins with a "disconcerting series of close-ups" (Greene 1990, 49), that "trademark of his cinematographic gaze" (Schwenk 2005, 42). This deliberately disorienting strategy is evident in the eroticization of certain characters. For example, although the hero of *Accattone* is supposedly in love with Stella, the camera caresses not Stella, the object of *his* desire, but Accattone himself. Some have suggested that this strategy is an indication of a "homosexual sensibility," a disposition toward subtext (a kind of "cruising") created by an oppressive social field (Boone 1993, 28).

La ricotta (1962), Pasolini's second film, is judged by some critics to be one of the "high points" of Pasolini's cinema (Greene 1990, 60; Viano 1993, 100). As noted, the film provoked a trial in which Pasolini was given a four-month suspended prison sentence. "I still can't say exactly why they tried me at all," he observed years later, "but it was a terrible period for me. I was slandered week after week, and for two or three years I lived under a kind of unimaginable persecution" (quoted in Greene 1990, 61). Even under the archaic clerical laws then in force in Catholic Italy (and Fascists still serving as magistrates: Chiesi and Mancini 2007, 164), Pasolini's sentence was extreme. Viewers misunderstood *La ricotta*; the film does not desacralize religion (Viano 1993, 104). Rather, the film portrays the degraded position to which religion had been relegated in postwar, capitalistic Italy (Greene 1990).

The fate of religion in neocapitalism underscores the political problem of the artist. In *La ricotta*, Pasolini asks how an artist can create authentic culture in a consumer society that renders everything profane, a grotesque society in which, as Luigi Faccini observed, "religious values can be recuperated only through cultural images" (quoted in Greene 1990, 65). This political, artistic, and cultural question will remain with Pasolini for the rest of his life. Indeed, his final film—*Salò*—may be regarded as his most desperate attempt to avoid "consumption" (Greene 1994; Pinar 2001, 24). In *La ricotta*, Pasolini confronts desacralization by shocking his viewers. Actors in the film could not be further removed from the biblical characters they are asked to represent. The vulgarity of Christ, for example, is matched only by the unpleasant egocentricity of Mary Magdalene, who is played, in still another layer of self-conscious autobiographical irony, by a close friend of Pasolini's, the actress-singer Laura Betti[37] (Greene 1990).

In the film-within-the-film, Pasolini mocked what he called the "worst" side of his own art. Through exaggeration, he parodied his "mannerist"[38] inclination for startling contrasts and hieratic poses, for cultural echoes and layers of pastiche, for a deeply estheticized and stylized reconstruction of reality. The maker of the "artificial" film, played by Orson Welles, resembles Pasolini.[39] He, too, is a solitary intellectual estranged from the very people with whom he identifies and who need him most (Greene 1990). This distance from the masses may be inevitable for one who confronts the presentism of consumer capitalism by reminding audiences of the past. The filmmaker—also an accomplished poet—announces himself: "I am a force of the Past./ Tradition is my only love./...I roam in search/ of brothers that are no more" (quoted in Greene 1990, 64).

The problem of representation was not only political for Pasolini, it was stylistic as well. At this stage in his work, he wrestled over the issue, thinking that it might be possible to re-enter the past, to represent it as it was, and in so doing, remind us of what we are not but can no longer be. Pasolini regarded the issue of representation as so crucial that he found it "painful" (Greene 1990, 65). And no subject matter made these issues more sharp, more momentous, than biblical material, and in particular, the personage of Jesus. Pasolini became very interested in the problem—at once stylistic, political, religious—of representing Jesus "directly," *not* through layers of cultural appropriation. He was interested in moving past "cultural images" in order to portray the "reality" of Christ directly.[40] What Pasolini wanted was to evoke "an idea of Christ/which precedes every style, every twist of history,/... I want this Christ to appear as did Christ in reality" (quoted in Greene 1990, 66). Pasolini insisted that representation was "hypocrisy" (Greene 1990, 67). But even in what may be his most conventionally political film (*La rabbia*, 1963), Pasolini was hardly ready to renounce his interest in stylistic experimentation.

La rabbia is "one of Pasolini's highest achievements," Viano (1993, 114) asserts, a "stunningly beautiful and moving visual poem." The commentary in *La rabbia* exhorts us not to close our eyes to the problem of the so-called Third World—the "emergence of people of color"—and its suffering masses. "A new problem is exploding in the world," says the narrator, "it is called: color. We must accept infinite stretches of real lives which ask, with a ferocious innocence, to enter our world." The commentary tells us that "Armstrong triumphed over Marx" (quoted passages in Greene 1990, 68), jazz over armed struggle. The juxtaposition of nuclear explosions and stills of Marilyn Monroe, however, underscore the vulnerability of beauty (Ryan-Scheutz 2007, 204). The film's "non-narrative nature" enabled Pasolini to convey in images "meaning which exceeds verbal and logical discourse" (Viano 1993, 115).[41]

Another "profoundly subversive" (Restivo 2002, 73) film appeared in 1964, this one focused on sexuality. In *Comizi d'amore* (*An Inquiry into Sexuality*), Pasolini uses *cinéma vérité* to explore Italian attitudes toward sex. Revealing a fascination with faces, Pasolini interviewed Italians—on the beach, in the street—creating an "indirect" national-sexual scene. Alberto Moravia (Pasolini's friend and a "champion of rationalism and an advocate of libertarian stands in sexual matters" [Viano 1993, 122]) and Cesare Musatti (an orthodox Freudian analyst and the so-called "father of Italian psychoanalysis" [Viano 1993, 122]) appear with Pasolini, punctuating the interviews with commentary.[42] From the film's beginning, when Sicilian children are asked how babies are born, viewers are "forced to see how the Symbolic Order is an arbitrary covering-over of some traumatic Real—of the body, of sexuation, of history" (Restivo 2002, 78).

Pasolini speaks through others, indirectly. The notion of the "indirect"— discourse, subjectivity—becomes key. As the adjective itself implies, he does not intend it as merely a reflection (or representation) of something else, as, for instance, Italian faces as somehow substitutes for "pure" sex. For Pasolini the face *is* sexual, as is speech. And sex is not, as in the Christian dualism, "physical" while the soul resides elsewhere. As for Robert Musil, for Pasolini sex is soulful; it is poetical. He writes:

> [T]hings in themselves are profoundly poetic: a tree photographed is poetic, a human face photographed is poetic because physicity is poetic

in itself, because it is an apparition, because it is full of mystery, because it is full of ambiguity, because it is full of polyvalent meaning, because even a tree is a sign of a linguistic system. But who talks through a tree? God, or reality itself? (quoted in Snyder 1980, 28).

In *Comizi d'amori*, people are sometimes defensive and embarrassed about sex. In the face of their apparent (pretended?) indifference and complacency, even during expressions of homophobia, Pasolini remains imperturbable, encouraging, the curious interviewer. Greene (1990, 69) characterizes the film as "a portrait of prejudice and conformism." In 1982, Michel Foucault suggested that "what is running through the film is not, I think, an obsession with sex, but a kind of historical apprehension, a premonitory and confused hesitation in the face of a new regime that was taking place then in Italy, namely the regime of tolerance" (quoted in Greene 1990, 73). For this regime, Pasolini felt only contempt.

Semiotics

> Pasolini's semiology was really ahead of its time … it has important points of contact with contemporary poststructuralist theory.
>
> Patrick Rumble and Bart Testa (1994a, 88)

Pasolini's first major essay on film was delivered at the 1965 Pesaro Film Festival. Other participants included several of the most influential theorists of the 1960s: Umberto Eco, Galvano Della Volpe, and Christian Metz. The "impassioned" and "intensely personal" character of Pasolini's essays (Greene 1990, 93) left him vulnerable to accusations of being "unscientific," of approaching these issues as a "poet." It took two decades for it to become clear that the strength of these essays lay precisely in Pasolini's poetic preferences, his emphasis on the subjective, his refusal to separate linguistics from broader domains of human life and thought, preferences that would later characterize the cultural disciplines in the 1980s and 1990s (Greene 1990).

Pasolini's writings on film are less political than his literary theory of the preceding decade. One important essay, entitled "Technical Confessions," does focus on an ideological question that had preoccupied Pasolini throughout the 1950s: How, or in what ways, can intellectuals and artists play a social role? It is a question that has plagued many U.S. scholars since 1968. In "Technical Confessions" Pasolini has lost almost all faith in the concept of the intellectual's "mandate," a concept common to the preceding decade. As the essay proceeds, it becomes clear that Pasolini insists that, far from changing society, writers and filmmakers can do little more—and even this "little" is problematical—than offer creative resistance to triumph of technological neocapitalism (Greene 1990). It a conclusion I reached as well (recall Note 6, Chapter 1).

Undoubtedly the best-known figure among the militants, Jean-Luc Godard denounced so-called realistic films (especially U.S. productions) as allies of capitalism insofar as they created an illusion of reality that served to mask the real facts of existence—ideological and social in nature—from the viewer. (Has Hollywood changed?) Unlike Godard and other militant French theorists, Pasolini went beyond this overly simple equation between capitalism and realism. Pasolini did not view capitalism as a monolithic, unchanging entity. He distinguished between nineteenth-century "paternalistic" capitalism and contemporary "neo-capitalism." The latter has enabled new forms of expression, such as the "new novel": that of Robbe-Grillet, for instance. For Pasolini, the absence of plot and characters in these novels, their apparently realistic descriptions that sometimes have no obvious significance or function, reflect a world from which human elements, coherence, and meaning have disappeared: the world of contemporary capitalism (Greene 1990). Foucault's early attack on the "subject" could be viewed likewise (Paras 2006).

On this point, Pasolini's view paralleled that of Georg Lukács, who felt that modernism itself—a modernism evident, for example, in Samuel Beckett's plotless, semi-characterless novels (Doll 1988)—reflected the alienation associated with modern capitalism. In contrast to Lukács, Pasolini did not criticize Beckett or the "new" novelists specifically, nor did he come to the same conclusion (i.e., that one must return to the past, to the tradition of Mann rather than of Kafka and Beckett). Pasolini declared:

> The disappearance of characters [is] similar to the disappearance of individuals in monopolistic capitalistic societies. [The task is] to make such situations into the very object of the narrative. I must say that ideological irony—which takes as its subject the very problem of the novel or film—seems extremely fertile to me (quoted in Greene 1990, 95).

Pasolini is suggesting that the only way an artist can contest capitalistic society and create "non-bourgeois" films or novels is to take as the subject of a work the creation of the work itself.

In one of his most famous essays, "*Il cinema di poesia*," he would restate this strategy. That essay concludes with the speculation that his meta-cinematic idea of a "cinema of poetry" may well be part of a "possible revolution" in bourgeois culture. This "internal" revolution is precipitated by a "neocapitalism that questions and modifies its own structure and, in this case, restores to poets a late humanistic function: the myth and technical awareness of form" (quoted in Greene 1990, 95). Rooted in his lifelong interest in symbolist poetry, Pasolini is suggesting that though poets may not be able to intervene directly in cultural and political life, they can teach the awareness of form. Such awareness might allow us better to understand (and thereby alter) the forms of political and cultural life, perhaps even the structure of capitalism itself (Greene 1990).

Anticipating criticism of these views, Pasolini did not disagree with more traditional Marxist critics who viewed the late nineteenth-century preoccupation with poetic style and language as bourgeois. He knew he was on slippery ground when he created the concept of meta-cinema, a cinema devoid of traditional characters and stylistically self-conscious, and claimed a capability of ideological impact. He tried to move to a firmer footing by differentiating film from literature. Recall that Pasolini had departed literature for film. He argued: "The fact that cinema can resemble a narrative, but a narrative which is above all musical, might demonstrate that cinema possesses a certain irrational quality—archaic and fantastic—when compared to literature" (quoted in Greene 1990, 97). More ambitiously, he continued: "Cinema is a language. Cinema *reproduces* reality: image and sound! In reproducing reality, what does it do? Cinema expresses reality with reality" (Pasolini 2005 [1972], 133; quoted in Greene 1990, 98–99). Film versions of novels of interiority—I think of *Mrs. Dalloway*—suggest that Pasolini's exuberance has here led to exaggeration.

In language remarkably similar to the poststructuralist theory to become influential some two decades later (Pinar et al. 1995, 450–514), Pasolini wrote: "The written language of reality will make us know first of all what the language of reality is; and it will wind up modifying our way of thinking about it—transforming at least our physical relations with reality into cultural ones" (quoted in Greene 1990, 100). On another occasion, Pasolini puts the matter this way: "[C]inema is an infinitely long take ... the ideal, virtual and infinite reproduction by means of an invisible machine that faithfully reproduces all a man's gestures, acts, words, from his birth to his death" (quoted in Ward 1994, 129). Most simply, he declared that the "real structure of all work is its linguistic structure" (quoted in Schwartz 1992, 646).

As we become conscious of our "gestures, acts, words" through this cinematic "writing" or "representation," presumably we will be more able to recognize the ways in which our lives are immersed in *pragma*.[43] Pasolini asserted:

> [L]ife is clearly moving away from classical humanistic ideals and is becoming lost in *pragma*. Film (along with other audiovisual techniques) *seems to be the written language of this pragma*. But this may also be its salvation, precisely because *it expresses it*—and it expresses it from within: producing itself from it and reproducing it (quoted in Greene 1990, 100).

Recalling Sartre's idea that only at the moment of death can one judge the meaning of a life, as well as Cocteau's epithet that cinema captures "death at work," Pasolini contrasted the infinite long-take (or the so-called plenitude of the real) inherent in cinema and those limitations (culminating in death) imposed by montage in individual films. He stated, "It is therefore absolutely essential to die because, *as long as we are alive*, we lack meaning and the language of our life ... remains untranslatable—a chaos of possibilities, a quest for relations and meanings. *Death achieves a dazzling montage of our life. Thanks to death alone our life serves to express us*" (quoted in Greene 1990, 100–101).

This view of cinema as the written language of reality, focused by death, derived from Pasolini's "hallucinatory, childlike, and pragmatic love of reality. A religious love in that it somehow merged, by analogy, with an immense sexual fetishism" (quoted in Greene 1990, 101). The very violence of this "hallucinatory" love, this "fetishism," rendered its failure even more dramatic. That is, the more Pasolini fixed people and places with his camera as if seeking to identify or even to become one with them, the less his filmic world—where everything was, as he said, "stopped and isolated in the flux of time"—was recognizable to the masses (Greene 1990). The more political he became, the less political was the effect.

Pasolini's appreciation that the world can be deciphered like a text is echoed, Greene points out, in Roland Barthes' likening of structuralism's pursuit of meaning with the Greek sense that meanings are inherent in the natural world. For Barthes, as for Pasolini, structuralism did not exclude "a semiology of reality." "According to Hegel," Barthes writes, "the ancient Greeks were astonished by what was natural in nature; they constantly listened to it, interrogated the meaning of streams, mountains, forests, storms. He, too, listens to the natural in culture" (quoted in Greene 1990, 102, n. 20). Listening to the natural world typifies indigenous poetics and autobiography as well (Astrov 1962 [1946]; Krupat 1994).

Some critics decoded this equation of the natural with the cultural as only a homosexual adoration of the young male body, a view other critics have complicated (Duncan 2006, 87; Boone 1993, 28, 32 n. 10). Others—such as Emilio Garroni, a professor of esthetics at the University of Rome—took Pasolini to be equating reality with the surface of the body, a version of behaviorism. Though Pasolini's theorization of "reality" did privilege physical presence, Greene notes, nonetheless his postulation of a language of behavior and oral-written language underlined social and cultural elements. Pasolini foreshadowed poststructuralism (Bruno 1994, 88, 91, 95), a prescience made clear in an essay entitled "*I segni viventi e i poeti morti*," where he equates physical presence with "pure" language. He asks,

> While a poplar speaks a pure language, do I, Pier Paolo Pasolini ... speak a pure language? Obviously not. This pure language is contaminated above all by the first social contract, that is, by language, first in its spoken and then in its written form; and then by all the infinite nonsign languages which I experience as a result of my birth, my economic station, my education—by society and the historical moment in which I live (quoted in Greene 1990, 104–105, n. 27).

During the 1960s, Pasolini was alone in these views. Poststructuralism was yet to reach the center-stage of Theory. Critics and theoreticians (even the great Umberto Eco) mistook Pasolini's views as a primitive "empiricism," what we might today dismiss as positivism. Greene (1990) observes that, like his films, Pasolini's theories were concerned less with the surface of representation than with those mythic layers that underpin our inner selves, including our most rational thoughts and schemes. The only writer to appreciate Pasolini's theories early on was Gilles Deleuze. Greene (1990, 107) characterizes Deleuze as "another great iconoclast in revolt against the rationalist tradition of the Enlightenment." For Deleuze, the world revealed is not, or not necessarily, or not at first, a conceptual one. To use Pasolini's terms, it is a world of "physical presence," a pregrammatical and preverbal world where the "not-said" may be more important than the said, a world where bodies themselves "speak." Such cinema brings the world back, Deleuze believed, by "returning words to the body, to flesh" (quoted in Greene 1990, 109). For Deleuze, cinema, like thought itself, *precedes* language. This sounds to me like Musil, for whom reality and truth resided "elsewhere," in the attic room, in sado-masochistic homosexuality, in *Young Torless* (Musil 1955 [1905]; Pinar 2006c).

Félix Guattari takes Deleuze's conclusion one step further. He moves it onto a political terrain that was implicit in Pasolini's theoretical writings of the 1960s and that would become explicit in the 1970s (Chiesi 2007, 153). By focusing on the body in pre-signifiying ways, Pasolini challenged the prevailing social order. Guattari writes:

> If you want to make cinema into a totalitarian machine, simply bring it under the rule of signifying semiologies, because cinema fulfills its function first of all in the order of images, movement, and sounds, that is, of pre-signifying or a-signifying semiotics. The more cinema enriches itself in the domain of a-signifying semiotics and enlarges its range of esthetic possibilities, the more power tries to enslave it to a signifying semiologies, that is, to dominant meanings (quoted in Greene, 1990, pp. 109–110, n. 42).

To escape such enslavement, the filmmaker must make his points indirectly, shadow-boxing (as it were) with the dominant semiological system. In this respect, Pasolini's cinema recalls the theory of Mikhail Bakhtin. Indeed, the points of intersection between Pasolini and Bakhtin on the issue of free indirect discourse are striking: For Gilles Deleuze, in fact, Bakhtin is nothing less than "the best theoretician for 'free indirect discourse' before Pasolini" (quoted in Greene 1990, 110).

The "grammar" of indirect discourse is uncontainable, uncontrollable. For this reason, Pasolini—foreshadowing Deleuze—calls this realm not only "premorphological" but also "pregrammatical." Visual images, he asserts, are "crude, almost animalistic … prehuman, or at the border of what is human" (quoted in Greene 1990, 112). Pasolini wrote: "[i]ts foundation is the mythic and childlike film which, by the very nature of cinema, runs beneath every commercial film" (quoted in Greene 1990, 113). This visuality would seem to be rather different from what several philosophers have termed "ocularcentrism" (Pinar 2006a, 69–71).

Free indirect discourse is no simple combination, Deleuze explains, an admixture of "two totally constituted subjects of enunciation" but, rather, the "differentiation of two correlative subjects in a system which is itself heterogeneous." For Deleuze, free indirect discourse is then the "fundamental act of language" insofar as it "bears witness to a system which is always heterogeneous, never in equilibrium" (passages quoted in Greene 1990, 114). Free indirect discourse might be structured by "juxtaposition" (Pinar 2006a, vii), itself understood as the inscription of difference.

This socio-linguistic viewpoint of Pasolini (and Bakhtin) was indebted to Leo Spitzer and other German philologists (Greene 1990; for a brief history of philology's devolution: see Guillory 2002). Both men accorded an important role to speech, the changing patterns and different layers of which are emblematic (as Pasolini had always insisted in his remarks about dialects) of the ways that language itself is intertwined with social and political structures. For Bakhtin, individual consciousness is shaped by language and, specifically, by speech, both of which, in turn, are embedded in politics and history. Bakhtin writes: "The evolution of individual consciousness will depend upon the evolution of language, in its grammatical structures as well as its concretely ideological ones. Personality evolves along with language" (quoted in Greene 1990, 113, n. 51). This "fundamental act of language" is—as Bakhtin's analyses make clear—simultaneously meta-literary and social. As the Soviet theoretician observed, whenever and however a text conveys another's speech or discourse—whether in a direct or indirect manner—it always involves a "discourse about discourse, an enunciation about enunciation" (quoted in Greene 1990, 114).

Also an indication of class relations, the bond between, for instance, hero and author or between narrator and speaker may well contribute to the heightened quality of imagination that, for Bakhtin, is an important feature of free indirect discourse:

> In truth, for the artist involved in the creative process, his phantasms constitute reality itself: he does not only sees them, he also hears them. He does not give them words as in indirect discourse, he hears them speak. What he seeks is not to relate a fact or some product of thought but to communicate his impressions, to awaken in the soul of the reader images and living representations. He does not speak to reason but to imagination (quoted in Greene, 1990, 114–115).

Maxine Greene (1995) and Kieran Egan (1992) would agree. For Pasolini, such speech recalled the oneiric and barbaric character of cinema, to the "*monstrum*" lying beneath every film.[44] Pasolini explained that free indirect subjectivity, which conveys a "gaze" or set of feelings not contained in the narrative, allows the "*monstrum*"—the "expressive possibilities stifled by the convention of traditional narrative"—to come to the fore (quoted in Greene 1990, 116).

For Deleuze, (written) free indirect discourse is stylistic rather than linguistic: "Free indirect discourse does not fall within the jurisdiction of linguistic categories because these only concern homogeneous or homogenized systems. It's an affair of style, of stylistics, as Pasolini says" (quoted in Greene 1990, 116, n. 58). Furthermore, Deleuze asserts that

> The camera does not simply give a vision of the character and his world; it imposes another vision in which the first vision is transformed and reflected. This doubling is what Pasolini calls "free indirect subjectivity"... it is a question of going beyond the subjective and the objective toward a pure Form which rises up as an autonomous vision of the content (quoted in Greene 1990, 117).

Free indirect discourse is a juxtaposition of heteronymous elements—an expression of "free indirect subjectivity"—I employed to teach the curse of the Covenant in *Race, Religion and Reparation* (Chapter 3) and worldliness here. For me, a constant characteristic of the "free indirect" is self-reconstruction, as it supports a reflexive arc that refracts one's extension into the world—say, Bragg's Boxes—back into the psyche, restructuring subjectivity after alterity. "Patterns of self-inscription … inform Pasolini's evolving notion of education," Gordon (1996, 38) notes, as the teacher "stimulates curiosity through scandal, revelation and drama." For Pasolini, subjectivity was always worldly; he rejected any "exaltation of the self" (quoted in Gordon 1996, 52 n. 47).

Pasolini would employ these three strategies to "teach" the bourgeoisie about subproletariat. "If Antonioni was the anatomist of middle-class alienation, and Fellini the master of spectacle," Greene (1990, 53) suggests, "then Pasolini was the poet of the Roman *borgata*." This distinction is revealed in Pasolini's examination of Antonioni, Bertolucci, and Godard. Pasolini observed that their films are populated by neurotic, bourgeois characters. Through these characters, each director communicates an irrational, even obsessive, relation to reality. In each of the three directors, Pasolini theorizes a strong link between free indirect subjectivity—which implies a degree of mimesis between the author's vision and that of his neurotic protagonists—and what he terms an "abnormal" stylistic freedom. Such freedom of subjective expression, Pasolini suggests, reveals an obsessive relationship with reality even as it breaks with the traditions of film syntax. It is this stylistic freedom that is the core of the "cinema of poetry" for, through it, the director creates the "second" film, an "authentic" and "irrational" film that springs from cinema's deepest, and perhaps most essential poetic subtext. This "second" film—one that the "author would have wanted to make even without the visual mimesis of his protagonist"—is "totally and freely of an expressive-expressionist sort" (quoted in Greene 1990, 120). This "other" film is created through formal means. Its protagonist—and, by extension, the protagonist of the cinema of poetry—is style itself. And this style is a stylistic freedom that calls attention to itself by violating convention (Greene 1990).

Unlike the notion of the Lacanian "real"—the repression of which makes possible the social field, or, in the present case, the expressed narrative form—the stylistic disruption Pasolini postulates makes necessary the eruption of the "real" (in the Lacanaian sense) into the everyday, the taken-for-granted. For instance, by depicting sub-proletarian characters in his early films or, in the case of films made after 1966, bourgeois characters too grotesque to permit the audience's identification with them, Pasolini contests the assumption that the "bourgeoisie constitutes all of mankind" (quoted in Greene 1990, 122). By what stylistic means did Pasolini disallow bourgeois identification with his characters? Deleuze explains:

> What characterizes Pasolini's cinema is a poetic awareness which ... is mystical or "sacred." This allows Pasolini to carry the neurosis of his character to a level of lowness and bestiality ... while illuminating them in a pure poetic awareness impelled by something which is mythic or "sacred making." Here is the permutation of the trivial and the novel, the connection between the excremental and the beautiful, and the projection into myth that Pasolini diagnosed in free indirect discourse (seen) as the essential form of literature. And he succeeds in making it into a cinematographic form capable of grace as much as of horror (quoted in Greene 1990, 123).

In Pasolini's cinema, the sacred graces the horror of the contemporary age, with its victims across the class spectrum. Horror characterizes the bourgeoisie (as in *Teorema*), and the sacred resides in the despised, as in *La ricotta*, wherein a vulgar man with a gluttonous appetite is in fact a Christ figure. That "didactic" (Viano 1993, 100) film "does not deny the Passion," Viano (1993, 104) points out, "it just shows that it is not where we normally look for it."

La ricotta recalls Bakhtin's notions of the carnivalesque, Rohdie (1995, 149) notes, as it contains various elements of carnival: "derision, orgy, excess, blasphemy, reversal of the normal, parody, the sacred paradox." There are, then, intersections between Pasolini and Bakhtin, especially concerning the interminglings of different languages or stylistic registers. Throughout his career, he employed parody, pastiche, and dialect, implying that one language is "enunciated in light of another" or that two social languages are expressed "within one enunciation" (quoted in Greene 1990, 123–124). Even before he conceived of the idea of free indirect subjectivity, Pasolini's interest in plurilinguistic effects was clear. For instance, as early as 1959, Franco Fortini remarked that "linguistic plurality" and "stylistic contamination" were among Pasolini's "expressive instruments" (quoted in Greene 1990, 124).

The Bakhtinian qualities of Pasolini's *oeuvre* are discernible in his understanding of scene. As a literary text that demands a visual embodiment, the scene, for Pasolini, is situated uneasily between two "languages ... a structure imbued with the will to become another structure" (quoted in Greene 1990, 124). As for the screenplay itself, it is located between biography and autobiography: "The characters are pseudo-objectifications of the author" (Pasolini, quoted in Greene 1990, 125). But to create the "hallucinatory immediacy of poetry", the "teeming details" of lived experience must portrayed through "slow rhythms" and "poetic fixations" (quoted in Greene 1990, 125). Like this synoptic text for teachers, the screenplay is a text that wants to become something else (Bruno 1994, 95; Note 18).

Like that of the great medieval poet Dante,[45] Pasolini's work discloses a blend of the temporal and the teleological, of the poetic and prosaic, of the allegorical and the naturalistic. Those critics who saw only the social and temporal side of, say, *Accattone* complained about the film's mythic overlay. They charged that Pasolini lacked a sense of historicity. After his death, when *Salò* was finally released, critics objected to the strong elements of history at the heart of an allegory (Viano 1993, 299 ff.). Of all his films, Greene (1990) characterizes *Uccellacci e Uccellini* as the most balanced between the realistic and the mythic, between poetry and prose, naturalism and allegory. Viano (1993, 54; see Steimatsky 1998, 245) argues that Pasolini employs the mythic in the service of "a certain realism."[46] The "lesson" in realism Pasolini taught in that film, Rohdie (1995, 136,137) suggests, was that "consumerism" had destroyed—through "depoliticization"—any possibility of socialism or revolution, thereby dissolving any popular (in a Gramscian sense) role for intellectuals.[47]

With the nation's political life destroyed, any intervention must occur outside what passes for politics, esthetic interventions that "contested the political real by being other to it, its complete ideal alterity" (Rohdie 1995, 137). Punctuated by extreme stylistic ruptures and expressive clashes, Pasolini's films of the late 1960s communicate the esthetic and existential issues articulated in his theory. In the films of this period, the savagery and barbarism that he locates at the core of cinema not only express the hypothetical "*monstrum*" behind each film but constitute the narrative itself. These narratives are laced by impulses that surface from the unconscious of individuals as well as from humankind's ancient past. History is the analogue of myth; allegory specifies the immediacy of the present. The linear and progressive sense of time characteristic of the Christian era is eclipsed by what Mircea Eliade—the famous ethnologist whose work Pasolini admired—calls, in a Nietzschean phrase, the "eternal return" of earlier religions (Greene 1990). To portray the eternal in the present (a present devastated by the cultural genocide that was neocapitalism: Rohdie 1995, 132), Pasolini visited places where capitalism had not destroyed humanity: Palestine (Viano 1993, 128–129), India (Rohdie 1995, 37; Viano 1993, 192–193), and Africa (Viano 1993, 118). It was in southern Italy (Steimatsky 1998, 244, 253), however, where he found the palimpsest that conveyed the simultaneity of temporality (Rohdie 1995, 161; Viano 1993, 138), and there he would film his *Il Vangelo*.

Visual Anthropology

Referring both to his representation of the *borgata* in his early films as well
as his evocation of ancient civilizations in the mythic quartet, Alessandro
Cappabianca[48] called Pasolini "the first and only great anthropologist
of cinema." In a seminar conducted at the University of Rome in 1984–
1985 devoted to "Visual Anthropology and Pasolini's Cinema," Massimo
Canevacci[49] suggested that *Medea*, the first of Pasolini's mythic quartet, is
a "masterpiece of visual anthropology." For Canevacci, the film's opening
sequence, depicting an act of human sacrifice, communicates fundamental
human rituals: the "Dionysian sacrifice of death and resurrection (mystical
and proto-eucharistic ecstasy), the great feast and the overturning of roles
(flogging, laughter and revelry), the exchange of identities (masks and proto-
theater), dances of mimicry (musical and bodily frenzy). A formal ritual that
has been perpetuated by cinema" (all passages quoted in Greene 1990, 127,
n. 2).

During the decade, Pasolini visited other countries in the "Third World."
His love for these places was interwoven with his filmmaking activities;
he used African and Middle Eastern locations for several of his films. He
was especially attracted to Africa: "Pasolini's unconscious is displaced in a
romance of Africa," Jennifer Stone (1994, 51) suggests. *Il padre selvaggio*
depicts a young African boy—Davidson—who is driven to the edge of
madness when, spellbound by the teaching of a handsome young European
schoolteacher, he begins to become estranged from his own culture (Greene
1990). It is estrangement from his own (bourgeois, capitalist) culture that
Africa offered Pasolini. Davidson resolves his crisis by writing poetry (Rohdie
1995, 103), a strategy Pasolini himself had employed when torn from his
beloved Friuli.

Pasolini imagines an "African alternative." This was the only place with
which "future history" can be imagined because it is the only place remote
from the bourgeois world of the so-called First World.[50] "And now ... the
desert, deafened/by the wind, the splendid, foul/sun of Africa, illuminating
the world,/Africa, my only/alternative" (quoted in Friedrich 1982, 17).
Pasolini would come to invest the peoples of the "Third World" with that
mythic and symbolic potential to exorcise his personal sins and his class guilt
as a bourgeois European intellectual (Friedrich 1982). In ancient art, Pasolini
asserts, we can discern traces of our prehistoric past:

> The Furies who dominated the whole first part of the tragedy as
> Goddesses of a Tradition—a Tradition which was, precisely, full of blood
> and permeated by terror—are not destroyed at the end by the Goddesses
> of reason, but transformed. Thus they remain irrational and archaic
> divinities; but instead of inspiring atrocious, obsessed, and degrading
> dreams, they reign over works of piety, of affective imagination (quoted
> in Greene 1990, 128).

It is not that the repressed returns; it is always already here, everywhere, suffused throughout our conscious rational life (Markell 2003, 192–193).

Like his love for Friuli or his obsession with the Roman *borgate*, Pasolini's attraction to the so-called Third World had profoundly existential roots. Sexual desire may have drawn him to the Third World, but it was not his only motive. As he was increasingly repelled by the Italy he saw emerging all about him, his longing for ancient civilizations grew. By the end of the decade, Pasolini saw that the homogenizing forces of bourgeois consumerism had all but obliterated those regional differences that had drawn him to his homeland. The imaginary ancient and barbaric civilizations portrayed in his films were envisioned, then, as polar opposites of a modern world he loathed: "In my films, barbarism is always symbolic: it represents the ideal moment of mankind" (quoted in Greene 1990, 129). An intensely symbolic moment in twentieth-century political history in the West proved to be a defining moment for Pasolini as well.

1968

[T]o love the world, it's a naïve/violent sensual love.
Pier Paolo Pasolini (quoted in Ahern 1983/1984, 111)

And what of the young, who were once my saviors?
Pier Paolo Pasolini (quoted in Mura 1989, 42)

At a time when filmmakers such as Godard, Costa-Gavras,[51] and Petri[52] were at their most politically "committed," Pasolini's cinema renounced history and politics. *Medea* appeared to reject the contemporary world for an imaginary past. Accusing him of leaving "Marx for Freud," critics in Italy (especially on the left) condemned his portrayal of ancient and mythic civilizations as "nostalgic" and "regressive." Voicing views shared by many, Goffredo Fofi[53] declared that Pasolini could no longer be considered an artist on the left. His films of the late sixties signaled, sadly, "a return to historical Italian decadentism" (quoted in Greene 1990, 168). Pasolini countered with arguments that were, some critics thought, even more scandalous than the films themselves. Defending his repudiation of conventional politics, Pasolini denounced the pretense to "committed" art. Such art was, he decried, the latest version of "socialist realism" promoted by "left-wing fascists." In polemical terms, he argued against a conventionally political cinema that "vulgarizes and simplifies problems."[54] The only accomplishment of such cinema was "to quiet the bad conscience of the bourgeoisie." As it is neocapitalism that prizes "action" and utility above everything else, by demanding political militancy one merely reproduces neocapitalist and bourgeois values: "Although they think [the young militants] are breaking the circle, they are only reinforcing it" (all quoted passages from Greene 1990, 168–169). In contrast to politically militant film and so-called "materialist" criticism, only authentic art—the art of innovation and controversy—can possibly subvert capitalist commodification. Only authentic art, he asserted, protests against the social and economic order (Greene 1990; Mariniello 1994, 110).

At this point (but not always: Ward 1995, 21–23), film critic and historian Lino Miccichè (1934–2004) spoke in Pasolini's defense. Comparing him to Theodor Adorno, Miccichè explained that Pasolini opposed not only the existing order of things but the "existing modes of opposing such an order." Perhaps, wrote Miccichè,

> the role of Pasolini can be explained in an Adornian key, if Adorno is seen as the man who best described contemporary society as one in which the order of the Enlightenment turned into barbarianism, where thought ceased to think itself, where the destruction of Myth ... created the new myth of reason (and its order of the "rational"). For Adorno, in fact, and in general for all "negative thought," the mandate of intellectuals and artists ... [to] merely oppose what exists ... winds up reflecting the barbarity of what exists (quoted in Greene 1990, 170).

In my terms, resistance[55] guarantees reproduction (Pinar 1994 [1983], 152).

For Pasolini, the contemporary period was unprecedented. The twentieth century was marked not only by the disappearance of the "people" but, anticipating a theme that would preoccupy him in the 1970s, by the "false democracy" of television. Pasolini insisted: "Where there are the ears and mouths of single individuals ... there can be no mass culture. It is for this reason ... that the 'theater of the Word'[56] affirms its real democracy, as opposed to the false democracy of the communications media that address the masses" (quoted in Friedrich 1982, 104). For Pasolini, democracy in culture signified the critical clarification of intellectual processes. Taking "history and society as his texts" (Ahern 1983/1984, 110), democracy, for Pasolini, required the advancement of knowledge for the purpose of freedom (Sicioliano 1982).

In 1968, much of the West was shaken by student protests. Outraged by what he perceived as the students' bourgeois smugness, Pasolini—to the disbelief of many—defended the police against the students. Although the police were "wrong" politically, he acknowledged, they were nonetheless the sons of poor peasants. He pointed out that the students came from middle-class backgrounds; their lives disallowed any real sympathy for the poor. Pasolini judged that they were acting out an exhibitionistic frenzy that could lead only to the "restoration of the bourgeoisie" (quoted in Greene 1990, 173). In the United States, it did exactly that, inaugurating, with the election of Richard Nixon, the nightmare that is the present. Pasolini expressed these judgments in a poem entitled *Il PCI ai giovani*: "You have the spoiled faces of your fathers..../I sympathized with the policemen!/Because policemen are sons of the poor" (quoted in Greene 1990, 174). Despite his class allegiance to the police, Pasolini was not without sympathy for the students, as their actions represented a "mythical moment of revolutionary potential" (Gordon 1996,

65). For many intellectuals, 1968 was the prelude to revolution. For Pasolini it was a time of anguish, "a moment of false promises" (Butler and Spivak 2007, 120). To his mind, the protests and demonstrations indicated not revolution but, instead, the final act of that postwar struggle for social justice and cultural rejuvenation that had been so compelling for him and other intellectuals and artists of his postwar generation (Ryan-Scheutz 2007, 117, 124; Rohdie 1995, 193 ff.). Ignorant of poetry, the generation of 1968, Pasolini predicted, would be "capable of creating only bureaucracy and organization" (Ahern 1983/1984, 116). As we saw in Chapter 3, that prediction proved prescient.

The 1970s

> Between 1961 and 1975 something essential changed:
> A genocide took place.
>> Pier Paolo Pasolini (quoted in Schwartz 1992, 634)

> Now the guiding spirit of language will no longer be literature but technology.
>> Pier Paolo Pasolini (2005 [1972], 19)

Events in the 1970s confirmed Pasolini's sense of despair that had alienated him from so many during the heady year of 1968. From 1969 to 1982, there was a steady escalation in terrorist activity: There were 14,225 attacks killing 415 persons. In 1982, Italian police managed a spectacular rescue of U.S. Army Brigadier General James Dozier, who was being held by members of the Red Brigade. Several of Dozier's kidnappers had cooperated with the police, who were then able to make a number of important arrests. Prophetically sensing this wave of left-wing terrorism, in 1974 Pasolini had remarked, "I know that pragmatism and empiricism are very dangerous: they burst out, they can burst out into the myth of irrational actions which then become the basis of fascism. Pragmatism becomes a kind of myth of action" (quoted in Greene 1990, 175–176). In the United States, as public schools receded from curriculum studies professors' jurisdiction, the demand for action—"practice" in parlance of politically impotent professors—intensified (Wraga 1999).

As the social climate in Italy turned liberal, Pasolini's role of *provocateur* (a role, Greene suggests, that was both forced on him and embraced by him) seemed less timely. Even his homosexuality was less controversial by the early 1970s, given what he regarded as the "false" tolerance of the new regime. For him, such tolerance was worse than repression; it was in fact the most "intolerable" and "humiliating thing in the world." (This is my experience living in Canada, where gay marriage is legal and tolerance typifies the public sphere. It is as if the matter were settled; there is no tolerance for flirtation, let alone for heterosexual destabilization.) In his view, Italy was undergoing a disastrous cultural and social leveling, or "homologization." Bitterly, he would observe that 1968 marked his transition from being a "son"—a symbol of revolt and "disobedience"—to being a "father" (all quoted passages in Greene 1990, 177).

Pasolini's contempt for "false tolerance" and other culturally devastating effects of mass consumerism paralleled the analyses of Herbert Marcuse and the American New Left generally (Restivo 2002, 149). His meditation on power resembled Michel Foucault's. His semiological readings of cultural phenomena evoked those of Roland Barthes's. In contrast to Barthes (who was frequently playful and detached), Pasolini was unrelentingly intense and polemical. "Fascism," Pasolini said, "did not even touch the Church, while, today, neocapitalism destroys it" (quoted in Greene 1990, 179). This intensity and polemicism brought a vicious response. Of course Pasolini understood about consumerism, critics responded; he has long been involved in the "market" of male prostitution (Greene 1990).

Most Italians interpreted the 1974 vote legalizing divorce as a victory for the Left. Pasolini, however, described the event as a triumph of "the hedonistic ideology of consumerism and [the] ensuing modernistic tolerance of the American sort." As for the legalization of abortion, which occurred the following year, Pasolini insisted that abortion was only a tool for "bourgeois" couples, who, unlike their proletarian counterparts, would rather consume than procreate. Just underneath the smiling face of this "new" tolerance he discerned repression and conformism, tendencies that "ignored and rejected all that is sexually different with a violence found only in ... the camps." He worried that this violence might be directed against homosexuals in particular. Homosexuals, he theorized, threatened the "repressive libidinal economy which supports the whole structure of industrial society" (all quoted passages in Greene 1990, 179–180). In this specific view, he anticipated the analysis of Guy Hocquenghem (1978; Marshall 1997).

Consumer capitalism, and the process of cultural leveling or "homologization" that accompanied it, signaled the end of traditional societies. In certain traditional societies (Pasolini was thinking of Sicily specifically), the sequestration of women had encouraged homosexuality. The assault on homosexuality was due not only to the new "tolerance." As regional differences disappeared and the media grew omnipresent, young men were increasingly pressured to reject the past, which had often included occasional homosexuality. Instead, they felt pressured to conform to the uniform model of life seen on television—a model typified by the bourgeois heterosexual couple (Greene 1990).

"Not to own a car," Pasolini pointed out, "and not to be in a couple, when everyone 'must' have a car and 'must' be in a couple (the two-headed monster of consumers), can only be regarded as a great misfortune, an unbearable frustration. Thus heterosexual love, so widely tolerated as to become obligatory has become a sort of 'social erotomania'" (quoted in Caesar 1999, 373). Pasolini's own sexual adventures became more dangerous. Knowing who he was, many young men tried to blackmail him after sexual encounters. These sexual difficulties were exacerbated by an intensifying concern with aging (he turned 50 in 1972). And Pasolini became "inconsolable" (Ahern 1983/1984, 120) over the marriage, in the early 1970s, of his beloved Ninetto Davoli (Greene 1990).

Sexual authenticity felt forever lost to Pasolini; only the "suicidal delusion" remained (quoted in Friedrich 1982, 38). "Besides," he declared in 1971, "the love of truth winds up destroying everything—because nothing is true" (quoted in Greene 1990, 181). Ninetto had represented for Pasolini a powerful and paradoxical union of eros and agape (Ahern 1983/1984, 117). It was during the filming of *I racconti di Canterbury* (The Canterbury Tales) that Davoli decided to get married. Pasolini's pain was not only personal, it was theoretical and political: Even the subproletarian class, represented by Ninetto, converts to conformism. And then there is a certain surrendering to time, expressed in the instinct to procreate, made possible in heterosexual union (Siti 1994).

In *The Canterbury Tales,* Pasolini looked away from the tragic universe of the mythic quartet. He looked away from those social and political concerns that preoccupied him as a journalist. He turned to sex. Indeed, this was the most "scandalous" aspect of the film. Pasolini depicted sexuality with an explicitness unprecedented in Italy. For the first time, Italian audiences saw nude scenes, frequent close-ups of genitals, erections, and lovemaking in every imaginable (and unimaginable) position. This "traumatic" rupture with the past was compelled "by Pasolini's desire for scandal and of his constant need for innovation" (Greene 1990, 181). Ninetto Davoli's abandonment of Pasolini for a woman may have been a factor as well. Critics responded quickly and harshly. They condemned the film, declaring it was pornography. "I prefer the vulgarity of pornography and the most traumatizing violence to the total absence of reality on TV," Pasolini countered. "Violence and vulgarity are at least sometimes mitigated by the fact that they belong, sadly, to reality: the falseness of television is truly immoral" (quoted in Greene 1990, 181, n. 19). If Pasolini were alive today, his horror would be complete, as violence and vulgarity, too, have been incorporated in the "absence of reality" heralded by Hollywood and shown (over and over) on the totalizing "completely self-referential system" (Restivo 2000, 91) that is television.

La trilogia della vita (The Trilogy of Life[57])—*Il Decamerone* (1971), *I racconti di Canterbury* (1972), and *Il fiore delle mille e una notte* (1974)—was influenced by these changes in Pasolini's life. These films, Pasolini explained, reflected both his political despair and what he experienced as the coming of age: "After a series of disillusionments you wind up by seeing reality as a horrendous, intolerable thing." And by "life," Pasolini was thinking especially of those physical or "ontological" realities embodied in the sexual act, the "corporeal moment by definition" (quoted passages in Greene 1990, 182). Sex, aging, politics, and discourse intertwine in the trilogy. He charged that it was "conformist" to suggest that sexual themes are less appropriate than, say, political or religious ones (Greene 1990). He saw them in some senses as indistinguishable. This view that one cannot always distinguish between social and sexual themes in cinema was endorsed by Félix Guattari, who declared that "all themes are at once social and transsexual" (quoted in Greene 1990, 182–183, n. 24).

At first, Pasolini insisted that his portrayal of sexuality was itself political. "A body," he asserted provocatively, "is always revolutionary because it represents what cannot be codified." How we perceive and represent sexuality is political. The links between sexuality and ideology are inseparable. He declared that the explicit sexuality of the trilogy represented a protest against the rigid moralism of the extreme Left. Marxism was itself reactionary due to its sexual puritanism. The trilogy stemmed from his interest to

> oppose both this excess of politicalization and utilitarianism on the part of leftists as well as the unreality of mass culture. To make films where you could find the existentialist sense of the body, of what is physical, the *élan vital* which is being lost. In my trilogy I tried—in a total and absolute way—to anchor myself in the existential. Now, the extreme point of corporeality is sex. Why haven't Marxist texts talked about free love for forty years? Why? It is that Marxism has re-absorbed the customs of the culture that gave birth to it (quoted in Greene 1990, 183).

Though Pasolini was disturbed by the constant left-wing attacks, he also might have taken pleasure in the opportunity they afforded for him to continue teaching the Italian public. Perhaps he felt at once vulnerable and triumphant. "Success," he remarked in the course of one television interview, "is but the other face of persecution" (quoted in Greene 1990, 183–184).

Did the crucifixion of Christ separate sexuality from spirituality, culturally substituting guilt and longing for passion and desire? (In *Race, Religion and a Curriculum of Reparation*, I answer yes.) "If you look at *Il Vangelo* and *Il Decamerone* with a critical eye," Pasolini said, "the style and the idea are the same: sex has taken the place of Christ, that's all, but it is not a big difference" (quoted in Greene 1990, 184). On another occasion, speaking of *The Canterbury Tales*, Pasolini asserted that Chaucer's narrators "chatter rather than narrate: the tales they recount are a pretext for marvelous comic-moralistic bravura pieces. [This] gives rise to the distance from one's own tale, the irony toward one's own tale, that is typical of Anglo-Saxon literature" (quoted in Greene, 1990, 188, n. 43).

For Pasolini, narrative structures and visual strategies imagistically replicate social structures. Rumble (1994) points out that in *Empirismo eretico*, Pasolini develops a theory of the homology, or structural parallel, between models of storytelling and models of social and economic aggregation. In so doing, Pasolini is suggesting there are political and ethical elements of style. *Il fiore* can be understood, Rumble continues, as an allegory of a text without an author and, in the parallel, a society without a state. Just as Pasolini celebrates the bodies and pleasures available in a pre-capitalist, non-industrialized society in *The Decameron*, in *Il fiore* he celebrates an analogous "peasant" or pre-capitalist culture (i.e., the "Third World" with which he came to identify more and more in the final years). Language as well as sex is a site of political and economic struggle, a struggle premodern societies are doomed to lose: "Today dialect provides a means to oppose acculturation. As always, it will be a lost battle" (quoted in Rumble 1994, 210). For Pasolini, dialect represents both his nostalgia for a non-industrial society and non-bourgeois expressions of sexuality (Rumble 1994).

Completed only weeks before Pasolini was murdered, *Salò*, in Greene's (1990, 196) judgment, is not only Pasolini's "most scandalous and chilling film but one of the most disturbing and radical films in the history of cinema." Nathaniel Rich [2007, 80] agrees: *Salò* is "arguably the darkest and most disturbing film ever made." Roland Barthes judged it "absolutely unredeemable" (Ahern 1983/1984, 124). *Le Monde* conceded: "It is difficult for the cinema to go further than this" (quoted in Schwartz 1992, 640). "Meticulous bureaucrats, banal torturers," Greene (1994, 235) points out, Pasolini's libertines are driven not by energy or the pulsing of desire but by impotence and frustration." She continues:

> Indeed, I would argue that if audiences experience a sense of numb and leaden helplessness as they watch this film, it is not only because of what they see but because of how they are positioned by *Salò*. For the very construction of the film gives rise to a terrifying web of complicity with the libertines, a web that forces us to see ourselves—and Pasolini—as among their number (Greene 1994, 237–238).

The film was banned in most countries on charges ranging from indecency and pornography to political subversion. Somehow *Salò* was shot during the same time when Pasolini was working on his 2,000-page novel *Petrolio* (Rumble and Testa 1994b, 11; Ryan-Scheutz 2007, 212 ff.).

Death

> [I] am adapting myself to the degradation and I am accepting the unacceptable.... Before me—little by little, slowly, without further alternatives—looms the present.
>
> Pier Paolo Pasolini (2005 [1972], xx)

> In photographs, you lean on your Romeo, /ruined by nights of sexual stalking/ Defiant.
>
> David Mura (1989, 1)

On November 3, 1975 a brutal assassination—apparently at the hands of a young male prostitute named Giuseppe Pelosi—ended the life of a man who, by the time of his death, was generally recognized not only as a great artist but one of the most important intellectuals of postwar Europe, occupying a position in Italy comparable to that of Sartre in France. In the small cemetery of Casarsa, Pasolini lies buried near his adored mother Susanna (Greene 1990).

One of Pasolini's oldest and closest friends (he had appeared in one of Pasolini's films, *Comizi d'amore*), Alberto Moravia, expressed his wish that the director's career had ended not with *Salò*, but instead, with *Il fiore delle mille e una notte*. Unlike *Salò*, Moravia explained, in *Il fiore delle mille e una notte*

> homosexuality is viewed ... with happiness, sympathy, with ingenuity and serenity. In *Il fiore*, for the last time, Pasolini liked himself, that is, his own life, his own destiny, his own way of being in the world. In *Salò*, on the other hand, he hated himself in the most radical way, to the point of self-calumny. I don't know why he did it. Probably from a sense of guilt (quoted in Greene 1990, 208–209).

Filmmaker Gideon Bachman interviewed Pasolini while he was making *Salò*. He, too, was distressed by Pasolini's despair: "Hearing him discuss Klossowski's ideas of the eternal, repetitiousness of the act of love, I realize the man is talking about himself, about his eternal reaching out, and his eternal disappointment. Disappointment in man and in God" (quoted in Greene 1990, 209).

Salò provoked a furor, but it did not compare to the scandal that was Pasolini's death. Many felt that that the prostitute may not have been the assassin or that he had not acted alone. Shrouded in mystery, Pasolini's death provoked the greatest controversy of his tumultuous career. Pasolini's alleged assailant insisted that he had murdered Pasolini rather than commit repellant homosexual acts. However disingenuous a defense this was—after all, as a "rent-boy," Pelosi's work *was* homosexual acts (Restivo 2002, 148)—in the eyes of homophobes, the murderer became a hero. The homophobia reached such a frenzy that Jean-Paul Sartre was moved to write an article pleading that the court "not put Pasolini on trial" (quoted in Greene 1990, 219).[58] After the murder, it became impossible to separate the sadomasochistic nightmare portrayed by *Salò* from how Pasolini lived his life and met his death. The many comparisons between art and life were inevitably confused by the bourgeois moralism he had fought since his days as a schoolteacher in Casarsa (Greene 1990).

Pasolini's constant persecution by the Right prompted many of his admirers to elevate his death to the status of martyrdom. Many homosexuals were, perhaps, the only ones who resisted the temptation to make Pasolini's death symbolic. Pointing out that murders such as Pasolini's took place nightly in every Italian city, many suggested that if Pasolini were a "martyr to a conformist and repressive society, so, too, were hundreds of nameless, faceless others" (quoted in Greene 1990, 219). As time passed, assertions of martyrdom became more and more insistent. In one retrospective of his cinema, an early film was shown superimposed onto the photographs of his corpse; at an exhibit in Rome, the blood-stained jacket he was wearing the night of his death was displayed as if it were a saint's relic; a Dutch documentary (*He who tells the truth shall die*) ends with frames from *Il Vangelo* that depict Christ's—and, by implication, Pasolini's—crucifixion (Greene 1990).

Naomi Greene (1990, 219) notes that "the notion of sainthood would not have displeased Pasolini." At times, she points out, Pasolini appeared to be obsessed with the idea of martyrdom. In a passage of his diary as a young man, he described a fantasy in which he identifies with Christ on the Cross. As he does so, he experiences a kind of sensual suffering. He confessed:

> This nude body, scarcely covered with a strange hand at the loins ... evoked in me thoughts which were not openly illicit and yet whenever I looked at this swathe of silk (as if a veil spread over a disquieting abyss) ... I would suddenly direct my feelings to piety and prayer. Then there would clearly appear in my fantasies the desire to imitate the sacrifice Jesus made for others, to be condemned and killed despite my total innocence. I saw myself hung, nailed, on the cross. My loins were scantily clad by this thin strip and an immense crowd watched me. My public martyrdom wound up by becoming a voluptuous image and, bit by bit, I was nailed up with an entirely nude body. With arms outstretched with hands and feet nailed, I was totally vulnerable, lost (quoted in Greene 1990, 219–220).

That final image—of arms outstretched—reminds one of the final scene in *The Trial*, but there are other associations besides Kafka. One is reminded of the "Miss Jesus" act in Paul Monette's *Halfway Home* and the conflation of Christ with a "hunk" on the cross in the mortuary scene in the Dutch film "The Fourth Man" (1983). The obsession with the crucifix is, I suggest (2006a), a compulsive repetition of the historic desecration of homosexual desire.

The mix of masochism-exaltation and mysticism-sensuality evident in the foregoing diary entry can be found in Pasolini's cinema. A few of his protagonists even die in the position of the cross: Greene thinks of homosexual burned at the stake in *The Canterbury Tales*. Other characters (Greene recalls Medea, taunt and frozen, or the young cannibal in *Porcile* with his arms outstretched) wait for their deaths in states of sensual suffering and pride. Moreover, it is not only Pasolini's cinematic images that portray masochism. Whether censored, banned, or (merely) denounced, the public history of nearly every Pasolini film illustrates this pattern of transgression and persecution, Greene observes. The pattern starts with the first showing of *Accattone*, precipitating a night of right-wing riots in Rome. The pattern ends with the banning of *Salò*. Judges, censors, and journalists all seemed eager to participate in this pattern, performing Pasolini's fantasy of persecution that, by the end, bordered on paranoia. In the year of his death, he told journalist Jean Duflot that Italian public opinion, aggravated by the media, regarded his homosexuality as "the very sign of an abominable human type" (quoted in Greene 1990, 220).

Though his persecution was sometimes unbearable, it was also, Greene suggests, in some way desired. It was almost as if Pasolini were compelled to transgress, to break nearly every social convention, to exhibit himself, so that others were forced to his *diversità* and punish him for it. "*Diversità*" meant not so much, or not only, homosexuality; it meant marginality. To be "different" meant being the social and psychological "negative" of others, one on whom others project the disavowed elements of their personalities (Friedrich 1982). An autobiography of alterity seeks to portray certain "negatives" (in the photographic not moralistic sense) of the autobiographer and, in so doing, reincorporate the experience projected onto "others" at the "margins." It is a form of self-reconstruction through self-shattering.

Probably this "need to violate" formed early. Recall that Pasolini's earliest poems were composed in a language that was officially frowned upon and that few could understand or appreciate.[59] Responding to the student protests of the late 1960s, he could have been describing the masochism implicit in his own position. For Pasolini, the student revolt was laced with a "presentiment of death, a mythical masochism. Killing the father, even in this way, represents an absolute masochism, a constant sense of guilt" (quoted in Greene 1990, 222). He appreciated that the revolutionary artistic process was sadomasochistic: sadistic in that it challenged the public's assumptions, masochistic in that the public rejects such challenges by attacking the artist. As Lawton (2005a, ix) points out: "Sadistically he was embroiled in endless polemics with everyone in Italy. Masochistically, he paid the price." Even the act of creation engaged the pleasure of suffering:

> In every author, in the act of invention, freedom presents itself as a masochistic loss of something certain. In the necessarily scandalous act of inventing he exposes himself, literally, to others; precisely to scandal, to ridicule, to reproach, to the feeling of difference, and—why ?—to admiration, even if it is sonewhat questionable. There is, in short, the "pleasure" that one has in every fulfillment of the desire for pain and death (Pasolini 2005 [1972], 268).

Many of the sexually charged scenes in Pasolini's movies, in Greene's judgment, were expressions of his own homosexual desire converted to be an acceptable currency: heterosexuality often portrayed as male camaraderie or recoded altogether (Viano 1993, xiii, 95). In the early films, the expression of male homosexual desire was indirect, evident in the camera's absorption in male characters (Restivo 2002, 149; Boone 1993, 27). Greene (1990) argues that despite Pasolini's continual defiance of Italian machismo, he was complicit with its logic. Probably his communism helped reduce the shock of his homosexuality to his contemporaries. In a way, communism became the alibi for his desire; it helped explain his obsession with the subproletariat.

Ideologically, his paternal benevolence, his altruistic interest in the boys of the *borgata* provided Pasolini the means to express desire they could tolerate. Despite his public visibility as a homosexual, Di Stefano (1993) suggests, he was not as radical as perhaps he wanted to be. Pasolini was self-divided, Di Stefano (1993) asserts, lacerated by a viciously homophobic society. Other critics suggest it was the modern division of sexuality itself that was as distressing as homophobia itself. "For Pasolini," David Ward (1995, 31) concludes, "whenever sexuality is classified into hetero- or homosexual categories, that is always a moment of loss."

Di Stefano, who reports having met and slept with Pasolini during his visit to New York (Chiesi and Mancini 2007, 75 ff.), speculates that both Pasolini's overwhelming love for his mother and his "predictable" hatred of his father disguised a more basic level of desire: love for the father. Addressing himself to Pasolini, Di Stefano (1993, 300) asserts that his father was "the man you desired the most and who you could never allow yourself to love, but had wished to possess.... Why did we never see this on the screen?" The question of his father aside, Di Stefano's question fails to appreciate the limits of Pasolini's historical situation, specifically the severity of homophobia in the 1950s and 1960s, perhaps especially in Italy. It was a time, Viano (1993, xiii) notes, when the representation of homosexual desire was, simply, "forbidden." Pasolini's friend Paolo Volponi (2007 [1976], 124) blamed not only historical moment but the bourgeoisie for Pasolini's sexual suffering; Cesare Musatti (the psychoanalyst who appeared in *Comizi d'amore*) cited the "hypermoralistic structure" of Italian society. History, class, and Catholicism notwithstanding, Pasolini's concern for sexuality was political (decidedly not identity politics), even religious, and though the setting for his films was postwar Italy, the scope of his knowledge and interest made the stage European history generally.

The issues of Pasolini's life and times and taught in his work cannot be reduced to gay advocacy. Even the more expansive concept of "queer" fails to capture the range and complexity of Pasolini's pedagogy.[60] Even when focused on his "private" life, Pasolini was always thinking of history and politics. During those nights when he moved about the city looking for boys, he was perhaps most aware of his fascination with violence, risk, intensity. In 1960, he wrote,

> I spend the greater part of my life beyond the edges of the city. I love life with such violence and such intensity that no good can come of it. I am speaking of the physical side of life: the sun, the grass, youth. It is an addiction more terrible than cocaine. It doesn't cost anything and it is available in boundless *quantities*. I devour it ravenously. How it will all end, I don't know (quoted in Snyder 1980, 19).

At other moments, he knew exactly how it would end (Schwenk and Semff 2005, 21; Kammerer and Zigaina 2005, 157).

The metaphor of life-as-ingestion ("devour"), as Snyder (1980) notes, took various forms in his films. The repetition of the supper image in its various forms—as spiritual hunger (*The Gospel According to Matthew*), as an act of communion (*The Hawks and the Sparrows*, 1966), as the hunger of poverty (*La Ricotta*), or as a natural metaphor of the animality of consumerism (*Salò* and *Porcile*)—would suggest it occupied a significant station in the imagination of the filmmaker: "I experienced reality by taking from it" (quoted in Snyder 1980, 19). Does the "worldliness of the imagination" (Radhakrishnan 2008, 13) require ravenous appetites?

Despite his pedagogical "interventions" in the artistic, political, and social life of postwar Italy, Pasolini seems to have remained, in his own phrase, "beyond the edges of the city," on the margins of the institutions he supported (such as the Partito Comunista Italiano (PCI)), yet precisely upon the edge of life, unowned by anyone, disowned by every system. He was a profoundly spiritual man banished from the Church. He was a Marxist and a committed Communist excommunicated by the Party. He shocked many by criticizing the leftist student movements of the 1960s, by rejecting the idea of a political cinema, by positioning himself outside those intellectual milieux with which one would normally associate him (e.g., those of Marx, Freud, Lévi-Strauss), partly because his "authorial intertext" was so "complex and inherently contradictory" (Viano 1993, 1). He provoked scandal as a consequence of his defiant homosexuality, horrifying many through his apparent compulsion to employ male prostitutes in the Roman subproleteriat. His own murder, apparently by one such young man, was complicated by the plausibility (in the minds of homophobes) of Pelosi's story that Pasolini had attacked him. After all, they assured themselves, not long before Pasolini had been convicted, despite rather bizarre circumstances, of brandishing a knife at a gas station attendant (Lawton 2005a, ix; Snyder 1980).

Pasolini knew that the twentieth-century crisis of European culture could not be solved in its self-presented categories. It could not be solved by a Marxist-minded resistance but, perhaps, by a constantly changing politics of style that affirmed the "authenticity" of archaic—pre-capitalist—civilizations.[61] Only by challenging the contemporary codes of Europe—its regimes of reason—could art possibly question and subvert that culture and society within which Europeans were embedded. Pasolini embraced "permanent invention" and "continuous struggle." In a statement that could have been made by Frantz Fanon, Pasolini declared,

> Every volunteer who seeks a meaningful death "as exhibition" must deliberately present himself on the firing life: there is nowhere else where he can so rigorously carry out his course of action. Only the hero's death is a spectacle; and it alone is useful. Therefore martyr-directors, by their own decision, always find themselves, stylistically, on the firing line, and thus at the front line of linguistic transgressions. By dint of provoking the code (and therefore the world which uses it), by dint of *exposing*

themselves, they wind up by obtaining what they desire so aggressively: to be wounded and killed with the weapons they themselves offer to the enemy (quoted in Greene 1990, 222).

The very personification of the "martyr-director" theorized here, Pasolini was continually and defiantly on the "front-lines" of artistic and of social-political struggle. In this sense, his cinema was but the most public and spectacular expression of his commitment to "permanent invention," a commitment constantly renewed and re-expressed as each new film opposed still another configuration of political and social codes and conventions. By creating those transgressions that opened those "infinite possibilities of modifying and enlarging the code," Pasolini identified and then challenged the political limits, indeed the social reality, reflected and perpetuated via cultural codes. His emphasis upon the moral elements of culture was, perhaps, frequently distressing, often unfashionable, but it was, in Naomi Greene's (1990) view, this very insistence that positions him one of the most important figures of the twentieth century. Solitary and resolute, he stood, as journalist and parliamentarian Maria-Antonietta Macciocchi[62] astutely observed, at the intersection of "three great protests against the power of the state: political, sexual, and mystic" (quoted passages in Greene 1990, 222).

Pasolini knew that freedom in any society is measured by the freedom of women. Throughout Pasolini's films, there is the inescapable sense that the exploitation of man by man inherent in a capitalist economy begins with the exploitation of women by men. The relationship of prostitute to pimp is the model of sexual and social relationships generally. In both *Accattone* and *Mamma Roma* (1962), women exist to support men economically and satisfy them sexually. Pasolini cannot imagine a tale of social progress or self-liberation that is not also a narrative of women's emancipation. His most positive film, *Il fiore delle mille e una notte* (1974), is the story of a female slave who triumphs over a male-dominated world. The exceptions to this observation include *Teorema* (1968) and *Il Vangelo secondo Matteo* (1964). However, even Pasolini's Christ exhibits sufficient femininity to have provoked one critic to allege that Pasolini portrayed Jesus as an "obvious" homosexual. The handsome stranger in *Teorema* is no affirmation of heterosexuality, however: After having sex with the female servant, the daughter, and her mother, this Gnostic God seduces the son and his father (Testa 1994, 203). Each disintegrates, to be "born again" in a post-bourgeois state (Testa 1994, 201–202).

Pasolini's scandalous art restates private passion as public service. If homosexual desire drew him to Africa, his love for the "Third World" led to unforgettable films portraying the crisis of European civilization. An intensified and self-divided sensibility, a piercingly sharp sense of the otherness within and around him, enabled him to discern the fascism of the present. Whatever their psychological prerequisites, his denunciations of the media (and television specifically) and his contempt for cultural standardization

Made a classroom of Italian Society

and homogenization were deeply moral judgments. Pasolini was hardly the first prophet whose vision and commitment accrued from an inner crisis. As André Gide wrote in a study of Dostoyevsky, "If we really look, at the origin of every great ethical reform we find a little physiological mystery, a dissatisfaction of the flesh, an unease, an anomaly." Perhaps it was a certain "dissatisfaction of the flesh," an "inner disequilibrium," that made of Pasolini not only a poet—a creature Walter Benjamin called the "most different of living creatures" (quoted passages in Greene 1990, 223). In a November 3 obituary, Bengt Holmquist wrote, "His was a talent of seldom-seen breadth ... to get the equivalent, you would have to have Sartre, Böll, Bergman in the same person" (quoted in Schwartz 1992, 8).

It was Pasolini's worldliness—his ambivalent but passionate embrace of sexuality, his devotion to the subproletariat, his attunement to history, his compulsion to engage the public pedagogically—that enabled him to make a classroom of Italian society. In his cosmopolitan curriculum, art is central (not marginalized by mathematics, as in Bush's terrorized America: Dillon 2007a). In poetic, fictional, essayistic, journalistic, and cinematic "lessons"— instructive works of art addressed to the world—he juxtaposed images exposing the Right and the Left as entangled in the very cultural systems they claimed, respectively, to defend and critique. His films positioned viewers as questioning reality (Viano 1993, x), in part owing to his "incessant" use of "juxtaposition" (Ryan-Scheutz 2007, 222; Rohdie 1995, 123). His *borgata* boys—members of the lumpenproletariat—provided Pasolini opportunities not only for pleasure but for self-restructuring, affirming his own peasant past, his commitment to the poor in the present.

For the boys, in Pasolini they found not only pleasure (and payment) but opportunities for upward mobility, much, in the case of Giovanni ("Ninetto") Davoli, to Pasolini's horror (Schwartz 1992, 25). Evidently Ninetto's marriage and parenthood (the couple had two children, the first of whom was named Pier Paolo) did not end the intimacy. When Pasolini went to Stockholm in October 1975 (days before his murder), he took Ninetto with him; they shared a hotel room (Schwartz 1992, 7). Ninetto was "poetry in the form of a young man's body" (Mura 1989, 38). Pasolini admitted: "it is the world I love in him" (quoted in Schwartz 1992, 31). It is the world in Pasolini that demands our devotion today.

Epilogue

Passionate
Engagement
with the
world

> The past, or prehistory, survives as a negative, immanent power that revitalizes, but also dissolves the present.
>
> Robert S. C. Gordon (1996, 127)

"The future appears to be out of favor today," Fuyuki Kurasawa (2007, 94) suggests, "now the province of mystics and scientists", not of ordinary citizens I would add. Though no ordinary citizens, Pasolini, Bragg, and Addams personified what Nussbaum (1997, 8) depicts as "reflective citizenship," a state of civic commitment that "liberates the mind from the bondage of habit and custom, producing people who can function with sensitivity and alertness as citizens of the whole world." Addams, Bragg, and Pasolini were reflective citizens; each understood the subjective project of public service as the education of the public, a concept not limited to the classroom (although each worked in classrooms) but enacted as a way of life (Seigfried 1996, 58) inspired by, drawn to, otherness (Rohdie 1999, 181). In our time, "the cultivation of humanity" (Nussbaum 1997, 8) calls for the cultivation of subjectivity informed by academic study and lived experience, inspired by sexuality, spirituality, and sustainability. A state of mind more than a set of behaviors, such subjectivity—individuated states of voluptuousness—consecrates life through "the eroticization of otherness" (Nava 2007, 71). This knowledge—recalling the Grumet sentence with which I opened the book—derives from passionate engagement with the world. This knowledge is worldliness.

Cosmopolitanism involves not only understanding "one's own localism ... as part of a larger world of differences," Mayer, Luke and Luke (2008, 92) note, it implies as well a "cultural and political perspective on the social subject and on issues of 'global' governance." One such perspective is that of Fuyuki Kurasawa. "Cultivating a farsighted cosmopolitanism" (2007, 157), Kurasawa (2007, 6) is interested in "how sociopolitical actors situated in dense and meaningful lifeworlds engage in practices to counter structural and situational forms of violence and to advance emancipatory projects." Such projects, he continues, constitute "social labor" toward global justice "from the ground up" (2007, 6). What he summarizes as "formalism"[1]—both philosophical normativism (that cosmopolitanism I would associate with Appiah or Nussbaum) and "politico-legal institutionalism" (a Habermasian emphasis upon democratic procedures and transnational infrastructure)—is global justice "from above," abstractions not grounded in the "ethical and political soil" in which they might take "root" (2007, 6; see Gilroy 2005, 67). Neither of these "can adequately account for what makes up the substance of global justice and for the arduous processes that lead to it constitution in specific moments and places" (2007, 6). Despite this acknowledgement of specificity, Kurasawa (2007, 13–14) provides a typology of social actions in service to global justice, among them,

> bearing witness (testimonial acts in the face of extreme human rights violations); forgiveness (collective processes by which perpetrators of grave injustices ask to be forgiven and are granted such requests); foresight (farsighted forms of prevention of, or protection against, atrocities and disasters); aid (assigning persons living though humanitarian crises); and solidarity (the creation of a sense of global responsibility and a planetary consciousness).

These, he insists, do not constitute an "abstract norm" or "institutional outcome" but, rather, "a multidimensional, socially and historically constructed project produced by various forms of social action and ethico-political labor" (2007, 14). Such labor presupposes the recognition of "cultural pluralism" as a perquisite for "solidarity" (2007, 161).

Endorsing a "robust" (2007, 186), an "aesthetic"[2] (2007, 187) and, finally, a "critical" (2007, 194) cosmopolitanism, Kurasawa (2007, 169) names three "distinctive" elements of "cosmopolitan solidarity." The first is dialogue: "intersubjectivity" (2007, 64) and an "inner voice" (2007, 53) infuse the "struggle" that constitutes the "core" of global justice's "enactment" (2007, 15). Second is public practice, whereby civil groups negotiate a "sense of togetherness and common purpose." Third, "as a mode of social action, cosmopolitan solidarity is transnational in scope" (2007, 169). "As a mode of practice," Kurasawa (2007, 160) explains, "cosmopolitan solidarity engages in socio-political tasks that confront three distinct sets of perils: cultural homogenization, political fragmentation and social thinness." Addressing these is his critical cosmopolitanism, emphasizing the social labor of global justice (2007, 210) while avoiding "aforementioned traps of structuralist and voluntarist accounts of social life" (Kurasawa 2007, 12). For Kurasawa (2007, 15), "integral to the work of global justice is the fact that struggle represents the core of its enactment."

Kurasawa's insightful analysis suffers the dispositions of his discipline. Focused on the social, he associates subjectivity only with voluntarism, when not subservient to structure (Popkewitz 2008, xiii). It is in a sociologist's imagination wherein we live today, one in which the individual can only be "possessive," dedicated to "the maximization of self-interest" (Kurasawa

Global Justice

2007, 41). Can we describe Jane Addams in such terms? Laura Bragg? Cynics would associate Pasolini with self-interest, but it is clear he impaled himself on the cross of, if not humanity, the *borgatae*. Global justice *is* social labor—that is Kurasawa's powerful lesson—but social labor is, in part, pedagogical, and it is conducted by *individual* teachers committed to the education of the public. Such teaching constitutes a "relocation" of the personal (Kamler 2001), composed of acts of self-expression (and disclosure) in situations of "complicated conversation" with the public. (On that parenthetical point Seigfried [1996, 168] quotes Dewey: "What is sometimes called an act of self-expression might better be termed one of self-exposure: it discloses character—or lack of character—to others.") Like art, subjectivity brings truth into being (Radhakrishnan 2008, 190).

The social labor of global justice requires, then, the cultivation of cosmopolitan subjectivity. As an expanded notion of free indirect subjectivity implies, the sphere of the subjective is "where" one's lived experience and academic knowledge of the world can be understood, reconstructed, and expressed indirectly, through teaching (Green and Reid 2008, 22). As it did for Edward Said, to teach means "to hold a certain faith, a belief or principle, and to hold it rigorously and in complexity, but in love of the world" (Radhakrishnan 2008, 116–117). Ours is a profession enacted by sometimes heroic individuals creatively and critically engaged with the world. For us, as it was for Said, the "book, necessary and precious as it as, was also at the same time a very special point of entry into the worldliness of the world" (Radhakrishnan 2008, 117). As Grumet reminds, schooling is not about itself; it provides passages to the world.

That world is not only human. As urgent as worldwide political action is, I do not worship nature (Radhakrishnan 2008, 246). Like Radhakrishnan (2008, 236), I do not succumb to the "evangelical authority of biocentric theorists." Radhakrishnan (2008, 247) points out that "nature is as nature does," and as the terrorism of the 2004 Indian Ocean earthquake and tsunami suggest, again after Radhakrishnan (2008, 247), "in the context of nature, the human response has to be rigorously ambivalent and contradictory." Academic study and political action must intensify. But without subjective structures of sustainability, sexuality, and spirituality, political action is inevitably enervated.

It is the name of the political that heroic individualism proclaims the poetical. "[A]n untrammeled poetic subjectivity" (Radhakrishnan 2008, 216) testifies to the worldliness of life on earth. No nostalgic gesture toward what is forever lost, a poetic individualism appreciates the educational significance of the structures of knowledge. "Even though the world is descriptively and objectively out there," Radhakrishnan (2008, 224) notes, "it is still a matter of how and in what genre or modality the human subject accesses the world." Addams's, Bragg's, and Pasolini's experimentalism—in social relations, curricular objects, and in esthetic forms—enabled each to teach the "unique historicality of the moment" (Radhakrishnan 2008, 226). Each personified the epiphanic intersection between "the I am and the I think" (Radhakrishnan 2008, 230) in their commitments "to realize knowing as transformation" (Radhakrishnan 2008, 232).

The transformation of reality through human agency occurs, then, poetically. "The everyday and every person need to be poetized into their authentic historicality," Radhakrishnan (2008, 231) observes. It is the immanence of the esthetic that becomes translated into the historicality of being-in-the-world. Global justice requires social labor animated subjectively; political action requires the subject to "dwell totally in the antagonism of the moment, that is, ... embrace antagonism as process" (Radhakrishnan 2008, 85–86). The social labor of global justice requires ethical, existential, and creative acts of heroic individualism, a concept—an aspiration—we must disinter from its theoretical grave and acknowledge as vital to all "radical or radicalized thought" (Cusset 2008, 336). "We must," Cusset (2008, 336) pleads,

> reconcile heroism with the here and now and free its motives from suspicion and guilt. Or, more precisely, we must keep heroism and its beautiful ecstatic energy, but free it from a certain submission to negative concepts (the reference, the Father, action considered as other and always to occur in the future....

Immanence, not transcendence, informs the worldliness that knows that struggle for global justice is to be conducted from everywhere: from below, from above, from all points in between, *working from within* to redress the injustice that defines the world. Through such subjective labor—including that pedagogical labor undertaken by the heroic individual, in (and out of) school classrooms—the cultivation of humanity occurs. Radhakrishnan's (2008, 24) question specifies this pedagogical project of cosmopolitanism: "Does the human become human in the act of letting the world speak through her or him?" This "worlding" of subjectivity renders into practice the "Marxian dictum that to know something is to transform it" (2008, 25). Such "worlding" is enacted through the free play of indirect subjectivity, as the heroic individual "talks back" to the world that has confounded—made a "problem" of—one's life and flesh. "Selfhood," Williams (2007, 42) points out, "is also work: producing, consuming, doing all the things we do, having feelings, having thoughts, all of which contributes to—indeed, sustains—culture." The sustainability such subjective labor engenders represents passionate life in public service, an ongoing cosmopolitan education. A person who knows *that* is engaged with the world.

Notes

Preface

1. François Cusset's (2008, 4) patronizing reference to "the whole American machinery of fashionable citations and the splicing together of texts" persuades me to comment on my own citational practices in this text. Working in a field defined by the phrase "complicated conversation" obligates me to "perform" that definition textually. Extensive referencing is, then, an acknowledgement of the dialogical character of the curriculum, that it is, indeed, a conversation requiring acknowledgement of other interlocutors, past and present. To that basic professional obligation I have added a second (not uncommon) practice: listing page numbers after sentences that are not quotations. In a work that offers itself as synopsis of scholarship for reconstruction by individual teachers as curriculum, page numbers should speed and ease the work of those who wish to pursue particular points in their original or an associated formulation. The curriculum I have composed here constitutes notes for teachers who are able to honor their obligation to devise what they teach after their own interests attuned to their students and schools. Multiple references after the same sentence represent less a form of "triangulation" (an ugly methodological term I always associate with strangulation) than an acknowledgment that more than one scholar has addressed the issue. These citational practices are, then, hardly anonymous, as Cusset's use of "machinery" implies. They are, rather, my personal notes to teachers working on their own curricular projects. I do share Cusset's disdain for "fashionable" citations (and the avant-gardism that practice represents) from which his work and the work he discusses have profited so considerably.

2. I think of my own public-school teachers. My public-school education—in 1950s Westerville, Ohio—was "traditional," focused on textbooks, emphasizing memorization. While "school" as a social organization was sometimes awful, my teachers—whose daily individuated efforts can never be summarized by the totalizing term "traditional"—were remarkable in their steady, sometimes fervent, determination to teach. Perhaps this imbrication of tradition and innovation is why I cannot separate the knower from the known. I experienced no contrast between "the transfer of a static body of knowledge" and "teaching how it is one comes to know—how knowledge is constructed, and with what effects" (Davies 2008, 184): my public-school education persuades me that "what" and "how" are inseparable. The "aftermath of transmission" can indeed be "creative and singular acts of learning" (Pitt 2008, 195).

   In this regard, I recall the calm and comprehensive lectures of my tenth-grade world history teacher—Mrs. Sarah Ott—that, in a twelfth-grade honors government class she also taught, converted to conversation. In that latter class, I was introduced to Marx (and Adam Smith) and first glimpsed the curriculum as a multiply referenced conversation. Mrs. Near strained to teach us Spanish through repetition *and* spontaneous speech, at one point breaking down in sobs over our ineptitude: She was, for me, mesmerizing. There are others whose names remain with me today, among them Mr. Detamore (P.E. and biology), Mr. Stallings (English), Mr. Shade (football coach and American history), Mr. Becker (band), Miss Staats (to become Mrs. Morgan: English), Miss Chapman (sixth grade), Mrs. Kempshall (Latin), Mr. Starr (chemistry), Mr. Short (algebra). In his or her own individual ways, each of these teachers demonstrated fidelity to their subjects (both their school subjects and to us students). Each was dedicated to daily expressions of quietly passionate public service. A footnote hardly suffices as tribute: Laura Bragg becomes my emblem for those unacknowledged by the public but gratefully remembered in private (McWilliam 2008, 35). When I defend teachers (in Chapter 4, for example), I am thinking of these teachers as well as my colleagues at Paul D. Schreber High School, where I taught secondary English. Given these teachers' public service and professional accomplishment, school deform represents outrageous fortune, indeed.

3. The fundamental curriculum question invokes not only history but politics and ethics expressed through academic knowledge in the service of subjective and social reconstruction. Its degraded version—"*Whose* knowledge is of most worth?" (Buras and Apple 2006, 3, 18, emphasis added)—collapses curriculum into identity politics, as who "owns" the knowledge is more important than the disciplinary and educational significance of the knowledge itself. By arguing that "curricula were no more than a reflection of the interests of those in power," Michael F. D. Young (2008, 94) points out, "power, not knowledge" became what counts in education, leading to a "relativism that was not, to say the least, very helpful in debates about the future of curriculum." He emphasizes: "[k]nowledge cannot be reduced to the activities and interests of those who produce or transmit it" (Young 2008, 94).

4. I am following here Appiah's (2005, 230) distinction between "morality, which has to do with what we owe to others, and ethics, which has to do with what kind of life it is good for us to lead." Appiah (2005, 233) acknowledges that "moral obligations must discipline ethical ones."

5. "Significantly," Young-Bruehl (1996, 18) points out, "American anti-ethnocentrism education efforts in the 1950s went under the title 'intracultural education,' a term that implies bridge building among groups that have been out-groups to each other. This approach differs quite strikingly from the present 'multicultural education' promoted by minority groups, which is an effort to maintain pluralism and give minority cultures recognition." As indicated in Chapter 2, contemporary identity politics represents the devolution of a cosmopolitan multiculturalism with its ancient antecedents (Nussbaum 1997, 53, 55); Nussbaum (1997, 111) endorses "the world-citizen, rather than identity-politics, form of multiculturalism as the basis for our curricular efforts."

1   "The Problem of My Life and Flesh"

1. See, for instance, Nava (2007) and Tickner (2001). Feminist scholars in International Relations, J. Ann Tickner (2001, 3) observes, "focus on how world politics can contribute to the insecurity of individuals, particularly marginalized and disempowered populations." As well, feminists study how dominant forms of masculinity influence foreign policies of various states, resulting in the overuse of "state violence for domestic and international purposes" (2001, 4). This association of masculinity with war has been "central" to feminist research, Tickner (2001, 57) informs us. Mica Nava (2007, 3, 8) theorizes cosmopolitanism

as a "structure of *feeling*," in which difference is valorized positively, engendering "attraction for and identification with otherness ... intimate and visceral." She demonstrates this thesis historically, recalling that

> Between 1942 and 1945 many thousands of black American servicemen were stationed in the UK and received, on the whole, a remarkably warm welcome from across the class spectrum of the indigenous population, and particularly from women, with whom many developed romantic and sexual relations (Nava 2007, 9).

Cosmopolitanism, then, has not always been associated with elitism but, rather, with forms of popular culture (Nava 2007, 37), including women's shopping (2007, 19 ff.) and esthetic expressions of "the eroticization of otherness" (2007, 71). For Nava (2007, 12), "cosmopolitanism ... is not only visceral and vernacular but also domestic."

2. Distinguishing black cosmopolitanism from Pan-Africanism, Ifeoma Kiddoe Nwankwo demonstrates an ambivalence [2005, 205) toward the term, at one point defining it as "not in the race of the individuals who express it" (2005, 10) but "not ... as a race-less" (2006, 11), "one of the master's tools (Blackness being another) that people of African descent tested for its possible usefulness in attempting to at least get into the master's house" (2006, 11). Though the "complicity between culture and imperialism" (Radhakrishnan 2008, 179) is well established (Said 1993), Nwankwo (2006, 163) argues that "imperialism and colonialism themselves are forms of cosmopolitanism. Responses and resistance to these forms, then, are often also cosmopolitanism." Like Thomas Popkewitz (2008, 40, 111, 172), Nwankwo inflates the term so that contains its contraries. Historicizing particularizes the concept, and it becomes clear that "the cosmopolitanism of modernity, of the early decades of the century, was not about the erosion of difference" (Nava 2007, 6) but, indeed, about its attractiveness (2007, 91).

   In addition to black cosmopolitanism, there is a Native American form of cosmopolitanism, *avant la lettre*, evident in *Ohiyesa*'s (later Charles A. Eastman's) reminiscence regarding his self-formation as a Sioux: "After arriving at a reverent sense of the pervading presence of the Spirit and Giver of Life, and a deep consciousness of the brotherhood of man, the first thing for me to accomplish was to adapt myself perfectly to natural things—in other words, to harmonize myself with nature" (quoted in Krupat 1994, 260). Here are two of the three structures of subjectivity worldliness cultivates (as I discuss in this chapter).

3. Humanism's dismissal owing to its association with racism, imperialism, and colonialism is rhetorical excess, Appiah (2005, 250) implies: "But, of course, Hume's or Kant's or Hegel's inability to imagine that an African could achieve anything in the sphere of 'arts and letters' is objectionable not because it is humanist or universalist but because it is neither." Like the subject (Jay 2005, 2007 ff.), humanism has—thanks, in part, to Edward Said (2004)—reemerged in recent years (Radhakrishnan 2008, 6, 20, 139 ff.), derived from "the complex and forbidding 'new humanism' of Frantz Fanon" (Gilroy 2005, 40). Its "point of launch" is the "very legacy" of colonialism that accompanied humanism (Radhakrishnan 2008, 18). The revival of humanism today is also part of a larger project, as Amanda Anderson explains.

> Partly in reaction to the excesses of identity politics, and partly in response to the political and ethical impasses of a strictly negative critique of Enlightenment, a number of theorists have begun to reexamine universalism, asking how we might best combined the critique of partial or false universals

with the pursuit of those emancipatory ideals associated with traditional universalism (2006, 69).

That combination would include, but not be subsumed by, questions of identity. Indeed, after the "undoing of identity politics" (Gilroy 2005, 79), the new humanism reemerges as a "post-posthumanism" in the "aftermath of poststructuralism" (Lather 2007, 3, 1), and now that feminism has become "a dinosaur discourse" (Lather 2007, 12; for a contrasting assessment of feminism: see Seigfried 1996, 259; for a critique of Lather's feminism, see Grande 2004, 23, 148 ff.). Curiously, Lather's "postmodern mantras" (Cusset 2008, 284) disappear in an interlude of "straight talk," naked in a hot tub replying to female colleagues' questions. Catching the inconsistency, she claims she didn't mean it: "An apparent nakedness is but a mask that conceals a will to power" (Lather 2007, 17). Naked or not, poststructuralism's political potential has, evidently, evaporated (Fish 2008), exposed as "a post-representational form of narcissism that could keep multiplying its textual pleasures, aporias, and indeterminacies in an atmosphere of wall-to-wall discourse" (Radhakrishnan 2008, 21). The stage is now set for an "unabashed humanism" informing a worldliness that might be summarized as "planetarity" (Gilroy 2005, xv, 79, 151), in which the particular does not disappear in a fetishizing of "undecidability" (Radhakrishnan 2008, 38). "[T]he universal," Sekyi-Otu (1996, 202) notes, "is generated out of the constituent assembly and acts of the 'many ones'." No dinosaurs here: Humanism's affirmation of "the irreducible value of each person's experience is also central to feminist theory" (Seigfried 1996, 223). "Worldliness," as Radhakrishnan (2008, 128) notes (in reference to Said but relevant here): "precedes any other kind of determination or fixation."

Addams was inspired by nineteenth-century humanism, including Mazzini's "heartfelt humanism" (Appiah 2005, 241). A "product of northern progressivism" (Allen 2001, 50), Bragg was imprinted by Addams and Dewey. Pasolini's intellectual development was influenced by the humanism at the "core" of the Italian school curriculum (Viano 1993, 3, 5). Later, humanism signified "human" resistance against neocapitalism in this "Era of Applied Science" (Pasolini 2005 [1972], 30). Gilroy's (2005, xv–xvi) "unabashed humanism" is "derived from an explicit moral and political opposition to racism, and projects a different humanity, capable of interrupting the liberal, Cold War, and exclusionary humanisms that characterize most human-rights talk." Linking it with cosmopolitanism (2005, 4), Gilroy (2005, 40, 79, 151) characterizes his position specifically as a "planetary humanism," recalling Spivak's (2003, 71) conception of "planetarity." She suggests that the "sacred" is "a name for nature as radical alterity" (Spivak 1999, 319, n. 10). A form of cosmopolitan consciousness, then, the new humanism—an "ethico-political stance" (Radhakrishnan 2008, 155)—acknowledges species' interrelatedness and embeddedness in the biosphere while affirming the sacredness of the individual person (Seki-Otu above; Jay 2005, 328).

4. There is here an instance of metalepsis: the transformation of an effect into a cause (Anderson 2006, 49). It may be that certain personalities are drawn to conservative religion, as certain personalities are drawn to racism, misogyny, homophobia (Young-Bruehl 1996). Listening to testimonies of the "saved," it seems to me that a mix of cruel circumstances and personal ineptitude drives some into the various cults constitutive of conservative Christianity (Stein 2001, 120, 122).

5. Though a method for unearthing the past (the regressive phase), discovering one's sense of the future (the progressive moment), constructing self-understanding (the analytic phase) and enacting self-mobilization (the synthetic moment),

currere has never been a formula, as my transposition of the autobiographical into a collective reflexivity makes clear (Pinar 2004). No guide to how to live or formula for producing "revolution,"[6] these portraits of passionate lives do demonstrate that public service is not separable from private subjective life, as the case of Jane Addams makes clear (Lasch 1965, 2). Recasting cosmopolitanism as worldliness enables us to envisage "working from within" (Pinar 1994 [1972], 7ff.) as simultaneously subjective and social, recalling "the distinctive *worldliness* of Du Bois' humanist thinking" (Gilroy 2005, 33, 35), and Pasolini's appreciation that one must "retrogress" in order to be "progressive" (Gordon 1996, 66).

6. Denise Taliaferro Baszile (2006, 8, 18) is compelling in her discussion of cultural perquisites of social change, including the lighting of "fire" within. Zitkala-Ša tells us that she was "keenly alive to the fire within" (quoted in Krupat 1994, 282). "Fire" is passion, without which "nothing is called into existence" (Garrison 1997, 80). While affirming the significance of "fire" or passion, I disagree with Baszile that "revolution" should be an educational "purpose." Not only does such a conception relegate revolution to an objective of instrumental action (a profoundly anti-revolutionary scheme in a neo-capitalist regime that reduces all action to an ends-means illogic), it ignores the totalizing triumph of capitalism ("nothing can be exterior to capital anymore" [Cusset 2008, 213]), "the impossibility of meaningful action" (Gordon 1996, 180). There is, no longer, "any space outside the totality, whether one looks inwardly … or outwardly.… [I]nstitutions of power will quickly soak up any alterity, homogenize it, and allow it to circulate harmlessly in electronic space as a sign of 'progressivism' or daring" (Restivo 2002, 66). Even Michael F. D. Young (2008, 102) now calls for an "evolutionary" rather than "transformative … model of educational change."

Today the term *revolution* seems more suitable for Hollywood, including those "action" sit-coms called "critical pedagogy," a conspicuous example of what Pasolini (2005 [1972], 125) termed a "decoy-concept," this one compensating for professors' "*powerlessness*" (Cusset 2008, xii, 213). Incantations of "democracy" are also meaningless, since, as a way of life (Seigfried 1996, 58, 68), democracy has been replaced with consumerism, religious fundamentalism, and identitarianism. Education in schools disappears as well, replaced by test taking, rendering titles like *Reclaiming Education for Democracy* (Shaker and Heilman 2008) quixotic indeed. "Today," Mariniello (1994, 114) points out in a different but related context, "factories and business firms replace universities in spreading culture and a new, completely different, society is coming to life." Acknowledging the anthropological catastrophe that is the triumph of consumer capitalism, in September 1968 Pasolini observed: "we shall only ever be able to know reality 'through' the system, never 'beyond' the system" (quoted in Gordon 1996, 64). I focus on the past, not as a "golden age" gone by but as provocation for persistence now that hope is gone. Despite his enormous appeal, Barack Obama affords me little comfort, given the historic readiness of the Democrats to abdicate education to the right wing. To wit, in his Denver speech accepting the Democratic Party's presidential nomination, Obama called for "an army [!] of new teachers." While he pledges to pay teachers "higher salaries and give them more support," he also pledges to "ask for higher standards and more accountability" (accessed on August 30, 2008, from http://www.gantdaily.com/news/68/ARTICLE/29352/2008-08-28.html). No "change" here: even Obama succumbs to the rhetoric of school deform. Under these circumstances, "revolution" exists only as "writing" (Cusset 2008, 213): an educational objective on a syllabus in Oxford, Ohio.

7. Abandoning any struggle to coincide with ideals severed from flesh and fellowship, worldliness accepts the sensual and sublime as intertwined. "We insist," Nussbaum (2006, 278) asserts, "that need and capacity, rationality and

animality, are thoroughly interwoven, and that the dignity of the human being is the dignity of a needy enmattered being." For the worldly-wise, there can be no definitive distinction between sexuality and spirituality, between sustainability and subjectivity, reason and emotion (Garrison 1997, 33). Though worldliness is a given, it is also a state of being expressed through individuated aesthetic and intellectual forms. Thus, as Radhakrishnan (2008, 130) points out, "[t] here is no way of separating the reality of the world from the modal theoretical practices that establish a certain relationship to the real. It is within modality that the world becomes worldly." For Addams, it was social ethics performed through Hull-House; for Bragg, her boxes and exhibits; for Pasolini, his movies, poems, novels, newspaper articles, and theoretical essays. For us teachers, it is the curriculum that enables us to establish (and reestablish, again and again, in individuated ways) for our students and ourselves "a certain relationship to the real." It is through academic study structured by lived experience that the world becomes accessible.

"The worldliness of American curriculum studies" is a phrase Janet L. Miller (2005, 249) conceived to acknowledge not only 9/11 and its aftermath but, in education, "school deform" (that phrase is mine) through high-stakes testing and curricular standardization. As her scholarship demonstrates, that worldliness is autobiographical, political, and aesthetic, rendering curriculum "accountable to the outside" (Radhakrishnan 2008, 131). For the field's intellectual history and present circumstances see: Pinar et al. 1995, 2008, Autio 2005; Malewski in press; Pinar 2003.

8. For insightful discussions of "distance" see Taubman 1990, 127; Nussbaum 1997, 57–58; Kögler 1999, 174; Gilroy 2005, 67; Jay 2005, 333; Anderson 2006, 1; Seigfried 1996, 93. "There is," Anderson (2006, 70) reminds, "a term that throughout its long philosophical, aesthetic, and political history has been used to denote cultivated detachment from restrictive forms of identity, and that term is 'cosmopolitanism'." Such detachment—"a distinctive introspective space" (McBride 2006, 112)—is not indifference, but intensified engagement with the world, creating crevices through the apparently impenetrable present. Roberto Unger (2007, 121) suggests "we cannot escape the gravitational field of the present situation by a methodological maneuver or a conceptual stipulation at the outset of our intellectual and political work… We can escape it only by a relentless campaign within the context, uncovering its fault lines and discovering its hidden opportunities of transformation." This I take as an endorsement of immanence over transcendence, a pragmatist restatement of psychoanalytic insight. The "examined life" (Nussbaum 1997, 8) —as represented by the academic study of philosophy—is now, evidently, chosen more often by U.S. university students who have, since 1968, often emphasized business (Donadio 2007; Hu 2008b), unsurprising in that during these decades the university itself has become another business (Finder 2008).

9. Academic knowledge faces an uncertain future in public schools, as the marketplace—a cover for right-wing efforts to control the curriculum, stripping it of its critical capacities—rules without competition. What students are to "learn" is not knowledge but "skills," a vacuous concept meaning whatever standardized test profiteers take it to mean. Now it is time for progressives to appropriate Spencer's question—what knowledge is of most worth?—to affirm academic freedom (Petrina 2008; Goodman 2006, 52; Seigfried 1996, 234), that is, the intellectual independence of individual teachers and students committed to study what arts, humanities, and sciences scholars have discovered, summarized by curriculum developers (Pinar 2006b).

10. To help us understand the nightmare that was the present, I invoked the psychoanalytic notion of "deferred action" (*Nachtraglichkeit*), a term Freud had

formulated to specify how the experience of trauma is deferred—and, I would add, displaced—into other subjective and social spheres, where it is often no longer readily recognizable. I argued that the gendered "trauma" of the Cold War in the 1950s and the 1954 U.S. Supreme Court decision to desegregate the public schools (coupled with the visibility of college students in 1960s civil rights struggles) was "displaced and deferred" onto public education. In the aftermath of these "trauma," public education was racialized and gendered in the American popular imagination. Bluntly stated, we can understand the nightmare that is our subjugation in the present only if we appreciate that teachers are the victims of displaced and deferred misogyny and racism (Pinar 2004). Though the genesis of teachers' "gracious submission" differs, in Canada the consequence—the erasure of academic freedom as the curriculum is linked to students' scores on standardized examinations—seems the same (Mahoney and Peritz 2008).

11. The lives of Addams, Bragg, and Pasolini communicate distinctive meanings of passion, including that associated with the suffering of Jesus between the night of the Last Supper and his death (Jay 2005, 95). Dating from his 1940s poetry and fiction (Viano 1993, 41), Pasolini's passion (Rohdie 1995, 51, 109, 183; Viano 1993, 39) led him to identify with the suffering of Christ: He had his mother play Mary in his film version of *The Gospel According to St. Matthew*. I am "still surviving,/in a long extension/Of unexhausted,/inexhaustible passion/that almost has its roots in another time," Pasolini (quoted in Ryan-Scheutz 2007, 29) wrote. In *Teorema*, Viano (1993, 212) points out, "passion for the life of the body is also the passion for the absolute." Spiritual and sexual passion converge in Pasolini. "[T]here is no wisdom without passion and imagination," Jim Garrison (1997, 20) asserts.

    Addams and Bragg suffered as they struggled with their psychic legacies and public circumstances. Though the term's meaning as "suffering" is considered obsolete (by Merriam-Webster's dictionary), it is not irrelevant here, as suffering seems inevitable to those whose lives are lived passionately. Despite being vilified for her pacifism, Addams's "passionate devotion to the ideals of democracy" (Lasch 1965, 21) became compassion (Lasch 1965, xiii) for democracy's victims; Bragg's passion for experimental art and social activism cost her her position. Emotion is another concept associated with passion (and intelligence: see Garrison 1997, 95), as in an intense or overmastering feeling or conviction, including an outbreak of anger (Boler 1999, 190). "[A]n amalgam of rage, passion, and the deep desire for self-dignity," Baszile (2006, 9) declares, "have led many to re/claim the power to define one's own reality, the power to do, the power to be agentive, the power to pursue a freedom dream." Also included in Merriam-Webster's definition of passion is "ardent affection," as in a strong liking or devotion to some activity, object, or concept, as in deep interest. Passion is an expression of interiority through intense engagement with the public world, as through a "freedom dream." Passion also refers to the state or capacity of being acted on by external agents or forces. Those agents—parents, teachers, loved and loathed ones—and forces—politics, history, culture—form the psychic and social subject matter with which public servants—including teachers—labor in service to others.

12. Recent scholarship regarding public service emphasizes its democratic, even transformational, potential. "*Public servants*," Denhardt and Denhardt (2007, xi) emphasize, "*do not deliver customer service; they deliver democracy*." Public service is an expansive concept that includes teaching (Denhardt and Denhardt 2007, 4). From their studies of "transformational" public servants, King and Zanetti (2005, 117) conclude that "they are deeply passionate about their work," as well, "they are deeply relational: their work and their rewards come out of relationships." Each had, at some point, been "cast in the role of a scapegoat"

(King and Zanetti 2005, 131), a fate shared by Addams, Bragg, and Pasolini. "Self-reflective work" (2005, 134)—including a gendered subjective restructuring (2005, 136)—is recommended in preparation for public service, work requiring, King and Zanetti (2005, 138) suggest, balancing passion with "acceptance" and "detachment." Reminding me of the autobiographical tradition in curriculum studies, King and Zanetti (2005, 146) assert: "To practice our work in the public interest, we have to first (and always) practice our work on ourselves." In concert with curriculum theory's repudiation of the business model of education (Pinar 2004, 235), Denhardt and Denhardt (2007, 3) assert: "Government shouldn't be run like a business; it should be run like a democracy." There are other parallels between the two fields, including an acknowledgement that the work of public servants cannot "be made predictable and objective" (Denhardt and Denhardt 2007, 124). Committed to serve citizens as "stewards of public resources (2007, 152), public servants "must share power and lead with passion, commitment, and integrity" (2007, 154), facilitating "citizenship and democratic dialogue" (2007, 152). Understanding "public service as an extension of citizenship" (2007, 53) recalls Knight's characterization of Jane Addams as, above all, a citizen.

13. "For in virtually all of its manifestations," Martin Jay (2005, 158) points out, "aesthetic experience meant a privileging of the subject, whether contemplative, productive, or self-fashioning, over the art object." As in the project of teaching curriculum theory (Pinar 2004) or whiteness (Pinar 2006) or racial violence (Pinar 2001), I teach the subject at hand—in the present instance, the worldliness of a cosmopolitan education—through juxtapositions of the summarized scholarship of others. "The strategy of juxtaposition," Janet Miller (2005, 144) and her colleagues suggest, "is one that invites inconsistencies, ambiguities, ambivalence, and foregrounds the fact that there will always be 'unspoken themes' that cannot or will not be interrogated." Radhakrishnan (2008, 3) employs juxtaposition— whether of systems of thought or of individuals—to forefront the "complex, contradictory, and unpredictable relationships between the places" people inhabit and the "spaces where they think." In Pasolinian terms, the "juxtaposition of languages where reality is differentially represented" discloses "the real ... beyond the confines all language, so that reality as no longer symbolized but is purely itself" (Rohdie 1995, 63; 30, 32; Viano 1993, 115; Fabbri 1994, 84). Juxtaposition enables "contamination" (Rohdie 1995, 123; Gordon 1996, 116; Note 32, Chapter 7). As in his 1964 *Comizi d'amore* where the various voices of the film 'rub against one another,' juxtaposition "illustrates ... *the very problem of the constitution of the object of study*" (Restivo 2002, 79). How? As the juxtaposition of heteronymous elements, Jacques Rancière (2008) pointed out, collage renders discernible interrelationships among apparently unrelated subjects. So conceived, collage contests the equivalence of constituent elements through the contiguity of apparently incommensurable subjects. Abrogating a simplistic narrativism (typical of so-called narrative inquiry: see Clandinin and Connelly 2004) that fails to appreciate narrative's genesis in self-difference and conflict (Britzman and Gilbert 2008, 200-1), juxtaposition creates split spaces among contiguous, perhaps dissonant, elements of difference that enable readers to breathe (Pinar 2004, 2)—no airtight argument here—by positioning elements in "creative tensionality" (Aoki 2005 [1986/1991], 161–164). Such curriculum design is no recipe for academic "success": As intellectual labor rather than bureaucratic protocol, juxtaposition constitutes an aesthetic-inspired reconfiguration of scholarship that invites complicated conversation among students and teachers focused on the texts that speak to them and through which they find their voices: curriculum development as a "theoretical practice" (Cusset 2008, 240). Juxtaposition has also been associated with the practices of "DJs." In his discussion of "French theory" in the United States, Cusset (2008,

[handwritten marginal note: Juxtaposition creates a third place]

258) describes the practice of a DJ named "Spooky" who juxtaposes Duchamp with Fanon, Nietzsche with Philip Glass, haiku with jazz, inspired by "theories of excess and creative misreading." The combination, Cusset (2008, 258) continues, produces "a real event" associated with a "culture of subversion." I am not suggesting that curriculum developers—or teachers—become DJs, but the association may underscore those elements of aesthetic play and communication in planning the complicated conversation that is curriculum.

14. The evidently disguised danger in the term *learning* (as it is deployed today) is missed by many education professors, despite the great curriculum theorist Dwayne Huebner's explicit warning over three decades ago (1999, 133–136). Among his concerns was that the term (as usurped by educational psychology) distracted educators from "the fact that man is above all else a being caught in succession and duration," a distraction disabling us from "find[ing] a means to express his concern for man's temporality" (136). Instead, as Markell (2003, 22) suggests, "[s]ocial subordination can be understood as a means of avoiding or disavowing the open-ended temporality of human action by converting that existential problem of time into the technical problem of the organization of social space." The link between "subordination" and contemporary conceptions of "learning" becomes explicit: First, "learning" elides the question of what knowledge is of most worth as it directs attention to the acquisition of whatever knowledge is taught. For the teacher, the point becomes "how" to teach whatever must be taught, foreclosing her academic freedom by enlisting her in an instrumentalist effort to implement the directives of policy makers dissociated from the academic disciplines and from the specificity of individual teachers and students in actual classrooms. Dissociation is the second issue: Stripping students and teachers of their agency, the press is to acquire quickly and much, today meaning "skills" not knowledge. As Addams autobiographically records, what is lost is emotion, the opportunity to work through (on one's own and with others) what one has undertaken to study, including working through those gendered emotions that could enable ethical inventiveness and moral responsibility (Lasch 1965, 16–17). Addams's concern for temporality of educational experience is refracted, we could say, through Pasolini's struggle to understand the present by studying strategies of signification in texts (Fabbri 1994, 79) as well as his call for a "discursive reinscription of the past" (Bruno 1994, 102). Private study is paramount. Pasolini never stopped studying: "every day he studied for long hours" (Volponi 2007 [1976], 126).

15. Readers will learn the circumstances in Chapter 7, but here I want to note that Pasolini's political excommunication has been repeated, this time owing to ideological rather than sexual deviance, and performed not by Party hacks but by scholars Zgymunt Barański (who complains that Pasolini's oeuvre is marred by "self-centeredness" [1999b, 33]) and Joseph Francese (who convicts Pasolini of "Crocean idealism" [1999, 132], a crime that presumably condemned him to a misreading of Gramsci [1999, 135, 138], a "misappropriation" [Rhodes 2007, 58], an "agonistic" (Gordon 1996, 35) or "creative" (Cusset 2008, 117) misreading Pasolini in fact self-consciously claimed: "I strayed from Gramsci," he explains, "because objectively I was not facing the same world as Gramsci" [quoted in Mariniello 1994, 113]. Like Gramsci, Croce regarded passion—see Chapter 1, note 11—as structuring individuals' engagement with the world [Viano 1993, 321, n. 34; Jay 2005, 219]. But Pasolini was critical of Croce's "metahistorical" historiography (Jewell 1992, 31, 245). Francese [1999, 157 n. 12] tries to hedge his bets in a footnote.)

16. Indirectness, says Barthes, has two functions: to permit communication and to preserve subjectivity (Moriarty 1991, 107). The two are not mutually exclusive: The reconstruction of subjectivity—one's ongoing self-formation—takes place

through communication with others, including deceased others through their works, and others yet to appear, as we imagine the world "not yet," as Maxine Greene has eloquently emphasized.

17. "[T]he abiding appeal of autobiography," Krupat (1994, 8) observes, "is exactly the sense we have of an encounter with lives other than and apart from our own." Pasolini was horrified by cultural homogenization, a problem that required attention both to the intellectual and stylistic history of culture and of the genre of poetry in relation to the realities of cultural hegemony. His notion of "free indirect style" in prose narrative and a parallel subjective camera style in cinema conveys his conviction that ideology and representations of subjectivity cannot be separated. For Pasolini, Jewell (1992) emphasizes, ideologies of poetic subjectivity must be grasped historically, since history is the site of their transmission and transformation. Moreover, Gordon (1996, 39) observes, Pasolini "insists on anchoring the ideological validity of an intellectual position in an operation of subjective introspection."

Though acknowledging Croce's influence (1999, 331) in Pasolini's intellectual formation, David Ward points out that Marxism is "of interest to Pasolini not as a totalizing ideology which will provide an ultimate new interpretation of the world" but, rather, as providing an opportunity for "rupture ... within dominant bourgeois ideology" (1999, 333). "The Communists," Pasolini declared, "are fighting for civil rights in the name of an *otherness*" (quoted in Meekins 1999, 242). "In other words," Ward (1999, 334) continues,

> Pasolini is willing to stay within Marxism as long as the task it sets itself is that of deconstructing dominant ideology. When, however, Marxism establishes itself to such an extent that it constructs an alternative orthodoxy, then Pasolini is quick to proclaim his ideological independence.

For the doctrinaire, this is a "so-called Marxism" (Francese 1999, 134). For educators, such "rupture" illustrates the educational significance of autobiographical labor.

18. For Barthes as for Pasolini, writing was no simple communication of a message but "an ongoing process engaging multiple incommensurable codes, thus untranslatable in terms of a global signified, thus splitting and disturbing the Western symbolic regime" (Moriarty 1991, 115). Writing in his diary in 1910, Robert Musil reminds that "One should not paint mood but allow the desired measure of lyricism to grow from the shaping of facts" (quoted in McBride 2006, 59). Likewise, subjectivity is expressed autobiographically but indirectly, through the ideas narrated and juxtaposed in synoptic texts, that classic medium of curriculum development (Pinar 2006b). So structured, the textbook, like Pasolini's (2005 [1972], 192) screenplay,

> expresses *"a will of the form to become another" above and beyond the form; that is, it captures "the form in movement"*—a movement that finishes freely and in various manners in the fantasy of the writer and in the cooperating and friendly fantasy of the reader, the two coinciding freely and in different ways.

The synoptic textbook—including this one—is structured (through juxtaposition) to precipitate complicated conversation. "This inscription of will or desire into a text," Gordon (1996, 221) observes, "can be taken as coterminous with the inscription of subjectivity into a text."

2   On the Agony and Ecstasy of the Particular

1. An earlier version of the first section of this chapter was presented to the Provoking Curriculum Conference on February 24, 2007, Banff, Alberta, Canada. Entitled "Curricular Absence: Indigenous Concepts of Citizenship and Community in the Context of Trans-National Inquiry," that session featured papers by Dwayne Donald (University of Alberta), Nicholas Ng-A-Fook (University of Ottawa), and Makere Stewart-Harawira (University of Alberta). I had access to the Ng-A-Fook and Donald papers beforehand. Though designated a discussant, I took the occasion to discuss the general matter of identity politics, not only a problem (see Alcoff et al. 2006 for a "defense" that illustrates the problem, namely that "the politics of recognition ... is at odds with itself" [Markell 2003, 59], obliterating identity in the name of identity) in curriculum studies that demanded attention, in my view, as the allegation, made during the 2006 Purdue University Conference, that U.S. curriculum studies paid no substantive attention to race. This unsubstantiated claim—such a claim cannot, in fact, be substantiated (Pinar, et al. 1995, 315 ff., for example)—was part of a larger identity politics event at the Purdue Conference during which several self-designated "representatives" of various victimized groups voiced indignation at their alleged under-representation at the conference and in the field (not exactly a novel gesture: Cusset 2008, 169, 173). One of participants in this identity politics event later rewrote the conference as exemplary multiculturalism (Gaztambide-Fernández 2006, 63)! Aside from curriculum studies sounding white (2006, 61), Gaztambide-Fernández's primary complaint appears to be that some mispronounce his first name (2006, 62). One year after this nonsense, I found myself positioned in the Alberta session (February 24, 2007) as the "fall guy" for another "curricular absence," this time inattention to indigenous peoples. In tandem with the Bush Administration's sustained assaults on U.S. public schools and on schools of education, identity politics (never mind its misuse of "strategic essentialism": jagodzinski 2006, 55)—performs a parody of professional ethics. As the above misconduct makes clear, professional ethics are replaced by opportunistic acts of indignation in the service of a cynical careerism (Young 2008, 198; Cusset 2008, 189).

2. Virtually every non-white group gets funneled into the concept—"culturally-responsive pedagogy"—eliding not only distinctive cultural characteristics between and within these groups but erasing as well specific histories of victimization, resistance, and triumph. By the "logic" of culturally responsive pedagogy, students of European descent should study only European and European-American history and culture. By failing to focus on larger issues of social reconstruction—economic justice, for instance—Gay lends credence to conservatives' assertion that teachers alone are responsible for students' academic underachievement. There is no self-criticism, disabling parents from taking any authority in—and responsibility for—their children's achievement. Students are likewise absolved of any responsibility. One would conclude that academic underachievement is solely a function of teachers' malpractice and that with the implementation of Gay's model, test scores would soar. Poverty and other legacies of racism—not to mention class size, the erudition and the ethics of the teacher, the intellectual quality of curricular materials—are all sidebars: Only "culturally-responsive pedagogy" matters.

3. Zitkala-Ša's three autobiographical essays, along with a fourth autobiographical piece, short stories, and a political tract, were published as *American Indian Stories* in 1921 (Katanski 2005, 132). Several of these are available online: http://www.wsu.edu/~campbelld/amlit/zitkala.htm Krupat (1994, 3) notes "that the genre of writing referred to in the West as *autobiography* had no close parallel in

the traditional cultures of the indigenous inhabitants of the Americas, misnamed 'Indians.'" That Zitkala-Ša wrote autobiographical essays indicates her active engagement with the world Europeans enforced. The earliest Native American autobiography, Krupat (1994, 5) tells us, was composed in 1768 by the Reverend Samson Occom, a Mohegan.

4. Emily Katanski (2005, 122) tells us that Zitkala-Ša's fluency in English did not automatically alter her "way of thinking or make her more amenable to the schools' assimilating project." The stigma of assimilation—associated with studying "whitestream" language and culture—may be fading among some Native Americans (Johnson 2008) at the same time many emphasize the particularity of Native American voices through poetry (Frosch 2008).

5. Dakota and Lakota are Siouan languages of the Great Plains. They are so closely related that most linguists consider them dialects of the same language, similar to the difference between British and American English. There are some differences in pronunciation, but they are very regular, and Dakota and Lakota Indians can almost always understand each other. The Nakota languages—Stoney and Assiniboine—are also related languages but are impossible for a Dakota or Lakota Sioux speaker to understand without language lessons, as Dutch is for English speakers. There are a combined 16,000 speakers of Lakota and Dakota Sioux in the north-central United States and southern Canada. Accessed on February 17, 2007 from http://www.native-languages.org/dakota.htm

6. http://www.wsu.edu/~campbelld/amlit/zitkala.htm (accessed on February 21, 2007).

7. "[R]acial branding," Nussbaum (1995, 95) notes, "eclipses personal identity," and thereby "prevents ... [any] common view of humanity" (1995, 96). After the repudiation of the racism that accompanied imperialism and colonialism, in subsequent stages of theorizing alterity, the "other" remained de-individuated, conflated with radical difference, with utterly inscrutable alien reality, denoted by the capital "O." Levinas comes to mind; Spivak (1999, 283) declared that "knowledge of the other subject is theoretically impossible." To the extent that is true (I think Spivak overstates the case), a politics of recognition—on which identity politics is, in part, based—becomes impossible. Perhaps this problem is a factor in prompting Patchen Markell to prefer a politics of acknowledgement, a conception that follows from her conviction that "the source of relations of subordination lies not in the failure to recognize the identity of the other, but in the failure to acknowledge one's own basic situation and circumstances" (2003, 7). Autobiography would seem central to such a politics.

8. Kant's fantasy—his 1795 essay is entitled *Toward Perpetual Peace*—was that cosmopolitanism would follow a world federation of republican nation-states trading with each other: Marshall, 1997, 62; Pojman 2005). Pheng Cheah (2006, 81) is convinced that

> Any contemporary revival of cosmopolitanism, however, must take a critical distance from the ancestor cosmopolitanism of philosophical modernity best represented by Kant's project for perpetual peace.... The history of colonialism has disproved Kant's benign view of the unifying power of international commerce and discredited the moral-civilizing claims of cosmopolitan culture.

It is Cheah's (2006, 5ff.) critique of cosmopolitanism—and its reliance upon transcendence—that first focused my interest in worldliness.

9. One problem with identity politics is that it converts such complexity to simplicity and in so doing reduces the other to its identitarian positioning, thereby disqualifying her or him from extending solidarity to others or taking

individual action. Moreover, in emphasizing victimhood, identity politics often fails to articulate the complexity and specificity of post-colonial and specifically diasporic moments for historically victimized groups, as it freezes and congeals "fractured and mingled identities" into collectivized abstractions. As Appiah (2006, 113) notes: "Cultural purity is an oxymoron."

10. Recall that even the "official curriculum" (Garrison 1997, 29) is a "complicated conversation" (Pinar et al. 1995, 848). The curriculum is a central site where the cultivation of cosmopolitanism can be undertaken.

11. Elizabeth Macedo (in Pinar 2007a, xxiv) theorizes the school curriculum as a "space of enunciation" providing political and intellectual opportunities for subjectively-existing individuals to testify to the lived experience of public events through the discursive means the academic disciplines supply.

12. Affirming the prerogative of the particular to negotiate its relation to the abstract is Sneja Gunew's (2004, 54) suggestion that "[I]nternationalization could perhaps be reserved for the ways in which each nation state (and smaller groupings) chooses to respond to globalization, as far as possible, on its own terms." Illustrating its potential to perturb the provincialism of the local is Daniel Tröhler's (2003, 778) characterization of internationalization as "international discussion among scholars who are historically self-aware of their own traditions, not in order to defend them, but—on the contrary—to allow different or foreign arguments to be understood." For more information regarding the Centre, visit http://csics.educ.ubc.ca/

13. It is the nation-state that provides the organization for the federally funded (by the Social Sciences and Humanities Research Council of Canada) study I am now conducting concerning the internationalization of three nationally distinctive curriculum studies fields: those in South Africa, Brazil, and Mexico. I am hardly idealizing the nation-state, however: as Benhabib (2006, 177) points out, its political sovereignty is being privatized and corporatized. Still, as an "imagined community," the nation-state remains a key site for understanding curriculum: "[e]ducation remains a resolutely local and national project" (Mayer, Luke and Luke 2008, 91).

14. Accessed on December 26, 2007 from http://www.historyguide.org/intellect/fourier.html

15. Accessed on December 20, 2007 from http://www.historyguide.org/intellect/lecture21a.html

16. First among worldliness' synonyms is "earthly," reminding us that worldliness concerns not only the social sphere but the biosphere as well. Huebner blurs the distinction between "transcendence" and "worldliness" when he writes: "Education is the lure of the transcendent—that which we seem is not what we are, for we could always be other" (1999, 360).

17. Accessed on December 13, 2007 from http://www.raystedman.org/misc/worldly.html Another view of the Christian life is to enter the world fully, filled with faith, provoked by passion: "To be a Christian does not mean to be religious in a particular way, to cultivate some particular form of asceticism ... but to be a [person in the world]. It is not a religious act that makes a Christian what he [or she] is, but participation in the suffering of God in the life of the world" (Bonhoeffer 1953, 166-7).

18. For Pasolini (quoted in Rohdie 1995, 4), the lumpenproletariat—because they are "outside bourgeois consciousness"—are "always in a certain measure 'pure.'" In particular, Pasolini felt the speech of peasants and pimps to be closest to an "earthy real," and he made films as a "homage to the primitive," as well as a "contestation of the communicative, unreal, functional unpoetic languages of the bourgeoisie: the languages of reason, of modern society, of capitalism, of exploitation, of politics" (Rohdie 1995, 49; Greene 1990, 17; Ryan-Scheutz

2007, 12). For Pasolini, the *borgate* [slum] was "a world of fierce and generous instincts" (quoted in Rohdie 1995, 49). In the New Orleans Old Quarter, I spent several years among the local lumpen, whom I would not claim to know, except poetically (Rohdie 1995, 96). No generalizations, then, only memories, as Pasolini emboldens me:

> For the lumpen I knew
> money was a means to pleasure, only.
> No shop-keepers, school-teachers
> parceling out commodities,
> storing up dreams.
> No, they were
> giving and taking
> in moments like these.
> Anxieties released, never
> stored up for Thee.

February 12, 2008

19. In Fall 1972, in a *Black Scholar* article entitled "On Lumpen Ideology," Cleaver—introduced as "internationally known as a black revolutionary and theoretician" (Rout 1991, 171)—expanded his definition of the lumpenproletariat: He asserted that "the Lumpen condition" is "basic" to all "dispossessed people," even though some "lift themselves out" and into "the proletarian condition," sometimes only temporarily. Thus, the lumpen, "understood in its broader sense," were what used to be called the proletariat, some of whom were always unemployed. For the lumpen, it is just to demand "to be cut in on Consumption in spite of being blocked out of production." This, he asserted, "is the ultimate revolutionary demand." Wealth *is*: No one needs to produce it, as Kathleen Rout summarizes this scheme. "The point is not," Cleaver clarified, "equality in Production, which is the Marxist view and basic error, but equality in distribution and consumption." Future labor will be unnecessary, thanks to "technological advances," and while we wait for that future, the unemployable have a right to consume (quoted passages in Rout 1991, 141-142).

Rout (1991, 171) suggests that this essay is the "clearest" and "most extreme" expression of Cleaver's anti-proletarian, pro-lumpen preference, which, she notes, dates back to at least 1968. Cleaver declares that the members of the working class to be "a part of the system that has to be destroyed" because they claim a share in that system. Cleaver: "The real revolutionary element of our era is the Lumpen, understood in its broad sense," that is, as "the vast majority" of mankind. True "Lumpen consciousness" assumes that "the Lumpen, humanity itself, has been robbed of its social heritage by the concentration and centralization of technology." All the wealth technology produces belongs to "the people." "The point is not equality in Production, which is the Marxist error, but equality in distribution and consumption": Those who produce nothing have the same "right to consume" as those who do. His view, claims Cleaver, is "more advanced" than the "job-seeking, fringe benefit consciousness of the AFL/CIO/ Communist Party/Working Class accommodationist movement"; this is "the ultimately revolutionary demand" (quoted passages in Rout 1991, 171).

20. "Deculturation" is hardly limited to the lumpenproletariat, of course; it describes as well the traumas undergone, for instance, by the indigenous population of Canada. Accessed on December 20, 2007, from (http://www.canadiana.org/citm/ themes/aboriginals/aboriginals9_e.html

21. Before working with Tosquelles, Fanon studied Sartre, Heidegger, Jaspers, Kierkegaard, and Merleau-Ponty. For Fanon, existentialism was, Geismar (1971,

125) suggests, "the basis of politics." His political education had already begun in Lyon (where he studied medicine), as he read Lenin, Marx, and Trotsky while studying Freud and Lacan. Fanon's studies traversed the psychiatric and the political, the subjective and the social, stressing the compulsory continuity between individual and political freedom (Verges 1996).

22. McCulloch points out that Fanon was sensitive to the problems posed by psychological features of the lumpenproletariat; many of his patients at Blida were drawn from this traumatized class. In revolutionary Algeria, the lumpen were often refugees from a devastated rural economy, now landless peasants populating urban slums (McCulloch 1983, 154). McCulloch credits Fanon with being the first to identify the numerical significance and political potential of the lumpenproletariat.

23. That concept suggests one point of studying the lumpenproletariat for the bourgeoisie, the incorporation of that class's acceptance of the flesh, i.e. the cultivation of a "sexual cosmopolitanism" (Savran 1998, 152). Not without its risks (Lane 2002, 301ff.), voluptuous is defined as (1) a: full of delight or pleasure to the senses: conducive to or arising from sensuous or sensual gratification: luxurious <a voluptuous dance> <voluptuous ornamentation> <a voluptuous wine> b: suggesting sensual pleasure by fullness and beauty of form <voluptuous nudes> and (2) given to or spent in enjoyment of luxury, pleasure, or sensual gratifications. The genealogy of whiteness led me to conclude, "voluptuousness, not renunciation, engenders reparation" (Pinar 2006a, 182) The embodiment of immanence, voluptuousness as a state in which self-differentiation of the "collectivity of the individual" (Radhakrishnan 2008, 75) is always already under reconstruction, in part through regression, progression, analysis, and synthesis. Self-shattering, eroticization, and democratization are, then, reciprocally related.

24. Kögler (1999, 246–247) reminds us that "the abstract and pure individual is just as empty and 'transcendental' ... as the concept of total or absolute power; both power and individuality are instead always situated in symbolic order, within which the antagonism between complete conformity to a system and individual self-realization is capable of first being ignited." Like worldliness, individuality is always particularistic, concrete, transitory, situated, its "disunity" (McBride 2006, 111) capable of agency through reconstruction (Seigfried 1996, 251). Finally, it bears repeating that "individuality" is no recent bourgeois fabrication; recall that the concept dates at least to ancient Greeks and their belief that at birth each of us is seized by a daemon that determines our unique potential and destiny (Garrison 1997, 168).

3   Only the Sign is For Sale

1. Darren Lund studies teachers' and students' activism, on one occasion (2003) listing ten suggestions for forming a "Multicultural Action Group." Student activism can be laudable, but teachers' encouragement of it raises questions of professional ethics. Certainly that was Dewey's (and others') concern with Counts's challenge to U.S. schools to build a new social order (1978 [1932]; Perlstein 2000, 51). Lund (2003) relies on Banks's advocacy of schools as "units of change." Lund is hardly alone in risking indoctrination: see Anyon 2005, 178, 188.

2. If one wants to complain about titles, how about *The Subaltern Speak*? Never mind that in Spivak's initial formulation it is not obvious the subaltern *can* speak; worse, in this collection, the subaltern "speak" through professors and graduate students, a glaring example of the "intellectual imperialism" Spivak has so adamantly opposed (Cusset 2008, 200). The term loses its specificity

when forced to represent various "oppressed" groups (among them conservative Christian home-schoolers: Apple 2006). Spivak deplores such sloppy uses of the term, Michael Kilburn (1996) points out, especially its misappropriation to designate marginalized but not specifically "subaltern" groups. "Simply by being postcolonial or the member of an ethnic minority," Spivak (1999, 310) makes clear, "we are not 'subaltern'." (For a more general intellectual history of the concept, see Jay 2005, 242 ff.; Radhakrishnan 2008, 28; for the Buras-Apple "defense" of their (mis)use of the term, see 2006, 19ff.) Michael F. D. Young (2008, 198) criticizes scholars who assume "that their identification with the powerless or with a particular disadvantaged group brings them automatically closer to the truth."

3. Accessed on January 13, 2008, from http://www.websophia.com/faces/kierkegaard.html Even when "signs" post appealing messages, they fail to represent the lived experience and academic knowledge rendering them real. Cosmopolitan teachers, Mayer, Luke and Luke (2008, 81) tell us, will move easily between the local and the global, engaging "with the broad flows of knowledge and information, technologies and populations, artifacts and practices that characterize this historical moment." Such cosmopolitan teachers will form "a new community" that "would work, communicate and exchange ... across national and regional boundaries with each other, with educational researchers, teacher educators, curriculum developers and, indeed, senior educational bureaucrats" (2008, 81). This is a job description substituting behaviors for erudition.

   Focusing on the sign, not the substance it represents, is, in part, a consequence of education's institutionalization. Jane Addams and Ellen Gates Starr appreciated the distraction institutionalization constructs. As they conceived Hull-House, "not being an organization would become a kind of mantra to them, signifying the informal, creative, spontaneous, natural life they wished to lead and the centrality of human relationships to their work." Exemplifying my sense of "free indirect subjectivity," Addams and Starr sought to "achieve influence through their personalities" (Knight 2005, 193), not through bureaucratic protocols regulating (even "progressive") attitudes and behavior. "Institutional time," the Chippewa writer Gerald Vizenor (in Krupat 1994, 426) points out, "belies our personal memories, imagination, and consciousness." Focusing on the institution rather than on the intellectual substance it houses replaces knowledge with protocols, freedom with compliance.

4. When Bill Moyers asked Newark Mayor Corey Booker (on PBS on March 28, 2008) what can be done in Newark (for a history of school reform efforts there: see Anyon 1997), Booker replied that "we" should "look in the mirror," a "we" that obviously encompassed African- and European-Americans. At one point, he offered: "It's all about the spirit." Having lost faith in the usefulness of public debates regarding "race," Booker appreciated that reducing race to sociological determinism blocks individual efforts at political activism and cultural renewal. In her study of Newark schools (1997) and in a subsequent study (2005), Anyon focuses on poverty—clearly key—but barely mentions curriculum and seems altogether unmindful of "spirit" or subjectivity.

5. Restating Huebner (1999, 405) in even stronger terms, Kieran Egan (2002, 113) asserts: "The dominant position that psychology has held in educational thinking consequently seems to me to have been, and continues to be, a bit of a disaster." The inculcation of a content-less concept of "skills" is one consequence of the "disaster," as is "teacher education" empty of specific academic content.

6. To ascribe causal status to the curriculum—whether looking for a scapegoat for military (Sputnik) or economic setbacks (during the early Reagan years) or creating future prosperity (America 2000)—is to invoke the most intellectually

dishonest forms of social engineering. Egan (2002, 115) blames Spencer and his progressive descendents for our contemporaries to be able to imagine the curriculum as "an agent of the economy, of civic virtue, of political responsibility, of technological progress, and of much else." The progressives are hardly the only blameworthy group (radicals like Eugene Debs had little patience for the idea that social reform could be accomplished through education: Cremin 1961, 89); in our time it is conservative Republicans (with help from naïve Democrats) who invoke the association with education and progress to their political advantage. Curiously, while Egan (2002, 147) underscores "the very considerable difficulty of tying educational cause to social effect," he claims to have done so, linking the "educational ideas of progressivism and their less than wonderful educational effects." If the curriculum cannot be the means to the future, it cannot be imagined to have been the conveyance to the present. Evidently confession constitutes absolution: "No doubt I am guilty of the simplistic cause-and-effect connecting I complained about just above" (Egan 2002, 148). One is then free to "sin" again (Egan 2002, 176).

7. Jeff was disappointed to learn that the fabled 40-acres-and-a-mule story was just that: http://www.emergingminds.org/magazine/content/item/1303

8. Kieran Egan (2002, 74) thinks "progressivism got two connected things wrong." The first was the conviction that there is something "natural" about learning and that such natural learning offers a model for how teachers should teach children in school. The second was the conviction that the "scientific study of the nature of human learning will lead to principles for effective teaching." The second error is hardly limited to "progressivism"; it informs much of Bush-era educational research in the U.S. (see Slavin 2008 for an intellectually deadening illustration of the profession's opportunistic complicity with that fascistic administration). Historically, the quixotic quest for a "science" of education has been a gendered folly (Seigfried 1996, 194).

9. Demonstrating his penchant for titles, Lund (2006) writes —in "Waking Up the Neighbors: Surveying Multicultural and Antiracist Education in Canada, the United Kingdom, and the United States"—that he hopes to "stimulate further conversation between theorists and practitioners committed to ideals of equity and fairness in education." His acknowledgement that "only by learning more about our differing histories, perceptions, and social circumstances—along with the overlapping and intersecting aspects of our various interests—can we enhance the collaborative aspect of this challenging and important work"—furthers the cause of cosmopolitanism (and, more specifically, that of "internationalization" among curriculum studies scholars: Pinar 2008, 501), but it appears to focus on "ideals" spilt off from the academic knowledge that makes them intelligible. Spare me, Foucault pleaded, this "morality of bureaucrats and police" that requires philosophers [and teachers] "to remain the same" (quoted in Cusset 2008, 280).

4   A Declaration of Independence

1. This chapter is a speech, delivered on July 6 and 16, 2006 to the Leadership Academy, Massachusetts College of Liberal Arts.

2. There are other exceptionalisms, among them Japanese (Yoshimoto 2002, 374), South African (Muller 2000, 3), Jewish (Gollaher 2000, 9), even gay (Mendelsohn 1996, 31) exceptionalism. For W. E. B. Du Bois, the "problem" of being black was "an issue of both commonality and exceptionalism" (Carby 1998, 31). Spivak (2003, 98) suggests that Du Bois shifted from exceptionalism to egalitarianism: advocating for "the talented tenth" in his early, communism in his later, years. Exceptionalism evidently structures the interdisciplinary field known as American

Studies (Bové 2002, 218) and, allegedly, U.S. progressivism (Tröhler 2006, 94; Hirsch 1999, 95), including multiculturalism (Rowe 2002, 74).

3. Accessed on April 2, 2008, from http://www.whitehouse.gov/history/presidents/jk35.html Regarding Sputnik's role in U.S. curriculum reform, see Pinar 2004, 65 ff; Dean 2007.

4. This is a reference to the 1944 film "Gaslight," directed by George Cukor, starring Charles Boyer, Ingrid Bergman, and Joseph Cotten. By creating the illusion that reality is not what she knows it to be, a husband drives his wife to the brink of madness.

5. I am thinking of right-wing ideologues who bear no obvious Confederate connection, among them, for instance, John Yoo and Dick Cheney. Historian Richard Hofstadter (1996 [1965], 43) would prefer the concept of "pseudo-conservative," a term he borrowed from *The Authoritarian Personality* (published in 1950 by Theodore W. Adorno and his associates), to underscore that although "conservatives" often believe themselves to be conservative and even employ the rhetoric of conservatism, "they have little in common with the temperate and compromising spirit of true conservatism in the classical sense of the word." The current crop of "conservatives" seems more extreme, even more dangerous to the republic the founding fathers labored to establish, than those demonstrating a "paranoid style" in 1950s and 1960s American politics whom Hofstadter (1996 [1965], 29) was describing. Naming the present crop as "Confederate" and "fascist" is not only analytically accurate and psychologically resonant (as Hofstadter's term is, too) but underscores their specific historical antecedents.

6. As noted, the "trauma" of the Cold War in the 1950s and the 1954 U.S. Supreme Court decision to desegregate the public schools (coupled with the primacy of students in 1960s civil rights struggles) was "displaced and deferred" onto public education (Pinar 2004).

7. Art educator Rita L. Irwin has theorized the generative interrelations among the roles of artist, teacher, and researcher in what she terms A/R/Tography (Irwin and de Cosson 2004; Springgay et al. 2008).

8. The material conditions in which especially poor students study must be improved as well, as Jonathan Kozol, among others, has observed. Instead, politicians—and policymakers and professional educators who believe them—focus on classroom learning measured by test scores as the lever for eradicating poverty and, even, improving moral character (Yu 2003). This expensive quixotic search for "what works" derives from an early twentieth-century gendered (Seigfried 1996, 194) faith that "the scientific study of the nature of human learning will lead to principles for effective teaching" (Egan 2002, 74). Ignorant of the intellectual history of the academic field of education, politicians (and those practitioners who believe them) plod on: One New York City charter school promised to pay teachers $125,000 plus a potential performance bonus (Gootman 2008a). Alas, "performance" is not individual but school-, even district-wide, and defined as raising students' test scores, not offering an intellectually provocative curriculum (Hu 2008a; Schemo 2007). Not only has New York City Mayor Michael R. Bloomberg wanted teachers' salaries linked to their students' scores standardized exams (Gootman 2007b), he proposed that tenure be likewise linked! That latter demand was rejected by New York State legislators, although not, evidently, owing to concerns for academic freedom (Hakim and Peters 2008). In one survey, an overwhelming majority of teachers disagreed that the emphasis on testing had improved the quality of education in the schools where they taught (Gootman 2008b). "What works" doesn't, as Bush's billion-dollar reading boondoggle makes clear: Dillon 2008b. Complementary to the obsession with "what works is the fantasy that new teachers from elite institutions can pull rabbits out of hats, a pedagogical version of *noblesse oblige* (Dillon 2008d).

5 Jane Addams

1. Jane Addams was so described in an 1894 newspaper article. The journalist described Addams as "lacking Suavity and graciousness of manner but the impression soon wears away before [her] earnestness and honesty." The journalist was also struck by Addams's paleness, her "deep" eyes, her "low and well-trained voice," and how her face was "a window behind which stands her soul" (quoted in Knight 2005, 313–314). In emphasizing this status for Addams as an extraordinary individual, I could be accused of making her a hero as Carlyle was for her during her Rockford years, as Lincoln was for her father (and herself). Roberto Unger (2007, 46) warns against a "nostalgic-heroic reading of pragmatism" that, "under the pretext of venerating the classic American pragmatists," renders pragmatism "a fossil" and obscures from view "the most disquieting, perplexing, and energizing elements in their doctrine." For me, the recent scholarship on Addams—the work of Munro, Elshtain, Knight, and Brown—functions to make vivid these "disquieting, perplexing and energizing elements" of her astonishing accomplishment. It is true that Addams disapproved of individualism recoded as "self-seeking" (Elshtain 2002, 25), the so-called cult of individualism. A rationale for exploiting others economically and, in fact, a demand for social conformity, the "cult of individualism" is, I point out, not only misnamed but also gives "individuality"—the psychological, even spiritual process of self-differentiation and individuation—an undeserved bad name.
2. At the 2006 meeting of the American Association for the Advancement of Curriculum Studies, the general membership approved my proposal to undertake a curriculum studies canon project. One point of the Project, I noted (Pinar 2007a, xviii), was to ensure that excluded scholarship—such as that on Addams and Du Bois—was officially instantiated as central to the reconceptualized field of curriculum studies. On March 23, 2008, during the seventh annual meeting of the Association, members of the Canon Committee—William H. Schubert (2008), Rubén Gaztambide-Fernández, Ming Fang He, William H. Watkins—stripped this intention from the Canon Project by acting as if in ignorance of it, repeating well-known facts about the concept's legacies of imperialism, racism, and misogyny. This defiant disinclination to undertake the work their membership on the Canon Committee obligated them to undertake leaves in place precisely the canon they criticized. Despite complaining that students of curriculum studies are not expected to know the work of Du Bois, Gaztambide-Fernández (2006, 61) misses entirely the implication of his remark, namely that the establishment of a revised canon is urgent if curriculum studies students are to know the work of Du Bois and others now marginal to the field.

     Contradicting my characterization of him (Pinar 2007a, 182), Schubert (2008, 3) confessed that he thought the Canon Project was "merely" a "literary device." Despite its having been approved by the General Membership, evidently Schubert intends to dispose of it by making it so broad as to include the "spontaneous interest[s] of children" (2008, 35)! It is as if the conservative accusation that education professors know nothing had become internalized, then defensively re-expressed as education professors must know everything (even "what is worthwhile" [2008, 32]), an absurd ambition that acknowledges that one knows—and that one will only know—nothing. As Michael F. D. Young (2008, 23) observes, "tradition, though capable of preserving vested interests, is also crucial in ensuring the maintenance and development of standards … as well as being a condition for innovation and creating new knowledge."

     Left unaddressed, the "canon" becomes a version of those "popularity contests" Rosenbaum (2008, xv) decries as too often constitutive of canonization in film studies. In curriculum studies, such "contests" include instructors (pressured by students threatening poor teaching evaluations) choosing "accessible" texts their students will tolerate, texts composed by themselves, their Ph.D. supervisor, or other members of their academic "tribe" (those who took their degree at the same institution or with the same supervisor). There are, too, avant-gardists who select books they think catch the next "breaking wave" in the field and/or that reply to the politics of school deform. The intellectual advancement of the field seems rarely a consideration.

What curriculum scholars have in common is not the present but the past. It includes the legendary curriculum scholarship Philip Jackson (1992) reviews in his, yes canonical, essay on the state of the field. By acting in defiance of their charge, Schubert and his complainants ensure that the problem that Kliebard (2000 [1970], 40) identified 40 years ago—"an ahistorical posture"—remains unaddressed by the professional association whose *raison d'être* is the intellectual advancement of the field.

3. It is precisely this independence of mind identity politics threatens, and not only among whites but among some African Americans as well. In his discussion of settlement houses, for example, Watkins (2001, 104, emphasis added) informs us that "settlement house proponents, including Jane Addams, *claimed* to be expanding social opportunity and elevating the masses in the difficult new industrial society." True to the conspiratorial tenor of his book—even when whites donated money and thought they were contributing to improvements in African Americans' education, they were really only racists committed to racial subjugation—Watkins implies here (with his use of the verb "claimed") that Addams was insincere in her efforts. No matter how "progressive," no one—not Addams, not Watkins, not I—is finally free of the racial assumptions of their day, but Addams can hardly be accused of being insincere. Nor can Hull-House's contributions can be summarized as a "civilizing mission" (Watkins 2001, 104). As her biographers point out, Addams saw herself as the student of her immigrant neighbors, a student of life itself. Moreover, the curriculum she and Starr taught was simultaneously "cross-cultural" as well as "defiant of the usual class barriers" (Knight 2005, 206). Nobody's fool, Ida B. Wells (no Booker T. Washington, the sign of racial subservience for Watkins) thought Addams was the greatest woman in America.

4. The "snare of preparation" (Elshtain 2002, 15, 74; Brown 2004, 116) is the phrase Addams invoked to depict the "inactivity" of academic life, its deferral of engagement, disabling Addams to "reduce"—a word, Elshtain (2002, 28) points out, she used in a sense we have largely abandoned, meaning to "distill"— her ideas into action. Elshtain (2002, 18) points out that Christopher Lasch criticized Addams's psychological motivation and identified a certain "anti-intellectualism" in her extolment of "applied knowledge." "To his credit," Elshtain continues, "Lasch got Addams's hard-won purposes right," in Lasch's words "not so much ... helping the poor as ... understanding them," and "bridging the chasm that industrial and had opened between the social classes." Lasch is not alone in underscoring Addams's commitment to consequences; Victoria Bissel Brown (2004, 295) notes that "in all of her [Addams's] writings, she weighed social practice by social outcomes." What many scholars have under-emphasized, Elshtain (2002, 28) asserts, "is just how much hers was a literary mind." (Interesting, given Elshtain's characterization, is Nussbaum's (1995, 92) argument that "literary understanding ... promotes habits of mind that lead toward social equality in that they contribute to the dismantling of the stereotypes that support group hatred.") The remarks of Addams's friend, the social worker Mary Simkovitch, suggests that her "literary understanding" was dispersed throughout her subjective presence: "Jane Addams was an intellectual woman, but I don't think we think enough about that, perhaps because she was so natural" (quoted in Lasch 1965, xiii).

5. After Hull-House was established and Addams had become an overscheduled public figure, she took a third tour during summer 1896, the guest of her future "devoted life partner" (Knight 2005, 278) Mary Rozet Smith and Smith's parents (Knight 2005, 368). Though Smith framed the trip as a vacation, Addams viewed it as an educational venture (Jay 2005, 256), one dedicated to (1) the study of social movements in Europe, in particular those in London; (2) a meeting with philosopher Edward Caird (1835–1907) of Oxford University, whose books she admired; and (3) a meeting with Leo Tolstoy, whose revision of Christian conscience she had long admired (Knight 2005, 371–375).

6. I am employing "passion" in a theological sense, implying self-sacrifice (although Lasch [1965, xiii] would disagree, asserting she "had no taste for self-sacrifice"), even suffering, in the service of others. Though she was not Christ, it is difficult not to accept Addams's service as self-sacrificing and involving suffering, certainly physical (she was constantly overscheduled) and psychological (given her empathetic tendencies toward others).

   Addams was drawn to stories of the early Christians, their humility, their poverty and courage (Brown 2004, 264; Knight 2005, 138, 152, 163, 253; Lasch 1965, 25), stories inspiring her to work in the world. (Recall that Foucault's interest in the early Christians had to do with their location of truth within themselves, in contrast to the Roman emperor Severus's search for it in the world: Paras 2006, 112. Evidently Pasolini, too, was drawn to gnostic mysticism of early Christianity: Kammerer and Zigaina 2005, 167.) Inspired by stories of early Christians, Addams searched the truth of herself in the world, through public service. In 1910, Addams professed "an almost passionate devotion to the ideals of democracy" (quoted in Lasch 1965, 21). Curious in light of Addams's private devotion to Starr then Smith is Daniel Boyarin's (1997, 78) argument that

   > Both early rabbinic Jews and early Christians performed resistance to the Roman imperial power structure through "gender bending"—males consciously renouncing the markers of masculinity and adopting practices that signified them as female within the economy of Roman gender models—thus marking their own understanding that gender itself is implicated in the maintenance of political power. Various symbolic enactments of "femaleness"—as constructed within a particular system of genders—among them asceticism, submissiveness, retiring to private spaces, (ostensible) renunciation of political power, exclusive devotion to study, and self-castration were adopted variously by Christians or rabbinic Jews as acts of resistance against Roman culture and the masculinist exercise of power.

   It would seem the early Christians anticipated Addams's "passion" more than she might have known.

7. As noted earlier, Addams may seem to some an odd choice to personify "worldliness," as—except for a probably fabricated story about taking opium (Brown 2004, 103)—her life does not exactly coincide with the common view of the worldly as dissolute. Her entrance into the world (through Hull-House) was, moreover, delayed. For that, Addams blamed the isolation of her academic experience (at Rockford Seminary) and its otherworldly principal Miss Sill (Brown 2004, 108). Her judgment is, I think, unfair, as it was at Rockford that she herself became a heroic individual. As a consequence of academic study and lived experience (including travel) Addams embraces the world, including its alterity (personified by her Nineteenth Ward neighbors and her African American colleagues, such as Ida B. Wells). Against essentialism, Addams' initial absorption in the nineteenth-century mythology of "heroic individualism" was

linked to the "masculine" (Brown 2004, 166), specifically to Thomas Carlyle who (like Matthew Arnold, another "old humanist," reclaimed in our time by Edward Said: see Radhakrishnan 2008, 118) opposed a depersonalized, scientific modernity (Guillory 2002, 24). (As would Pasolini a century later.) In "Signs of the Times" (1829), Carlyle had advised that the "individual's wisest response to the 'mechanical' age is to cultivate 'the mysterious springs of Love, and Fear, and Wonder, of Enthusiasm, Poetry, Religion, all [of[which have a truly vital and infinite character'" (Lane 2002, 294). Sounds like spirituality to me.

8. "Experience," Martin Jay (2005, 6–7) explains, "is at the nodal point of the intersection between public language and private subjectivity, between expressible commonalities and the ineffability of the individual interior." However much it may be imagined as a "personal possession," he (2005, 7) continues, experience is "inevitably acquired through an encounter with otherness, whether human or not." We might say that the alterity of actuality constitutes the prerequisite for experience, itself derived from the Latin *experientia*, which denotes "trial, proof, or experiment" (Jay 2005, 10). Dewey's linking of education with experience is, then, genealogically indicated. Experience is not always safe; Jay (2005, 10) points out that

    > Insofar as "to try" (*experei*) contains the same root as *periculum*, or "danger," there is also a covert association between experience and peril, which suggests that it comes from having survived risks and learned something from the encounter (ex meaning a coming forth from).

    Perhaps it was the apparent absence of danger at Rockford Seminary that led Addams to conclude she had been snared there by preparation for a life that never seemed to come.

    In sharp contrast to its degraded usage in too many U.S. schools of education (where it links depersonalized objectives to standardized assessment), the verb *learned* in Jay's sentence emphasizes the individual's subjective capacity for self-reflexive agency, including the exercise of interest in choosing what experience to undertake and deciding by what terms to assess its significance. The self-reflexive element in experience is genealogically implied by the Greek antecedent to the Latin, *empeiria*, which, as Jay (2005, 10) points out,

    > also serves as the root for the English word "empirical".... Here a crucial link between experience and raw unreflected sensation or unmediated observation (as opposed to reason, theory, or speculation) is already evident. So too is the association between experience as dealing more with specific than general matters, with particulars rather than universals.

    The particularity of individual experience requires academic study to understand both its specificity and relative universality. In study, however, the vividness and immediacy of experience are not to be demeaned; thus the relevance of the phrase "lived experience" in denoting embodied, emotional, even ineffable engagement with the natural (in which is subsumed the human) world. Jay (2005, 11) notes that *Erlebnis* contains within it the root for life (*Leben*) and is sometimes translated as "lived experience." Moreover, "because it can encompass what is being experienced as well as the subjective process of experiencing it, the word can sometimes function as an umbrella term to overcome the epistemological split between subject and object" (Jay 2005, 12).

9. "At the heart of Jane Addams's education," Brown (2004, 10) suggests, "was her struggle with faith and religion." After rejecting the "shallow piety" she encountered at Rockford, Addams was "compelled to dig deeper, and that excavation strengthened her soul, giving her the spiritual stamina for a lifetime of

rough and dirty work" (Brown 2004, 10). After leaving Rockford (and through reading and conversation with Ellen Gates Starr), Addams became interested in the early Christians, discovering through that study "a faith founded by a community of people from all walks of life who wishes to help each other, even at great personal cost" (Knight 2005, 138). In *The Subjective Necessity for Social Settlements* (1892), Addams (in Lasch 1965, 29) lists "a certain renaissance of Christianity, a movement toward its early humanitarian aspects," as the third "great line" informing the "subjective pressure" toward Social Settlements. In contrast to a self-centered obsession with personal "salvation," Addams declared that the "impulse to share the lives of the poor, the desire to make social service … express the spirit of Christ," and that "revelation" occurs through "action" (in Lasch 1965, 40). This "renaissance of the early Christian humanitarianism" was occurring, she offered, in America, indeed, in Chicago (Lasch 1965, 40).

10. Besant was hardly the only influence, only the most perfectly timed. Addams was also influenced by Tolstoy (with whom she had a memorable dinner: Knight 2005, 373–374), whose book, *What Then Must We Do*, had appeared in English in 1887. Building upon his argument in *My Religion,* Tolstoy expressed the view that work on others' behalf was the only true source of happiness. Contact with his "powerful prose," Brown (2004, 213) suggests, persuaded Addams that working alongside the masses was, in and of itself, "an anodyne" for the "misery" of pampered luxury (quoted in Brown 2004, 213).

11. Hull-House was a "complex intercultural space" (Elshtain 2002, 22). What was life like there? We get a glimpse from Knight's summary of a reporter's account (1895):

> The front doors were wide open, she wrote. She could hear snatches of music and glimpse pictures, statuary, and "well-filled" bookcases. People of all ages came and went. Inside, she found the German reception underway in the library and the Italian reception underway in the dining room. A woman (it was Ellen Gates Starr) was teaching a class on Dante in the Octagon, a young man was giving a lecture in the drawing room on Bohemian history, and a young woman was teaching cooking in the kitchen. A girl's club was meeting in one of the halls, and in the Butler Art Gallery a French reading was going on in one room and a class in English and letter writing in another. (Knight 2005, 344)

If educators were authorized to create curricula according to community concerns, students' interests and their own, this might be a description of a public school. On rare occasion it is (Goodman 2006, 90, 109; Nossiter 2007).

12. Though I have used the concept of "interest" to specify the centrality of subjectivity in study, I believe Pasolini's concept of the "free indirect subjectivity" conveys with more subtlety and force the creative presence of the individual in the forms—institutional, as in Hull-House, and intellectual, as in the curriculum—s/he creates. Imagine Addams and Starr and their colleagues being asked to document their compliance with bureaucratic standards, as U.S. public-school teachers are routinely asked to do, or being forced to read a "scripted" curriculum, or to employ's Tyler's bureaucratizing "rationale!"

13. Knight (2005, 81) describes Anna Sill as a woman of "unrelenting moral purpose, deeply Christian evangelical faith, and great organizational skill." Brown (2004, 58) points out that Sill provided Jane Addams with an "impressive" example of an unmarried career woman running an institution with more determination than money, a woman who "breathed tangible reality into her philosophical convictions." Because her conservative religious convictions required her to disclaim her achievements, Sill was, Brown (2004, 58) acknowledges, a "confusing, even maddening" model of female leadership.

14. By "study," I invoke a confluence of self-cultivation through self-reflection and social service threaded through intellectual labor (Pinar 2006b, 109–120). One source for this concept is Michel de Montaigne (1533–1592), as elaborated by Robert McClintock (1971). Montaigne's celebrated *Essays* conclude, Martin Jay (2005, 23) points out, with a long meditation written in 1587–88 when he was 56, entitled "Of Experience," a title (Jay continues), "suggesting exploratory, tentative experiments rather than settled dogma—document[ing] his journey of self-discovery, as well as his extraordinarily keen observations about the human condition." Although returning to public service for periods in the 1580s, Montaigne ensured he enjoyed the leisure prerequisite to study his experience, asserting "I do not portray being: I portray passing" (quoted in Jay 2005, 24). As he affirmed the plenitude of momentary experience (rather than its endless deferral in expectation of an afterlife), Montaigne likewise inhabited his body "fully as a lived reality," anticipating the twentieth-century phenomenology of Maurice Merleau-Ponty (Jay 2005, 27). The accelerating "prestige" of science, Jay (2005, 40) reminds, "meant jettisoning Montaigne's preoccupation with introspection and self-discovery; to be worthy taking seriously, experience had to be public, replicable, and verified by objective instruments." For constructing understandings of the natural world, this was obviously a welcome epistemological development; for understanding educational experience, it has proven a complete catastrophe.

15. In 1912, she may have been "one" of several, but by the end of her life, Brown (2004, 295) concludes, it was the "amplification of her activism through her published writings that make the most compelling argument for Addams as a blue-ribbon figure in the history of the Progressive Era, in the history of American pragmatism, in the history of international pacifism, and in the history of democratic campaigns for the rights of workers, women, ethnics, and nonwhites." Later in this chapter, I review her civil rights activism, one exceptional for the era but not without its "occasional failures" (Seigfried 1996, 235).

16. Though specifying experience that is subjectively undergone, the phenomenological phrase "lived experience" is also an "umbrella" concept, thereby "shielding" us from the specificity of such experience as it incorporates the social and the historical. (Indeed, there is, Martin Jay [2005, 192] notes, a "leftist appropriation of a politics of experience ... most explicit in two of the founding texts of British Marxist humanism, Williams' *Culture and Society* of 1958 and Thompson's *The Making of the English Working Class* of 1963 (see Jay 2005, 196ff for an intellectual history of the concept, including the debates this particular appropriation set off among British Marxists, and its repudiation by "structural Marxism" of Louis Althusser). My use of "lived experience" is here focused on the life history antecedents of Addams's later activism. To take one example, consider her pro-mediation inclinations, the life history antecedents of which can be discerned in Addams's childhood. Brown's (2004, 297) observes that "taking the high ground won her psychic safety in the conflicted Haldeman-Addams household and earned Pa's grateful approval as well."

17. Not only Addams's view of ethics was revised over the years. Knight (2004, 54) notes that while she was "rarely seen to be angry when older, she was angry often enough when she was young." And the distance from other women that she carefully maintained during her years at Rockford slowly closed as she became intimate first with Ellen Gates Starr, then Mary Rozet Smith (Brown 2004, 253 ff.; Knight 2005, 228, 250–251). Specific attitudes changed as well, among them a childhood disdain felt toward immigrants, evidently inherited from her father (Knight 2005, 68). Nor was poverty much on her mind during her youth. Addams's letters to her friends, Lasch (1965, 2) points out, "show her to have been a pious

young woman conscientiously pursuing a program of self-education in the cultural classics esteemed by the genteel tradition in which she was brought up." Part of Addams' genius was to bring to bear on the problems of poverty her knowledge of cultural classics. Perhaps reconstruction, not revision, more dramatically describes the dramatic changes Addams underwent and fashioned in her self.

18. Christopher Lasch (1965, xiii, xiv) characterizes Addams as a social critic and, more importantly, as "theorist and intellectual—a thinker of originality and daring" (xv). For Jean Bethke Elshtain (2002, 24), Addams was a "first-rate thinker and a gifted writer with extraordinary social and political influence," someone who "share[s] with Walt Whitman a lyrical evocation of American possibility" (Elshtain 2002, 25; regarding Whitman see Robertson 2008). Petra Munro (1999, 23) points out Addams "pioneered sociological field methods" and "contributed to the birth of pragmatism." Victoria Bissel Brown (2004, 8) depicts the "most famous" and "most influential woman in America" as a "democratic pacifist" and "philosopher." Brown (2004, 8) is also intrigued by Addams's "elusive personal style, her capacity for inspiring others' love and devotion while never quite revealing herself." No wonder Emily Balch[19] asserted (when Addams died) that Addams's "greatness has been veiled by her goodness" (quoted in Lasch 1965, xiii).

19. Working closely with Jane Addams and other social reformers at Hull House, Balch studied the life of immigrants in Chicago. Her research resulted in the book, *Our Slavic Fellow Citizens* (1910). A committed pacifist, Balch opposed U.S. involvement in World War I and was a member of the Woman's Peace Party (WPP) and the Women's International League for Peace and Freedom (WILPF). As a result of her anti-war activities, Balch was dismissed as professor of political economy at Wellesley College. Secretary of the Women's International League for Peace and Freedom (1918–22 and 1934–35), Balch won the Nobel Peace Prize in 1946. Taken on January 23, 2008 from http://www.spartacus.schoolnet.co.uk/USAWbalch.htm

20. Critics have noted the conservative character of Arnold's emphasis upon the moral function of culture, specifically his presentation of "political restiveness as a symptom of cultural anarchy." It would take the inclusion of class, gender, and racial content to "break the back of the Arnoldian curriculum, which asserts that education exists to filter the values of a dominant class downward to other classes" (both passages from Viswanathan 2002, 179). An exclusively conservative interpretation of Arnold would be misleading, however, as Christopher Lane (2002, 284) points out:

> Social inequalities and mass illiteracy appalled Arnold, who scorned the "incomparable self-satisfaction" of the Victorian middle class that permitted both. Spending much of his career trying to reform Britain's elitist education system, he attacked "the hideous and grotesque illusions of middle-class Protestantism" in order to diminish its "pedantry, bigotry, and narrowness."

There are cosmopolitan credentials as well: Lane (2002, 284) recalls Arnold's "disdain" for British parochialism, his "admiration" for European and Asian thought.... [H]e favored parody over snobbery, debate over demagoguery, flux over rigidity, and inquiry over philistinism." Arnold "presciently" appreciated that literary study was becoming a secular version of Christian knowledge (Viswanathan 2002, 182), a transmutation that would animate Addams' move into Chicago's Nineteenth Ward.

21. During the summer of 1886, Addams emerged from five years of depression (Knight 2005, 146). Knight attributes this event to breaking free of family responsibilities, including a proposal of marriage made by her stepmother's son

George. Her movement away from Anna and George enabled her to imagine a new life (Knight 2005, 157, 196, 270).

22. Knight (2005, 173, 174) tells us that Addams supplemented Fremantle and Westcott's "middlebrow version of social Christianity" with the "method of cooperation" endorsed by Toynbee Hall's founders Samuel and Henrietta Barnett (and articulated later by contemporary neo-pragmatists such as Roberto Unger: 2007, 171). Recall that the East End Settlement House (founded in 1884) had been named in honor of Arnold Toynbee, the Oxford political economist credited with coining the phrase "the industrial revolution" and who then called for a fundamental revision in modern class relations. Inspired by Toynbee's conviction that the privileged classes needed to move away from patronizing stewardship and toward relations of democratic mutuality with the working classes, the Barnetts addressed a wide range of issues: housing, sanitation, and education among them (Brown 2004, 200–202). In their efforts at school reform in London, for instance, the Barnetts sought cooperation among parents, teachers, administrators and students. "With, not for" was, Knight (2005, 174) reports, their "motto." "The most interesting thing we have done in London," Jane Addams wrote to her sister Alice just five days back in the city, "was to visit Toynbee Hall in the East End" (quoted in Brown 2004, 201). As for her hosts, Henrietta recorded her and her husband's first impression of Addams: "[W]e realized," she wrote, "that she was a great soul, and took pains to show her much and tell her more" (quoted in Knight 2005, 169).

23. I have suggested the term *seduction* communicates the aggressive love pacifism implies. When it is a reply to violence, seduction is not free of anger (Pinar 1994, 158 ff.), but it beckons post-coital conversation ("pillow talk") and reflection (Seigfried 1996, 166–167). Pasolini appreciated the significance of refusing to reproduce patriarchy through resistance:

> Perhaps the homosexual has the sense of the sacred origin of life more than those who are narrowly heterosexual. Respect for the sanctity of the mother predisposes him to a particular identification with her; I would say, in fact, that at the core of the homosexual there is, unconsciously, a reassertion of chastity: the desire for purity. In a rather obscure way the homosexual seeks himself in the other (the other-same), a partner with whom he does not risk reproducing the terrible power of the father, of the profaner. I would say that the homosexual tends to preserve life, not contributing to the cycle of procreation-destruction, but rather substituting the coherence of a culture, the continuity of consciousness, for the survival of the species. (quoted in Rohdie 1995, 70)

"[T]he rebellion of the son against the father," Gordon (1996, 163) observes in a different but not unrelated context, "is only a hidden mechanism for the transformation in turn of the son into the father." Seduction of (rather than resistance to) the father implies the son's identification with the mother, ending the reproduction of patriarchy, not for the sake of the "child" (that split-off sacrifice of the present for a future that never comes: Edelman 2004), but for the "love for the world" (Gordon 1996, 166).

24. Pasolini, too, focused on the plight of daughters, daughters of the post–World War II Italian bourgeoisie: Ryan-Scheutz 2007.

25. The character of Addams's contribution to the cause of peace is not, perhaps, self-evident. No "sentimental pacifist," Lasch (1965, 218) points out, she did not oppose war on religious grounds either, but because war was a "wasteful" and "ineffective" means of solving social problems. Indeed, war created more problems than it solved.

26. In her conception of "culturally-responsive pedagogy," Geneva Gay (2004) seems to argue for the school's mirroring the culture students bring to class, rather than enabling one to incorporate the culture of one's upbringing into a broader, more cosmopolitan, understanding of oneself and others. Likewise, there are reading specialists who argue that the secret to literacy instruction is reducing the gap between home and school, reminiscent of Egan's (2002, 59) critique of progressivism, namely its assumption "that learning in school settings must be made to conform as closely as possible to this [children's] early effortless learning." Michael F. D. Young (2008, 82) is emphatic: "[b]ecause the world is not as we experience it, curriculum knowledge must be discontinuous, not continuous with everyday experience." I suspect teachers can usefully (imaginatively, as Egan would have it) draw upon literacy practices (and other knowledge) employed in the home and neighborhood, but doing so as starting points for journeys whose destinations are, hopefully, more worldly than those the domestic sphere often allows, as the case of Jane Addams illustrates (Brown 2004, 214, 278). Despite assumptions that esoteric mathematics can be taught by means of everyday examples (Muller 2000, 67), at least one study has suggested otherwise (Chang 2008).

27. Addams and Dewey became close friends (Ryan 1995, 151). Dewey's second daughter, Jane Mary, was named Jane (and Mary after Addams's second partner). Dewey missed her and Hull-House "dearly" when he moved to New York to take up his lifelong post at Columbia (Westbrook 1991, 167). It was not a friendship without incident, however. Ryan (1995, 29) reports that Dewey's support for the World War I "nearly wrecked his friendship" with Addams. In 1935, Dewey dedicated *Liberalism and Social Action* "To the Memory of Jane Addams" (Seigfried 1996, 45). In 1945, Dewey wrote the foreword to Addams's republished *Peace and Bread* (1922), underscoring that for her, "social advance depends as much upon the process through which it is secured as upon the result itself" (quoted in Seigfried 1996, 75).

28. Ryan (1995, 29) tells us that, Dewey "lost his faith in 1894 ... he explicitly abandoned his church membership."

29. Not unlike the "subprime" mortgage crisis in the United States (exported worldwide), overleveraged businesses in the East precipitated the economic collapse of 1893, felt intensely in Chicago, where unemployment soon hit 20 percent. Thousands demonstrated, demanding food and jobs, including 25,000 protestors on the lakefront; the mayor was assassinated on October 29.
   By the end of the summer, homeless mothers had inundated Hull-House, camping in the nursery school; by December, Hull-House had opened a shelter. The Pullman Palace Car Company was not immune to the effects of the Depression; it laid off 3,400 of its 4,500 workers and slashed the wages of those remaining by as much as 40 percent. Despite his reputation as a generous employer, George Pullman refused to reduce rents in company housing to reflect either the wage decline or the rent reductions in adjacent areas. Moreover, the company's layoff and rehiring polices gave preference to those who remained in the company town and paid high rents from low wages. Understandably, the workers felt exploited and betrayed. Addams met with workers and attempted to meet with Pullman, but he snubbed her; she wrote him, to no avail. Violence ensued, and the federal government intervened, imprisoning the union leader (Eugene Debs) and using soldiers to break the strike (Brown 2004, 279 ff). The Pullman Strike, Knight (2005, 322) summarizes, was "a national tragedy that aroused fierce passions and left many scars." As Brown (2004, 295) observes:

   Amid the din of competing voices that cried out for peaceful, democratic reform in the decades following the Pullman strike, Jane Addams both acted and spoke in a singular, consistent, trustworthy tone that often served as the conscience of the nation and has seldom been heard with such clarity since.

In our own nightmare time, such a tone—"singular, consistent, and trustworthy"—may be just the right tone for us to hear—as Ted Aoki (2005 [1978]) wanted us to—curriculum in a new key.

30. Ryan (1995, 153) attributes Dewey's acceptance of conflict to his Darwinian disposition, evident in his early interest in the Herbartians: Kliebard 1999 [1981].

31. Addams predisposition to compromise followed her father's "political orientation ... of stewardship, harmony, and principled compromise" (Brown 2004, 20). In the biographies of Addams I studied (Brown's, Elshtain's, Knight's), her father, John (an Illinois state senator, one-time teacher and wealthy businessman), emerges as the decisive figure—"the center of her emotional life" (Knight 2005, 2)—in Jane Addams's self-formation. His "deep civic involvement clearly influenced" Jane Addams's disposition toward public life (Elshtain 2002, 2). When he died suddenly in August 1881 ("the greatest sorrow that can ever come to me" Jane Addams wrote Ellen Gates Starr [quoted in Knight 2005, 114]), Addams received a letter from her brother-in-law, the Reverend John Linn. In it is what Brown (2004, 13) regards as "the single most explicit and sustained comment on this father-daughter bond." Linn suggested that the "poignancy" of Jane Addams' grief arose from "the fact that your heart and life were wrapped up with your Pa." Addams' identification with her father (young Jane Addams had centered upon her father "all that careful imitation which a little girl ordinarily gives to her mother's ways and habits" [quoted in Brown 2004, 23]) was strong because, Linn offered, "your life aims were high enough and your plans broad enough so that he could take an interest in them and it was his great delight to prepare you for your mission" (quoted passages in Brown 2004, 13). (As Brown [2004, 13] adds, in August 1881, neither Lin nor Jane Addams knew what her "mission" might be.) "Only much later," Brown (2004, 37) notes, would Addams "realign her loyalties and identify with an assertively female political culture."

Knight (2005, 165) points out that embracing her father's dedication to work in the public domain enabled her to dis-identify with the "female ideal" of "duty to family" that she had spent most of her post-Rockford years trying to honor. Addams would never abandon certain elements of the female ideal, Knight (2005, 165) observes, "particularly self-sacrifice and sympathy." The identificatory through-line seems, clearly, her father (Elshtain 2002, 2). Addams would awaken herself at three o'clock because that was when her father awoke (Elshtain 2002, 33). Declining the invitation of the National Cathedral of Washington, D.C., to be interred there, Addams requested to be buried beside her father in the small Cedarville graveyard that was his resting place; this is where her remains rest today (Knight 2005, 12). There was, for Addams, no contradiction between being her father's daughter and feminist activism. John Addams bequeathed to his daughter a "passionate desire" to be "morally excellent" (Knight 2005, 27). He believed that children needed to be "listened to" and "taken seriously" (Brown 2004, 25), and he expected his daughter to be as "level-headed" and "responsible as a son" (Brown 2004, 26). Since the 1870s, John Addams had favored women's suffrage (Knight 2005, 32, 62). Enjoying the support of an enabling father was not distinctive to Jane Addams, as Laura Bragg enjoyed such a father, and one can argue that an enabling mother made possible Pasolini's accomplishment.

32. The 1964 Democratic National Convention approved a compromise crafted by Minnesota Senator Hubert Humphrey seating the Mississippi regulars in exchange for a written commitment to back the national ticket and a pledge that,

in all future conventions, delegations from states that allow racial discrimination in voting will not be recognized. All but four members of the regular Mississippi delegation refused to sign the pledge and left the Convention; the Freedom Democrats rejected the compromise as well. Accessed on January 14, 2008 from http://edition.cnn.com/ELECTION/2000/conventions/democratic/features/convention.history/index.html#1964]

33. Addams had been present at discussions concerning the founding of the *Crisis*; she had been skeptical that the new organization could financially support its own publication: Wells 1970, 327.

6 Religion, Love, and Democracy in Laura Bragg's Boxes

1. As an adult, Bragg built her own library; at her death, she owned 5,000 books (Allen 2001, 11), filling every "corner and nook" (Allen 2001, 202) of her modest living quarters. Focused on books (and money), 25 years of correspondence between Bragg and her father have survived (2001, 33). Still, her father's influence was not complete: Bragg rejected her father's organized religion. In its place, she explored Chinese culture and religion, an interest animated by her relationship with a young Chinese man named Chia Mei who, Allen (2001, 111) reports, "became increasingly important in Bragg's life, as she did in his." The echo of Addams's life is loud enough: the centrality of the father in the daughter's upbringing, specifically her education; the daughter's modification (in Addams's case) of the father's religious faith; and the embrace of cultural and generational difference.

2. As Allen (2001, 33) points out, at this time it was not uncommon for libraries and museums to operate as single institutions and "with a freer atmosphere than existed in the public schools of the day." The latter is not difficult to imagine.

3. "This shift in emphasis [for museums] from an exhibitionist to an educational function," Allen (2001, 35) explains, "brought with it social implications." In Charleston, for instance, Bragg worked to extend the reach of the Museum into the community, seeking patrons not known before. Though this progressive reformulation of the museum as educational (as well as exhibitionist and archival) was new to museums in the Northeast, it was, Allen (2001, 35) acknowledges, "almost unheard of in the South, due to the poverty, isolation, and racism that predominated in the region."

4. Daniel Tröhler (2006, 95) points to the influence that Whitman had on Dewey by quoting a letter that he wrote to his wife, Alice Chipman Dewey, on April 16, 1887: "I have been reading Walt Whitman more and find that he has a pretty definite philosophy. His philosophy of democracy and its relation to religion strikes me as the thing." "Dewey's deep trust in Whitman continued throughout his life," Tröhler (2006, 95) writes, referring to him once as the "seer" of democracy (Westbrook 1991, 552). That trust, Tröhler continues, "is an expression of the dominant discourse in the United States at the turn of the twentieth century that bound together the chief architects of the Pragmatism." How important were homoerotic elements in this discourse? For Whitman, they were important (Robertson 2008, 195; Pinar 2001, 354–356).

5. Though never becoming secular (as Tröhler argues liberal Christianity did), even conservative Christianity exhibited socially progressive elements during the late nineteenth century (Haynes 1998). Not so in our time: see Worthen 2007; Stein 2001.

6. In addition to opening the Museum to black patrons, Bragg wanted a free library open to all of Charleston's citizens (Allen 2001, 127). She and other community leaders obtained several thousand signatures, including those of prominent

Charlestonians and educators who supported the funding of such a library. On January 1, 1931, the Charleston Free Library opened (Allen 2001, 128).

7. A multiculturalist *avant la lettre*, at least during the Charleston years, Bragg was focused especially upon African Americans. In addition to sending the traveling school exhibits to both black and white schools and working for a free library open to all citizens, Bragg introduced African American art to the Museum, exhibiting the pottery of a slave named Dave, now recognized, Allen (2001, 140) tells us, as the "outstanding African American potter of his time." His very large jars remain among the largest utilitarian vessels made in the United States. Allen (2001, 140) credits Bragg as a "preservationist," but her progressive racial views (at least for the time) must have been in play as well. Nor did her racial views disappear when she moved to Massachusetts. Just before her retirement in 1939, Bragg told an interviewer: "Let's not have one more lynching!!" (quoted Allen 2001, 196).

8. Chia Mei was like Bragg's son, Allen (2001, 114) tells us. During the summer of 1930, while training at Kelly Air Field in San Antonio, Chia Mei was involved in a plane accident. In Washington at the time, Bragg took a train to his bedside, spending her month's vacation nursing him back to health. Bragg wrote many letters from the hospital, writing to, among others, Robert Marks, another of "her boys" (Allen 2001, 115). Chia Mei was, Allen (2001, 115) tells us, "one of the few people in her life for whom she expressed her compassion and sympathy."

9. By today's standards, Bragg was not entirely progressive in her multiculturalism. "Among the most perplexing paradoxes" of Bragg's character, Allen (2001, 114) suggests, was her opposition to mixed-race relationships and marriages.

10. The Rosenwald Fund was established in 1917 by Julius Rosenwald, part-owner and later president of Sears, Roebuck and Company. Committed to education for African Americans, the Rosenwald Fund financed the building of more than 5,000 schools in Southern states. After obtaining his Ph.D., Horace Mann Bond represented the Fund (Pinar 2001, 659).

11. Allen (2001, 171) interprets Bragg's invitation to speak before the Progressive Education Association as "acceptance" of her educational programs—the Boxes prominently among them—"as examples of progressive educational reform." Bragg's Boxes were esthetic as well as educational exhibits, disclosing her liberal arts education and disposition, her embrace of art as experience. ("For Dewey," Garrison [1997, 20] reminds, "artistic creation and aesthetic appreciation are the source of all meaning and value." Indeed, "the self is created through its own creations" [1997, 168].) In contrast, social efficiency was to be realized through scientific curriculum making focused on adults' activities (Pinar et al. 1995, 90 ff.)

12. For me (Pinar 2006a), one teaches understanding *through* facts.

13. Many political conservatives cynically exploit Americans' faith in education to displace accountability for the fate of the poor from themselves and their anti-poor, anti-working class policies of the past 25 years (Pinar 2004).

14. Evidently, "Americanization" was not a cause limited to newly arrived immigrants only. Allen (2001, 216) tells us that Bragg wanted to "Americanize the southerners who did 'not know even the heroes and myths of our culture,' as she wrote Mayor Grace [of Charleston] on one occasion." The former Confederacy has never wanted to be Americanized, repudiating Washington's efforts at Reconstruction after the Civil War, then, since 1976, occupying Washington with a series of increasingly conservative (decoded as "Confederate," as I argue in Chapter 4) Southern presidents, culminating (one hopes) in George W. Bush.

15. The last exhibit before her retirement—"The World of Today"—portrayed "the problems, ideas, creative forces, and crises of the real world" (Allen 2001, 195). Dedicated to Bragg— "Because she has the vision to perceive art's function and

the courage to act on her vision, this exhibit is dedicated to Laura M. Bragg: a fearless progressive and humane museum director" (quoted in Allen 2001, 196)—the exhibit was judged by the public as "frightful" and contained labels presumably "criticizing government and the capitalists for the treatment of the poor." In response, the trustees became "violently opposed to the use of the name of the Berkshire Museum in connection with the circulation of the 'World of Today.' The labeling of this exhibit, as you know, refers to matters other than Art alone" (quoted passages in Allen 2001, 196). The "World of Today" went next to Vassar, where museum-goers also judged it as too radical; it was not shown anywhere else (Allen 2001, 197).

16. Funding was a perennial problem for Bragg. Bragg's Boxes could have reached more children "if the power structure had not chosen to stonewall every effort to seek state funding" (Allen 2001, 218). Even when the General Assembly passed a resolution praising the traveling school exhibits, the state's financial support "never materialized." No doubt, Allen (2001, 218) points out, "Bragg's gender also played a role in her inability to gain funding."

17. Did the Boston-educated Bragg suffer "culture shock" upon moving to Charleston? "The fetishization of objects," Ann Cvetkovich (2003, 118) reports, "can be one way of negotiating the cultural dislocation produced by immigration." Related to trauma more generally, we can appreciate that Freud considered fetishism to be "one of the chief modes of reparation" (Young-Bruehl 1996, 284).

18. Behind Winnicott's formulation, Derrick (1997, 229 n. 20) points out, is the work of Melanie Klein. Klein's work suggests that the child's first object relations involve the internalization of gendered objects such as the breast and that such internalizations involve crucial subsidiary processes such as splitting, projection, reparation, and mania.

19. In Freud's initial formulation, as David Eng (2001, 152) succinctly summarizes, "fetishism functions to normalize the white heterosexual relations on which the paternal legacy is built through the management of female sexual difference and the simultaneous denial of female castration and lack."

20. Joseph Schwab (1978, 109), too, linked Eros with education, with liberal education more specifically: "Not only the means, however, but also the ends of liberal education involve Eros. For the end includes not only knowledge gained but knowledge desired and knowledge sought" (see Block 2004, 131). Garrison (1997, xiii) puts the matter more bluntly: "Our destiny is in our desires."

7 Pier Paolo Pasolini

1. *Officina* means "workshop," or "atelier," and captured the sense of process its founders were after (Schwartz 1992, 287). *Officina* was "a twice-monthly publication of poetry" and printed a steady stream of new verse and theoretical essays (Schwartz 1992, 290). (For Dewey, too, "poetry and prophecy went together" [Garrison 1997, 134].) Pasolini cofounded *Officina* with the two of the same colleagues (Francesco Leonetti and Roberto Roversi) with whom he had planned in 1941–1942 the unrealized journal *Eredi* (*Heirs*), whose modest agenda was to revisit the literary canon. (Blocked by wartime paper shortages, the project did lead, in 1942, to the private publication of Pasolini's first collection of poems in Friulan dialect, *Poesie a Casarsa*: Gordon 1996, 12). After *Officina*'s demise, Roversi told an interviewer from *L'unita*` that their intention had been "to correct Croce with Gramsci, to leaven Italian classical idealism with a nationalist but humanist Marx—all without being sucked into the PCI's intellectual vacuum cleaner" (Schwartz 1992, 291). (This comment is doubly interesting in light of later accusations that Pasolini suffered from Crocean

idealism, as noted in Note 15, Chapter 1.) *Officina*'s distribution was never more than a thousand copies, and as many were given away as sold; it was "talked about far more than the circulation suggests; influence was its business, and it thrived that way, as one of the voices at the very center of a crucial debate about culture and society" (Schwartz 1992, 291). Gordon (1996, 43) attributes the journal's demise to the "collapse" of its "editorial consensus," an event that, in his judgment, "pointed up the inherent instability in Pasolini's eclectic and polemical approach." Pasolini's model was based on an "anachronistic, Romantic model, guided only by literary taste and a diffidence of genuinely 'avant-garde' cultural militancy" which rejected the "scientific" or "technical" model of the intellectual championed by Calvino and Vittorini (Gordon 1996, 46).

2. His early life marred by tragedy (both of his parents died as well as five of his brothers and sisters), Giovanni Pascoli (1855–1912) remains one of Italy's revered poets. It was Pascoli's fresh vision of detail and of the linguistic object— Ryan-Scheutz (2007, 19) tells us he "also wrote in a maternal dialect"—that attracted the young Pasolini: "Pascoli's characters and his settings, his children, the birds and all that, his magical and highly artificial world, which is falsely ingenious—all this was very close to my taste" (quoted in Peterson 1994, 91; Rohdie 1995, 186; Ryan-Scheutz 2007, 233).

3. One of the great Italian art historians, the "charismatic" Roberto Longhi had a major influence on Pasolini, who attended his lectures in a state of "febrile excitement" (Schwartz 1992, 120; Gordon 1996, 185). Longhi also loved the movies: He was famous among his students for making a special trip to Paris to see Renoir's *Grand Illusion* and Chaplin's *The Great Dictator*, both banned in fascist Italy. He made a short film entitled *Carpaccio* (1948), composed of detail shots of paintings by the Renaissance painter "enlivened with Baroque music"; the film expresses "Longhi's interest in endowing the imagistic work of a past epoch with a direct, living effect for the modern observer" (Weis 2005, 62). Pasolini began a thesis on modern Italian art under Longhi but in fact completed a thesis under Professor Carlo Calcaterra on the poet and professor of classics Giovanni Pascoli (1855–1912). Pasolini paid direct homage to Longhi in *Mamma Rosa* (Rohdie 1995, 186).

4. "As so many of his poems, novels, essays, and interviews reveal," Ryan-Scheutz (2007, 222) points out, "he was driven to self-study and self-affirmation. From his earliest verses, autobiographism was implicit in all he did." It seems to me that Pasolini's commitment to self-understanding underlay his later formulation of free indirect subjectivity: "The use of the 'free indirect point-of-view shot' is the cinema of poetry, as I have repeated several times, is pretextual. It serves to speak indirectly—through any narrative alibi—in the first person singular" (Pasolini 2005 [1972], 185, 113).

5. Pasolini fell in love with one of his students: Tonuti Spagnol (Rhodes 2007, 20). Ryan-Scheutz (2007, 234, n. 30) reports that "their teacher-student pedagogical bond was matched by a reciprocal physical attraction." At that time, in that place, such a relationship was considered a form of *amicizia*, or friendship, in this instance expressed also by the boy's affiliation with Pasolini's efforts on behalf of the Friulian language (De Mauro 2007 [1976], 112). Tonuti Spagnol would later deny that their relationship was sexual (Schwartz 1992, 196; Duncan 2006, 97).

6. Despite this experience of what he would later call "leftwing fascism" (quoted in Viano 1993, 8) and "leftist blackmail" (quoted in Viano 1993, 268), Pasolini remained close to the Communist Party throughout his life. After his murder, Lawton (2005b, xxxix) points out, the PCI buried him "with full party honors." For Pasolini, fascism did not disappear with Mussolini: "Did Nazism ever die? Were we not crazy to believe it an episode? Isn't it Nazism which defined the petite bourgeoisie as 'normal' and which continues to define it?" (Pasolini

2005 [1972], 138). Fascism's omnipresence constituted a "new phenomenon," Pasolini (2005 [1972], 162) asserted, partly because the threat was now not direct oppression as an "indirect one of allure" (Lawton 2005b, xxx). Co-opting its victims through the exploitation of fantasy, neocapitalism coverts consumers into "willing participants" in the self-destruction of their values (Lawton 2005a, x). Because the traditional family is the structural backbone of capitalism, the traditional family becomes one target of anti-capitalist action. How do you destroy patriarchal family values? Pasolini's answer, at least initially, was "sex, the more unconventional the better" (Lawton 2005a, x). It was "unconventional sex" that had led to Pasolini's excommunication from the PCI in 1949.

7. An "intimate" friend of Pasolini's (Jewell 1992, x), Attilio Bertolucci (1911–2000) was an Italian poet, literary critic, and translator (and the father of Bernardo, whom Pasolini introduced to filmmaking). Pasolini, Mario Luzi, and Bertolucci strongly influenced postwar cultural history. The work of these three poets, perhaps Pasolini most prominently, dispelled what then became a leftist cliché that "civic" verse must be narrative and realistic, as each was quite aware that history is inscribed in literary forms and that literary forms are formative in the epistemological underpinnings of the writing of history. Like Pasolini, Bertolucci and Luzi were attentive to the sedimented history of forms from Antiquity through to the medieval, Renaissance, baroque, neoclassical, and modern periods. This history is visible in many parts of Italy by simply walking down the street. The architectural simultaneity of past and present in Italy no doubt prompted Pasolini to model his Roman poems as palimpsests (Jewell 1992, 24). "These attempts by Pasolini, Bertolucci, and Luzi to reconceptualize history through specific generic experiments" Jewell (1992, 4) calls "the *poiesis*, or the poetic composition, of history."

8. One of Pasolini's oldest and closest friends (he appears in one of Pasolini's films, *Comizi d'amore*), Alberto Moravia was a journalist, short-story writer, and novelist.

9. Italian novelist (*La Storia*, 1974), short-story writer, and poet, Elsa Morante (1912–1985) was best known for the epic and mythical quality of her work, often focused on the young struggling to come to terms with the world (http://www.britannica.com/eb/article-9053663/Elsa-Morante). Alberto Moravia's common-law wife, Morante shared with Pasolini an appreciation for the quasi-religious mystery of life and a passion about writing that some thought even more intense than Moravia's. Pasolini found in her, Schwartz (1992, 293) tells us, a woman who was both his "intellectual equal and spiritual soul mate," someone with whom he shared a "sometimes abrasive commitment to complete openness, a lust for frankness at any price," a preference "for which each became famous, and one which finally cost them their friendship." Morante joined Pasolini and Moravia during their trip to India in 1961; she and Moravia separated that year, after 25 years together, and Moravia (then 55) set up a household with the writer and feminist Dacia Maraini, with whom Pasolini would also become friends (Schwartz 1992, 360; Ryan-Scheutz 2007, 35). Maraini co-authored with Pasolini the screenplay for his *Il fiore delle Mille e una notte* (Ryan-Scheutz 2007, 189; Viano 1993, 342).

10. Paolo Volponi (1924–1994) was a writer and lawyer who worked for Olivetti and then FIAT before joining the Communist Party; he was elected senator in 1983. Although he began his literary career as a poet with *Il ramarro* (1948), he is best known for his novels. In Volponi's view, cinema diverted Pasolini's attention from "serious" poetic pursuits (Gordon 1996, 19).

11. Federico Fellini (1920–1993) is considered as one of the most influential filmmakers of the twentieth century. Pasolini built an "odd, wary friendship" with Fellini (Schwartz 1992, 349). After winning the 1957 Viareggio Prize for

Poetry for *Le ceneri di Gramsci*, Pasolini drove to Viareggio to collect his prize money (a million lire) in his Fiat 600 given to him by Fellini during the making of *Le notti di Cabiria* (Schwartz 1992, 309). Despite the gift, the friendship did not survive Fellini's dislike of *Accattone* (Schwartz 1992, 357; Gordon 1996, 189). Pasolini came to regard Fellini as "neodecadent," submerged in his own "fantastic imagination" (Viano 1993, 158). Despite their disagreements, Fellini defended Pasolini when his third film—*La ricotta*—was condemned, asserting that the condemnation was "incredible, unacceptable, a source of anguish...it seems the best spirits are always blocked by the obtuse... those people are putting him [Pasolini] in a condition to express in his coming film on the *Gospel* exactly what is the sadness of not being understood" (quoted in Schwartz 1992, 419). Both Pasolini and Fellini embraced the creativity of the irrational: Though the latter "threatens disorder" it also "promises pleasure"; even more importantly, it is the "source of the poetic" (Rohdie 1995, 88). For Rohdie, their view of the irrational stemmed from the presence within Catholicism of an earlier paganism.

12. While working on *Le notti di Cabiria*, Pasolini had come to know Mauro Bolognini (1922–2001). When Pasolini was ready to direct his own film, Bolognini helped him find a producer—Alfredo Bini—who agreed to finance *Accattone* (Schwartz 1992, 360).

13. Franco Rossi (1919–2000) was an Italian film screenwriter and director.

14. Florestano Vancini (1926-) is an award-winning Italian film director and screenwriter.

15. Bernardo Bertolucci was born on March 16, 1940 in Parma, Italy. His accomplished father—Attilio—encouraged Bernardo's childhood interest in films by taking him to film screenings (http://italian.vassar.edu/bertolucci/bertbio.html). The young Bertolucci accompanied Pasolini to the set of *Accattone*, where Pasolini allowed him to assist and learn what he could; Bertolucci remarked that being his assistant was like witnessing the invention of cinema anew (Viano 1993, ix). In 1955 Pasolini dedicated a poem "*A un ragazzo*" to the young Bernardo (Schwartz 1992, 301–311). Years later (in 1972), when Bertolucci showed his "Last Tango in Paris" to Pasolini (before its release), his former friend and teacher told him it was "merely mass entertainment ... a subcultural product" (quoted in Schwartz 1992, 606). Bertolucci was a pallbearer at Pasolini's funeral; he later recalled feeling that he might be swept off his feet at any moment (Schwartz 1992, 87). Along with Bertolucci's *Novecento*, Pasolini's last film—*Salo`*—was shown at the Fifteenth New York Film Festival in October 1977 (Schwartz 1992, 689).

16. "*Ragazzi*" means "young male hustlers" (Pasolini 2005 [1972], 21 n. 14). These characters may be "ragged and cruel," Rich (2007, 79) notes, but they serve as "symbols of purity and even classical beauty."

17. Born in Bologna in 1923, Roberto Roversi is a writer and poet. Roversi, Leonetti, and Pasolini started the journal *Officina* in May 1955. "In an arrogant, intolerant era," Roversi (2007 [1978], 132) wrote, "what I call Pasolini's *vital tenderness* was under constant attack. He was indisputably excluded from his time; whenever he offered a helping hand, out of his passion for knowledge, he was rejected harshly and resentfully."

18. Francesco Leonetti (1924–) is a writer and poet.

19. Franco Fortini (1917–1994) was an essayist, literary critic, and poet.

20. Pasolini characterized his theoretical practice as a "heretical empiricism," Viano (1993, 38) explains, owing to the primacy of embodied experience, a view that contradicted Marxist rationalism. His empiricism was "heretical" because it challenged the value-neutrality of empiricism as it positioned "experience" as situated within historically specific contexts and worldviews. If the concept *empiricism* evoked the Anglo-Saxon philosophical tradition opposing *idealism*,"

Viano (1993, 38) continues, the adjective "heretical" conveyed a religious animation in contestation of "hierarchical structures from below," from the subproletariat and from an archaic past but from subjective experience as well. His "heresy" was not only epistemological and religious, then, it was Marxian, for Pasolini would provide Marxism with the subjectivity it had eradicated (Viano 1993, 38).

It is the erasure of subjective experience in the reduction of the school curriculum to considerations of "class" (for an acknowledgment of the complexity of the concept see Goodman 2006, 10 ff.) or "ideology" (Apple 2004) that renders such subsumption a version of "leftwing fascism" (Pasolini, quoted in Viano 1993, 8). (Apple's performance of ideology critique is contradicted by his exhibitionistic invocation of an apparently ideology-free individual—himself!: see Apple 2004, 159 ff. For examples of self-reference serving a scholarly purpose: see Grande 2004, 91–92, 159–160; Howard 2008, ix–xv.) Such ideology critique, Michael F. D. Young (2008, 164) points out, demotes the curriculum to a "positioning device … "promoting the interests and advantages of some groups rather than others." Young (2008, 199) likens such analysis to "muckraking journalism rather than social science," and, he adds, Apple's work is "the most sophisticated and influential example of this genre" (2008, 226 n. 3). In Young's (2008, 165, 199) judgment, then, "ideology critique" is "seriously flawed"; it is part of "what went wrong with the sociology of knowledge in educational studies."

21. As early as 1951, Pasolini published articles in a wide range of newspapers (Barański 1999c, 255). During the 1960s, he was a regular contributor to *Vie Nuove* (a leftwing weekly magazine), replying to readers' queries regarding social and cultural matters. In the June 5, 1960 issue, for instance, Pasolini replied to a reader's question concerning sexual intolerance: "But irrationality (in which the problem of sexuality is involved) is a category of the human spirit: thus it is a problem which is always current and urgent" (quoted in Rohdie 1995, 128). The form of this column was a dialogue, but the practice of it was monologic. Pasolini spoke to himself as if he were speaking to another, Rohdie (1995, 128) tells us, at times in his own tongue, at times even in the dialects of others.

During 1974–75, Pasolini regularly contributed articles to the daily *Corriere della Serra*, a national newspaper (like *The New York Times*) located in Milan. Pasolini's contributions to *Corriere* were "controversial," including a series of anti-abortion articles at the time of the referendum of legalization (Rohdie 1995, 180). From March to June 1975, not six months before he was murdered, Pasolini contributed a series of fourteen articles to *Corriere* under the general title "Gennariello." These—they constitute, for Viano (1993, 31), a "pedagogical treatise"—were later collected and published in an anthology of Pasolini's late writings as *Lettere luterane* (1976). The last one is dated October 29: "My Proposals for School and TV" (Rohdie 1995, 181). The core of the *Lettre*, "Gennariello" ("an affectionate Neapolitan name" [Rohdie 1995, 181]) is in the form of a "primer," composed of "didactic letters" addressed to a young man trying to find his way in contemporary Italy. "Short lessons" that provide "tools necessary to resist assimilation into the dominant culture" (Viano 1993, 31), they were also "partly love letters" (as Rohdie [1995, 181] depicts them), "paternal" and "affectionate" as they "instruct" and "seduce." Rohdie (1995, 181) observes that "Pasolini assumed the role of teacher was to help Gennariello become conscious of himself and of the world around him," as well as conscious of the "father" who was teaching him (Pasolini). But consciousness was often a "dangerous instrument for Pasolini, necessary, but potentially lethal." Why? "The ability to learn about your innocence and the gracious gift it is," Rohdie (1995, 182, emphasis added) explains, entails the acquisition of the knowledge which would put an end to the innocence the knowledge was acquired to protect. But consciousness was less a threat than a necessary defense of an irrational severely threatened by a capitalism which would obliterate all otherness including the preciousness of Gennariello's Neapolitanism. *Reason was a means for rescuing the irrational....* Writing then, and poetry in all its forms, was an existential and even revolutionary necessity. It was a way to save your soul.

The "forces" of passion and intellect combine (Ryan-Scheutz 2007, 94, 103, 125–126; Viano 1993, 108–110, 117, 239). As Robert Musil (1990 [1922],131) put the matter: "We do not have too much intellect and too little soul, but too little intellect in matters of the soul."

22. Lawton (2005a, vii) characterizes Pelosi as a "seventeen-year-old two-bit punk," accompanied by "several unidentified associates." Beaten "viciously with a nail-studded board," Pasolini was run over repeatedly with his own Alfa Romeo." On May 7, 2005, Pelosi retracted his confession, precipitating investigators in Rome to reopen the inquiry. Sergio Citti (1933–2005), a film director who had worked closely with Pasolini, claimed five men murdered Pasolini, using Pelosi as "bait" (http://news.bbc.co.uk/1/hi/entertainment/film/4529877.stm) and (http://film.guardian.co.uk/news/story/0,12589,1590898,00.html).

   Pasolini's life-long friend Giuseppe Zigaina (2005; Kammerer and Zigaina 2005) alleged that Pasolini arranged his own murder, a view contradicted by Pasolini's determination to finish *Petrolio* and his plans to shoot, during spring 1976, a new film (Chiesi 2007, 103; Welle 1999, 121). Volponi (2007 [1976], 128) asserts: "his death was a political act ... that stemmed from the collective unconscious of the sanctimonious, self-satisfied bourgeoisie." There is a film focused on the murder, *Pasolini, un delitto italiano* (1995), directed by Marco Tullio Giordana. With assistance from a journalist, Pelosi wrote *Io, angelo nero* (*I, Black Angel*, 1995; Duncan 2006, 135–136).

23. In performing *Petrolio*'s "pedagogical function" (Ward 1995, 107), Pasolini prophetically poses petroleum as the "hidden protagonist" behind the political and economic problems of Italy (Lawton 2005a, xiii), among them "kidnappings, petty crime, and *terrorism*" (Ahern 1983/1984, 123). Splitting the two "souls" of St. Paul (Siti 1994, 68), the autobiographical male protagonist can only achieve authenticity by becoming a woman, both in body and spirit (Ryan-Scheutz 2007, 11, 212 ff.). For Pasolini, Ryan-Scheutz (2007, 12) asserts,

   the tragedy of contemporary society was encapsulated by the fact that people no longer recognized their own potential for authenticity. Even worse than not actively desiring or embracing more genuine ways of being, most people seemed increasingly blind or immune to their existence.

Thirty years ago, that fact prodded me to redefine curriculum as *currere* and propose autobiography as a means of remembering—and reconstructing—one's lived experience as a teacher. In *Petrolio*, Pasolini "establishes a clear ideological connection between subjectivity, sexuality, and gender" (Ryan-Scheutz 2007, 270 n. 32). Like the self-shattering prerequisite to the dissolution of whiteness (Pinar 2006a), "only the cancellation of one's identity, as achieved through ...—a radical change, degradation, or symbolic death—can free the human subject from his role as dictated by the dominant culture" (Ryan-Scheutz 2007, 220). That curricular agenda, Ryan-Scheutz suggests, is the message of *Petrolio*. It is accomplished, in part, through a narrative form which is sensitive to what Gian Carlo Ferretti in his review of *Petrolio* has described as the "boiling, lava-like river the 'lived'" (quoted in Ward 1995, 108). Ward (1995, 112) points out that, for Pasolini, "lived reality comes to our consciousness already filtered through and formed by the modes of representation available at a given historical moment."

Through the subjective labor of reconstruction one transfigures the lived into the historical, "lava" into transitional objects, including "public service." Subjective reconstruction is, in part, a restructuring of the modes of representation by which we experience the "lived" and from which we express it, thereby participating in the complicated conversation that is history. In this regard, self-referential "poetic expressivity" is no relic of nineteenth-century "heroic individualism" but a progressive political practice amid the crimes of collectivism, including those that have preoccupied me here: identity politics, bureaucratism, and school deform. The teacher—drawing inspiration from Pasolini's characterization of a "genial analytic mind"—becomes "a figure who quite literally takes control over a mass of heterogeneous information and works this material into a coherent and plausible narrative form" (Ward 1995, 132). The teacher does more that fulfill this structuring function, but it is true that she or he "aims to weave the most crucial and significant moments of a given [intellectual] event into narrative form" (Ward 1995, 133). That narrative is his or her subjective reply to the ongoing—situated, existential as well as historical and intellectual—curricular question "what knowledge is of most worth"? Teaching as "the free play of indirect subjectivity" bears no relation to the instrumentalism of "pedagogical content knowledge" (Shulman 1987); it exhibits a playful self-reflexive appreciation for the power chance stimulates (Radhakrishnan 2008, 61). "To affirm chance," Radhakrishnan (2008, 62) suggests, "would be to achieve a higher and truer level of agency than that allowed by the merely political."

24. Though there are connections between Pasolini's concerns and feminist issues (Bruno 1994, 98), feminism was not a key influence for him (Ryan-Scheutz 2007, 35). Interviewed by Dacia Maraini, Pasolini acknowledged that "yes, perhaps it is true that I accept a certain condition of inferiority for women." Pasolini attributed this view to his "ontological love for the past" (quoted in Viano 1993, 342). Only in *Appunti per un'Orestiade Africana* does Pasolini's camera focus on women (Viano 1993, 256). With the exception of *Salò*, Pasolini's films ignore lesbian love (Viano 1993, 291). Still, "while numerous male figures were central to the expression of his world view," Ryan-Scheutz (2007, 4) argues, "women and the female sphere were equally and uniquely important." Moreover, "his portrayal of and identification with female characters onscreen neither conflicted with nor inhibited his political mandate as male writer, critic, and director" (Ryan-Scheutz 2007, 8). In his unfinished novel (*Petrolio*), Pasolini still associated humanity with the presence and subjectivity of women (Ryan-Scheutz 2007, 201). In her study of "five predominant female character types found in Pasolini's films—mothers, prostitutes, daughters, saints, and sinners (2007, 11)—Ryan-Scheutz (2007, 12–13) concludes:

> Thus, no matter what their social status or occupation, no matter how degraded, hypocritical, or coerced their activities, Pasolini considered women—their actions and existential domains—an undying source of goodness both for himself, as individual and artist, and for the world around him. Attracted to life and emotionally invested in the hope of recovering genuine human relations, Pasolini used female figures and their modes of self-expression to articulate his personal longings, to express his political convictions, and to engage directly and metaphorically with the uncorrupted roots of Italian society.

"My love," Pasolini admitted, "is only for woman" (Ryan-Scheutz 2007, 4, 225). "The most important thing in my life has been my mother," Pasolini (quoted in Chiesi and Mancini 2007, 11) confided, adding "joining her, just now, is Ninetto."

25. In October 1962, while a guest in Assisi of the Pro Civitate Christiana, an institution for the promotion of Catholic culture in Italy, Pasolini read the Gospel he found at his bedside; he experienced "a sense of religious possession, interchangeable in his mind with an aesthetic revelation" (Steimatsky 1998, 240). With the support of the Pro Civitate Christiana, Pasolini undertook the filming of *Il Vangelo secondo Matteo*, which he dedicated to the memory of John XXIII. Read through a Gramscian lens (Testa 1994, 184), Pasolini's Christ is a "social reformer within a magical, sacred world, the world that produced the Gospels" (Rohdie 1995, 161). The film was the first "Jesus film" that went directly to scripture for the text (Testa 1994, 182); it emphasized "Matthew's abrupt style" as it "conformed to Matthews's elliptical and episode structure" (Testa 1994, 1888). Though the jury of the *Ufficio Cattolico Internazionale del Cinema* awarded a prize, conservative Catholics were horrified, as were secular leftists (with the prominent exception of Sartre: Viano 1993, 331 n. 5).

26. In the slums or *borgate*, Pasolini focused on the lumpenproletariat, precisely "*because they do not work*": pimps, thieves, prostitutes, the unemployable are not integrated in capitalist modes of production, "unemployed parasites in a Pasolinian Utopia" (Rohdie 1995, 121). Because they are "useless," they are admirable, as they contradict a capitalism where "use" and "function" govern all activity. For Pasolini, the lumpenproletariat were, in effect, "analogies of poets" (1995, 121), not "modern but ancient and with an ancient purity to stand against a contemporary corruption" (1995, 123).

27. As it did with other young women in his life, Pasolini's friendship with Silvana Mauri (1920–2008) took the form of conversations about literature and art. In the case of Mauri, these conversations focused on questions of reality (or "actuality" as Pasolini at times preferred: Rohdie 1995, 121). Ryan-Scheutz (2007, 22) reports that she "fell in love" with Pasolini, knowing he could not reciprocate her feelings. In an early 1950 letter, Pasolini acknowledged that "you have always been for me the woman I could have loved, the only one who has made me understand what a woman is" (quoted in Sicioliano 1982, 159). Though he did have a "unique regard" for Mauri, it is not clear that, as Ryan-Scheutz (2007, 23) suggests, she was "the only woman for whom he ever felt something very close to love." Others have suggested that he loved Maria Callas—the star of his *Medea*—as well.

28. A committed Communist Party leader with ideologically impeccable credentials, Teresina Degan objected "long" and "loudly" to Mautino's railroading of Pasolini's expulsion. Despite lodging formal complaints that a quorum had not been present, that the "debate" had not met the PCI's own procedures, Degan—the "sole woman in the [Party] leadership"—was "ignored" (Schwartz 1992, 227). Rohdie (1995, 26) suggests that it was the "poet Pasolini" who was even more annoying to the Party than the pederast Pasolini.

29. Dino Campana (1885–1932) was an Italian poet who led a wandering existence and died deranged.

30. For Pasolini, poetical labor was an expressive, but not narrative, undertaking. He was critical of Hollywood films for their reliance on story, for failing to honor cinema's "oneiric" and "barbaric" nature, to compose filmic poems whose structure did not communicate as much as "subvert" subjectivity (Rumble 1994, 211; Jay 1993, 255). By "poetry," Viano (1993, 54) suggests, Pasolini came to mean "a film style, a "cinema of poetry" that underscored "subjactivity," Viano's neologism for subjectivity as "compelling action," including its modification—and the world's—by "passion" (1993, 42, 45), a "passion … for reality" (1993, 47). In my terms, this is worldliness.

31. Despite the pervasiveness of neo-capitalism in the post-war era, Ryan-Scheutz (2007, 12) reminds, women remained, for Pasolini, "living signs of innocence and integrity in the most basic and universal of senses." (Ninetto Davoli also signaled innocence: Viano 1993, 180; Lawton 1980–81, 168.) Though representing "vitality" (Pasolini, quoted in Ryan-Scheutz 2007, 94, 95, 98), women were also real (Ryan-Scheutz 2007, 41, 75). His intense and life-long relationship with his mother and with a series of (non-sexual) intimacies with women (Ryan-Scheutz 2007, 23, 43) structured Pasolini's gendered understanding of cultural crisis (Ryan-Scheutz 2007, 35).

32. These various processes Pasolini specified in one concept—*contaminazione* (contamination)—a process central to Pasolini's notion of free indirect discourse: "it describes the interlacing of voices, high and low, literary Italian and dialect intertwined in free indirect discourse without thereby neutralizing the specificity of each voice" (Steimatsky 1998, 241). Pasolini asserted: "The sign under which I work is always contamination" (quoted in Rhodes 2007, 56). In its specialized linguistic meaning, "contamination" lacks the pejorative meaning it connotes in English translation; in Pasolini, it refers to the action of one element on another with which it finds itself associated (Lawton 2005b, xxxii). Rhodes (2007, 56–57) accords the concept a material basis in the reality of Rome, an ancient city reconfigured by Mussolini and, after World War II, by bureaucrats and capitalists accommodating the city's influx of immigrants from the South. Like the palimpsest Rome is (Jewell 1992, 14), Pasolini's contamination juxtaposes "the high with the low ... the center with the periphery"; it is his stylistic strategy for engaging the world, for entering history:

> The objects comprising the world exist in relation to traces ("fossils," or "ruins") that contain the lost utopian impulses of earlier epochs; when a painting or a poem sets in motion a dialect between object and the failed dreams of the past, we become conscious of our immersion in history, not simply as dead weight, but as a redemptive future project (Restivo 2002, 54).

For me, the presence of the past postulates reparation as redemption.

The practice of juxtaposition, with its "intercalating of idioms and registers to create a dynamic linguistic energy" (Gordon 1996, 43), demonstrates Pasolinian contamination; it "thereby conflates categories, defies logic, exceeds order; it turns language inside-out, topsy-turvy; as dialect, from below, from a nether world beneath the bourgeois one, corrupts the official bourgeois language that dominates at the top" (Rohdie 1995, 11). In *Accattone* (1961), Pasolini registered his "signature" performance of "contamination" by juxtaposing sacred music to scenes of "instinctive, irrational behavior," recalling Christian redemption during the most base moments of a character's existence (Ryan-Scheutz 2007, 8, 66, 79).

33. "The assemblage of the film must never add anything to the existing reality," asserted André Bazin (1918–1958), the influential French film critic and theorist (quoted in Viano 1993, 88). Bazin's statement specified Italian neorealism, often associated with Roberto Rossellini (1906–1977), and specifically his movie *Rome, Open City* (1945), neo-realism's "founding text" (Viano 1993, 85). ("Rossellini *is* neorealism," Pasolini once asserted [quoted in Viano 1993, 86].) "Although neorealists and Bazin were never as naive as their detractors portrayed them to be," Viano (1993, 88) explains, "their emphasis on immediacy undeniably engendered a dangerous conflation of realism and empiricism: reality is what we see, and what we see is real" (cf. Pinar 2004, 257). In the first films—*Accattone* and *Mamma Roma*—Pasolini makes, Viano (1993, 87; Ryan-Scheutz 2007, 242 n. 10) argues, a "rather harsh" critique of *Open City*'s portrait of the lower

classes as "basically immune from greed," and that immorality was external in origin. "The enemy," Pasolini is clearly asserting, "is within" (Viano 1993, 88).

Only *Accattone*, *Mamma Roma*, and *Il Vangelo secondo Matteo* are taken as tributes to neorealism, Viano (1993, 53) continues. He acknowledges that this view of Pasolini's career as breaking with realism can be documented by several of his declarations. These occasional repudiations of realism, Viano (1993, 54) cautions, must be contextualized as his "love for reality." For example, speaking to a French journalist after the release of *Teorema* in Paris, he declared:

> The only expression which still interests me is poetry, and the more meaning is complex the more poetic it is. I am discovering a reality which has nothing to do with realism. And it is precisely because this reality is my only great concern that I am increasingly drawn to the cinema: it apprehends reality even beyond the will of the director and the actors (quoted in Viano 1993, 54).

This revised realism—what Viano (1993, 54) terms "a certain realism"—recast reality in a "problematic" and "open form," as historicized, as the "courage of seeing and saying things which must be seen and said" (Viano 1993, 328, n. 3), a version of autobiographical demand (Casemore 2008) that Pasolini would later theorize as "free indirect discourse" (Restivo 2002, 54). It was Pasolini's "attachment to the 'things of the world' and to their incarnate images" that expressed itself in his "twofold commitment to the 'realist' and 'reverential,' deeply intertwined in Pasolini's thinking, the one contaminating the other" (Steimatsky 1998, 245). Pasolini pointed out that what constituted realism in 1945 was no longer true in 1960: "every epoch has something to unmask; for power, by definition, only tends to produce representations instrumental to its reproduction" (Viano 1993, 69). In theoretical terms, Viano (1993, 70) explains:

> neorealism relied on the plenitude of the represented image, that is, on its hoped-for monosemic status. Inevitably, the audience was also thought of as unified, as an undifferentiated mass bound to experience a common (because natural) reaction in the face of a universal signifier.

Not only did the "plenitude" of the image (and the undifferentiated viewer) splinter and multiply, the narrative cohesiveness—specifically the "connective logic" between shots—dissolved, as Pasolini "reinscribed the sacred by his dissolution of perspective" (Rohdie 1995, 22). The shot became the analogue of a painting—this he learned from Longhi (Weis 2005, 58, 59 n. 29)—and these separate framed images (in their "anticipation" and "intensification" [Weis 2005, 58]) replaced transcendence with immanence.

A "trademark of his cinematographic gaze" (Schwenk 2005, 42), Pasolini's "concentration of action in an image" is discernible, Schwenk (2005, 45) suggests, in Pasolini's writings as well, including his early novel, *Il sogno di una cosa* (The Dream of a Soul, 1962), and his drawings (Semff 2005, 121). A decade earlier, Pasolini had spoken of "moments in which time, filled up, purifies itself and overflows into the absolute," of "moments of richness in which is prophesied the mystery which is not understood," and lastly of "stoppages, the *intermittences du coeur* in which the gestures, because it is so wonderfully integrated into the anonymous body of the day, would have been all but overlooked and stands out, isolated, in a kind aureole of consciousness" (quoted in Schwenk 2005, 46). Worldliness is not only being transfigured by experience, but consciously intensifying experience, as Pasolini describes here (Schwenk 2005, 47–48).

34. In Pasolini's judgment, television was installing *one* bourgeois model, a totalizing totalitarianism posing as entertainment (Viano 1993, 267–268). Pasolini

asserted: "TV has so codified a kind of 'unreality' that its unique human model is more and more the hypocritical, conformist petit bourgeois" (quoted in Viano 1993, 268). Pasolini's point is well-taken, if exaggerated.

35. Ninetto Davoli *became* a professional actor, as did Sergio and Franco Citti (Ryan-Scheutz 2007, 76). On occasion, Pasolini did employ professional actors, among them Anna Magnani (who starred in *Mamma Roma*) and Terrace Stamp (who starred in *Teorema*), both of whom were "imposed by the producers" (Gordon 1996, 192). His friend and legendary opera star Maria Callas starred in *Medea*. To encourage working from within, Pasolini refused "preparation, emotional or otherwise, in the actors" (Gordon 1996, 194). Pasolini's most significant appearances in his films are in *Edipo* and *Il Decameron* (Gordon 1996, 197).

36. Pasolini's "method" is the "collage," Rohdie (1995, 32) explains, "the embeddedness of things, their overlap. His art is an art of superimpositions.... It is like an archaeological site. An all-at-onceness of differences which repeat and mirror each other on various historical levels, but all contained within the one fiction." In my clumsy way, I employ this "method" in the composition of synoptic textbooks for teachers (like this one), summarizing scholarship, then arranging it, if not always contrapuntally, inspired by Aoki's "generative tensionality" (quoted in Pinar and Irwin 2005, 161, 164, 211). The juxtaposition of heteronymous elements ("holes" [Pinar 2004, 2] in the argument) precipitates passages to understanding. As in Pasolini's films (as Rohdie [1995, 21] points out), "there *are* connectives between shots, but they are not narratives ones; the connectives are poetic in the way I have described them, that is they sound, they rhyme, they echo, and they do so not narratively, that is semiotically, but irrationally, that is mimetically." In the tensions juxtapositions create, students may experience the subjectivity of study, its oneric origins transfigured by knowledge of the world. To compose a synoptic text structured like subjectivity, I follow Pasolini's advice:

> The book must be written in layers; each new version must be in the form of a dated note, so that the book comes across almost as a diary.... At the end, the book must appear to be a chronological stratification, a living formal process—where a new idea does not erase an earlier one, but rather corrects it or indeed lets it stand unaltered, thereby conserving it formally as a document of thought's passage (quoted in Jewell 1992, 25).

Reminiscent of a Roman ruin, such a textbook resembles the reality it represents.

The extensive footnoting—a customary practice in scholarship generally but atypical in textbooks, especially in textbooks for teachers (see Ayers 2004, for instance)–contradicts the inattention to academic knowledge typical of teacher education scholarship; extended endnotes perform the palimpsest that was, as Rhodie notes above (and elsewhere: 1995, 63, 109, 123, 161), the model for Pasolini's "method" of juxtaposition. As Jewell (1992, 24) notes, "*palimpsest* can also refer to a superimposition of texts and, etymologically, to the newly erased, to subtractions. It evokes, then, a hermeneutical question and leads to inquiries about the nature, motivations, and results of textual representations." Such inquiries constitute, in part, the complicated conversation that is a curriculum of cosmopolitanism, disinterring the buried in order to reanimate the present (Jewell 1992, 52).

Like Pasolini's *contaminatio*, the synoptic text is no flat surface, however, as it "favors pluralizing literary superimpositions ... over mimetic models of representation" (Jewell 1992, 13): My referencing of newspaper articles emphasizes the past's indissoluble structuring of the present. In a different but related context, Rohdie (1995, 9) observes: "Citation broke with representation and, thus, with its history." Disarticulating the narrative into "mannerist"

fragments performs the "coded nature of reality itself" (Rumble 1994, 218).
In Pasolinian terms, footnoting represents (as it suppresses) the "temptation"
(Pasolini 2005 [1972], 180, 182) to compose another text.

37. Pasolini met Laura Betti (born Maura Trombetti) in 1958; she became his
confidante (Schwartz 1992, 67; Ryan-Scheutz 2007, 43). Often seen together,
the pair was "tailor-made" for the tabloids and gossip columns: he, the "avowed"
homosexual, Betti, in "dramatic clothes, platinum blond straight hair, and as
likely to kick a reporter as to ask him for supper in her Bolognese kitchen"
(Schwartz 1992, 321). In private settings (at Pasolini's 1974 New Year's Eve
Party, for instance), too, she could be "the life of the party" (Taviani and Taviani
2007 [1994], 5). In *Teorema*, Betti plays the peasant servant Emila, for which
she received the Venice Festival's Volpi Cup as best actress of the year (Schwartz
1992, 522). In *I racconti di Canterbury*—the "Wife of Bath's Prologue"—she
plays the leading role (Ryan-Scheutz 2007, 185). After his murder, Betti would
work to honor his memory (Ryan-Scheutz 2007, 237 n. 65), pressing the PCI to
commemorate him (Schwartz 1992, 80), then founding the Pasolini Foundation
(Schwenk and Semff 2005, 21).

38. Mannerist painters often painted religious subjects, Viano (1993, 107) tells us,
but their angels had blackened wings and "estranged faces," disclosing "not
seraphic bliss" but "doubt," even "torment." The Mannerists questioned the
possibility of objective representation by portraying a "simultaneity of points
of view" and by conveying an "expressionist dissonance" (Viano 1993, 108).
Pasolini called himself a Mannerist, and he was called a Mannerist by critics
(owing to his citations of Mannerist paintings in his films: Rohdie 1995, 145). In
Mannerist paintings (1520–1600), compositions can have no focal point, space
can be ambiguous, figures can be characterized by bending and twisting with
distortions, exaggerations, an elastic elongation of the limbs, bizarre posturing
on one hand, graceful posturing on the other hand, and a rendering of the heads
as uniformly small and oval. The composition is jammed by clashing colors,
which is unlike what one sees in the balanced, natural, and dramatic colors of the
High Renaissance. Mannerist artwork seeks instability and restlessness. There
is also a fondness for allegories that have lascivious undertones. Accessed on
February 28, 2008, from http://www.artmovements.co.uk/mannerism.htm

    For Pasolini, Gordon (1996, 148) suggests, "Mannerist, formal patterns ...
create a profound, ontological link with the real, without recourse to mimesis,
representing reality always with the imprint of subjectivity."

39. George Orson Welles (1915–1985) was an Academy Award-winning director,
writer, actor, and producer for film, stage, radio, and television. Naomi Greene
points out the resemblance in position between Welles and Pasolini; at one point
Pasolini has Welles declare: "Italy has the most illiterate masses and the most
ignorant bourgeoisie in Europe.... The average man is a dangerous criminal, a
monster. He is a racist, a colonialist, a defender of slavery, a mediocrity" (quoted
Rich 2007, 79). Schwartz (1992, 411) suggests that Pasolini chose Welles because
he resembled Fellini.

40. "Directly" meant through "analogy" (Barański 1999d, 286). Though faithful
to the "narrative flow" of the Gospel, the film is not strictly organized after
the Gospel (1999d, 289): "[i]t becomes difficult not to see his film taking on a
dialectical relationship with its source rather than passively repeating its rhythms
and its message" (1999d, 294). Moreover, Barański (1999d, 313–314) suggests,
the film calls into question Matthew's authority.

41. *La rabbia* is Pasolini's "many-faceted experiment" stylistically focused on the
"signifying power of montage, both as linkage of images and juxtaposition
of images with sound and spoken commentary." The newsreel images that
provide "visual evidence" for "documentary truth" are edited by Pasolini into

"new sequences, where they acquire different meanings" (all quoted passages are Viano 1993, 114). Unanimously acknowledged by critics and by Pasolini himself, the Marilyn Monroe sequence is the "highest achievement" in *La rabbia* (Viano 1993, 115; Ryan-Scheutz 2007, 40). Viano (1993, 115) suggests that Monroe's suicide provides a sublime example of death as "refusal," not only of the corruption of Hollywood (Ryan-Scheutz 2007, 40) but of capitalism's co-optation of the body and desire as well. For Pasolini, Marilyn Monroe was a "martyr" and a "witness" to the "wreckage of the culture industry" (Viano 1993, 115; Ryan-Scheutz 2007, 41).

42. Shortly before making *Comizi d'amore*, Viano (1993, 122) tells us, Pasolini saw *Chronicle d'un été* (*Chronicle of a Summer*, 1960), the French documentary that initiated *cinéma vérité*. In that film, the anthropologist Jean Rouch and the sociologist Edward Morin interviewed several Parisians and, afterward, invited the participants to watch a rough cut of the filmed material. The participants' reactions to the rough cut were also filmed, then discussed by the authors in the final sequence. Intrigued by the potential of *cinéma vérité*—I am still following Viano's narration (1993, 122)—Pasolini "embraced Morin's and Rouch's suggestion that the only possible documentary truth was one that included the filmmaker's presence." Moreover, he derived from *Chronicle d'un été* the strategy of discussing the film *in* the film. Viano suggests that to accentuate Pasolini's "self-reflexiveness" (1993, 122), he enjoined Moravia and Musatti in discussion of the film.

During the film, Pasolini also interviews the journalist Oriana Fallaci (Restivo 2002, 78). Ryan-Scheutz (2007, 41) notes that while *La rabbia* expresses Pasolini's "trope of (female) vitality and goodness by referring to real women worldwide," *Comizi d'amore* focuses on the women of Italy. For Ryan-Scheutz (2007, 41), the film is an "important work" in Pasolini filmography owing to its interview format in which actually existing Italians of all ages, classes, and occupations speak and because he used the film to probe public views on controversial subjects such as sexual freedom, homosexuality, divorce and prostitution: "A crusade against ignorance and fear, then!" (Pasolini, quoted in Viano 1993, 122). *Comizi* reveals the particular nature of Pasolini's documentary. He wants to "document a certain reality" as he labors to "fight" and "leave a mark" on "reality" (Viano 1993, 123). In this respect, *Comizi d'amore* is the chronicle of Pasolini's mounting frustration at the sight of people's refusal to acknowledge sexuality as a problem, "one of few films at the time to solicit and ponder women's views" (2007, 41). In it, Pasolini links women's onscreen iconographic expressivity with their historical reality in 1960s Italy (Ryan-Scheutz 2007, 41).

The "value" of *Comizi d'amore*, Viano (1993, 123) suggests, is its "immediacy." He quotes Foucault's 1977 observation that "the faces of these kids" with whom Pasolini begins the film "do not even try to give the impression that they believe what they say" (quoted in 1993, 123). It becomes obvious that nearly everyone Pasolini interviews is withholding or disguising the truth; what Pasolini documents, then (as Viano notes), is the mask 1960s Italy wore. Evidently Pasolini had this in mind, as he wrote in the preparatory notes:

> The questions must be stinging, malicious, impertinent, and fired point-blank (they can be toned down in the dubbing if necessary), so as to wring from those interviewed, if not the truth in the logical sense, at least psychological truth. An expression in the eyes, a scandalized angry reaction, or a laugh, can say more than words (quoted in Viano 1993, 123).

Viano (1993, 123) suggests that in *Comizi d'amore*, Pasolini begins to appreciate what he can achieve with cinema that he could not achieve through literary means: He can portray an order of subliminal truth through "an expression in the eyes." Not for the first time, Viano (1993, 123) points out that Pasolini makes a distinction between a verbal and visual truth, a distinction that "foreshadows" the future direction of his film theory and practice.

43. A Greek word (πραγμα), the root meaning of *pragma* is "that which has been done, an act, a deed, a fact" (Cherryholmes 1999, 25). Here Pasolini seems interested in those meanings associated with "practicality" (not philosophical pragmatism, the subject of Cherryholmes's study: 1999, 25) or instrumentality. Like Pasolini, the great curriculum theorist James B. Macdonald (1995, 4) worried over anti-humanist consequences of "technological rationality." Like Pasolini, Macdonald (1995, 2) faced reality: "The school exists to bring learners in contact with reality, of which our society, ourselves, and our cultural heritage are parts."

44. "Monstrum" refers to "monster," evidently, to "unusual phenomena" (Pasolini 2005 [1972], 172; 287). Associated with the French "monere," it also connotes portent or warning: to remind (Doll 1995, 102; Jardine, Clifford, and Friesen (in press), 70).

45. Dante was a "constant presence" in Pasolini's career (Welle 1999, 115). To my astonishment, during a keynote address at the 2008 Conference on Globalization, Diversity, Education (organized by Washington State University), multicultural advocate Professor James A. Banks dismissed Dante (and Shakespeare!) as "traditional academic knowledge." On occasion, the excess of contemporary identity politics becomes comic.

46. Is "a certain realism" a form of worldliness? Speaking to a French journalist after the release of *Teorema* in Paris, Pasolini declared: "I am discovering a reality which has nothing to do with realism" (quoted in Viano 1993, 54). Pasolini historicized realism—as he did reality—when he asserted, "There is no absolute Realism that is valid for all epochs. Every epoch has its own realism. And this is because every epoch has its own ideology" (quoted in Viano 1993, 69). Pasolini's presence (and the particular role he plays) in *Edipo re* (his most autobiographical film: Viano 1993, 2) indicates to Viano (1993, 175) that "a certain realism" has taken the "road of autobiography" (1993, 177). On other films it requires preoccupation with sexuality (Viano 1993, 121). Pasolini coined the phrase "a certain realism" in his 1968 interview with Oswald Stack (Viano 1993, 200), when he was focused on the question of what we can know after certainty is no longer possible (Viano 1993, 200; Muller 2000, 145). Myth (especially as the prehistory of the present) and allegory (the abstract in the concrete)—in *Teorema* they are represented by the recurrent image of the desert (Viano 1993, 131)—return our gaze to the historical present as it transports our attention to other—enduring—human preoccupations: "As the image of what exceeds, defines, and awaits the characters," Viano (1993, 204) explains, "the desert transposes the story into another, a nonrealistic dimension; it is the key to the allegory." For Pasolini, Viano (1993, 165) continues, "realism is what conveys 'the essential humanity of an action'."

47. It was during the late 1960s that many on the "new" Left began to argue that the cause of revolution was best served not by street struggle but by interventions in the "superstructure" (Pinar et al. 1995, 245) (i.e., the domains of culture: cinema, language, painting, theater, literature, television). More so than economic structures, the argument went, culture forms consciousness; no longer was it possible to insist that cultural labor was a subordinate political activity, that culture and ideology were merely epiphenomenal to economic forces. "Theory," Rohdie (1995, 140) explains, "became a political activity in its own right," employing conceptual tools outside Marxism proper, among them semiotics, structuralism, linguistics, psychoanalysis. Now political work included restructuring those codes of representation that conveyed the ideology of neocapitalism by—in

Pasolini's terms—"scandalizing" them, thereby influencing how people think. No longer did it make political or historical sense for intellectuals to identify themselves with the working class; now it made sense for intellectuals to distance themselves from the working class. (In consciousness, the U.S. working class became petit bourgeois, vulnerable to the self-serving fantasies of that formation: Witness the Ronald Reagan phenomenon in the 1980s.) Intellectuals assumed an "autonomous critical-revolutionary role independent of a class politics" (Rohdie 1995, 140). In the United States, those adjectives may disappear with those who came of age in the 1960s (Cohen 2008).

"Theory" was often "French theory," decontextualized then reworked for reuse in America. In the U.S., Cusset (2008, 279) points out, Foucault's work has functioned as theoretical support for condemnations of universalism, rationalism, and humanism as discourses of conquest and colonialism, as well as affirmation for allegations that exclusion (of the insane, of criminals, of homosexuals) produces the norm (reason, justice, heterosexuality). "This interpretation of Foucault," Cusset (2008, 280) continues,

> provided his American readers with a veritable *conspiracy theory*, in the name of which they scoured society to uncover its aggressors and victims. American cultural studies or minority studies texts inspired by Foucault consistently focus on the notion of "unmasking" or "delegitimizing" some form of power that is "stifling" or "marginalizing" one oppressed minority group or another—an approach that stands in direct opposition to Foucault's genealogical method.

Though there are intellectually rigorous studies faithful to Foucault's complex oeuvre (see Baker 2001), too often in U.S. schools of education, it has been employed in just this fashion.

48. Alessandro Cappabianca is an architect and film critic.
49. Massimo Canevacci teaches cultural anthropology in the Department of Sociology at the University of Rome. He is the director of the journal *Avatar*.
50. In *La rabbia*, as in *Appunti per un'Orestiade Africana* (a "most unusual and beautiful film": Viano 1993, 251), Viano (1993, 118, 256) points out, the color black symbolizes Pasolini's fantasy that the black race could transform the Western, white scene. In this year's U.S. presidential campaign, featuring for the first time an African American candidate, does the color "black" symbolize the same?
51. Constantinos Gavras (born February 13, 1933), better known as (Constantin) Costa-Gavras (and other variants), is a Greek-French filmmaker best known for films with political themes, most famously *Z* (1969). Many of his movies were made in French and released with English subtitles; starting with *Missing* (1982), several were made in English.
52. Elio Petri (1929–1982) was an Italian filmmaker and screenwriter whose work is intensely political, dominated by the themes of exclusion and divided lives.
53. An Italian film and drama critic, Goffredo Fofi (1937-) has focused—as did Pasolini—on the relationship between social reality and its representation in the arts. He has been actively engaged in the politics of Italian culture through many articles, speeches, and other initiatives, such as publication of new magazines (among them *The Earth Seen from the Moon* and *The Stranger*).
54. In the United States, the educational Left is often guilty of such simplification. Its obsession with "social justice" reiterates the right-wing's claim that schools—not government—are responsible for redressing the inequities of the present. Rather than constructing new forms of representation—such as a reconceptualized synoptic text, a form of contemporary curriculum development—by means of

which teachers might construct curricula focused on social justice, too many have regressed to the self-indulgent indignation offered by identity politics.

55. Pasolini's "resistance" to the hegemony of the bourgeoisie was, Rohdie (1995, 13) suggests, through "poetry." It was his

> language [that] refused to succumb; it stood firm as a point of resistance, or it fought back; it adulterated, defiled, desecrated, violated, besmirched, befouled, parodied, burst into laughter, became tumescent, buggered, proliferated. This was the scandal of his writing. And though it was writing at the highest literary and filmic levels, it imitated styles and perspectives which were base, which were in the muck, in a homage to baseness.

In *Accattone*, it is the pimp who is sacred (Rohdie 1995, 5), precisely because he exists outside the social. It is the "dream of conformity" that "destroys" Mamma Roma, Rohdie (1995, 12) notes: it kills her son Ettore.

56. In his "*Manifesto per un nuovo teatro*," Pasolini connects his theatrical project to the reabsorption of dissidents into the bourgeois power structure and the destruction of the excluded. Opposition to such hegemony is futile, Pasolini lamented, as all ritual, including theater, functions finally to assimilate difference. Despite this political pessimism, Pasolini maintained a Gramscian spiritual optimism, which became invested in the possibility of a "cultural rite" or "Theater of Speech" (or the "Word"). Such a theater represented for Pasolini a return to authenticity expressed in those "texts based on (a perhaps poetic) speech and themes that might typify a lecture, an ideal conference or a scientific debate" (quoted in Peterson 1994, 214; Bertolucci 2007 [1977], 120; Pinar 2006b, 173–176). Conscious of his appropriation by the power structure, the revolutionary playwright must identify those social hypostases in society that intensify stress in the bourgeois individual (Peterson 1994). The new theater, Pasolini asserts, is to be a forum that gives voice to intellectuals—"the progressive group of the bourgeois"—who otherwise have no meaningful role in society. For Pasolini, intellectuals are the survivors, those idiosyncratic figures whose marginality has meant that though they have not been taken over by the dominant ideology, they have been forced to the edges and no longer have a voice. Perhaps the major aim of Pasolini's "Manifesto," Rumble and Testa (1994a) suggest, is to recover these marginalized intellectuals and bring them into purposeful debate on the issues of the day. Pasolini's new theater is then, first and foremost, a site of dialogue, not a theater of scenic action. It is "the place where language comes into its own as a means of sustaining dialogue" (Rumble and Testa, 1994a, 153–154). For Pasolini,

> The theater, then, is seen as a natural meeting place between poetic words and vital speech. Through dramatic fiction, speaking is restored to the character's being, since the character has no real existence outside of performance. The drama is always a sacred drama: the word made flesh (Roncaglia 2007 [1978], 122).

Pasolini was characteristically provocative: "*signore* dressed in fur coats are required to pay thirty times the price of the ticket (which will normally be very low). On the other hand, the sign will also say that fascists (as long as they are under twenty-five) can come in free" (1994 [1968], 156). There are, he complained, two types of conventional theater, the theater of "Chatter" and the theater of the "Gesture" or the "Scream." His theater will be different: "The theater of the World has no interest in spectacle or worldliness, etc.: its only interest is cultural, shared by the author, actors, and public who, therefore, when they gather, take part in a 'cultural rite'" (Pasolini 1994 [1968], 170).

57. The Trilogy made Pasolini one of the wealthiest filmmakers in Italy (Viano 1993, xviii, 269). Later, while acknowledging that the films had contributed to the "democratization of the 'right to self-expression' and then for sexual liberation" (2005 [1972, xvii), Pasolini (2005 [1972], xvii) would announce: "I repudiate the *Trilogy of Life*, even though I do not repent having made it. I cannot, in fact, deny the sincerity and the necessity that drove me to the representation of bodies and their culminating symbol, the sexual organs." By the early 1970s, Pasolini had decided, the hegemony of bourgeois culture had rendered the notion of sexual freedom worthless. No longer a source of vitality or a site of spiritual renewal, the human body and its passions had become as degraded as the rest of neocapitalist life (Ryan-Scheutz 2007, 174; Lawton 1980–81, 173 n. 14). Viano is critical of the Trilogy (1993, 266, 270; and of *Medea*: a "lofty bore," he judges [1993, 280], too severely I think) on esthetic grounds: *Il Decamerone* fails because it presents Pasolini's private preferences as "epiphanies of the real" (1993, 273); *I racconti di Canterbury* was "probably Pasolini's most uninteresting film" (1993, 280); *Il fiore delle mille e una notte* was "irritating and somewhat preposterous" (1993, 286).

58. On May 10, 2005, the BBC reported that investigators in Rome had reopened the inquiry into Pasolini's murder. That decision followed Pelosi's insistence that he did not kill Pasolini. According to Pelosi, three unnamed men beat Pasolini to death on a beach while shouting abuse and insults such as "dirty communist." A group of 30 MPs asked Prime Minister Silvio Berlusconi what steps he intends to take to solve the crime. Accessed on January 5, 2008, from http://news.bbc. co.uk/1/hi/entertainment/film/4529877.stm

    Recall that Giuseppe Zigaina (2005) alleged that Pasolini contracted for his own death (Note 22).

59. Pasolini recalled his embrace of the Friulian dialect (technically it was not a dialect but a minor language) as a political act within the context of the linguistic policies of fascism. (Under Mussolini, the "particular was not-national" and unpatriotic: Rohdie 1995, 28.) Rather than shedding dialect as the fascist state demanded, Pasolini acquired it (Rohdie 1995, 118). As Rohdie (1995, 28; see, also, Jewell 1992, 111) points out, his embrace was also personal:

    The links between dialect, the peasantry, the rural were connected to Pasolini's closeness to his mother; these, in turn, were analogues of poetry. Hence dialect, in and of itself, had a poetic value. Negatively, Poetry and Mother were contrasts to Father: militarist, fascist.... Insofar as dialect was an illegal, even scandalous activity for Pasolini, it was because dialect was a poetic activity, and a private one.

    In this regard, Friulian represented a "regression outside history and symbolic speech" (Rohdie 1995, 29). In another sense, this regression—psychological exile—enabled his return to engagement with the world, as Pasolini notes: "For me it [Friulian] was the highest point of hermeticism, of obscurity, of a refusal to communicate. Instead, something happened that I didn't expect. The use of this dialect gave it a flavor of life and realism" (quoted in Rohdie 1995, 118).

60. Despite denying the pedagogical intentions of his work (during an interview in New York: Chiesi and Mancini 2007, 91), most critics and scholars appreciate Pasolini's production as "broadly pedagogical (Restivo 2002, 152), based on love, "scandalous" in its "sexuality or ideology, and aimed at mutual transformation" (Gordon 1996, 78), "less interested in consciousness than in subconscious impulses" (1996, 212). Though Pasolini's pedagogy was indeed public, addressed to the citizens of Italy, his educational experience had been, at least initially, intensely private. Ryan-Scheutz (2007, 16–17) tells us that Pasolini's mother Susanna

fostered her son's talents and intellectual growth as much as she could. She loved poetry and taught Pier Paolo what she knew about rhyme and meter. During his elementary school days, Susanna introduced him to literature in her own modest way by reading and writing short poems. At age seven, Pier Paolo reciprocated his mother's gesture by writing her a poem of his own. Later in life, he recalled his future jobs that same year: he would become a navy captain and a poet. While this declaration innocently embraces both parental spheres, it also reveals the division he already perceived as existing between his mother's loving demeanor and aesthetic sensitivities and his father's military career and authoritative presence. Over time, this emotional-perceptual distinction in the private sphere would coincide with the civic division between the male and female domains in his larger poetic vision.

Pasolini understood both his private passion and public service as avenging the structural position of "woman," transposing the female body into a boy's (Duncan 2006, 104 n. 28). Despite the animus toward his father and the patriarchal polis, the "father-son dyad ... gradually comes to dominate Pasolini's entire late oeuvre" (Gordon 1996, 78, 134), supporting Di Stefano's suspicion.

61. The "soul" Pasolini discerned in the Third World he had found earlier in the Rome *borgate*. During his 1966 trip to New York, he also found this "vitality" (Viano 1993, 299) among African Americans living in Harlem (Rohdie 1995, 80). In 1968, Pasolini sketched out a plan for a film—tentatively entitled called "Notes for a Poem on the Third World"—he never made. It was to have been structured by five episodes focused on different parts of the Third World: India, Africa, the Arab countries, South America, and the African-American ghettoes. The theme concerned the spiritual price of integration within a global capitalism, with each episode emphasizing a particular problematic: religion and famine in India, white rationality and black pre-industrial consciousness in Africa, nationalism in Arab countries, guerrilla warfare in Latin America, and dropping out among impoverished blacks in America (Rohdie 1995, 81). Before his eyes, Rohdie (1995, 13) notes, the Third World was "lost to a global capitalism," and Pasolini turned to "myth" in order to evoke that "archaic" world that had been exterminated. Pasolini knew, Rohdie (1995, 110) thinks, that the past he evoked had never existed, that its value was "mythological" and "hypothetical." It functioned as a "defense against the present" (Rohdie 1995, 100; Cvetkovich 2003, 49).

62. Maria Antonietta Macciocchi edited the PCI weekly mass-circulation (350,000 readers) magazine *Vie nuove* (New pathways), founded in 1946 "with a declared pedagogical ambition to educate and inform party members" (Gordon 1996, 47). Macciocchi offered him a column—"Pasolini in Dialogue"—that continued (despite a long interruption) from May 1960 until September 1965 (Gordon 1996, 47). Among the topics Pasolini discussed were erotic literature, "southern machismo," prostitution, women's rights, racism, and sexual taboos, often clashing with the editors (Gordon 1996, 51). In 1977, Macciocchi was expelled from the Party for "ideological deviance" (Schwartz 1992, 366).

Epilogue

1. "Formalism" Kurasawa (2007, 168) summarizes as "institutional cosmopolitanism," global justice that is the "outcome of proper organizational design and mechanisms, or of procedurally legitimate political consensus." Because these organizational designs and mechanisms are "socially thin" they are "reminiscent of its normative counterpart." Kurasawa (2007, 168) observes:

"There is more to creating bonds of mutual commitment and responsibility between citizens of the world than elaborating an ideal-typical model of global governance or specifying the democratic procedures to produce a justifiable body of international law." For him that "more" is social labor. I can accept that concept, but I insist it involves pedagogy by individuals. There is no guarantee that "students" learn what "teachers" teach, but then there is no reason for faith in "social action" either. If "emancipation has to be built from the bottom up" (Dimitriadis and McCarthy 2001, 32), there will be none. In the academic field of education, "struggle" has become a cliché, referencing various social movements but in fact the notion registers a recoding of the individual's scholar's presumed radicalism. Specific individuals—such as Freire or Che Guevara—disappear into "legacies" of "critical pedagogy" (McLaren 2000, 184, 192, xvii; McLaren 1997, 105, 107; Buras and Apple 2006, 31). The gratuitous appropriation of the famous and the naive use of the first-person singular discloses that, despite the rhetoric of "revolution" and "ideology," these "critical" pedagogues are academic versions of consumers, displaying their "critical" commodities for public consumption.

2. For Kurasawa (2007, 187), "aesthetic cosmopolitanism" refers to forms of popular (and possibly high) culture, including "world music, literature and cinema (including hybrid genres), in addition to the Euro-America phenomena of alterative overseas travel and backpacker counter-cultures (the Lonely Planet and Rough Guide audiences, so to speak)."

Given my study of Addams, Bragg, and Pasolini, I link esthetic cosmopolitanism with politics: "the aesthetic becomes the *prerequisite* for a meaningful politics: as if not political rhetoric but art itself provides us with the fundamental experience of freedom out of which the political act can be projected" (Restivo 2002, 149). That the free play of indirect subjectivity is central to creative and pedagogical expression is by now, I trust, obvious.

Bibliography

Addams, Jane (1912, November). The progressive party and the negro. *The Crisis* V, 30–31.

Addams, Jane (2002 [1902]). *Democracy and social ethics*. Urbana: University of Illinois Press.

Adorno, T. W., et al. (1950). *The authoritarian personality*. New York: Harper.

Ahern, John (1983/1984). His poems, his body. *Parnassus: Poetry in Review*, 103–126.

Alcoff, Linda Martín, Hames-García, Michael, Mohanty, Satya P., Moya, Paula M. L. (Eds.) (2006). *Identity politics reconsidered*. New York: Palgrave Macmillan.

Alford, C. Fred (2002). *Levinas, the Frankfurt School, and psychoanalysis*. Middletown, CT: Wesleyan University Press.

Allen, Beverly (1982) (Ed.). *Pier Paolo Pasolini: The poetics of heresy*. Saratoga, CA: Anma Libri and Co.

Allen, Louise Anderson (2001). *A bluestocking in Charleston: The life and career of Laura Bragg*. Columbia: University of South Carolina Press.

Allen, Louise Anderson (2002). Laura Bragg and the Charleston Museum. In Alan R. Sadovnik and Susan F. Semel (Eds.), *Founding mothers and others* (177–200). New York: Palgrave Macmillan.

Anderson, Amada (2006). *The way we argue now*. Princeton, NJ: Princeton University Press.

Anderson, Amanda and Valente, Joseph (Eds.) (2002). *Disciplinarity at the fin de siècle*. Princeton, NJ: Princeton University Press.

Angier, Natalie (2008, May 27). Curriculum designed to unite art and science. *The New York Times* online: http://www.nytimes.com/2008/05/27/science/27angi.html?ex=1212552000&en=ce1212f40c83f0ae&ei=5070&emc=eta1

Anyon, Jean (1997). *Ghetto schooling*. New York: Teachers College Press.

Anyon, Jean (2005). *Radical possibilities*. New York: Routledge.

Aoki, Ted T. (2005 [1978]). Toward curriculum inquiry in a new key. In William F. Pinar and Rita L. Irwin (Eds.), *Curriculum in a new key* (89–110). Mahwah, NJ: Lawrence Erlbaum.

Aoki, Ted (2005 [1986/1991]). Teaching as indwelling between two curriculum worlds. In William F. Pinar and Rita L. Irwin (Eds.), *Curriculum in a new key* (159–165). Mahwah, NJ: Lawrence Erlbaum.

Appiah, Kwame Anthony (2005). *The ethics of identity*. Princeton, NJ: Princeton University Press.

Appiah, Kwame Anthony (2006). *Cosmopolitanism*. New York: Norton.

Apple, Michael W. (2004). *Ideology and curriculum*. New York: RoutledgeFalmer.
Apple, Michael W. (2006). "We are the oppressed": Gender, culture, and the work of home schooling. In Michael W. Apple and Kristen L. Buras (Eds.), *The subaltern speak* (75–93). New York: Routledge.
Aptheker, Bettina (1977). Introduction to Jane Addams and Ida B. Wells' *Lynching and Rape*. Chicago: University of Illinois, Occasional Paper No. 25.
Associated Press (2008, May 11). Los Angeles high school breaks out in violence. *The New York Times* online: http://www.nytimes.com/2008/05/11/education/11school. html?ex=1211169600&en=b03aa5025956e14c&ei=5070&emc=eta1
Astrov, Margot (Ed.) (1962 [1946]. *American Indian prose and poetry*. New York: Capricorn Books.
Autio, Tero (2005). *Subjectivity, curriculum, and society*. Mahwah, NJ: Lawrence Erlbaum.
Ayers, William (2004). *Teaching the personal and the political*. New York: Teachers College Press.
Baker, Bernadette M. (2001). *In perpetual motion: Theories of power, educational history, and the child*. New York: Peter Lang.
Banerjee, Neela (2008, March 6). District to settle Bible suit. *The New York Times* online: http://www.nytimes.com/2008/03/06/us/06bible.html?ex=1205470800& en=e83eb9fdc2bd4b04&ei=5070&emc=eta1
Barański, Zygmunt G. (Ed.) (1999a). *Pasolini old and new*. Dublin: Four Courts Press.
Barański, Zygmunt G. (1999b). Introduction: The importance of being Pier Paolo Pasolini. In Zygmunt G. Barański (Ed.), *Pasolini old and new* (13–40). Dublin: Four Courts Press.
Barański, Zygmunt C. (1999c). Pasolini, Friuli, Rome (1950–1951): Philological and historical notes. In Zygmunt G. Barański (Ed.), *Pasolini old and new* (253–280). Dublin: Four Courts Press.
Barański, Zygmunt C. (1999d). The texts of *Il Vangelo secondo Matteo*. In Zygmunt G. Barański (Ed.), *Pasolini old and new* (281–320). Dublin: Four Courts Press.
Barry, Dan (2008, March 24). A boy the bullies love to beat up, repeatedly. *The New York Times* online: http://www.nytimes.com/2008/03/24/us/24land.html?ex=120 7022400&en=afe416f794889421&ei=5070&emc=eta1
Baszile, Denise Taliaferro (2006). A fire inside. *JCT* 22 (3), 7–25.
Beil, Laura (2008, June 4). Opponents of evolution adopting a new strategy. *The New York Times* online: http://www.nytimes.com/2008/06/04/us/04evolution.html?ex =1213243200&en=d69e762a05629f91&ei=5070&emc=eta1
Benhabib, Seyla (2006). *Another cosmopolitanism* [with Jeremy Waldron, Bonnie Honig, & Will Kymlicka. Edited by Robert Post]. Oxford: Oxford University Press.
Berliner, David C. and Biddle, Bruce J. (1996). *The manufactured crisis*. Cambridge, MA: Perseus.
Bersani, Leo (1995). *Homos*. Cambridge, MA: Harvard University Press.
Bertolucci, Attilio 2007 [1977]. Pasolini's theater. In Roberto Chiesi and Andrea Mancini (Eds.), *Pier Paolo Pasolini: Poet of ashes* (120). San Francisco: City Lights Books.
Bhabha, Homi K. (1996). Day by day: With Frantz Fanon. In Alan Read (Ed.), *The fact of blackness: Frantz Fanon and visual representation* (186-205). Seattle: Bay Press.
Block, Alan A. (1997). *I'm only bleeding*. New York: Peter Lang.
Block, Alan A. (2004). *Talmud, curriculum, and the practical: Joseph Schwab and the Rabbis*. New York: Peter Lang.

Bloom, Harold (1994). *The Western canon*. New York: Harcourt Brace.

Blumenthal, Ralph (2007, December 7). Official leaves post as Texas prepares to debate science education standards. *The New York Times* online: http://www.nytimes.com/2007/12/03/us/03evolution.html?ex=1197435600&en=230a48e0aa41a67a&ei=5070&emc=eta1

Boa, Elizabeth (1996). *Kafka*. Oxford: Clarendon Press.

Boler, Megan (1999). *Feeling power*. New York: Routledge.

Bonhoeffer, Dietrich (1953). *Prisoner for God*. New York: Macmillan.

Boone, Joseph A. (1993). Framing the phallus in the Arabian Nights. In Valerie Wayne and Cornelia Moore (Eds.), *Translations/transformations: Gender and culture in film and literature East and West* (23–33). Honolulu: University of Hawaii East-West Center.

Borgna, Gianni (2007). Pasolini and music. In Roberto Chiesi and Andrea Mancini (Eds.), *Pier Paolo Pasolini: Poet of ashes* (140–144). San Francisco: City Lights Books.

Bové, Paul A. (2002). Can American studies be area studies? In Masao Miyoshi and D. H. Harootunian (Eds.), *Learning places: The afterlives of area studies* (206–230). Durham, NC: Duke University Press.

Boyarin, Daniel (1997). *Unheroic conduct: The rise of heterosexuality and the invention of the Jewish man*. Berkeley: University of California Press.

Boyd, Todd (1997). *Am I black enough for you?* Bloomington: Indiana University Press.

Britzman, Deborah P. (2006). *Novel education*. New York: Peter Lang.

Britzman, Deborah P. and Gilbert, Jen (2008). What will have been said about gayness in teacher education. In Anne Phelan and Jennifer Sumsion (Eds), *Critical readings in teacher education* (201–215). Rotterdam: Sense.

Brown, Elaine (1992). *A taste of power*. New York: Pantheon.

Brown, Victoria Bissell (2004). *The education of Jane Addams*. Philadelphia: University of Pennsylvania Press.

Brundage, W. Fitzhugh (Ed.). (1997). *Under sentence of death*. Chapel Hill: University of North Carolina Press.

Bruno, Giuliana (1994). The body of Pasolini's semiotics: A sequel twenty years later. In Patrick Rumble and Bart Testa (Eds.), *Pier Paolo Pasolini* (88–105). Toronto: University of Toronto Press.

Bulhan, Hussein Abdilahi (1985). *Frantz Fanon and the psychology of oppression*. New York: Plenum Press.

Buras, Kristen L. and Apple, Michael W. (2006). Introduction. In Michael W. Apple and Kristen L. Buras (Eds.), *The subaltern speak* (1–39). New York: Routledge.

Butler, Judith (2004). *Undoing gender*. New York: Routledge.

Butler, Judith and Spivak, Gayatri Chakravorty (2007). *Who sings the nation-state?* London: Seagull.

Caesar, Michael (1999). Outside the palace: Pasolini's journalism (1973–1975). In Zygmunt G. Barański (Ed.), *Pasolini old and new* (363–390). Dublin: Four Courts Press.

Carby, Hazel V. (1998). *Race men*. Cambridge, MA: Harvard University Press.

Casemore, Brian (2008). *The language and politics of place*. New York: Peter Lang.

Caughie, Pamela L. (1999). *Passing and pedagogy*. Urbana: University of Illinois Press.

Chang, Kenneth (2008, April 25). Study suggests math teachers scrap balls and slices. *The New York Times* online: http://www.nytimes.com/2008/04/25/science/25math.html?ref=education

Cheah, Pheng (2006). *Inhuman conditions*. Cambridge, MA: Harvard University Press.

Cherryholmes, Cleo H. (1999). *Reading pragmatism*. New York: Teachers College Press.

Chiesi, Roberto (2007). The body's truth: Notes on Angelo Novi's still photography from *Mamma Roma* (1962) to *Teorema* (1968). In Roberto Chiesi and Andrea Mancini (Eds.), *Pier Paolo Pasolini: Poet of Ashes* (153–158). San Francisco: City Lights Books.

Chiesi, Roberto and Mancini, Andrea (Eds.) (2007). *Pier Paolo Pasolini: Poet of ashes*. San Francisco: City Lights Books.

Clandinin, D. Jean and Connelly, F. Michael (2004). *Narrative inquiry*. San Francisco, CA: Jossey-Bass.

Cohen, Patricia (2008, July 3). The '60s begin to fade as liberal professors retire. *The New York Times* online: http://www.nytimes.com/2008/07/03/arts/03camp.html?e x=1215748800&en=e79ccff072f04f31&ei=5070&emc=eta1

Conn, Steven (2004). *History's shadow*. Chicago: University of Chicago Press.

Counts, George S. (1978 [1932]). *Dare the school build a new social order?* Carbondale, IL: Southern Illinois University Press.

Crary, Jonathan (1999). *Suspensions of perception*. Cambridge, MA: The MIT Press.

Cremin, Lawrence A. (1961). *The transformation of the school*. New York: Alfred A. Knopf.

Cusset, François (2008). *French theory* [trans. by Jeff Fort]. Minneapolis: University of Minnesota Press.

Cvetkovich, Ann (2003). *An archive of feelings*. Durham, NC: Duke University Press.

Daignault, Jacques (1992). Traces at work from different places. In William F. Pinar and William M. Reynolds (Eds.), *Understanding curriculum as phenomenological and deconstructed text* (195–215). New York: Teachers College Press.

Davies, Bronwyn (2008). Re-thinking "behavior" in terms of positioning and the ethics of responsibility. In Anne Phelan and Jennifer Sumsion (Eds.), *Critical readings in teacher education* (173–186). Rotterdam: Sense.

Dean, Cornelia (2007, September 25). When science suddenly mattered, in space and in class. *The New York Times* online: http://www.nytimes.com/2007/09/25/ science/space/25educ.html?ex=1191384000&en=9087d0b360bab414&ei=507 0&emc=eta1

Dearborn, Mary V. (1999). *Mailer*. Boston: Houghton Mifflin.

de Bolla, Peter (1996). The visibility of visuality. In Teresa Brennan and Martin Jay (Eds.), *Vision in context* (63–81). New York: Routledge.

de Lauretis, Teresa (1994). Habit changes. *Differences* 6 (2+3), 296–296–313.

De Mauro, Tullio (2007 [1976]). Pasolini: From the stratification of tongues to the unity of language. In Roberto Chiesi and Andrea Mancini (Eds.) *Pier Paolo Pasolini: Poet of ashes* (110–113). San Francisco: City Lights Books.

De Mauro, Tullio (1999). Pasolini's linguistics. In Zygmunt G. Baranski (Ed.) *Pasolini Old and New: Surveys and Studies* (77–90) Dublin: Four Courts Press.

Denhardt, Janet V. and Denhardt, Robert B. (2007). *The new public service*. Armonk, NY: M.E. Sharpe.

Derrick, Scott S. (1997). *Monumental anxieties*. New Brunswick, NJ: Rutgers University Press.

De Veaux, Alexis (2004). *Warrior poet: A biography of Audre Lorde*. New York: Norton.

Dewey, John (1991 [1927]). *The public and its problems*. Athens: Ohio University Press.

Dillon, Sam (2007a, July 25). Focus 2r's cuts time for the rest, report says. *The New York Times* online: http://www.nytimes.com/2007/07/25/education/25child.html?ex=1186027200&en=0e0e16cc81a804e2&ei=5070&emc=eta1

Dillon, Sam (2007b, August 27). With turnover high, schools fight for teachers. *The New York Times* online: http://www.nytimes.com/2007/08/27/education/27teacher.html?scp=22&sq=Sam+Dillon&st=nyt

Dillon, Sam (2007c, December 23). Democrats make Bush school act an election issue. *The New York Times* online: http://www.nytimes.com/2007/12/23/us/politics/23child.html?pagewanted=1&ei=5070&en=76984bece2297a70&ex=1199077200&emc=eta1

Dillon, Sam (2008a, April 23). Education secretary offers changes to "No Child" law. *The New York Times* online: http://www.nytimes.com/2008/04/23/washington/23child.html?ex=1209614400&en=1abe0e8e185aa72a&ei=5070&emc=eta1

Dillon, Sam (2008b, May 2). An initiative on reading is rated ineffective. *The New York Times* online: http://www.nytimes.com/2008/05/02/education/02reading.html?ex=1210392000&en=e8bc59baa29e7af0&ei=5070&emc=eta1

Dillon, Sam (2008c, June 12). Democrats offer plans to revamp schools law. *The New York Times* online: http://www.nytimes.com/2008/06/12/us/12education.html?ex=1214020800&en=dc8d9bae7aa00e66&ei=5070&emc=eta1

Dillon, Sam (2008d, June 19). 2 school entrepreneurs lead the way on change. *The New York Times* online: http://www.nytimes.com/2008/06/19/education/19teach.html?ex=1214539200&en=2557882d57f2286d&ei=5070&emc=eta1

Dimitriadis, Greg and McCarthy, Cameron (2001). *Reading & teaching the postcolonial*. New York: Teachers College Press.

Di Stefano, John (1993). My affair with Pasolini. In Martha Gever, Pratibha Parmar, and John Greyson (Eds.), *Queer looks* (292–300). Toronto: Between the Lines.

Doll, Mary Aswell (1988). *Beckett and myth*. Syracuse, NY: Syracuse University Press.

Doll, Mary Aswell (1995). *To the lighthouse and back*. New York: Peter Lang.

Doll, William E. Jr., Fleener, M. Jayne, Trueit, Donna, and St. Julien, John (Eds.). (2005). *Chaos, complexity, curriculum, and culture*. New York: Peter Lang.

Donadio, Rachel (2007, September 16). Revisiting the canon wars. *The New York Times* online: http://www.nytimes.com/2007/09/16/books/review/Donadio-t.html?ex=1190692800&en=90c93017172d2e7d&ei=5070&emc=eta1

Donald, Dwayne (2007, February 24). On making love to death. Paper presented to the Provoking Curriculum Conference, Banff, Alberta.

Duke, Lynne (1995, September 9). Mugabe makes homosexuals public enemies. Washington, DC: *The Washington Post*, A19, A24.

Duncan, Derek (2006). *Reading and writing Italian homosexuality*. Hampshire, U.K.: Ashgate.

Earle, William (1972). *The autobiographical consciousness*. Chicago: Quadrangle.

Edelman, Lee (1994). *Homographesis*. New York: Routledge.

Edelman, Lee (2004). *No future*. Durham, NC: Duke University Press.

Edgerton, Susan Huddleston (1996). *Translating the curriculum*. New York: Routledge.

Egan, Kieran (2002). *Getting it wrong from the beginning: Our progressivist inheritance from Herbert Spencer, John Dewey, and Jean Piaget*. New Haven, CT: Yale University Press.

Egan, Kieran (1992). *Imagination in teaching and learning.* Chicago: University of Chicago Press.

Egéa-Kuehne, Denise (2008). Levinas's quest for justice: Of faith and the "possibility of education." In Denise Egéa-Kuehne (Ed.), *Levinas and education* (26–40). London: Routledge.

Elshtain, Jean Bethke (1993 [1981]). *Public man, private woman.* Princeton, NJ: Princeton University Press.

Elshtain, Jean Bethke (2002). *Jane Addams and the dream of American democracy.* New York: Basic Books.

Eng, David L. (2001). *Racial castration: Managing masculinity in Asian America.* Durham, NC: Duke University Press.

Epstein, Helen (2008, August 14). Fatal misconception. *The New York Review of Books* LV (13), 57–59).

Eribon, Didier (2004). *Insult and the making of the gay self* [trans. Michael Lucey]. Durham, NC: Duke University Press.

Fabbri, Paolo (1994). Free/indirect/discourse. In Patrick Rumble and Bart Testa (Eds.), *Pier Paolo Pasolini: Contemporary perspectives* (78–87). Toronto: University of Toronto Press.

Fanon, Frantz (1967a). *Black skin, white masks* [trans. by Charles Lam Markmann]. New York: Grove Weidenfeld. [Originally published in French under the title *Peau Noire, Masques Blancs*, copyright 1952 by Editions du Seuil, Paris.]

Fanon, Frantz (1967b). *Toward the African revolution.* [Trans. Hakkon Chevalier.] New York: Grove Press. [Originally published in France under the title *Pour la revolution Africaine*, 1964, by François Maspero.]

Fanon, Frantz (1968). *The wretched of the earth* [preface by Jean-Paul Sartre; trans. by Constance Farrington]. New York: Grove Press. [Originally published by François Maspero éditeur, Paris, France, under the title *Les damnés de la terre*, 1961.]

Fichte, Hubert (1996). *The gay critic* [trans. by Kevin Gavin; introd. by James W. Jones]. Ann Arbor: University of Michigan Press.

Finder, Alan (2008, May 22). At one university, tobacco money is a secret. *The New York Times* online: http://www.nytimes.com/2008/05/22/us/22tobacco.html?ex=1212120000&en=f207e2acce96fc17&ei=5070&emc=eta1

Fish, Stanley (2008, April 6, April 20). French theory in America. *The New York Times* online: http://fish.blogs.nytimes.com/2008/04/06/french-theory-in-america/?ex=1208232000&en=3ddacee7197b8e0c&ei=5070&emc=eta1

Flatley, Jonathon (1996) Warhol gives good face: Publicity and the politics of prosopopoeia. In Jennifer Doyle, Jonathan Flatley, and José Esteban Munoz (Eds.), *Pop out: Queer Warhol* (101–133). Durham, NC: Duke University Press.

Foster, Thomas (2005). *The souls of cyberfolk.* Minneapolis: University of Minnesota Press.

Foucault, Michel (1995 [1979]). *Discipline and punish* [trans. by Alan Sheridan]. New York: Vintage.

Foucault, Michel (1997 [1982]). Sex, power, and the politics of identity. In Paul Rabinow (Ed.), *Ethics, subjectivity, and truth* (163–177). New York: The New Press.

Francese, Joseph (1994). Pasolini's "Roman novels," the Italian Communist Party, and the events of 1956. In Patrick Rumble and Bart Testa (Eds.), *Pier Paolo Pasolini* (22–39). Toronto: University of Toronto Press.

Francese, Joseph   (1999). The latent presence of Crocean aesthetics in Pasolini's "Critical Marxism." In Zygmunt G. Barański (Ed.), *Pasolini old and new* (131–162). Dublin: Four Courts Press.

Freud, Sigmund (1955). *The standard edition of the complete works of Sigmund Freud*, vol. 17 [ed. James Strachey]. London: Hogarth Press.

Friedman, Lawrence J. (1970). *The white savage*. Englewood Cliffs, NJ: Prentice-Hall, Inc.

Friedrich, Pia (1982). *Pier Paolo Pasolini*. Boston: Twayne Publishers.

Frosch, Dan (2008, June 17). Young American Indians find their voice in poetry. *The New York Times* online: http://www.nytimes.com/2008/06/17/us/17slam.html?ex =1214366400&en=77923995951d89ea&ei=5070&emc=eta1

Gallagher, Catherine and Greenblatt, Stephen (2000). *Practicing new historicism*. Chicago: University of Chicago Press.

Gaztambide-Fernández, Rubén A. (2006). Regarding race. *Journal of Curriculum and Pedagogy* 3 (1), 60–65.

Garrison, Jim (1997). *Dewey and eros*. New York: Teachers College of Press.

Gay, Geneva (2000). *Culturally responsive teaching*. New York: Teachers College Press.

Geismar, Peter (1971). *Fanon*. New York: The Dial Press.

Gendzier, Irene L. (1973). *Frantz Fanon*. New York: Pantheon Books.

Gilmore, David D. (2001). *Misogyny: The male malady*. Philadelphia: University of Pennsylvania Press.

Gilroy, Paul (2005). *Postcolonial melancholy*. New York: Columbia University Press.

Gollaher, David L. (2000). *Circumcision*. New York: Basic Books.

Gombrowicz, Witold (1989). *Diary*, vol. 2 [trans. Lillian Vallee]. Evanston, IL: Northwestern University Press.

Goodman, Jesse (2006). *Reforming schools*. Albany: State University of New York Press.

Goodwin, Jeff, Jasper, James M., and Polletta, Francesca (Eds.) (2001). *Passionate politics*. Chicago: University of Chicago Press.

Gootman, Elissa (2007a, September 7). Survey reveals student attitudes, parental goals and teacher mistrust. *The New York Times* online: http://www.nytimes.com/2007/09/07/nyregion/07schools.html?_r=1&ex=1189828800&en=7b3bd e5a06440b46&ei=5070&emc=eta1&oref=slogin

Gootman, Elissa (2007b, October 17). Bloomberg unveils performance pay for teachers. *The New York Times* online: http://www.nytimes.com/2007/10/17/ nyregion/17cnd-teachers.html?ex=1193284800&en=618598100e2da13c&ei= 5070&emc=eta1

Gootman, Elissa (2008a, March 7). At a charter school, higher teacher pay. *The New York Times* online http://www.nytimes.com/2008/03/07/nyregion/07charter. html?_r=1&ex=1205557200&en=7ce008c928e7f083&ei=5070&emc=eta1 &oref=slogin

Gootman, Elissa (2008b, June 27). Survey of teachers shows dissatisfaction with Klein. *The New York Times* online: http://www.nytimes.com/2008/06/27/ education/27school.html?ex=1215230400&en=9ee843942d5ba09b&ei=5070 &emc=eta1

Gordon, Robert S. C. (1996). *Pasolini: Forms of subjectivity*. Oxford: Clarendon Press.

Gouldner, Alvin W. (1970). *The coming crisis of Western sociology*. New York: Basic Books.

Gough, Noel (2004). Editorial: A vision for transnational curriculum inquiry. *Transnational Curriculum Inquiry* 1 (1) 1–11, online at http://nitinat.library.ubc.ca/ojs/index.php/tci/

Grande, Sandy (2004). *Red pedagogy*. Lanham, MD: Rowman & Littlefield.

Grant, Agnes (1995). The challenge for universities. In Marie Battiste and Jean Barman (Eds.), *First nations education in Canada* (208–223). Vancouver: University of British Columbia Press.

Green, Bill and Reid, Jo-Anne (2008). Method(s) in our madness: Poststructuralism, pedagogy and teacher education. In Anne Phelan and Jennifer Sumsion (Eds), *Critical readings in teacher education* (17–31). Rotterdam: Sense.

Greenberg, David F. (1988). *The construction of homosexuality*. Chicago: University of Chicago Press.

Greene, Maxine (1995). *Releasing the imagination*. San Francisco: Jossey-Bass.

Greene, Naomi (1990). *Pier Paolo Pasolini: Cinema as heresy*. Princeton: Princeton University Press.

Greene, Naomi (1994). "Salò": The refusal to consume. In Patrick Rumble and Bart Testa (Eds.), *Pier Paolo Pasolini* (232–242). Toronto: University of Toronto Press.

Grosz, Elizabeth (1994). The labors of love. Analyzing perverse desire: An interrogation of Teresa de Lauretis's *The Practice of Love*. *Differences* 6 (2+3), 274–295).

Grosz, Elizabeth (1995). *Space, time, and perversion*. New York: Routledge.

Grumet, Madeleine R. (2006, Fall). Where does the world go when schooling is about schooling? *JCT* 22 (3), 47–54.

Grumet, Madeleine R. (2007). Foreword. Paul M. Slavio's *Anne Sexton* (ix–xi). Albany: State University of New York Press.

Guillory, John (2002). Literary study and the modern system of the disciplines. In Amanda Anderson and Joseph Valente (Eds.), *Disciplinarity at the fin de siècle* (19–43). Princeton, NJ: Princeton University Press.

Gunew, Sneja (2004). *Haunted nations*. London: Routledge.

Hakim, Danny and Peters, Jeremy W. (2008, April 9). Legislators balk at tying teacher tenure to student tests. *The New York Times* online: http://www.nytimes.com/2008/04/09/nyregion/09albany.html?ex=1208404800&en=981296ec84dc63be&ei=5070&emc=eta1

Hansen, Emmanuel (1977). *Frantz Fanon*. Columbus: Ohio State University Press.

Harootunian, H. D. (2002). Postcoloniality's unconscious/area studies' desire. In Masao Miyoshi and D. H. Harootunian (Eds.) *Learning Places: The Afterlives of Area Studies* (150–174). Durham, NC: Duke University Press.

Harris, Frederick C. (2001). Religious resources in an oppositional civic culture. In Jane Mansbridge and Aldon Morris (Eds.), *Oppositional consciousness* (38–64). Chicago: University of Chicago Press.

Haynes, Carolyn A. (1998). *Divine destiny*. Jackson: University Press of Mississippi.

Hirsch, Jr., E. D. (1967). *Validity in interpretation*. New Haven, CT: Yale University Press.

Hirsch, Jr., E. D. (1999). *The schools we need: And why we don't have them*. New York: Anchor Books.

Hlebowitsh, Peter S. (2005). *Designing the school curriculum*. Boston: Pearson.

Hocquenghem, Guy (1978). *Homosexual desire*. London: Allison and Busby.

Hoffman, Jan (2008, May 4). I know what you did last math class. *The New York Times* online: http://www.nytimes.com/2008/05/04/fashion/04edline.html?ex=12 10478400&en=6f141afcc14d28cb&ei=5070&emc=eta1

Hofstadter, Richard (1996 [1965]). *The paranoid style in American politics and other essays*. Cambridge, MA: Harvard University Press.

Holmes, David L. (2006). *The faiths of the founding fathers*. New York: Oxford University Press.

Howard, Adam (2008). *Learning privilege*. New York: Routledge.

Howard, John (1999). *Men like that: A southern queer history*. Chicago: University of Chicago Press.

Hu, Winnie (2008a, March 25). State identifies failing school districts. *The New York Times* online: http://cityroom.blogs.nytimes.com/2008/03/25/state-identifies-failing-school-districts/?ex=1207108800&en=5be60f174d37807b&ei=5070& emc=eta1

Hu, Winnie (2008b, April 6). In a new generation of college students, may opt for the life examined. *The New York Times* online: http://www.nytimes.com/2008/04/06/education/06philosophy.html?ex=1208145600&en=1c3585fc82773e7f&ei=50 70&emc=eta1

Hu, Winnie (2008c, May 16). Districts puts all the world in classrooms. *The New York Times* online: http://www.nytimes.com/2008/05/16/education/16global.html ?ex=1211601600&en=868f0e90087bc044&ei=5070&emc=eta1

Huebner, Dwayne E. (1999). *The lure of the transcendent*. Mahwah, NJ: Lawrence Erlbaum.

Irwin, Rita L. and Alex de Cosson, Alex (Eds.). (2004). *A/r/tography: Rendering self through arts-based living inquiry*. Vancouver, B.C.: Pacific Educational Press.

Jackson, Philip W. (1992). Conceptions of curriculum and curriculum specialists. In Philip W.

Jackson (Ed.), *Handbook of research on curriculum* (3–40). New York: Macmillan.

jagodzinski, jan (2006, Fall). Jacque Lacan as queer theorist: Is there a "beyond" to identification politics in education?" *JCT* 22 (3), 55-70.

Jardine, David W., Clifford, Patricia, and Friesen, Sharon (in press). *Back to the basics of teaching and learning*. New York: Routledge.

Jay, Martin (1993). *Downcast eyes: The denigration of vision in twentieth-century French thought*. Berkeley: University of California Press.

Jay, Martin (2005). *Songs of experience*. Berkeley: University of California Press.

Jewell, Keala (1992). *The poesis of history: Experimenting with genre in postwar Italy*. Ithaca and London: Cornell University Press.

Johnson, Kirk (2008, May 25). On the reservation and off, schools a changing tide. *The New York Times* online: http://www.nytimes.com/2008/05/25/education/25hardin. html?ex=1212379200&en=9ebf52ac2d97699d&ei=5070&emc=eta1

Johnston, Adrian (2004). The cynic's fetish: Slavoj Žižek and the dynamics of belief. *Psychoanalysis, Culture & Society* 9, 259–283.

Jonsson, Stefan (2000). *Subject without nation*. Durham, NC: Duke University Press.

Kamler, Barbara (2001). *Relocating the personal* [foreword by Michelle Fine]. Albany: State University of New York Press.

Kammerer, Peter and Zigaina, Giuseppe (2005). In the firing line: Pasolini's signs of life and death. Peter Kammerer in Conversation with Giuseppe Zigaina. In Bernhart Schwenk and Michael Semff (Eds.), *Pier Paolo Pasolini and death* (157–171). Munich: Hatje Cantz.

Katanski, Amelia V. (2005). *Learning to write "Indian."* Norman: University of Oklahoma Press.

Kellogg, Charles Flint (1967). *NAACP: A history of the National Association for the Advancement of Colored People, Vol. I: 1909–1920.* Baltimore: Johns Hopkins University Press.

Kesteloot, Lilyan (1991). *Black writers in French.* Washington, DC: Howard University Press.

Kilburn, Michael (1996, Spring). Glossary of key terms in the work of Gayatri Chakravorty Spivak. Retrieved on April 29, 2008 from http://www.english.emory.edu/Bahri/Glossary.html

King, Cheryl Simrell and Zanetti, Lisa A. (2005). *Transformational public service.* Armonk, NY: M.E. Sharpe.

Kliebard, Herbert M. (2000 [1970]). Persistent issues in historical perspective. In William F. Pinar (Ed.), *Curriculum theorizing* (39–50). Troy, NY: Educator's International Press.

Kliebard, Herbert M. (1999 [1981]). Dewey and the Herbartians. In William F. Pinar (Ed.), *Contemporary curriculum discourses* (68–81). New York: Peter Lang.

Kliebard, Herbert M. (2000 [1970]). Reappraisal: The Tyler Rationale. In William Pinar (Ed.), *Curriculum studies* (70–83). Troy, NY: Educator's International Press.

Knight, Louise W. (2005). *Citizen: Jane Addams and the struggle for democracy.* Chicago: University of Chicago Press.

Kögler, Hans-Herbert (1999). *The power of dialogue.* Cambridge, MA: MIT Press.

Kovach, Gretel C. (2008, May 12). To curb truancy, Dallas tries electronic monitoring. *The New York Times* online: http://www.nytimes.com/2008/05/12/education/12dallas.html?ex=1211256000&en=183b5e509c03d62d&ei=5070&emc=eta1

Kridel, Craig and Bullough, Robert V. Jr. (2007). *Stories of the eight-year study.* Albany: State University of New York Press.

Krupat, Arnold (1994). *Native American autobiography.* Madison: University of Wisconsin Press.

Kumashiro, Kevin, et al. (2005). Thinking collaboratively about the peer-review process for journal-article publication. *Harvard Educational Review* 73 (3), 257–285.

Kurasawa, Fuyuki (2007). *The work of global justice.* Cambridge: Cambridge University Press.

Lane, Christopher (2002). The Arnoldian ideal, or culture studies and the problem of nothingness. In Amanda Anderson and Joseph Valente (Eds.), *Disciplinarity at the fin de siècle* (283–311). Princeton, NJ: Princeton University Press.

Laplanche, J. and Pontalis, J. B. (1973). *The language of psychoanalysis* [trans. by Donald Nicholson-Smith]. New York: Norton.

Lasch, Christopher (Ed.). (1965). *The social thought of Jane Addams.* Indianapolis: Bobbs-Merrill.

Lasch, Christopher (1978). *The culture of narcissism.* New York: Norton.

Lasch, Christopher (1984). *The minimal self.* New York: Norton.

Lather, Patti and Smithies, Chris (1997). *Troubling the angels.* Boulder, CO: Westview Press.

Lather, Patti (2007). *Getting lost.* Albany: State University of New York Press.

Lawton, Ben (1980–81). The evolving rejection of homosexuality, sub-proletariat and the Third World in Pasolini's films. *Italian Quarterly* (82–83), 167–173.

Lawton, Ben (2005a). Why add "Repudiation of the Trilogy of Life" to the 2005 edition of Pasolini's *Heretical Empiricism?* In Pier Paolo Pasolini's *Heretical Empiricism* (vii–xv). Washington, DC: New Academic Publishing, LLC.

Lawton, Ben (2005b). Introduction to Pier Paolo Pasolini's *Heretical Empiricism* (xxvii–xlii). Washington, DC: New Academic Publishing, LLC.

Layton, Lynne (2004). A fork in the royal road: On "defining" the unconscious and its stakes for social theory." *Psychoanalysis, Society & Culture* 9, 33–51.

Lepri, Loris (2005). The changing of culture by the "new fascism." In Bernhart Schwenk and Michael Semff (Eds.), *Pier Paolo Pasolini and death* (175–180). Munich: Hatje Cantz.

Lewin, Tamar (2008, May 27). 2 colleges end entrance requirement. *The New York Times* online: http://www.nytimes.com/2008/05/27/education/27sat.html?ex=12 12552000&en=4e9a596c6abd0086&ei=5070&emc=eta1

Lewis, Magda (1999). The backlash factor: Women, intellectual labor and student evaluations of courses and teaching. In Linda K. Christian-Smith and Kristine S. Kellor (Eds.), *Uncommon truths* (59–82). Boulder, CO: Westview Press.

Lukacher, Ned (1986). *Primal scenes*. Ithaca, NY: Cornell University Press.

Lund, Darren E. (2003). Engaging student leaders in social responsibility. *Electronic Magazine of Multicultural Education.* Retrieved in January 2008 from File:/// Users/williampinar/Desktop/Worldliness/lund.html

Lund, Darren E. (2006). Waking up the neighbors: Surveying multicultural and antiracist education in Canada, the United Kingdom, and the United States. *Multicultural Perspectives* 8 (1), 35–43.

Lund, Darren E. (2007, June 4). *TC Record.* Retrieved on September 18, 2007 from http://www.tcrecord.org/content.asp?contentid=14510

Macdonald, James B. (1995). *Theory as a prayerful act* [edited by Bradley Macdonald; introduced by William F. Pinar]. New York: Peter Lang.

Macedo, Elizabeth (2007). Personal communication.

Mahoney, Jill and Peritz, Ingrid (2008, April 30). Quebec students' top rank tied to course reform. *Toronto Globe and Mail* online: http://www.theglobeandmail.com/ servlet/story/RTGAM.20080430.wscores30/EmailBNStory/National/Quebec

Mailer, Norman (1957). *The white negro*. San Francisco: City Lights.

Malewski, Erik (Ed.) (in press). *Curriculum studies: The next moment.* New York: Routledge.

Mansbridge, Jane (2001). The making of oppositional consciousness. In Jane Mansbridge and Aldon Morris (Eds.), *Oppositional consciousness: The subjective roots of social protest* (1–19). Chicago: University of Chicago Press.

Mansbridge, Jane and Morris, Aldon (Eds.) (2001). *Oppositional consciousness: The subjective roots of social protest.* Chicago: University of Chicago Press.

Markell, Patchen (2003). *Bound by recognition*. Princeton, NJ: Princeton University Press.

Marshall, Bill (1997). *Guy Hocquenghem*. Durham, NC: Duke University Press.

Mariniello, Silvestra (1994). Toward a materialist linguistics: Pasolini's theory of language. In Patrick Rumble and Bart Testa (Eds.), *Pier Paolo Pasolini* (106–126). Toronto: University of Toronto Press.

Mayer, Diane, Luke, Carmen and Luke, Allan (2008). Teachers, national regulation and cosmopolitanism. In Anne Phelan and Jennifer Sumsion (Eds), *Critical readings in teacher education* (79–98). Rotterdam: Sense.

McBride, Patrizia C. (2006). *The void of ethics*. Evanston, IL: Northwestern University Press.

McClintock, R. (1971). Toward a place for study in a world of instruction. *Teachers College Record* 73 (20), 161–205.

McCulloch, Jock (1983). *Black soul white artifact*. Cambridge: Cambridge University Press.

McKnight, E. Douglas (2003). *Schooling, the Puritan imperative, and the molding of an American national identity*. Mahwah, NJ: Lawrence Erlbaum.

McLaren, Peter (1997). *Revolutionary multiculturalism*. Boulder, CO: Westview.

McLaren, Peter (2000). *Che Guevara, Paulo Freire, and the pedagogy of revolution*. Lanham, MD: Rowman & Littlefield.

McWilliam, Erica (2008). Making excellent teachers. In Anne Phelan and Jennifer Sumsion (Eds), *Critical readings in teacher education* (33–44). Rotterdam: Sense.

Medina, Jennifer (2008, July 2). Students, teachers, and parents weigh in on the state of the schools. *The New York Times* online: http://www.nytimes.com/2008/07/02/ducatione/02survey.html?ex=1215662400&en=e342eb52622607df&ei=5070&emc=eta1

Meekins, Angela C. (1999). Pier Paolo Pasolini: *Narcis Tal Friul*. In Zygmunt G. Barański (Ed.), *Pasolini old and new* (229–251) Dublin: Four Courts Press.

Mendelsohn, Daniel (1996, September 30). We're here! We're queer! Let's get coffee! *New York Times Magazine*, 26–31.

Mercer, Kobena (1994). *Welcome to the jungle*. New York: Routledge.

Merrill, James (1993). *A different person*. New York: Alfred A. Knopf.

Miller, James E. (1993). *The passion of Michel Foucault*. New York: Simon & Schuster.

Miller, Janet L. (2005). *The sound of silence breaking and other essays*. New York: Peter Lang.

Mitchell, W. J. T. (1994). *Picture theory*. Chicago: University of Chicago Press.

Miyoshi, Masao (2002). Ivory tower in escrow. In Masao Miyoshi and D. H. Harootunian (Eds.), *Learning places: The afterlives of area studies* (19–60). Durham, NC: Duke University Press.

Moravia, Alberto (2007 [1978]). Pasolini as civic poet. In Roberto Chiesi and Andrea Mancini (Eds.), *Pier Paolo Pasolini: Poet of ashes* (108–109). San Francisco: City Lights Books.

Moriarty, Michael (1991). *Roland Barthes*. Stanford: Stanford University Press.

Morris, Aldon and Braine, Naomi (2001). Social movements and oppositional consciousness. In Jane Mansbridge and Aldon Morris (Eds.), *Oppositional consciousness* (20–37). Chicago: University of Chicago Press.

Morris, Marla (2001). *Holocaust and curriculum*. Mahwah, NJ: Lawrence Erlbaum.

Mosse, George L. (2000). *Confronting history*. Madison: University of Wisconsin Press.

Muller, Johan (2000). *Reclaiming knowledge*. London: Routledge.

Munro, Petra (1998). Engendering curriculum history. In William F. Pinar (Ed.), *Curriculum* (263–294). New York: Garland.

Munro, Petra (1999). Political activism as teaching: Jane Addams and Ida B. Wells. In Margaret Smith Crocco, Petra Munro and Kathleen Weiler (Eds.), *Pedagogies of resistance: Women educator activists, 1880–1960* (19–45). New York: Teachers College Press.

Mura, David (1989). *After we lost our way*. New York: Dutton.

Murphy, Kevin P. (1998). Socrates in the slums: Homoerotics, gender, and settlement house reform. In Laura McCall and Donald Yacovone (Eds.), *A shared experience* (273–296). New York: New York University Press.

Musil, Robert (1955 [1905]). *Young Torless* [preface by Alan Pryce-Jones]. New York: Pantheon Books Inc.

Musil, Robert (1990). *Precision and soul* [edited and translated by Burton Pike and David S. Luft]. Chicago: University of Chicago Press.

Naldini, Nico (1994). Pier Paolo, my cousin... In Patrick Rumble and Bart Testa (Eds.), *Pier Paolo Pasolini* (14–21). Toronto: University of Toronto Press.

Nava, Mica (2007). *Visceral cosmopolitanism*. Oxford and New York: Berg.

Newman, Saul (2004). Interrogating the master: Lacan and radical politics. *Psychoanalysis, Culture & Society* 9, 298–314.

Ng-A-Fook, Nicholas (2007a). *An indigenous curriculum of place: The United Houma Nation's contentious relationship with Louisiana's educational institutions*. New York: Peter Lang.

Ng-A-Fook, Nicholas (2007b, February 24). Provoking A "Complicated Conversation": Curricular Absence, Migrancy, and Indigenous Communities. Paper presented to the Provoking Curriculum Conference, Banff, Alberta.

Nossiter, Adam (2007, September 24). A tamer of schools has plan in New Orleans. *The New York Times* online: http://www.nytimes.com/2007/09/24/education/24orleans.html?ex=1191297600&en=0924ee47fc79ca1a&ei=5070&emc=eta1

Nussbaum, Martha C. (1995). *Poetic justice*. Boston: Beacon Press.

Nussbaum, Martha C. (1997). *Cultivating humanity*. Cambridge, MA: Harvard University Press.

Nussbaum, Martha C. (2006). *Frontiers of justice*. Cambridge, MA: Harvard University Press.

Nwankwo, Ifeoma Kiddoe (2005). *Black cosmopolitanism*. Philadelphia: University of Pennsylvania Press.

Paras, Eric (2006). *Foucault 2.0*. New York: Other Press.

Parry, Benita (2002). Signs of our times: A discussion of Homi Bhabha's The Location of Culture. In Masao Miyoshi and D. H. Harootunian (Eds.), *Learning places: The afterlives of area studies* (119–149). Durham, NC: Duke University Press.

Pasolini, Pier Paolo (1985). *A violent life* [trans. by William Weaver]. Manchester, UK: Carcanet Press Ltd. [First published in U.K. in 1968; published in Italy in 1959 by Aldo Garzanti Editore.]

Pasolini, Pier Paolo (1986). *Roman poems* [trans. Lawrence Ferlinghetti and Francesca Valenta; preface by Alberto Moravia]. San Francisco: City Lights Books.

Pasolini, Pier Paolo (1994 [1968]). Manifesto for a new theatre [trans. by David Ward]. In Patrick Rumble and Bart Testa (Eds.), *Pier Paolo Pasolini* (152–170). Toronto: University of Toronto Press.

Pasolini, Pier Paolo (1997). *Petrolio* [trans. by Ann Goldstein]. New York: Pantheon.

Pasolini, Pier Paolo (2005 [1972]). *Heretical empiricism* [trans. by Ben Lawton and Louise K. Barnett]. Washington, DC: New Academic Publishing, LLC. [First published in 1972 by Aldo Garzanti Editore; first English edition in 1988 by Indiana University Press.]

Pedersen, Christopher (1998, October 23). Repressive desublimation. Retrieved on January 8, 2008 from http://archives.econ.utah.edu/archives/theory-frankfurt-school/1998m10/msg00016.htm

Perlstein, Daniel (2000). "There is no escape … from the ogre of indoctrination": George Counts and the civic dilemmas of democratic educators. In Larry Cuban and Dorothy Shipps (Eds.), *Reconstructing the common good in education* (51–67). Stanford, CA: Stanford University Press.

Peterson, Thomas Erling (1994). *The paraphrase of an imaginary dialogue.* New York: Peter Lang.

Petrina, Stephen (2008). Academic freedom for K-12 teachers. In Sandra Mathison and E. Wayne Ross (Eds.), *Battleground: Schools* (1–11). Westport, CT: Greenwood Press.

Pinar, William F. (1991). Curriculum as social psychoanalysis: On the significance of place. In Joe L. Kincheloe and William F. Pinar (Eds.), *Curriculum as social psychoanalysis* (167–186). Albany: State University of New York Press.

Pinar, William F. (1994). *Autobiography, politics, and sexuality: Essays in curriculum theory 1972-1992.* New York: Peter Lang.

Pinar, William F. (2001). *The gender of racial politics and violence in America.* New York: Peter Lang.

Pinar, William F. (Ed.) (2003). *International handbook of curriculum research.* Mahwah, NJ: Lawrence Erlbaum.

Pinar, William F. (2004). *What is curriculum theory?* Mahwah, NJ: Lawrence Erlbaum.

Pinar, William F. (2006a). *Race, religion and a curriculum of reparation.* New York: Palgrave Macmillan.

Pinar, William F. (2006b). *The synoptic text today and other essays.* New York: Peter Lang.

Pinar, William F. (2006c). Literary study as educational research: "More than a pungent school story." In Kenneth Tobin and Joe L. Kincheloe (Eds.), *Doing educational research* (347–377). Rotterdam: Sense.

Pinar, William F. (2007a). *Intellectual advancement through disciplinarity.* Rotterdam: Sense.

Pinar, William F. (2007b). Cultures of torture. In Joy James (Ed.), *Warfare in the American homeland* (290–304). Durham, NC: Duke University Press.

Pinar, William F. (2007c). Curriculum leadership then and now. In William Smale and Kelly Young (Eds.), *Approaches to educational leadership* (110–125). Calgary, Alberta: Detselig.

Pinar, William F. (2007d). Punk'd. In Nelson M. Rodriguez and William F. Pinar (Eds.), *Queering straight teachers* (155–182). New York: Peter Lang.

Pinar, William F. (2008a). Curriculum theory since 1950: Crisis, reconceptualization, internationalization. In F. Michael Connelly, Ming Fang He, and JoAnn Phillion (Eds.), *The Sage Handbook of Curriculum and Instruction* (491-513). Los Angeles: Sage.

Pinar, William F. (2008b). The subjective violence of decolonization. In Ali A. Abdi and George Richardson (Eds.) *Decolonizing Democratic Education: Trans-disciplinary Dialogues* (34-45). Rotterdam and Tapei: Sense Publishers.

Pinar, William F. and Grumet, Madeleine R. (2006 [1976]). *Toward a poor curriculum.* Troy, NY: Educator's International Press.

Pinar, William F. and Irwin, Rita L. (Eds.) (2005). *Curriculum in a new key.* Mahwah, NJ: Lawrence Erlbaum.

Pinar, William F., Reynolds, William M., Slattery, Patrick, and Taubman, Peter M. (1995). *Understanding curriculum.* New York: Peter Lang.

Pitt, Alice J. (2003). *The play of the personal.* New York: Peter Lang.

Pitt, Alice J. (2008). Reproducing authority: Revolts against transmission. In Anne Phelan and Jennifer Sumsion (Eds.), *Critical readings in teacher education* (187–200). Rotterdam: Sense.

Pojman, Louis P. (2005, Spring). Kant's perpetual peace and cosmopolitanism. *Journal of Social Philosophy* 36 (1), 62–71.

Popkewitz, Thomas S. (2008). *Cosmopolitanism and the age of school reform.* New York: Routledge.

Radhakrishnan, R. (2008). *History, the human, and the world between.* Durham, NC: Duke University Press.

Rancière, Jacques (2008, March 7). The contemporary misadventures of critical thinking. Lecture at the University of British Columbia. Video available online at: http://www.youtube.com/watch?v=1tCCoS87pws

Ransom, John S. (1997). *Foucault's discipline.* Durham, NC: Duke University Press.

Restivo, Angelo (2002). *The cinema of economic miracles.* Durham, NC: Duke University Press.

Revkin, Andrew C. (2008, April 10). A textbook case of downplaying global warming. *The New York Times* online: http://dotearth.blogs.nytimes.com/2008/04/10/a-textbook-case-of-downplaying-global-warming/?ex=1208491200&en=c17df03 5aa975d7e&ei=5070&emc=eta1

Rhodes, John David (2007). *Stupendous miserable city: Pasolini's Rome.* Minneapolis: University of Minnesota Press.

Rich, Nathaniel (2007, September 27). The passion of Pasolini. *New York Review of Books* LIV (14), 77–80.

Robertson, Michael (2008). *Worshipping Walt.* Princeton, NJ: Princeton University Press.

Rohdie, Sam (1995). *The passion of Pier Paolo Pasolini.* Bloomington: Indiana University Press.

Rohdie, Sam (1999). Neo-realism and Pasolini: The desire for reality. In Zygmunt G. Barański (Ed.), *Pasolini old and new* (163–183). Dublin: Four Courts Press.

Roncaglia, Aurelio (2007 [1978]). Poetic word and vital discourse. In Roberto Chiesi and Andrea Mancini (Eds.), *Pier Paolo Pasolini: Poet of ashes* (121–123). San Francisco: City Lights Books.

Rosenbaum, Jonathan (2008). *Essential cinema: On the necessity of film canons.* Baltimore: Johns Hopkins University Press.

Rout, Kathleen (1991). *Eldridge Cleaver.* Boston: Twayne Publishers (G. K. Hall and Co.).

Roversi, Roberto (2007 [1978]). The vital tenderness of Pasolini. In Roberto Chiesi and Andrea Mancini (Eds.) *Pier Paolo Pasolini: Poet of Ashes* (132-134). San Francisco: Titivillus Mostre Editoria and City Lights Books.

Rowe, John Carlos (2002). *The new American studies.* Minneapolis: University of Minnesota Press.

Rumble, Patrick (1994). Stylistic contamination in the "Trilogia della vita": The case of "Il fiore delle mille e una notte." In Patrick Rumble and Bart Testa (Eds.), *Pier Paolo Pasolini* (210–231). Toronto: University of Toronto Press.

Rumble, Patrick and Testa, Bart (Eds.). (1994a). *Pier Paolo Pasolini.* Toronto: University of Toronto Press.

Rumble, Patrick and Testa, Bart (1994b). Introduction. In Patrick Rumble and Bart Testa (Eds.), *Pier Paolo Pasolini* (3–13). Toronto: University of Toronto Press.

Ryan, Alan (1995). *John Dewey and the high tide of American liberalism*. New York: Norton.

Ryan-Scheutz, Colleen (2007). *Sex, the self, and the sacred*. Toronto: University of Toronto Press.

Said, Edward W. (1996). *Representations of the intellectual*. New York: Vintage.

Said, Edward W. (1993). *Culture and imperialism*. New York: Alfred A. Knopf.

Said, Edward (2004). *Humanism and democratic criticism*. New York: Palgrave Macmillan.

Salas, Charles G. (2007). Introduction: The essential myth? In Charles G. Salas (Ed.), *The life & the work* (1–27). Los Angeles: Getty Publications.

Salvio, Paula M. (2007). *Anne Sexton*. Albany: State University of New York Press.

Sartre, Jean-Paul (1981). *The family idiot: Gustave Flaubert 1821–1857* [trans. by Carol Cosman]. Chicago: University of Chicago Press.

Savran, David (1998). *Taking it a like a man*. Princeton, NJ: Princeton University Press.

Schemo, Diana Jean (2007, October 16). Failing schools strain to meet U.S. standard. *The New York Times* online: http://www.nytimes.com/2007/10/16/ education/16child.html?ex=1193198400&en=0db7921503e02bc1&ei=5070 &emc=eta1

Schreber, Daniel Paul (2000 [1903]). *Memoirs of my nervous illness* [introduction by Rosemary Dinnage; trans. and edited by Id Macalpine and Richard A. Hunter]. New York: New York Review Books.

Schubert, William H. (2008). The AAACS Curriculum Canon Project: Divergent and convergent possibilities and evolutions. Paper presented to the seventh annual meeting of the American Association for the Advancement of Curriculum Studies, New York, March 23rd.

Schwab, Joseph J. (1978). *Science, curriculum, and liberal education: Selected essays*. [Edited by Ian Westbury and Neil J. Wilkof.] Chicago: University of Chicago Press.

Schwartz, Barth David (1992). *Pasolini requiem*. New York: Pantheon.

Schwenk, Bernhart (2005). The chosen image: Pasolini's aesthetic of the drawn-out moment. In Bernhart Schwenk and Michael Semff (Eds.), *Pier Paolo Pasolini and death* (41–49). Munich: Hatje Cantz Publishers.

Schwenk, Bernhart and Semff, Michael (2005). Introduction. In Bernhart Schwenk and Michael Semff (Eds.) *Pier Paolo Pasolini and death* (18–22). Munich: Hatje Cantz Publishers.

Seigfried, Charlene Haddock (1996). *Pragmatism and feminism*. Chicago: University of Chicago Press.

Seixas, Peter (2004). Introduction. In Peter Seixas (Ed.), *Theorizing historical consciousness* (3–20). Toronto: University of Toronto Press.

Sekyi-Otu, Ato (1996). *Fanon's dialectic of experience*. Cambridge, MA: Harvard University Press.

Semff, Michael (2005). A dialect of the "language of poetry": On the drawings of Pier Paolo Pasolini. In Bernhart Schwenk and Michael Semff (Eds.), *Pier Paolo Pasolini and death* (119–127). Munich: Hatje Cantz Publishers.

Shaker, Paul and Heilman, Elizabeth E. (2008). *Reclaiming education for democracy*. New York: Routledge.

Shulman, Lee (1987). Knowledge and teaching. *Harvard Educational Review*, 57 (1), 1–22.

Sicioliano, Enzo (1982). *Pasolini* [trans. by John Shepley]. New York: Random House.

Silverman, Kaja (1988). *The acoustic mirror.* Bloomington: Indiana University Press.

Silverman, Kaja (1992). *Male subjectivity at the margins.* New York: Routledge.

Silverman, Kaja (2000). *World spectators.* Stanford, CA: Stanford University Press.

Sitney, P. Adams (1994). "Accattone" and "Mamma Roma." In Patrick Rumble and Bart Testa (Eds.), *Pier Paolo Pasolini* (171–179). Toronto: University of Toronto Press.

Siti, Walter (1994). Pasolini's "second victory." In Patrick Rumble and Bart Testa (Eds.), *Pier Paolo Pasolini* (56–77). Toronto: University of Toronto Press.

Sizer, Theodore R. (2004). *The red pencil.* New Haven, CT: Yale University Press.

Slattery, Patrick (2006). *Curriculum development in the postmodern era.* New York: Routledge.

Slavin, Robert E. (2008). What works? Issues in synthesizing education program evaluations. *Educational Researcher* 37 (1), 5–14.

Snyder, Stephen (1980). *Pier Paolo Pasolini.* Boston, MA: Twayne Publishers.

Spivak, Gayatri Chakravorty (1999). *A critique of postcolonial reason.* Cambridge, MA: Harvard University Press.

Spivak, Gayatri Chakravorty (2003). *Death of a discipline.* New York: Columbia University Press.

Springgay, Stephanie, Irwin, Rita L., Leggo, Carl, and Gouzouasis, Peter (Eds.) (2008). *Being with a/r/tography.* Rotterdam: Sense.

Stack, Oswald (1969). *Pasolini on Pasolini: Interviews with Oswald Stack.* Bloomington, IN: Indiana University Press.

Steimatsky, Noa (1998). Pasolini on *terra sancta*: Towards a theology of film. *The Yale Journal of Criticism* 11 (1), 239–258.

Stein, Arlene (2001). Revenge of the shamed: The Christian Right's emotional culture war. In Jeff Goodwin, James M. Jasper and Francesca Polletta (Eds.), *Passionate politics: Emotions and social movements* (115–131). Chicago: University of Chicago Press.

Stokes, Mason (2001). *The color of sex.* Durham, NC: Duke University Press.

Stoler, Ann Laura (1995). *Race and the education of desire.* Durham, NC: Duke University Press.

Stone, Jennifer (1994). Pasolini, Zanzotto, and the question of pedagogy. In Patrick Rumble and Bart Testa (Eds.), *Pier Paolo Pasolini* (40–55). Toronto: University of Toronto Press.

Strange, Susan (1996). *The retreat of the state.* Cambridge: Cambridge University Press.

Strong-Wilson, Teresa (2007). *Bringing memory forward.* New York: Peter Lang.

Taubman, Peter M. (1990, 1992). Achieving the right distance. *Educational Theory* 40 (1), 121–133.

Taubman, Peter M. (2009). *Teaching by numbers.* New York: Routledge.

Taviani, Paolo and Taviani, Vittorio (2007 [1994]). New year's eve, 1974, with Pasolini. In Roberto Chiesi and Andrea Mancini (Eds.), *Pier Paolo Pasolini: Poet of ashes* (5–6). San Francisco: City Lights Books.

Testa, Bart (1994). To film a gospel ... and advent of the theoretical stranger. In Patrick Rumble and Bart Testa (Eds.), *Pier Paolo Pasolini* (180–209). Toronto: University of Toronto Press.

Tickner, J. Ann (2001). *Gendering world politics.* New York: Columbia University Press.

Tröhler, Daniel (2003). The discourse of German *Geisteswissenschaftliche Pädagogik* – A contextual reconstruction. *Paedagogica Historica* 39 (6), 759–778.

Tröhler, Daniel (2006). The "Kingdom of God on Earth" and early Chicago pragmatism. *Educational Theory* 56 (1), 89–105.

Trueit, Donna, et. al (Eds.) (2003). *The internationalization of curriculum studies.* New York: Peter Lang.

Tyler, Carole-Anne (1994). Passing: Narcissism, identity, and difference. *Differences* 6 (2+3), 212–248.

Tyler, Ralph (1949). *Basic principles of curriculum and instruction.* Chicago: University of Chicago Press.

Unger, Roberto Mangabeira (2007). *The self awakened.* Cambridge, MA: Harvard University Press.

Verges, Françoise (1996). Chains of madness, chains of colonialism. In Alan Read (Ed.), *The fact of blackness* (48–75). Seattle: Bay Press.

Verges, Françoise (1999). "I am not the slave of slavery": The politics of reparation in (French) postslavery communities. In Anthony C. Alessandrini (Ed.), *Frantz Fanon* (258–275). London: Routledge.

Viano, Maurizio (1993). *A certain realism.* Berkeley: University of California Press.

Viswanathan, Gauri (2002). Subjecting English and the question of representation. In Amanda Anderson and Joseph Valente (Eds.), *Disciplinarity at the fin de siècle* (177–195). Princeton, NJ: Princeton University Press.

Volponi, Paolo (2007 [1976]). Pasolini, teacher and friend. In Roberto Chiesi and Andrea Mancini (Eds.), *Pier Paolo Pasolini: Poet of ashes* (124–131). San Francisco: Titivillus Mostre Editoria and City Lights Books.

Wahrman, Dror (2004). *The making of the modern self.* New Haven, CT: Yale University Press.

Wang, Hongyu (2004). *The call from the stranger on a journey home.* New York: Peter Lang.

Ward, David (1994). A genial analytic mind: "Film" and "cinema" in Pier Paolo Pasolini's film theory. In Patrick Rumble and Bart Testa (Eds.), *Pier Paolo Pasolini:* (127–151). Toronto: University of Toronto Press.

Ward, David (1995). *A poetics of resistance.* Madison, NJ: Fairleigh Dickinson University Press.

Ward, David (1999). Pier Paolo Pasolini and the events of May 1968: The "*Manifesto per un Nuovo Teatro.*" In Zygmunt G. Barański (Ed.), *Pasolini old and new* (321–344) Dublin: Four Courts Press.

Watkins, William H. (2001). *The white architects of black education.* New York: Teachers College Press.

Webber, Julie A. (2003). *Failure to hold.* Landham, MD: Rowman & Littlefield.

Weintraub, Karl Joachim (1978). *The value of the individual.* Chicago: University of Chicago Press.

Weis, Marc (2005). Slide show inspiration: On the effect of Roberto Longhi's interpretation of art on Pasolini. In Bernhart Schwenk and Michael Semff (Eds.), *Pier Paolo Pasolini and death* (53–64). Munich: Hatje Cantz Publishers.

Welle, John P. (1999). Pasolini *traduttore.* In Zygmunt G. Barański (Ed.), *Pasolini old and new* (90–129) Dublin: Four Courts Press.

Wells, Ida B. (1970). *Crusade for justice* [edited by Alfreda Duster]. Chicago: University of Chicago Press.

Westbrook, Robert (1991). *John Dewey and American philosophy.* Ithaca, NY: Cornell University Press.
Whitman, Walt (1881). *Leaves of Grass.* London: James R. Osgood and Company.
Williams, Robert (2007). Leonardo's modernity: Subjectivity as symptom. In Charles G. Salas (Ed.), *The life & the work* (34–44). Los Angeles, CA: Getty Publications.
Williamson, Joel (1984). *The crucible of race.* New York: Oxford University Press.
Willis, Paul (1981 [1977]). *Learning to labour.* Hampshire, UK: Gower. [1977 edition published by Saxon House in Farnborough, UK.]
Winnicott, D. W. (1990). *Playing and reality.* New York: Routledge.
Worthen, Molly (2007). Onward Christian soldiers. *The New York Times* online: http://www.nytimes.com/2007/09/30/magazine/30Christian-t.html?ex=1192248 000&en=1f43ebf09e8d451e&ei=5070&emc=etal
Wraga, William G. (1999, January-February). Extracting sun-beams out of cucumbers": The retreat from practice in reconceptualized curriculum studies. *Educational Researcher* (28) 1, 4-13.
Yack, Bernard (1986). *The longing for total revolution.* Princeton, NJ: Princeton University Press.
Yoshimoto, Mitsuhiro (2002). Questions of Japanese cinema: Disciplinary boundaries and the invention of the scholarly object. In Masao Miyoshi and D. H. Harootunian (Eds.), *Learning places: The afterlives of area studies* (368–401). Durham, NC: Duke University Press.
Young, Michael F. D. (2008). *Bringing knowledge back in.* London: Routledge.
Young-Bruehl, Elisabeth (1996). *The anatomy of prejudices.* Cambridge, MA: Harvard University Press.
Yu, Tianlong (2003). *In the name of morality.* New York: Peter Lang.
Zahar, Renate (1974). *Frantz Fanon: Colonialism and alienation. Concerning Frantz Fanon's political theory.* [Trans. by Willfried F. Feuser.] New York: Monthly Review Press.
Zaretsky, Eli (2004). *Secrets of the soul: A social and cultural history of psychoanalysis.* New York: Knopf.
Zigaina, Giuseppe (2005). Pasolini and death: A purely intellectual thriller. In Bernhart Schwenk and Michael Semff (Eds.), *Pier Paolo Pasolini and death* (25–37). Munich: Hatje Cantz Publishers.
Zimmerman, Jonathan (2002). *Whose America? Culture wars in the public schools.* Cambridge, MA: Harvard University Press.
Žižek, Slavoj (1991). *Looking awry.* Cambridge, MA: The MIT Press.

Index

218   *Index*